D0953588

THE
BOOK
OF
SIGNS

THE
BOOK
OF
SIGNS

31 UNDENIABLE PROPHECIES
OF THE APOCALYPSE

DR. DAVID JEREMIAH

W PUBLISHING GROUP

AN IMPRINT OF THOMAS NELSON

Published in Nashville, Tennessee, by W Publishing, an imprint of Thomas Nelson.

Published in association with Yates & Yates, www.yates2.com.

Thomas Nelson titles may be purchased in bulk for educational, business, fund-raising, or sales promotional use. For information, please e-mail SpecialMarkets@ThomasNelson.com.

Unless otherwise noted, Scripture quotations are taken from the New King James Version®. © 1982 by Thomas Nelson. Used by permission. All rights reserved.

Scripture quotations marked ESV are from the ESV® Bible (The Holy Bible, English Standard Version®). Copyright © 2001 by Crossway, a publishing ministry of Good News Publishers. Used by permission. All rights reserved.

Scripture quotations marked KJV are from the King James Version. Public domain.

Scripture quotations marked NLT are from the Holy Bible, New Living Translation. © 1996, 2004, 2007, 2013, 2015 by Tyndale House Foundation. Used by permission of Tyndale House Publishers, Inc., Carol Stream, Illinois 60188. All rights reserved.

Scripture quotations marked NASB are from the New American Standard Bible®. Copyright © 1960, 1962, 1963, 1968, 1971, 1972, 1973, 1975, 1977, 1995 by The Lockman Foundation. Used by permission. (www.Lockman.org)

Scripture quotations marked NIV are from the Holy Bible, New International Version®, NIV®. Copyright © 1973, 1978, 1984, 2011 by Biblica, Inc.® Used by permission of Zondervan. All rights reserved worldwide. www.zondervan.com. The "NIV" and "New International Version" are trademarks registered in the United States Patent and Trademark Office by Biblica, Inc.®

ISBN 978-0-7852-2957-5 (eBook)
ISBN 978-0-7852-2223-1 (IE)

Library of Congress Control Number: 2018961060

ISBN 978-0-7852-2954-4

Printed in the United States of America
21 22 23   LSC   22

To four prophetic scholars who have greatly impacted my life:
Dr. J. Dwight Pentecost and Dr. Tim LaHaye
who are living in heaven, and
Dr. Ed Hindson and Dr. Mark Hitchcock who are living on earth.

CONTENTS

Prologue   ix

PART 1: INTERNATIONAL SIGNS

Chapter 1: Israel   3
Chapter 2: Europe   17
Chapter 3: Russia   30
Chapter 4: Babylon   44
Chapter 5: America   57

PART 2: CULTURAL SIGNS

Chapter 6: Materialism   73
Chapter 7: Immorality   85
Chapter 8: Radical Islam   97
Chapter 9: Persecution   110
Chapter 10: Spiritual Warfare   125
Chapter 11: Apathy   139

PART 3: HEAVENLY SIGNS

Chapter 12: Rapture   155
Chapter 13: Resurrection   168
Chapter 14: Heaven   181

CONTENTS

Chapter 15: Judgment Seat of Christ   193

Chapter 16: Rewards   205

Chapter 17: Worship   218

PART 4: TRIBULATION SIGNS

Chapter 18: Four Riders   233

Chapter 19: Antichrist   246

Chapter 20: False Prophet   259

Chapter 21: Martyrs   270

Chapter 22: 144,000   284

Chapter 23: Two Witnesses   298

Chapter 24: Dragon   311

Chapter 25: Mark of the Beast   324

Chapter 26: Armageddon   336

PART 5: END SIGNS

Chapter 27: Return of the King   351

Chapter 28: Millennium   364

Chapter 29: Great White Throne Judgment   378

Chapter 30: New Heaven and New Earth   391

Chapter 31: Holy City   405

Epilogue   419

Notes   425

Index   447

Acknowledgments   461

About the Author   465

PROLOGUE

Can you remember back to the last time you drove along an interstate or highway? Perhaps it was only a few hours ago, or perhaps significantly longer. Either way, I'm certain your driving experience included interacting with signs—probably quite a few signs if you live close to a major city, as I do.

Many of the signs posted along our modern roads are informational; they tell us what we need to know. "Interstate 5 San Diego," for example. Or "Exit 74, 5 Miles." Other signs are invitational; they seek to capture our attention and pique our interest. Think of signs such as "Welcome to Texas" or "Great Food This Exit!" Some of the most important signs we encounter on our highways are warning signs; they alert us to possible dangers on the road ahead. I pay attention whenever I see a sign marked "Detour," for example, or "Right Lane Closed."

Whether offered as information, invitation, or warning, each sign we encounter along the road is designed to help us move from where we are to where we want to be. In a similar way, God in His providence has placed a number of critical signs along the highway we call human history. We often think of these signs as prophecies, and we have been made aware of them through the prophetic vehicle of God's Word, the Bible.

Some of the signs we encounter in the Scriptures are informational, some are invitational, and many offer warnings about the road ahead—warnings that apply to both our present and our future. All of these signs are important, and none should be ignored.

That's why I've written this book.

WHY STUDY THE SIGNS?

Throughout the history of the church, the prophetic portions of Scripture have received an enormous amount of literary attention. Countless books claim to offer insight on the hundreds of topics related to biblical prophecy, all of them written from a wide variety of theological perspectives and positions on how to interpret Scripture. These studies can create a variety of questions, concerns, and even confusion in our minds. Sometimes it is difficult to see how obscure passages, distant places, and unfamiliar symbols can have any significance for our lives. After all, if we can't understand what the Bible is teaching, how in the world can it have any relevance to what we are experiencing today?

This drive to understand has been a major foundation of my ministry for decades—including the drive to understand and apply the truths communicated through biblical prophecy. My interest in that subject as a preacher and a writer has always been anchored in my love for the Bible, which I believe to be the inspired Word of God. I find it fascinating that the Bible dedicates more space to the subject of prophecy than almost any other. There are over eighteen hundred prophecies in God's Word concerning the first and second coming of Jesus Christ alone!

Obviously, prophecy is important to God, and He desires for us to understand His plans. He has given us His signs for a reason.

Not coincidentally, people have always been fascinated with the future. In the uncertain and often anxious times in which we live, all of us yearn to see ahead, to know, and perhaps to avert disaster. Therefore, I count it a privilege to help people find their place in the great pattern of prophetic events foretold by God's prophets, written out in Scripture, and confirmed in the headlines of the day.

As you read through *The Book of Signs*, you will find a comprehensive exploration of these prophecies and signs. You will see not only how God's Word offers insights into the future, but also how Scripture builds faith through the events of the past and encouragement in the uncertainty of the present.

WHAT ARE THE SIGNS?

Before we move forward, what do I mean by "signs"? The conventional definition of a biblical sign is somewhat broad. It can be an event, symbol, object, place, or person whose existence or occurrence indicates something important in God's plan for history. There are any number of ways such signs can present themselves, but all express a particular meaning, help us know what to pay attention to, or point to what will be coming.

You will discover in these pages that God has taken great care to communicate in a way we can understand. Jesus Himself talked about signs verifying His first coming, signs portending His second coming back to earth, and signs that outline both general and specific elements of the end of the age. We'll take a close look at those in these pages, as well as other Scripture passages in which signs are a major theme.

Just as importantly, Jesus told us to keep our eyes open so that we are not fooled by the signs indicating that the end times are near. As we get closer to that time, many people are going to claim to be the Messiah and claim to have the answers for a troubled world. As the signs in this book unfold, it will be revealed that we can expect a period of international and cultural chaos with the possibility of ceaseless, unending, terrible war. It appears that we are already preparing for this period as worldwide arms development continues—currently there is at least one military weapon and several thousand pounds of explosives for every man, woman, and child on earth. Finally, there will be more and more disease and devastation. Even today, millions of people in the world are being afflicted by insufficient food, the spread of new diseases, antibiotic resistance, and the devastating effects of natural disasters.

Seeing these signs played out in the news, on television, over the Internet, and even in our own lives can cause despair, anxiety, and confusion—not just because of the world situation but also over our concern for those who do not know the Lord and could be "left behind" to face the Tribulation. But when Jesus told us to open our eyes, He did so to encourage us to gaze upon Him—not because this will cause all the world's problems (and ours) to disappear, but because He is the Prince of Peace.

In the pages that follow, I encourage you to study with me as we discover together what Scripture reveals about the signs of the times and the signs of God's plan for the future—all the way to paradise regained. I am confident you will find, as I have, that understanding the signs presented in the five parts of this book will help you live with confidence, hope, and a renewed sense of purpose.

The end times may be near, but as Christians, our future is secure. Indeed, we live in a chaotic world, but we can be confident and at peace because God is the author of history, and because the return of the Prince of Peace may be closer than we think.

—Awaiting His return,
David Jeremiah

PART 1

INTERNATIONAL SIGNS

The thirty-one undeniable prophecies of the Apocalypse is a story that can be told in five acts. In the first act, five nations in particular emerge—Israel, Europe, Russia, Babylon, and America.

According to the Bible, the regathering of the Jewish people back to their homeland is predicted time and again as a precursor to the end times. We are also told that the consolidation of world power under a supreme leader in Europe is one of the essential preludes to the coming of the Antichrist. The prophet Ezekiel speaks of a day when Russia will lead an alliance of nations that will attack Israel, igniting a pivotal world war like none ever seen or imagined. And during the Tribulation period we can expect the final financial world order to be located in a city called Babylon, which will rise to power again as the rebuilt commercial capital of the world. And while America is not clearly mentioned in Bible prophecy, it will play a role in several ways—key alliances with other countries, a force behind world missions, and a friend to the Jewish people.

Let's look together at the international signs that will precede God's coming judgment.

CHAPTER 1

ISRAEL

May 14, 1948, was a pivotal day in human history. On that afternoon, a car carrying Jewish leader David Ben-Gurion rushed down Rothschild Boulevard in Tel Aviv and stopped at the Tel Aviv Art Museum. Four o'clock was only minutes away, and inside, Jewish leaders and press representatives from all over the world were assembled in an auditorium, awaiting his arrival. Ben-Gurion bounded up the steps. Precisely at four o'clock, local time, he stepped to the podium, called the meeting to order, and read these historic words:[1]

> This right is the natural right of the Jewish people to be masters of their own fate, like all other nations, in their own sovereign State.
>
> Accordingly we . . . are here assembled . . . and, by virtue of our natural and historic right and on the strength of the resolution of the United Nations General Assembly, hereby declare the establishment of a Jewish State in Eretz-Israel, to be known as the State of Israel.[2]

Six thousand miles away, President Truman sat in the Oval Office reading a statement. He signed his approval and noted the time: 6:10 p.m. One minute later, the White House press secretary read the release to the world. The United States had officially recognized the birth of the modern nation of Israel.

Isaiah's prophecy, written 740 years before the birth of Jesus, declared, "Who has heard such a thing? Who has seen such things? Shall the earth be made to give birth in one day? Or shall a nation be born at once?" (Isa. 66:8). Secular Israel was born that day.

In the past seven decades, this tiny nation with a population of 8.5 million has become the geopolitical center of the world.[3] Why is this so? Why is a fledgling country with a total land space smaller than New Jersey mentioned in the nightly news more than any other nation except the United States?

To answer these questions, we must understand what happened on that day in 1948, what is happening today in Israel, and how these events affect the entire world. For answers we turn not to the evening news or the front page of the newspaper but to the Bible.

THE ABRAHAMIC COVENANT

The story of Israel begins in the book of Genesis. The almighty God of heaven and earth made a binding covenant with Abraham, who was to be the father of the Jewish nation. The provisions of that covenant are recorded in Genesis 12:1–3, in which God said:

> Get out of your country,
> From your family
> And from your father's house,
> To a land that I will show you.
> I will make you a great nation;
> I will bless you
> And make your name great;
> And you shall be a blessing.

I will bless those who bless you,
And I will curse him who curses you;
And in you all the families of the earth shall be blessed.

God's covenant with Abraham consists of four unconditional promises. First, God promised to bless Abraham. That promise has been lavishly kept; Abraham has been blessed in many ways. For thousands of years, Abraham has been revered by Jews, Christians, and Muslims alike.

Second, God promised to bring out of Abraham a great nation. Currently, more than 6 million Jews live in Israel alone.[4] Another five million live in the United States, and a significant Jewish population remains scattered throughout the world.[5]

Third, God promised to make Abraham a blessing to many. Just think what the world would be missing had it not been for the Jews. Without the Jews, we would have no Bible. Without the Jews, there would be no Ten Commandments, the basis of jurisprudence among most of the civilized nations of the world. Without the Jews, there would have been no Jesus. Without the Jewish Jesus, there would be no Christianity.

Fourth, God promised to bless those who blessed Israel and curse those who cursed her. He has kept that promise faithfully. I believe one of the reasons America has been blessed as a nation is that she has become a homeland for the Jewish people. Here Jews can retain their religion. Here they have economic, social, and educational opportunities. Today, the Christian church in America stands firmly between the Jewish people and the repetition of any further anti-Semitism.[6]

God's covenant with Abraham reveals both the mission and future of God's chosen nation. Studying these promises will give us great help in understanding the present unrest in the Middle East, the future of the Israeli nation, and how the destiny of today's nations will be affected by their stance toward God's chosen people.

This historic document includes seven important features. The Abrahamic covenant is . . .

AN UNCONDITIONAL COVENANT

Seven times in Genesis 12:1–3 God declared in emphatic terms what He would do for Abraham. His covenant with Abraham was unconditional, and He ratified it in a ceremony described in Genesis 15. In *The Jeremiah Study Bible*, I explain the meaning of this ceremony:

> To establish and confirm a covenant in Abram's day, usually the two parties would walk between the pieces of the sacrificial animals, saying, in effect, "May what has happened to these creatures happen to me if I break the covenant." . . .
>
> Because this was Yahweh's sovereign covenant with Abram, not an agreement between equals, symbols of God (a smoking oven and a burning torch) passed between those pieces; Abram did not. The LORD made the covenant with no conditions—independent of Abram—and He would fulfill it in His time.[7]

No provision was made for this covenant to be revoked, and it was not subject to amendment or annulment.

A PERSONAL COVENANT

In His covenant with Abraham, God promised extravagant blessings not only to Abraham's descendants but also to Abraham himself: "I will bless you and make your name great" (Gen. 12:2).

In Genesis 12:1–3, God addressed Abraham using the personal pronouns *you* and *your* eleven times. The promises are ultimately far-reaching and eternal, but they were made first of all to Abraham personally and each has been fulfilled.

God directed Abraham to travel to the land He promised to his descendants, and Abraham found it to be, as Moses later described, a rich land "flowing with milk and honey" (Ex. 3:8, 17; 13:5; 33:3). His flocks and herds increased exponentially, and he became an extremely wealthy man (Gen. 13:2). Yes, this land would be the eternal possession of his descendants, but it was also Abraham's personal home throughout his life (25:7–8).

God's promise to make Abraham's name great has also been lavishly fulfilled. Even in his own time, Abraham was known throughout the land as a rich and powerful leader who was highly respected and feared.

A NATIONAL COVENANT

In the second verse of God's covenant with Abraham, He said, "I will make you a great nation." The ultimate greatness of the nation of Israel awaits the Millennium, but by all the common standards of evaluation, Israel is a great nation today. Professor Amnon Rubinstein gives us an impressive summary of Israel's national achievements:

> Minute in size, not much bigger than a sliver of Mediterranean coastline, it has withstood continuing Arab onslaughts, wars, boycotts and terrorism; it has turned itself from a poor, rural country to an industrial and post-industrial powerhouse. . . . It has reduced social, educational and health gaps . . . between Arabs and Jews. Some of its achievements are unprecedented.[8]

A TERRITORIAL COVENANT

Of all God's covenant promises to Abraham, I believe the most amazing is His promise concerning the land. God told Abraham to leave his country, his family, and his father's house and go "to a land that I will show you" (Gen. 12:1). God then led Abraham to the land that would belong to his descendants forever.

The land promised to Abraham and his descendants was described with clear geographical boundaries. It takes in all the land from the Mediterranean Sea as the western boundary to the Euphrates River as the eastern boundary. The prophet Ezekiel fixed the northern boundary at Hamath, one hundred miles north of Damascus (Ezek. 48:1), and the southern boundary at Kadesh, about one hundred miles south of Jerusalem

(v. 28). If Israelis were currently occupying all the land that God gave to them, they would control all the holdings of present-day Israel, Lebanon, and the West Bank of Jordan, plus substantial portions of Syria, Iraq, and Saudi Arabia.

The strange thing is, Israel has never, in its long history, occupied anywhere near this much land—not even at the height of its glory days under David and Solomon. This fact has caused many biblical scholars to spiritualize the meaning of the term *land* and equate it with heaven. Others claim these promises were conditional and were forfeited by Israel's disobedience. In refutation of these interpretations, Dr. John F. Walvoord wrote:

> The term *land* . . . used in the Bible, means exactly what it says. It is not talking about heaven. It is talking about a piece of real estate in the Middle East. After all, if all God was promising Abraham was heaven, he could have stayed in Ur of the Chaldees. Why go on the long journey? Why be a pilgrim and a wanderer? No, God meant land.[9]

Any normal reading of Scripture recognizes Canaan as an actual place, a piece of real estate, an expanse of soil that belongs to Abraham's descendants forever.

The fact that Israel has been dispossessed of the land in three periods of its history is not an argument against its ultimate possession. Occupation is not the same as ownership. After each dispossession, God brought Israel back to its originally promised land. God has consistently kept His promise to Abraham, and that gives us absolute assurance that He will keep it in the future.

The turmoil over Israel's right to its land will not cease till the end, for the land provision of the Abrahamic covenant is at the core of the hatred of Middle Eastern nations for Israel today.

But ignoring God's care and protection of Israel is extremely dangerous. The land of Israel is so important to God that, according to Deuteronomy

11:12, it is "a land for which the LORD your God cares; the eyes of the LORD your God are always on it, from the beginning of the year to the very end of the year."

A RECIPROCAL COVENANT

God also promised protection to the nation that would descend from Abraham: "I will bless those who bless you, and I will curse him who curses you" (Gen. 12:3). Leaders and nations that ally with Israel to preserve, protect, and defend it will likewise be preserved, protected, and defended. On the other hand, those who stand in the way of Israel's well-being will find themselves standing against God—which means they will not long stand at all.

The prophet Zechariah declared that God would plunder the nations that plunder Israel, "for he who touches [Israel] touches the apple of His eye" (Zech. 2:8). History tells the tragic story of what has happened to nations and leaders who dared to oppress Israel. Egypt, the first nation to enslave Israel, was brought to its knees by ten devastating plagues (Ex. 7–12). The Amorites, who resisted Israel's march toward their promised land, were soundly defeated (Num. 21:21–30).

One of the most notable examples of God's vengeance against an enemy of Israel was the annihilation of the Midianites who joined with Moab in trying to stop Israel. After their failure to bribe the prophet Balaam into pronouncing a curse on Israel, they used Midianite women to seduce Israel's men into immorality and idolatry. Moses prepared Israel for war "to take vengeance for the LORD on Midian" (Num. 31:3). The battle was quick and decisive. All the Midianite cities were burned to the ground, and the Israelites took as plunder massive amounts of gold, silver, bronze, tin, lead, and wood, along with cattle, sheep, and donkeys (Num. 31; Rev. 2:14).

Babylon, the empire that destroyed Jerusalem and deported the Jews from their homeland, was soundly defeated seventy years later by the Persians. And one of history's worst persecutors of the Jews, the Greek-Seleucid ruler Antiochus IV, died a horrible death shortly after hearing that his army had been defeated in the Jewish Maccabean rebellion.[10]

In modern times, Russia confined Jews to ghettos and harassed them with pogroms under the czars, who were overthrown in the communist rebellion of 1917. Under communism, the Jews were forbidden to practice their religious rites, and many were arrested, deported, or executed. Hitler's Germany, which destroyed some six million Jews, was crushed in World War II.

Israel's Six-Day War of 1967 stands today as the most spectacular modern example of God's punishment on those who curse Israel. Although Israel became an independent nation in 1948, the Palestinians and Islamic states surrounding it didn't recognize its statehood and vowed its extermination. In 1967, the United Arab Republic (UAR) allied with Jordan, Syria, and Palestinian guerrillas to attack Israel from the north, south, and east. Israel was hopelessly outmanned. The Arab armies numbered more than 500,000 men; Israel had only 75,000. The Arabs fielded 5,000 tanks and 900 combat aircraft, whereas the Israeli total was only 1,000 tanks and 175 planes. Yet when the smoke cleared six days later, the UAR had lost almost its entire air force (about 20,000 lives), and Israel had taken over significant Arab-controlled territory, including the Sinai Peninsula, Golan Heights, Gaza Strip, and West Bank.[11]

In a powerful speech to the United Nations General Assembly on October 1, 2015, Israeli prime minister Benjamin Netanyahu summarized the miraculous preservation of the Jewish people:

> In every generation, there were those who rose up to destroy our people. In antiquity, we faced destruction from the ancient empires of Babylon and Rome. In the Middle Ages, we faced inquisition and expulsion. And in modern times, we faced pogroms and the Holocaust. Yet the Jewish people persevered.
>
> And now another regime has arisen, swearing to destroy Israel. That regime would be wise to consider this: I stand here today representing Israel, a country 67 years young, but the nation-state of a people nearly 4,000-years-old. Yet the empires of Babylon and Rome are not represented

in this hall of nations. Neither is the Thousand Year Reich. Those seemingly invincible empires are long gone. But Israel lives. The people of Israel live.[12]

History records that Israel stands at the graves of all its enemies.

A UNIVERSAL COVENANT

Here we reach the overarching reason for all the promises we have studied in God's covenant with Abraham: "In you all the families of the earth shall be blessed" (Gen. 12:3).

This is the root of God's promise to Abraham and His purpose in creating a new people for Himself. Abraham's descendants were to become the repository of God's glory, wisdom, love, and redemptive grace. This saving grace was to overflow from the Jews to the rest of the world.

Through Abraham, God gave His written Word to the world. With the possible exceptions of Luke and Acts, every book of the Bible was authored by a Jewish writer.[13] And through Abraham, God gave His Son to the world, blessing all humanity with the means of escaping the grip of sin and death, "that the blessing of Abraham might come upon the Gentiles in Christ Jesus, that we might receive the promise of the Spirit through faith" (Gal. 3:14). All the other promises in God's covenant with Abraham are in support of this one universal promise that affects every person who has ever lived.

AN ETERNAL COVENANT

God's promise to Abraham came in three stages. It was initiated in Genesis 12:1–3, formalized in Genesis 15:1–21, and then amplified in Genesis 17:1–18:21. In Genesis 17, Abraham was approaching his one-hundredth birthday, and his faith was frail—it had been nearly twenty-five years since his first encounter with the Lord. Then God appeared, reminding Abraham that His promise was a forever promise, an eternal promise "between Me and you and your descendants after you in their generations, for an everlasting covenant, to be God to you and your descendants after you. Also I give to you and your descendants after you the land in which

11

you are a stranger, all the land of Canaan, as an everlasting possession; and I will be their God" (vv. 7–8).

The promise to Abraham is an everlasting promise because it is an unconditional covenant based on the grace and sovereignty of almighty God. There may be delays, postponements, and chastisements, but an eternal covenant cannot be abrogated by a God who cannot deny Himself.

WHY DID GOD CHOOSE ISRAEL?

When I first began studying prophecy, I remember reading an offbeat little rhyme about Israel by British journalist William Norman Ewer: "How odd of God to choose the Jews." When you think about it, this poetic quip expresses a valid observation. Doesn't it seem a little odd that of all the people on earth, God selected these particular people to be His chosen nation? Why would God choose the Jews?

The Bible tells us that His choice of Israel had nothing to do with merit. It was not because Israel was more numerous than other people in the world; it was the least (Deut. 7:7). It was not because Israel was more sensitive to God than other nations; Israel did not know Him (Isa. 45:4). It was not because Israel was more righteous than other nations; God called them a rebellious, stiff-necked people (Deut. 9:6–7).

Then why did God choose the Jews? The answer: because it was His sovereign purpose to do so.

THE RETURN TO THE GOD OF ISRAEL

During my years as a pastor, I have been asked many times whether I believe Israel's return to its land fulfills all the biblical prophecies concerning its future. What people are really asking is this: "Now that Israel is restored to its land, is this the end?"

Many assume it is, but I have to tell them the answer is no! What is happening in Israel today is primarily the result of a secular Zionist movement, whereas Ezekiel wrote about a spiritual return of God's people to Him:

> I will take you from among the nations, gather you out of all countries, and bring you into your own land. . . . I will give you a new heart and put a new spirit within you; I will take the heart of stone out of your flesh and give you a heart of flesh. I will put My Spirit within you and cause you to walk in My statutes, and you will keep My judgments and do them. Then you shall dwell in the land that I gave to your fathers; you shall be My people, and I will be your God. (Ezek. 36:24, 26–28)

The return of Jews to the re-founded nation of Israel is the first stage of that regathering, but it certainly does not fulfill the requirements of a spiritual return to the Lord. But we can be assured that it will happen, just as God promised:

- "I will pour on the house of David and on the inhabitants of Jerusalem the Spirit of grace and supplication; then they will look on Me whom they pierced" (Zech. 12:10).
- "And so all Israel will be saved, as it is written: 'The Deliverer will come out of Zion, and He will turn away ungodliness from Jacob; for this is My covenant with them, when I take away their sins'" (Rom. 11:26–27).

There are still two pivotal prophecies concerning Israel that have not yet been fulfilled: Israel does not yet occupy all the land originally promised to it, and its people have not yet turned to Christ. The numerous prophecies of Israel's return to its homeland were explicitly fulfilled in 1948 when Israel began to be restored to its land. This gives us assurance that full restoration is on the horizon and the prophecies concerning Israel's return to God will also be fulfilled.

As we wait for the fulfillment of these prophecies, Israel continues to grow as a nation. Against all odds, the people of Israel lead the Middle East in productivity, wealth, order, freedom, and military power. Yet as these assets increase, the nation becomes more and more isolated, continually terrorized by the murderous hostility of its surrounding neighbors.

The most dramatic events lie ahead of us. Israel today is an island of less than nine million immigrants surrounded by a sea of three hundred million enemies, many of them eager to wipe the tiny nation off the map. From a purely human point of view, it would seem inevitable that, sooner or later, Israel will be destroyed. Indeed, Israel has been attacked over and over since its founding, sometimes in all-out wars and incessantly by terrorists. The Jewish people have survived by remaining vigilant, but they long for peace. According to the Bible, a future leader will fulfill this longing by brokering a peace deal with Israel's enemies. But Scripture also tells us that this peace plan will be broken, and Israel will be attacked once again, this time as never before. Countless armies will amass against the boxed-in nation, leaving it with no human hope of victory. Only Christ's return, His judgment, and His reign will finally bring true peace to Israel.

It is then that God's covenant with Abraham will reach its ultimate fulfillment. The Jews will return to the Lord, and they will be His people, and He will be their God. The borders of the land will expand to the dimensions described in Genesis 15 and Ezekiel 48. Christ's return will also fulfill the prophecy that God would gather the Jews. "Behold, I will gather them out of all countries where I have driven them . . . I will bring them back to this place, and I will cause them to dwell safely. They shall be My people, and I will be their God" (Jer. 32:37–38).

Ezekiel makes it clear that this gathering means He will return every single living Jew back to the land. For he wrote that the Lord said He would gather them again to their own land "and . . . none of them [will be] captive any longer" (Ezek. 39:28).

Today we see this prophecy being fulfilled right before our eyes. In 2006, Israel became home to the largest Jewish community in the world.

From the 650,000 who returned when the Jewish state was founded in 1948, the population of Israel is expected to exceed 20 million by 2065.[14]

Israel's reemergence in her ancient homeland sets the stage for the final fulfillment of biblical prophecies. The return of the Jews to their homeland is also significant in another way: it pinpoints where we are on history's timeline. As Milton B. Lindberg pointed out, "Without the existence of the nation of Israel, we would not be able to say with certainty that we are in the last days. That single event, more than any other, is the most prominent sign that we are living in the final moments before the coming of Jesus!"[15]

WHAT DOES ALL THIS MEAN TO ME?

The fulfillment of God's covenant with Abraham greatly affects every one of us. We have shown why it's important for our nation to continue to support and protect Israel. Nations that befriend Israel will be blessed; those that do not will be cursed.

The playing out of prophetic events concerning Israel also places us in the last days of history's timeline. The miraculous survival of God's covenant people, the Jews, demonstrates God's ability to accomplish His purpose in the face of what seem to be impossible odds. The existence of Israel today is exhibit A that the Bible's prophecies concerning the future will be fulfilled. This means the future not only of Israel but also of our world and our nation, as well as your future and mine. The astounding history of the Jews reveals the reality of God—His overwhelming power, the authenticity of His promises, the certainty of His existence, the urgency of His call to us, and His claim on our very being.

That historic day in 1948, when Israel was re-established as a nation, has been described as "the most spectacular event in nearly two millennia of Jewish history."[16] When President Truman read that statement and the United States officially became the first nation to recognize the birth of the modern state of Israel, the 2,500-year-old prophecy of the Bible was at last fulfilled!

But here's the rest of the story. Later, when the Chief Rabbi of Israel, Isaac Halevi Herzog, called the White House, he told Truman, "God put you in your mother's womb so that you would be the instrument to bring about the rebirth of Israel after two thousand years." One of Truman's men reported that when he looked at Truman after the rabbi's statement, tears were running down his cheeks.[17]

I was seven years old when the nation of Israel was established in 1948. I now believe the restoration of the Jewish people to their land is the most important prophetic sign to have occurred in my lifetime. More than any other sign described in this book, the prophetic future of the nation of Israel answers the question, "Is this the end?" But an even greater prophetic fulfillment awaits an unknown future day: the return of the Jewish Messiah to the Jewish people!

CHAPTER 2

EUROPE

When he was a teenager, Albert Einstein had a dream that likely changed the course of scientific history.

In the dream, Einstein was walking through a field when he noticed a group of cows far away in the distance, all leaning against an electric fence. The cows were enjoying the grass that had previously been out of their reach because of the fence. Beyond the cows, Einstein saw a farmer working near the opposite end of the fence—presumably fixing whatever had caused the loss of electricity.

All of a sudden, Einstein saw the entire group of cows jump back from the fence at the same time. Rightly assuming that the fence had been repaired, Einstein walked on. When he reached the farmer, Einstein commented how humorous it had been to see all the cows jump back at the same time. But the farmer was confused. He told Einstein that's not what happened at all. From his perspective, the cows had jumped back one at a time, starting with the cow closest to him.

Upon waking, the dream stayed in Einstein's mind. In fact, he continued to ruminate about the dream for decades. Eventually, his continued meditations on that subject became one of the factors that contributed to his Theory of General Relativity.[1]

Can you imagine anyone having a more significant dream than that? Actually, I can.

More than two thousand years ago, God gave Daniel a vision that we recognize as the most comprehensive prophetic insight ever received. God also sent a similar dream to the most powerful man in the world at that time. Looking back, we can see the effects of those dreams rippling throughout history—and even into the future.

Specifically, Daniel's vision operates as a sign of what we can expect to happen in Europe before and during the end times.

DANIEL'S INTERPRETATION FOR THE KING

While it was not uncommon for God to communicate to His people through dreams and visions, it is astounding that He gave the greatest vision of all time not only to Daniel but also to one of history's most wicked Gentile rulers: King Nebuchadnezzar.

It was the second year of Nebuchadnezzar's rule over Babylon. Although all the king's enemies were subdued or in captivity, he nevertheless was anxious about the future. His anxiety stemmed from a dream sent to him by God—a nightmare he could not understand, though he sensed its ominous implications. So the king called in his counselors. Since he had forgotten important details of the dream, he demanded that his counselors not only interpret the nightmare but also give him a vivid description of it.

The king's demand was unprecedented, and his counselors thought it unfair. When they could not meet his demand, Nebuchadnezzar ordered the execution of all the wise men of Babylon (Dan. 2:12–13).

When the Jewish captive Daniel heard of the king's edict, he and his friends asked God for a vision of Nebuchadnezzar's dream and its interpretation. Then Daniel went to the executioner and said, "Do not destroy the wise men of Babylon; take me before the king, and I will tell the king the interpretation" (v. 24).

Daniel was soon standing before Nebuchadnezzar, who asked him if he could reveal the meaning of his dream. Daniel explained that he could not, but he had connections with Someone who could: "The secret which the king has demanded, the wise men, the astrologers, the magicians, and the soothsayers cannot declare to the king. But there is a God in heaven who reveals secrets, and He has made known to King Nebuchadnezzar what will be in the latter days. Your dream, and the visions of your head upon your bed, were these" (vv. 27–28).

As Daniel explained, just as God had sent the dream to Nebuchadnezzar, God had also revealed the dream and its interpretation to Daniel (v. 19). Then the Jewish prophet stood before the king and unfolded the future of his nation.

Daniel described the king's vision: "You, O king, were watching; and behold, a great image! This great image, whose splendor was excellent, stood before you; and its form was awesome. This image's head was of fine gold, its chest and arms of silver, its belly and thighs of bronze, its legs of iron, its feet partly of iron and partly of clay" (vv. 31–33).

This vision gives us the history of human civilization, written by God Himself.

Daniel told Nebuchadnezzar that his dream was about the kingdoms of this world. He explained that the metallic image represented four successive Gentile world powers that would rule over Israel in the days ahead.

DANIEL'S INSIGHT INTO THE FUTURE

Through Daniel, God gave King Nebuchadnezzar a history of the remaining days of the world. We know this because he spoke specifically of "days to come" (v. 28 NIV). He revealed the meaning of the statue in five sections:

the head of gold, the breast and arms of silver, the belly and thighs of copper and brass, the legs of iron, and the feet of part iron and part clay.

The first world empire, represented by the statue's head of gold, was Nebuchadnezzar's kingdom of Babylon. Daniel's words to the king are clear: "You, O king, are a king of kings. For the God of heaven has given you a kingdom, power, strength, and glory; and wherever the children of men dwell, or the beasts of the field and the birds of the heaven, He has given them into your hand, and has made you ruler over them all—you are this head of gold" (vv. 37–38).

Nebuchadnezzar would have understood that the head of gold referred to his kingdom, since the chief deity of Babylon was Marduk, known as "the god of gold." The historian Herodotus described the image of Marduk as a dazzling sight—a golden statue seated on a golden throne before a golden table and a golden altar. Pliny tells us that the robes of Marduk's priests were interlaced with gold.[2]

The second world empire revealed in the king's dream was represented by the image's chest of silver, from which two silver arms emerged (v. 32). This was the Medo-Persian Empire, which conquered Babylon in 539 BC and remained in power for approximately two hundred years. Later, Daniel stated clearly that the dual monarchy of the Medes and the Persians would take control of Nebuchadnezzar's empire (5:28). The two nations are again confirmed as Babylon's successor in Daniel 8:20.

The third world empire was represented by the image's belly and thighs of bronze. Daniel told the king it would be a "kingdom of bronze, which shall rule over all the earth" (2:39). This is the Greek Empire, the kingdom of Philip of Macedon and his son, Alexander the Great. Not only does history confirm Greece as the empire that succeeded the Medo-Persians, but Daniel named Greece specifically in Daniel 8:21. Under Alexander, the Greek Empire encompassed more territory than either of the previous empires. It is appropriate that this third kingdom was characterized by the image's bronze midsection. Alexander's soldiers armored themselves in bronze helmets and breastplates, and they carried bronze shields and swords.

The fourth empire in the image is symbolized by its legs of iron. Daniel describes this empire as "strong as iron, inasmuch as iron breaks in pieces and shatters everything; and like iron that crushes, that kingdom will break in pieces and crush all the others" (2:40). Historians tell us that Rome was not only the successor to the Greek Empire, but they often use iron to describe the strength of the Roman Empire: *Rome's iron rule. Rome's iron fist. Rome's iron legions.*

History confirms Daniel's explanation of Nebuchadnezzar's dream. The Babylonians were overthrown by the Medo-Persians, the Medo-Persians were conquered by the Greeks, and then the previous kingdoms were assimilated into one kingdom known as the Roman Empire. This empire came into existence fifty years before Jesus was born, and it continued in power throughout His earthly ministry. It was Roman rule that put Jesus on the cross. It was the Romans who ruled ruthlessly during the early days of the church.

The fact that Rome is represented in the statue by its two iron legs is also significant:

> By A.D. 395 the Roman Empire had split into two political areas of rule: the [Latin-speaking] West with its capital in Rome, and the [Greek-speaking] East with its capital in Constantinople (modern Istanbul, Turkey), which included the land of Israel. This division of the empire is depicted in the statue's two legs.[3]

This splitting of the mighty Roman Empire into two political units was not the last division that kingdom would suffer. Daniel noted that in the king's dream, the feet and toes were composed of a mixture of iron and clay. Though positioned at the bottom of the image, these extremities were apparently important, for Daniel said as much about the feet and toes as he said about all the other parts of the image combined.

Daniel explained to the king the meaning of the material composing the image's feet: "As the toes of the feet were partly of iron and partly of clay, so the kingdom shall be partly strong and partly fragile. . . . They will mingle with the seed of men; but they will not adhere to one another, just as iron does not mix with clay" (2:42–43).

According to Daniel, there is to be yet another division in the Roman Empire, symbolized by its ten toes. Daniel foretells a time when the Roman Empire will consist of ten kingdoms or leaders. Since the downward movement from one section of the statue to the next represents the passage of time, the "feet and toes" stage must follow the "legs" stage. But we find nothing in history that corresponds to a tenfold Roman coalition. That shows us that this fifth and final feet-and-toes-stage kingdom is yet to perform its prescribed role in human history.

Daniel gives us another piece of information that enables us to understand the timing of the events in Nebuchadnezzar's dream. He tells us that this final form of the Roman Empire will exist when God sets up His earthly kingdom. "In the days of these kings the God of heaven will set up a kingdom which shall never be destroyed; and the kingdom shall not be left to other people; it shall break in pieces and consume all these kingdoms, and it shall stand forever" (v. 44).

DANIEL'S INTENSE DREAM

Years after Nebuchadnezzar's dream of the image, Daniel had a vision of his own that expands our understanding of Nebuchadnezzar's dream. In Daniel's vision, a powerful wind stirred the ocean, and "four great beasts came up from the sea, each different from the other" (7:3). These beasts represented the same Gentile kingdoms as those depicted in the king's dream, but this time the character of those kingdoms was revealed. The first vision (Dan. 2) portrayed the kingdoms of the world as man assessed them—majestic, massive, and impressive in their accomplishments. In the second vision (Dan. 7), the kingdoms were shown as savage beasts, attacking one another and fighting to the death. This second vision gives us

God's appraisal of these kingdoms—destructive, divisive, and cruel. While the two visions were different in their presentation, both were given for the same purpose: to show Daniel and his people what in the world was going on!

Why did God choose that particular time to reveal so great a prophecy? His people were in a desperate moment of their history. Assyria had taken the Northern Kingdom of Israel captive in 722 BC, and two hundred years later, the Southern Kingdom of Judah was in captivity in Babylon. If you had been a Jew during that time, you might have wondered, *Is God finished with us?* Through these two visions, God assured His people, *This isn't the end. There will be a time when I will once again be involved with you as a nation. But I want you to know what will happen between now and then.*

Much of what was revealed to Daniel in these dreams has already happened. But not all of it. Three of the prophesied kingdoms have come and gone, and the fourth kingdom has also made its appearance in history. But Daniel's later vision included additional information about events that are yet in the future. Let's look at how Daniel described it: "I saw in the night visions, and behold, a fourth beast, dreadful and terrible, exceedingly strong. It had huge iron teeth; it was devouring, breaking in pieces, and trampling the residue with its feet. It was different from all the beasts that were before it, and it had ten horns" (7:7). Daniel explained that the ten horns are ten kings who will arise from this kingdom (v. 24).

We know this ten-kingdom prophecy of Daniel's remains in the future because not only has the ten-leader form of the Roman Empire not existed, but such a kingdom has not been suddenly crushed as Daniel 2 indicates it will be. The Roman Empire of Jesus' day did not end suddenly. It gradually declined over many centuries until the western part, the Western Roman Empire, fell in AD 476, and the eastern part, the Byzantine Empire, fell in AD 1453. We must conclude, then, that some form of the Roman Empire must emerge in the end times, for, according to Daniel, it will be in place prior to the coming of Christ to reign over the earth.

REBIRTH OF THE ROMAN EMPIRE

The future manifestation of the Roman Empire that Daniel prophesied will be a confederation of ten world leaders and will encompass the same territory as the historic Roman Empire. Today, we see that coalition taking shape before our eyes! It began as early as 1930, when French statesman Aristide Briand attempted to enlist twenty-six nations in what he first called "the United States of Europe" and modified to "the European Union." In his proposal, he said, "The nations of Europe today must unite in order to live and prosper." The European press gave Briand's idea little attention, and nothing came of it.[4]

But Briand's call for European unity was merely one world war ahead of the curve. Fewer than twenty years later, one of the world's most respected leaders issued the same call:

> In 1946, following the devastation of Europe during the Second World War, Winston Churchill forcefully asserted that "the tragedy of Europe" could only be solved if the issues of ancient nationalism and sovereignty could give way to a sense of European "national grouping." He said that the path to European peace and prosperity on the world stage was clear: "We must build a United States of Europe."[5]

Churchill's call initiated a series of steps toward unification. The Benelux Conference of 1948, held in Brussels, Belgium, laid the foundation for a new organization "to unite European countries economically and politically in order to secure a lasting peace."[6] Only three nations attended the meeting—the Netherlands, Luxembourg, and Belgium. These nations saw unity as their only hope of survival in the postwar world.

Another step was taken in April 1951, when these three nations signed the Treaty of Paris with three additional nations, West Germany, France, and Italy, forming a common market for coal and steel in an environment of peace.

March 25, 1957, saw a major step toward European unification when the Treaty of Rome was signed on Capitoline Hill, one of the famous seven hills of Rome. On this occasion, Italy, France, and West Germany joined the Netherlands, Luxembourg, and Belgium, creating the European Economic Community—the Common Market.

In 1973, the United Kingdom, Ireland, and Denmark joined the EEC, and Greece was added in 1981, making it a ten-nation confederation. On January 1, 1986, Spain and Portugal came into the union, and the EEC officially adopted the goal of a politically unified Europe. In 1987, the Single European Act was implemented. With the fall of the Berlin Wall in 1989, Germany was reunified, and East Germany was integrated into the membership. In 1993, the economic borders between the nations of the European community were removed. Austria, Finland, and Sweden joined the union in 1995. In 2002, eighty billion coins were produced for use in the nations of the eurozone, thus introducing the new monetary unit, the euro.

The march toward European unification continued on May 1, 2004, when Cyprus, the Czech Republic, Estonia, Hungary, Latvia, Lithuania, Malta, Poland, Slovakia, and Slovenia were added, bringing the total to twenty-five nations and expanding the EU's population to surpass North America as the world's biggest economic zone. Romania and Bulgaria were admitted to the EU in 2007, and Croatia joined in 2013, while the United Kingdom voted to exit in June 2016.[7]

Gradually yet steadily, the nations of Europe have come together, creating a modern replica of the Roman Empire. Europe is more integrated today than at any time since the days of ancient Rome. The European Union is considered by many to be the second most powerful political force in our world.

REINFORCEMENT OF THE EUROPEAN GOVERNMENT

Currently the EU government is organized into three bodies: the European Parliament, the Council of European Union, and the European Commission.

The Parliament consists of 751 elected members who pass laws in conjunction with the Council. Its president is elected to serve a two-and-a-half-year term.

The Council consists of the heads of government of each of the member states. This body participates with Parliament in passing laws and establishes common foreign policy and security policies.

The third body of EU government, the European Commission, consists of one commissioner from each EU country, who draft new laws and implement policies and funding. Other EU governmental entities include the Court of Justice, the Court of Auditors, the European Central Bank, and the European Investment Bank.[8]

As we track these developments toward more centralized power among European nations, we can see a new empire in the making—an empire that occupies the same territory as the ancient Roman Empire. Turning back to Daniel for insight into this rising coalition, we are intrigued by his description of it as a mixture of two incohering materials. We know that iron represented the strength of the old Roman Empire. In the newly constituted empire, however, the prophecy tells us that iron will be mixed with clay. Clay speaks of weakness and instability.

The best interpretation of this unstable mix is that it represents the diverse racial, religious, and political elements that will comprise this final form of the Roman Empire. That is, in fact, what we see today in the European coalition. While the EU has great economic and political clout, the cultures and languages of its various countries are so diverse that it cannot hold together any more than iron and clay unless unity is imposed and enforced by an extremely powerful leader.

RENEWED VIGILANCE

From this brief study of modern Europe and ancient Rome, we can begin to understand how Europe represents a key sign of the end times. Three things in particular emerge from our study that should increase our vigilance.

THE CONSOLIDATION OF WORLD POWER

Since the time of the Roman Empire, there has been no nation or empire with the power to govern the known world. But it is coming. In the future, the world will be unified under one dominant leader.

In Daniel's second vision, the fourth beast had ten horns growing from its head: "The fourth beast shall be a fourth kingdom on earth, which shall . . . devour the whole earth, trample it and break it in pieces. The ten horns are ten kings who shall arise from this kingdom" (Dan. 7:23–24). The fourth beast represents the fourth successive kingdom after Babylon, which history identifies as the Roman Empire. But since Rome was never ruled simultaneously by ten kings, we know that those kings are yet to arrive on the stage of world history to rule a newly formed empire that overlays the territory of the ancient Roman Empire.

Today, the concentration of power in the European Union signals the beginning of this new world order.

THE COMING OF ONE WORLD LEADER

According to Daniel's prophecy, a supreme leader will rise from among the ten-leader confederacy in Europe: "Another shall rise after them; he shall be different from the first ones, and shall subdue three kings. He shall speak pompous words against the Most High, shall persecute the saints of the Most High, and shall intend to change times and law. Then the saints shall be given into his hand for a time and times and half a time" (vv. 24–25). This leader will emerge from the group of ten to take control of the European coalition and become the final world dictator. We know him as the Antichrist. We must not miss this point: the European Union is a prelude to the coming of the Antichrist.

Paul-Henri Spaak, first president of the European Parliament, is credited with making this stunning statement: "We do not need another committee. We have too many already. What we want is a man of sufficient stature to hold the allegiance of all people, and to lift us out of the economic morass into which we are sinking. Send us such a man and be he god or devil, we will receive him."[9]

Statements such as this should chill us to the bone. It shows that the world will actually embrace the power that will seek to enslave it. The European Union is the kindling awaiting the spark of the Antichrist to inflame the world with unprecedented evil. It is certainly a time to be vigilant.

THE CONDITION FOR THE TREATY WITH ISRAEL

Daniel's prophecy tells us of a treaty that will be signed between the Jewish people and the leader of the realigned Roman Empire: "He shall confirm a covenant with many for one week; but in the middle of the week he shall bring an end to sacrifice and offering" (9:27). Israel will sign a treaty with the Antichrist, and this treaty will be forged to last for a "week"—in prophetic language, a "week of years," or seven years. This treaty will be an attempt to settle the Arab-Israeli controversy. After three and one-half years, that treaty will be broken, and the countdown to Armageddon will begin.

READ THE WARNING SIGNS

The stage is now set in Europe for these events to occur. Israel is back in her land, and the nations of the ancient Roman Empire are reunifying. Daniel's prophecies show us that the hands on the prophetic clock are moving toward midnight. The warning has been sounded, and we will do well to heed it.

As the prophetic clock moves toward its final strike, we must not wait until it's too late to move out of harm's way. The admonition of Paul should spur us to action: "It is high time to awake out of sleep: for now our salvation is nearer than when we first believed" (Rom. 13:11).

Today's headlines show the wisdom of Paul's warning—it is time for us to awake and realize that things will not go on indefinitely as they are now. As the signs from Daniel's prophecies show us, things are coming to a head. Events are moving us toward the moment when warnings will be too late, and we will be caught in the firestorm of a great evil that will trouble the world before Christ finally returns to set things right.

Are you heeding the warnings? Are you prepared to stand before God? Have you accepted His offer of salvation? He is telling us by the events that surround us that the window of opportunity will soon be gone. Please do not wait until it is too late!

CHAPTER 3

RUSSIA

Russian president Vladimir Putin stepped onto the swaying deck of a miniature submarine. He squeezed inside the capsule, and the craft descended into the Black Sea. The purpose of Putin's excursion, people were told, was to view the wreckage of an ancient ship. But it soon became clear that archeology was the last thing on Putin's mind. The craft leveled out and moved toward the Crimean coastal city of Sevastopol. It surfaced near a waiting yacht, which sped the Russian president to the seaport and deposited him on Crimean soil.

It was August 2015, less than eighteen months after Russia seized the Crimean Peninsula from its parent nation Ukraine. At the time of the takeover, Ukraine had been making overtures to the West with the possibility of joining the European Union. To prevent such a move, which would impede Putin's ambitions for a reunited Soviet bloc, he had not only annexed Crimea but also infiltrated eastern Ukraine with Russian soldiers. His purpose was to stir that nation, already reeling from political turmoil, into chaos. It was his way of saying, "Crimea is Russian territory. I don't need an invitation. I can come here any time I want in any way I want."

Moments after Putin landed at Sevastopol, a BBC reporter questioned the legitimacy of the takeover. Putin replied, "The future of Crimea was determined by the people who live on this land. They voted to be united with Russia. That's it."[1]

Given Putin's history, this aggressive takeover and hard-nosed attitude is not surprising. He began his career as a Russian KGB officer in 1975 when Russia, the ruling nation of the USSR (Union of Soviet Socialist Republics), was a major world power second only to the United States. Russia was feared around the globe for its massive nuclear armaments and threats of communist takeover. Putin retired from the KGB in 1991 and entered politics, rising to power under Boris Yeltsin's administration. When Yeltsin resigned in December 1999, Putin became acting president. He was officially elected in March 2000 and subsequently held the offices of president (2000–2008) and prime minister (2008–2012), before being elected president again in 2012 and reelected to another term in 2018.

At the midpoint of Putin's rise to power, President Ronald Reagan's policies brought down the Soviet-Russian threat without firing a shot. The fall of communism and the disintegration of the USSR must have been a bitter blow to the ambitious young politician. Many believe that from that moment on, Putin has been driven by his determination to restore Russia to its former glory.

THE RUSSIAN AWAKENING

Many of us remember the Cold War between Russia and the United States, which lasted from 1947 to 1991. During that period, the possibility of nuclear war loomed over the world like a dark cloud. But that fear was moderated by US military might and strong Western alliances. Now, in the absence of American will and the collapse of order in the Middle East, what will keep the world's old nemesis, Russia, from rising again?

It appears Putin realizes this is his moment of opportunity and is taking advantage of it. Under his leadership, Russia has become increasingly aggressive on the world stage—and increasingly dangerous. In March of 2018, a former Russian spy named Sergei Skripal was found on a park bench in Great Britain. His thirty-three-year-old daughter was found next to him. Both had been poisoned by a nerve agent, and both were hospitalized for weeks before being moved to a secure location. British police later connected this attack with a similar poisoning involving a woman named Dawn Sturgess and her partner, Charlie Rowley. Ms. Sturgess did not survive that attack, having been exposed to a nerve agent after handling a contaminated perfume dispenser.

After an extensive investigation, British intelligence identified two men as the primary suspects in both attacks—both thought to be members of the GRU, which is Russia's military intelligence service. British prime minister Theresa May said the attacks were "almost certainly" directed by senior members of the Russian government.[2]

Putin obviously wants to be recognized as a world leader of a world power. Where will his ambitions lead? As much as we would like to think Putin's manipulations merely reflect the antics of an overreaching dreamer, we have good reason to believe the Russian threat is real. In fact, we have evidence that, at some point, Russia will ignite a world war like none other. Russia's aggressive moves today cast a long shadow into a future described by the prophet Ezekiel.

THE RUSSIAN AGGRESSION

Approximately twenty-five hundred years ago, Ezekiel predicted Russia's return to power in the latter days. In chapters 38 and 39 of his prophecy, he described the invasion of Israel by ten entities, including Russia and a coalition of mostly Islamic nations.

The nation we know today as Russia figures prominently in these scriptures. In Ezekiel's list of ten names, the third name, Rosh, identifies the nation ruled by the leader of the coalition that will attack Israel.

We have at least two strong reasons for believing that Rosh and Russia are the same. First, it is not hard to see the phonetic similarity between Rosh and Russia. Dr. John F. Walvoord says, "In the study of how ancient words came into modern language, it is quite common for the consonants to remain the same and the vowels to be changed. In the word 'Rosh,' if the vowel 'o' is changed to 'u' it becomes the root of the modern word, Russia."[3]

Second, the Bible refers to the location of Israel as "the middle" of the earth: "Thus says the LORD God: 'This is Jerusalem; I have set her in the midst of the nations and the countries all around her'" (Ezek. 5:5). So whenever we find geographical directions in prophecy, they are given in relation to the position of Israel.

The prophet Daniel described the ruler who would lead an attack against Israel in the latter days as the "king of the North" (Dan. 11:5–35). Ezekiel's prophecy says the invading armies will come to Israel "from the far north" (Ezek. 38:6, 15). Only one country occupies a geographical position in the "far north" in relation to Israel. That nation is Russia, whose landmass stretches from the Baltic to the Bering Seas.

THE RUSSIAN ALLIANCE

Now that we have identified Ezekiel's Rosh as today's Russia, we will turn to the other nine names listed in his prophecy—names that identify the leader and the nations forming the alliance that will attack Israel.

THE COMMANDER OF THE ALLIANCE

The first two verses of Ezekiel 38 read, "The word of the LORD came to me, saying, 'Son of man, set your face against Gog, of the land of Magog, the prince of Rosh, Meshech, and Tubal.'" Unlike the other names in this prophecy, Gog refers not to a nation but to a person. The word *Gog* means "high" or "supreme." Some scholars believe that Gog is not a personal name but a title, such as "President" or "Pharaoh."

Gog is the leader of the armies that will invade Israel, and God commands Gog to be a guard, or commander, for these nations: "Prepare yourself and be ready, you and all your companies that are gathered about you; and be a guard for them" (v. 7).

THE COUNTRIES IN THE ALLIANCE

Here's what we know about the countries named in this future coalition who will attack the nation of Israel.

- **Magog:** According to Genesis 10:2, Magog was the second son of Japheth and the grandson of Noah. Most scholars identify the land that Magog founded as the domain of the Scythians, who lived in the mountains around the Black and Caspian Seas. I like to identify this area as the homeland of the "-stan" countries, which are all states of the former Soviet Empire: Kazakhstan, Kyrgyzstan, Uzbekistan, Turkmenistan, Tajikistan, and perhaps Afghanistan. According to Mark Hitchcock, "These nations today have one thing in common: Islam. And within their borders they have a combined population of 60 million."[4]
- **Meshech and Tubal:** Meshech and Tubal were the fifth and sixth sons of Japheth and, therefore, grandsons of Noah (Gen. 10:2). The descendants of these men established cities or territories bearing their names. C. I. Scofield identifies Meshech as "Moscow" and Tubal as "Tobolsk."[5] Other scholars identify them as territories in modern Turkey.
- **Persia:** According to Ezekiel 38:5, Persia will also participate in Russia's invasion of Israel. Persia changed its name to Iran in 1935 and then, in 1979, changed it again to the Islamic Republic of Iran. Iran and Russia will be the leading forces in this final attempt to wipe Israel off the map. Today, Iran is wielding its malevolent influence not only in the Middle East but in the West as well.
- **Ethiopia:** This is the first of two North African nations named as

part of this coalition. Ethiopia was founded by Cush, the grandson of Noah through his second son, Ham (Gen. 10:6). When Ezekiel made this prophecy, Ethiopia was the land south of Egypt. Today, that region is the modern country of Sudan. Along with Iran, Sudan is one of Israel's fiercest enemies.

- **Libya:** Libya is the land west of Egypt—the only country on Ezekiel's list that retains its ancient name. Like Ethiopia, it was founded by a son of Ham, in this case Put (Gen. 10:6). Today's Libya, along with Iran and Syria, is another of Russia's friends among the Islamic states.

   Modern Libya was ruled for forty-one years by notorious dictator Muammar Gaddafi. Even now Gaddafi's legacy continues to haunt Libya, which is still wracked by civil war and street violence as militant Islamists vie for control. What's more, the Libyan government has been renewing ties with Russia in hopes of purchasing military armaments.[6]

- **Gomer:** Gomer was the first son of Japheth and the grandson of Noah (Gen. 10:2). Because of the similarity between the words, many have taught that Gomer was the founder of the nation that is now Germany. Believing that Gomer represents modern Germany, John Phillips wrote of the death and chaos that nation has inflicted in the past: "A united and greater Germany ('Gomer, and all his bands') had come within a hair of winning World War II. . . . It had taken all the combined might of the British Empire, the Soviet Union, and the United States to fight Germany to a standstill. What if a united and anti-Semitic Germany were to seek its future fortunes while allied to an anti-Semitic Russia?"[7]

- **Togarmah:** Togarmah was the third son of Gomer, son of Japheth (Gen. 10:3), and the great-grandson of Noah. Ezekiel located this nation for us: "the house of Togarmah from the far north and all its troops" (Ezek. 38:6). Some commentators identify Togarmah with Turkey, noting a possible etymological connection between the name Togarmah and the names Turkey and Turkestan.[8]

These are the nations that will form a coalition and march against Israel, setting the stage for this gigantic world war focused on the Holy Land. Though the northern armies of Russia and Turkey will lead the coalition, they will be joined by Iran from the east, Sudan and Libya from the south, and (possibly) Germany from the west in the form of a revived European coalition of nations. To darken the picture for Israel, Ezekiel added that the nation will have "many peoples" on its side (v. 9).

THE RUSSIAN ATTACK

After listing the Russian allies, Ezekiel described the invasion of Israel (38:7–17). As you read this section of Scripture, remember that this is a prophecy against Russia and the invading nations. "Thus says the Lord GOD: 'Behold, I am against you'" (v. 3). The term *you* refers to Russia, and the terms *they* and *them* refer to Israel in this section.

WHY WILL RUSSIA AND ITS ALLIES ATTACK ISRAEL?

What is the purpose of this invasion? Ezekiel gave us three answers that spring from the evil hearts of Israel's attackers. (There is a fourth answer that springs from the heart of God Himself. That will be revealed later in this chapter.)

First, the Russians will go to seize Israel's land: "'I will go up against a land of unwalled villages . . .' to stretch out your hand against the waste places that are again inhabited" (vv. 11–12).

Second, the purpose will be to steal Israel's wealth: "To take plunder and to take booty . . . 'to carry away silver and gold, to take away livestock and goods, to take great plunder'" (vv. 12–13).

Third, the great army from the north will seek to slaughter Israel's people: "You will come up against My people Israel like a cloud, to cover the land" (v. 16). We have already noted the hatred of Israel, a hatred that has existed since Abraham exiled Ishmael (Gen. 21:8–19). That hatred can only be satisfied by the annihilation of the Jewish nation.

WHERE WILL THE INVASION OCCUR?

Ezekiel identified the country to be invaded as "the land of those brought back from the sword and gathered from many people on the mountains of Israel" (Ezek. 38:8).

At least five times in chapter 38, Ezekiel affirmed that Israel will be the target of the Russian coalition. This fact alone makes Ezekiel's prophecy amazing because Israel is one of the smallest nations on earth. Russia is nearly 800 times larger than Israel. Yet Israel is at the center of one of the world's final global wars, the target of a massive coalition led by a world superpower.

WHEN WILL THE INVASION OCCUR?

Ezekiel prophesied that three events must take place before Russia invades Israel. Two of these events have already occurred in history; the third is yet to be fulfilled.

First, Israel must be present in its own land. Ezekiel tells us repeatedly that the dispersed people of Israel will be regathered to their original homeland (twice in 38:8; then in 38:12; 39:25, 27, 28). He also recorded this promise of God in a previous chapter: "I will take you from among the nations, gather you out of all countries, and bring you into your own land" (36:24). Obviously, Ezekiel's prophecy could not have been fulfilled prior to 1948, for the Jews had not yet regathered to their ancient land.

Ezekiel added one more item concerning Israel's occupation of its land before the Russian invasion. He told us that Gog, the coalition leader, "gathered from many people on the mountains of Israel, which had long been desolate" (38:8). Not only will the Jews return to their homeland, but they will also occupy "the mountains of Israel." Mark Hitchcock explains how this prophecy has been fulfilled: "Before the Six-Day War the mountains of Israel were in the hands of the Jordanian Arabs, with the exception of a small strip of West Jerusalem. Only since that war have the mountains of Israel been in Israel."[9]

Ezekiel 36–37, the chapters preceding the description of the Russian invasion, predict the regathering of the nation of Israel, which has already occurred. Ezekiel 40–48, the chapters that follow Ezekiel's description of the invasion, is about the Millennium, which will be the time of Israel's spiritual rebirth. The invasion of Gog and Magog will take place between the national and spiritual rebirths of Israel.

Next, Israel must be prosperous in its land. Ezekiel further prophesied that when the Jewish people have returned to their homeland, God will bless them beyond anything they had previously known: "I will make you inhabited as in former times, and do better for you than at your beginnings. Then you shall know that I am the LORD" (36:11).

The reestablished Israel will become extremely wealthy and the envy of the hostile nations surrounding it. Today, Israel has the third most Nasdaq-listed companies in the world—just after the US and China.[10] It has "earned the moniker of 'Startup Nation' mostly because it has [the] largest number of startups per capita in the world."[11] Israel is also home to eighteen billionaires and more than 105,000 millionaires.[12]

The prosperity of today's Israel is beyond question. This is the second of the three conditions that will exist before the Russian invasion is in place.

The third condition of Israel that will be in place before the Russian invasion is peace. Ezekiel told us that the northern coalition will descend on a people whose peace is so secure that they do not maintain weapons or take defensive measures. Gog boasts, "I will go up against a land of unwalled villages; I will go to a peaceful people, who dwell safely, all of them dwelling without walls, having neither bars nor gates" (38:11).

This is one condition that has not yet occurred. There has never been a time in Israel's existence when it has not been concerned about its defense. Israel has always been surrounded by enemies. Even today, Israel is threatened from all sides by extremely hostile neighbors many times its size. It has already fought numerous wars in its brief modern history, and Israel's close neighbor, Iran, is eager to annihilate it. Israel is not at peace or anywhere close to it. That means the Russian invasion is not imminent.

A time is coming, however, when Israel will be at peace in its land. The prophet Daniel told us how this peace will come about: "He [the Antichrist] shall confirm a covenant with many for one week" (Dan. 9:27). When the Antichrist appears, one of his first projects will be to settle the Arab-Israeli dispute. On behalf of the European coalition of nations, he will make a covenant with the Jews to guarantee their safety. This covenant, which will be contracted for a period of seven years (v. 27), will cause Israel to let down its guard and turn its attention toward prosperity. Israel will, for the first time, be a nation of "unwalled villages" and, therefore, a ripe target for Russian aggression.

Thus we have the time of the Russian invasion of Israel pinpointed. It will come after Israel returns to its homeland, after it has become highly prosperous, and after the implementation of the seven-year peace treaty with the Antichrist.

THE RUSSIAN ANNIHILATION

Israel has always been outnumbered in its wars, but in this instance it will be so grossly mismatched that there will be no human way for the nation to survive. Here is Ezekiel's description of the coalition's advance: "Then you will come from your place out of the far north, you and many peoples with you. . . . You will come up against My people Israel like a cloud, to cover the land" (Ezek. 38:15–16). As a cloud covers the land with its shadow, so the massive armies of the Russian alliance will cover Israel.

But when all hope for Israel's survival is gone, God will intervene: "'And it will come to pass at the same time, when Gog comes against the land of Israel,' says the Lord God, 'that My fury will show in My face. For in My jealousy and in the fire of My wrath I have spoken'" (vv. 18–19).

Remember that when we were outlining the three reasons for Russia's attack on Israel, I alluded to a fourth reason that overrides the others. That reason is to set the stage for God's punishment of Russia and its allies for their history of rebellion against Him: "Then the nations shall know that I am the LORD, the Holy One in Israel" (39:7). God will use the evil tendencies of these allied nations to goad them into attacking Israel so He can execute His judgment against them for their history of human oppression.

Ezekiel described four calamities that will descend on the invading armies when God intervenes to protect His people.

MONUMENTAL CONVULSIONS

The first calamity Ezekiel prophesied was "a great earthquake in the land of Israel" (38:19). This earthquake will be like none ever seen on earth. It will register completely off the Richter scale. Towering buildings and even mountains will come crashing down. Though Israel will be the epicenter, every living creature on the earth will feel the effects of this colossal quake.

MILITARY CONFUSION

The movement, wreckage, and clouds of dust and smoke from the quake will generate mass confusion among the invading armies (v. 21). Dr. Walvoord explains, "In the pandemonium, communication between the invading armies will break down and they will begin attacking each other."[13] This event will be similar to one from Israel's history, but on an exponentially larger scale (see 2 Chron. 20:22–25). God will protect His people in the future as He has done in the past.

MAJOR CONTAGION

God's third weapon against the Russian coalition will be an epidemic breakout of disease: "I will bring him to judgment with pestilence and bloodshed" (Ezek. 38:22). Unburied dead bodies will lie everywhere, causing a malignant plague to infect the land. Thousands more of the invaders will die.

MULTIPLE CALAMITIES

A deluge of fire and brimstone will also fall on Russia and its allies just as God rained fire and brimstone down on Sodom and Gomorrah (v. 22). These God-inflicted calamities will extend to the Magog homelands as well. "I will send fire on Magog and on those who live in security in the coastlands. Then they shall know that I am the LORD" (39:6). Those who remain in Magog will not escape punishment.

THE RUSSIAN AFTERMATH

God's supernatural intervention to protect Israel and bring judgment on the Russian coalition will leave all of Israel's fields, mountains, plains, gullies, and lakes strewn and piled with the invaders' bodies. It will be a grisly testament to the ignoble end of those who defy God. The disposal of these corpses can be summed up in these words: birds, beasts, burning, and burials. Just as Ezekiel 38 details the destruction of the northern armies, chapter 39 describes their disposal.

THE BIRDS AND THE BEASTS

Ezekiel recorded God's invitation to all the birds of the world and the beasts of the field to come to Israel and devour the thousands of bodies that will be scattered across the land. God calls it a "sacrificial meal" for the scavengers that will do His bidding and clean up the land for His people (39:17–20).

THE BURNINGS

Not only will the failed Russian invasion leave masses of bodies, but it will also leave the coalition's military equipment littering the landscape. How will these now-useless weapons be discarded? Ezekiel says, "Those who dwell in the cities of Israel will go out and set on fire and burn the weapons, both the shields and bucklers, the bows and arrows, the javelins and spears; and they will make fires with them for seven years" (v. 9).

THE BURIALS

The vultures and scavengers God will invite to devour the bodies of the fallen invaders will leave a residue of bones and other inedible parts. It will be necessary for the Israelis to bury what the scavengers leave. God says, "I will give Gog a burial place there in Israel. . . . For seven months the house of Israel will be burying them, in order to cleanse the land" (vv. 11–12). The fact that it will take seven months to bury all of the dead gives us an indication of the gigantic size of the invading army. Only when the burials are complete can the land be declared ceremonially clean again (Num. 19:11–22).

THE RUSSIAN APPLICATION

In Ezekiel 38–39, we find a compelling prophecy about the ultimate destruction of Russia, a nation that has long been antagonistic toward God and disruptive to the world. Today, we can see the historical character of that nation asserting itself again as it seeks to expand its power and disruptive influence, especially in the Middle East. It is merely a matter of time before Russia stretches its claws toward the rich and free nation of Israel. But God has promised Israel a glorious future, and as these two prophetic chapters show, He will keep that promise in a spectacular and satisfying way.

The whole world will marvel at how God brings down a powerful enemy while preserving His people. When this happens, the world will stand in awe of the name and power of God: "Thus I will magnify Myself and sanctify Myself, and I will be known in the eyes of many nations. Then they shall know that I am the LORD" (Ezek. 38:23).

I can understand why people shudder at today's headlines. The daily news shows an alarming disintegration of world order and security. We see growing disorder now and chaos ahead, and we wonder whether God has turned His face away from us.

Some years ago, the late pastor Ray Stedman was scheduled to speak at a conference in England. Each session of the conference began with a song service. One night, the leader led the worshippers in the chorus "Our God Reigns." Stedman glanced at the song sheet, which had been prepared by the church staff. What he saw caused him to smile. Someone, intending to type the title as "Our God Reigns," had actually typed "Our God Resigns."[14]

Let me assure you that our God will never resign. We who trust Him have no reason to fear. As I have read Ezekiel 38–39, the one thing that stands out is the sovereignty of God. He is in control. God orchestrates this scenario to demonstrate to His people, Israel, that He is their God and worthy of their trust. Israel has no hope without God, and God will win the battle for the nation. Godless Russia is no match for the King of kings.

The God of Israel is also our God, which means whatever we fear is also no match for the King of kings. When it looks like there is no hope, hope is just waiting for the proper moment to show up. God can be trusted.

CHAPTER 4

BABYLON

When the luxury liner *Titanic* was launched in 1912, it was the largest and most magnificent ship ever built. Spanning the length of almost three football fields, it boasted an interior rivaling the most opulent mansions and offered its passengers unprecedented luxuries, including a heated swimming pool, a Turkish bath, a squash court, and a dog kennel. The first-class dining room served ten-course dinners. A first-class parlor suite cost today's equivalent of $50,000, but many of the world's wealthiest and most prominent people bought tickets to enjoy the prestige and luxury of the ship's maiden voyage.

The *Titanic* was touted to be unsinkable, thus it carried only twenty lifeboats, a fraction of the sixty-four needed to evacuate its 2,228 passengers. Because the ship was "unsinkable," the captain and crew members ignored warnings of drifting icebergs in the northern Atlantic and posted only a desultory watch on the fatal night when the ship struck a berg. Water immediately began gushing into the ship, flooding enough airtight compartments to make sinking inevitable. Evacuation began, but with limited lifeboat capacity and a crew untrained in evacuation, only 705 people were saved, leaving 1,523 to perish with the ship.[1]

The tragedy of the *Titanic* demonstrates how man's pride and arrogance leads to destruction. It was pride in the ship's prestige and opulence that prompted many rich and prominent people to make the voyage. It was arrogance to think the ship unsinkable, thus dismissing the need for lifeboats, plowing headlong through iceberg-infested waters, and neglecting to train the crew for evacuation.

As we will see in this chapter, early in our world's history a city was founded on this same pride and arrogance and was brought to a similar ignominious end. That city is none other than the infamous Babylon.

BABYLON

Babylon is the second most frequently mentioned city in the Bible. In the NKJV, it appears 287 times in 253 verses. These references are never positive. Babylon's origins were pagan, humanistic, and rebellious against God—unholy attributes permanently adhered to the city's name, making it perennially infamous.

Old Testament scholar Dr. Charles H. Dyer summarizes the early prominence of Babylon:

> For nearly two thousand years, Babylon was the most important city in the world. It was the commercial and financial center for all Mesopotamia, the center of a geographical "X" that linked the Orient with the Mediterranean and Egypt with Persia. Its scribes and priests spread its cultural heritage throughout the known world. The arts of divination, astronomy, astrology, accounting, and private commercial law all sprang from Babylon.[2]

Though Babylon no longer exists as a cultural and financial powerhouse, it has influenced the world in ways that continue even today. In the first book of the Bible we learn that Babylon was the site of the Tower of

Babel, man's first attempt to establish a world order devoid of God's influence (Gen. 11). In the last book of the Bible we see that a revived Babylon will be the center of a financial world order which will dominate the Tribulation period.

Why Babylon? What mystery lies dormant in this ancient, fallen powerhouse that will elevate it again to a position of world dominance? Dr. Henry Morris explains:

> Babylon is indeed a prime prospect for rebuilding, entirely apart from any prophetic intimation. Its location is the most ideal in the world for any kind of international center. Not only is it in the beautiful and fertile Tigris Euphrates plain, but it is near some of the world's richest oil reserves. . . .
>
> Babylon is very near the geographical center of all of the earth's land masses. It is within navigable distances of the Persian Gulf and is at the crossroads of the three great continents of Europe, Asia, and Africa.
>
> Thus there is no more ideal location anywhere for a world trade center, a world communication center, a world banking center, a world education center, or especially, a world capital! . . .
>
> The greatest historian of modern time, Arnold Toynbee, used to stress . . . that Babylon would be the best place in the world to build a future world cultural metropolis.[3]

BABYLON'S REBIRTH

The book of Revelation reveals that when the Antichrist seizes the reins of world government, his administration will be divided among three power centers. Rome will be his political base (Rev. 17); Jerusalem will be his control center for religion (2 Thess. 2:4); and Babylon will become his financial and economic hub (Rev. 18).

John lists twenty-eight commodities that will form the foundation of Babylon's worldwide commerce in the end times:

> Merchandise of gold and silver, precious stones and pearls, fine linen and purple, silk and scarlet, every kind of citron wood, every kind of object of ivory, every kind of object of most precious wood, bronze, iron, and marble; and cinnamon and incense, fragrant oil and frankincense, wine and oil, fine flour and wheat, cattle and sheep, horses and chariots, and bodies and souls of men. (Rev. 18:12–13)

The striking thing about this list is that these commodities are as desired today as they were in John's time. Clearly, the list is not only literal—identifying the possessions men have striven for throughout history—it is also symbolic of mankind's endless pursuit of material wealth. That pursuit will continue up to the moment of Christ's return.

Notice that the first items on the list are gold, silver, and precious stones. This may indicate a coming collapse of global currencies, forcing a reversion to perennial value standards such as precious metals and gemstones.

When Babylon becomes the world's commercial center, international banks and corporations will set up operations there. Henry Morris explains:

> The international bankers and the corporation directors and the mercantile barons and the shipping magnates and all their host of money-worshiping, power-seeking underlings, who once traversed their orbits around New York and Geneva, London and Paris, Moscow and Berlin, Johannesburg and Tokyo, now find it gloriously profitable to center it all in Great Babylon.[4]

To sum it up, look for Babylon to rise phoenix-like from its present obscurity to become the financial center of the world.

But God will not allow Babylon's incessant output of evil to plague the world forever. The destruction of Babylon will be total and irrevocable, desolating even the site where it once stood. According to the prophet Isaiah:

> It will never be inhabited,
> Nor will it be settled from generation to generation;
> Nor will the Arabian pitch tents there,
> Nor will the shepherds make their sheepfolds there.
> But wild beasts of the desert will lie there,
> And their houses will be full of owls;
> Ostriches will dwell there,
> And wild goats will caper there. (Isa. 13:20–21)

Jeremiah elaborates on the desolation of Babylon, describing it as a heap of ruins, a dry desert of horror and scorn, a lair of jackals and howling hyenas that travelers will avoid, a place never again to be inhabited (Jer. 51:26, 37, 43).

THE REASONS FOR BABYLON'S DESTRUCTION

In Revelation 18, the apostle John saw an angel descending to earth whose splendor was so radiant it illuminated the entire earth. This angel pronounces judgment upon the city of Babylon: "And he cried mightily with a loud voice, saying, 'Babylon the great is fallen, is fallen'" (Rev. 18:2).

The word for "fallen" used here is a word that means "to fall instantaneously." That is, the destruction of Babylon will not take place over a long period of time but will happen in a moment—actually, in one hour, we are told later in the chapter (18:19).

Why is God so determined to judge and destroy Babylon? It's because He cannot allow the influences of a city so antagonistic to His people to contaminate His coming kingdom. John identifies five of these influences, which we will consider one by one.

BABYLON WILL BE DESTROYED
BECAUSE OF HER INIQUITY

John writes, "Babylon . . . has become a dwelling place of demons, a prison for every foul spirit, and a cage for every unclean and hated bird!" (18:2).

In Daniel's time, Babylon was infested with magicians, soothsayers, and astrologers who served as King Nebuchadnezzar's close advisors. This demonic occultism will multiply exponentially when Satan's puppet, the Beast, co-opts the Babylonian system. A vast web of demonic activity centered in Babylon will reach out across the nations intent on possessing the minds of every person on earth.

BABYLON WILL BE DESTROYED
BECAUSE OF HER INFLUENCE

In the next verse John adds: "For all the nations have drunk of the wine of the wrath of her fornication, the kings of the earth have committed fornication with her, and the merchants of the earth have become rich through the abundance of her luxury" (18:3).

We can easily imagine newspapers and TV channels lauding Babylon for its enlightenment, openness, and tolerance—newspeak euphemisms for the rampant immorality and deep depravity that will ooze from the city like pus from a sore. Jetsetters will flock to Babylon to indulge in debaucheries that will make the debaucheries of Vegas, Paris, and Hong Kong seem bland. Governments and corporations will normalize these sordid pleasures, spreading their influence throughout the world.

Bible expositor John Phillips believes Babylon will become the world crime center: "The crime syndicate, already enormously wealthy and powerful, feudal, ruthless, and omnipresent, will move its headquarters to Babylon. There can be little doubt that the syndicate, controlling the vice traffic of the world and insinuating itself into all kinds of legitimate businesses, will ultimately look to the Beast as its head."[5]

In the Tribulation period, the diabolical influence of Babylon will dominate humanity's social, political, cultural, and economic life. The only way to rid the world of this toxic contamination is to destroy the city from which it spews.

BABYLON WILL BE DESTROYED BECAUSE OF HER INFIDELITY

The third reason for God's judgment against Babylon is that "her sins have reached to heaven, and God has remembered her iniquities" (18:5).

The Greek word here translated as "reached" presents a fascinating picture. It means "to be glued or welded together." It's a deliberate allusion to the ancient Tower of Babel, predicting that the revived Babylon will build its own tower of sins, stacking one upon the other like bricks until they reach heaven. Just as God destroyed Babel's original tower, He must also demolish this unholy replica to rid the earth of the diabolic infidelity of the Beast.

BABYLON WILL BE DESTROYED BECAUSE OF HER INSOLENCE

"In the measure that she glorified herself and lived luxuriously, in the same measure give her torment and sorrow; for she says in her heart, 'I sit as queen, and am no widow, and will not see sorrow'" (18:7).

The newly revived Babylon will actually glory in its opulence, its debauchery, its occultism, and its ruthlessness, thinking the power and awe it commands renders it superior and inviolable. But just as the unsinkable *Titanic* now lies at the bottom of the ocean, Babylon's pride will bring it down, as pride always does: "Pride goes before destruction, and a haughty spirit before a fall" (Prov. 16:18).

BABYLON WILL BE DESTROYED BECAUSE OF HER INHUMANITY

When I discussed the catalog of Babylon's global trade commodities, I withheld for present discussion the final, chilling item on that list: "bodies and souls of men" (Rev. 18:13). Babylon will be the hub of worldwide sex trafficking, abducting untold thousands of men and women into forced prostitution.

In the Tribulation period, Babylon will utterly disdain the idea that man is created in the image of God. The system will see humans as did the intelligent simians in the classic film *Planet of the Apes*—as nothing more than animals to be bought, sold, used, and discarded at will.

Babylon's inhumanity will also be revealed in its wholesale slaughter of God's people: "And in her was found the blood of prophets and saints, and of all who were slain on the earth" (18:24). "I saw the woman, drunk with the blood of the saints and with the blood of the martyrs of Jesus" (17:6). In the Tribulation period, Babylon will execute God's prophets and all who refuse the mark of the Beast. In fact, simply being a believer and standing for moral purity and Christian ethics will be enough to warrant execution.

THE REALITY OF BABYLON'S DESTRUCTION

Babylon's new tower of depravity, built from the bricks of her sins, will rise to unprecedented heights, finally prompting God to take action. John describes the suddenness of God's judgment in this way: "Therefore her plagues will come in one day—death and mourning and famine. And she will be utterly burned with fire, for strong is the Lord God who judges her" (18:8).

John goes on to describe the utter finality of Babylon's destruction:

Then a mighty angel took up a stone like a great millstone and threw it into the sea, saying, "Thus with violence the great city Babylon shall be thrown down, and shall not be found anymore. The sound of harpists, musicians, flutists, and trumpeters shall not be heard in you anymore. No craftsman of any craft shall be found in you anymore, and the sound of a millstone shall not be heard in you anymore. The light of a lamp shall not shine in you anymore, and the voice of bridegroom and bride shall not be heard in you anymore. (Rev. 18:21–23)

The word *anymore*, which occurs six times in this passage, is translated from the strongest Greek term available to express "not at all" or "never again." It's a picture of what happens when God pronounces judgment; it is sudden, thorough, and final.

In the moment before Babylon's destruction, the city will bustle with all the normal activities abounding in any metropolis, along with the world-shaping enterprises of its elite citizens—the wealthy and powerful, the rulers of nations and banking and commerce. People will be working, shopping, marrying, and attending parties, theaters, orchestral performances, and sports events. Thousands of communication lines will hum between banks, government agencies, corporate headquarters, and their subsidiaries around the world.

Then suddenly, in one short hour, it will all cease to exist. Babylon will be gone. And as the center of a vast web of interconnected globalism, it will pull the world down with it. Down will come the world's financial system and the global market. Banks and corporations will collapse. All corporate stocks and national currencies will become fireplace kindling. Bank accounts will evaporate, and workers will be abruptly unemployed. The destruction of Babylon will trigger a global depression far eclipsing any disaster the world has yet seen.

THE REACTIONS TO BABYLON'S DESTRUCTION

The world will react to Babylon's fall with shock and horror. Everyone will reel with the cataclysmic impact of it on their own lives. To grasp the extent of this impact, let's examine the reactions of three specific groups which will be most severely affected by the city's collapse.

THE MONARCHS WILL MOURN

"The kings of the earth who committed fornication and lived luxuriously with [Babylon] will weep and lament for her, when they see the smoke of her burning, standing at a distance for fear of her torment, saying, 'Alas, alas, that great city Babylon, that mighty city! For in one hour your judgment has come'" (18:9–10).

When the Beast's political and financial empire goes down with Babylon's destruction, all the power and wealth of the world's rulers will collapse, leaving them shattered in the wake of crushed dreams and lost glory.

THE MERCHANTS WILL MOURN

"And the merchants of the earth will weep and mourn over [Babylon], for no one buys their merchandise anymore. . . . The merchants . . . who became rich by her, will stand at a distance for fear of her torment, weeping and wailing, and saying, 'Alas, alas, that great city that was clothed in fine linen, purple, and scarlet, and adorned with gold and precious stones and pearls! For in one hour such great riches came to nothing'" (18:11, 15–17).

The word *merchants* used here is translated from the Greek *emporoi*, which specifically means wholesalers who trade massive quantities of goods. With the fall of Babylon, the world's stock markets will crash beyond recovery, drying up all possibility of investment in the merchants' businesses. With no more banks to issue credit, their ruin will be sudden and total. In one short hour, the god of mammon will be reduced to ashes.

THE MARINERS WILL MOURN

"Every shipmaster, all who travel by ship, sailors, and as many as trade on the sea, stood at a distance and cried out when they saw the smoke of her burning, saying, 'What is like this great city?' They threw dust on their heads and cried out, weeping and wailing, and saying, 'Alas, alas, that great city, in which all who had ships on the sea became rich by her wealth! For in one hour she is made desolate'" (18:17–19).

Imagine the captain of a merchant ship laden with imported goods sailing northwesterly through the Persian Gulf toward Babylon. The waterway is crowded with similar ships carrying Babylonian cargo. Suddenly the captain gapes in disbelief. Massive columns of black smoke rise high on the horizon, their undersides glowing orange from the angry flames devouring the city. The captain groans and tears at his hair as he grasps the meaning of the sight. The market for his cargo is destroyed. Financing for future shipments no longer exists. He is ruined, along with all the other maritime shippers of the world. All commercial shipping is suddenly—and literally—dead in the water.

THE REJOICING OVER BABYLON'S DESTRUCTION

When Babylon is destroyed, the monarchs, merchants, and mariners of the world will mourn. But the apostles and prophets in heaven will rejoice: "Rejoice over her, O heaven, and you holy apostles and prophets, for God has avenged you on her!" (18:20).

What a contrast of emotions! While the opportunists who profited from Babylon grieve its destruction, the apostles and prophets in heaven who were martyred by the Babylonian system will exult at the end of its diabolic wickedness. From the time of its founding, Babylon has unleashed on the world an unholy system of defiance against God. It has enslaved God's people, cut them to pieces, boiled them in oil, cast them into furnaces and lions' dens, nailed them to crosses, and will soon inflict similar horrors on all who refuse the mark of the Beast.

But God promises justice to those who suffer for Him. As He repeatedly assures us, "Vengeance is Mine, I will repay" (Heb. 10:30). During the Tribulation, the martyrs under the altar in heaven cry out for justice, asking "How long, O Lord, holy and true, until You judge and avenge our blood on those who dwell on the earth?" (Rev. 6:10). They are told to rest in confidence that God will indeed avenge their suffering at the proper time. That promised justice will come down hard and fast with the destruction of Babylon, raising a resounding cry of rejoicing from the apostles and prophets—not in vindictiveness for their persecution, but in gratitude that the earth is finally cleansed of an insidious evil.

When you are treated unfairly or endure some form of abuse, or when you see others promoted at your expense through underhanded means, do you wonder if God has forgotten you? Do you, like the martyrs waiting in heaven, wonder how long it will be before God sets things right? It's a common experience that often leads people to question Christianity. "If God is good, why doesn't He eradicate evil?"

The Bible addresses that age-old question extensively in the books of Job, Habakkuk, and in Psalm 73. But while pondering those deeper explanations, it helps to know that God never ignores evil. His judgment against those who wrong us may not be immediate. But the biblical record shows that when the time is right, He will avenge every evil committed against His own, beginning with Satan's seduction in Eden and culminating with the destruction of Babylon.

OUR RESPONSE TO BABYLON'S DESTRUCTION

Now that we've seen how kings, merchants, shippers, apostles, and prophets will respond to Babylon's destruction, one additional response remains to be addressed: how will you and I respond? John shows us the way when he writes, "And I heard another voice from heaven saying, 'Come out of her, my people, lest you share in her sins, and lest you receive of her plagues'" (Rev. 18:4). God calls us to get out of Babylon—that is, to separate ourselves from the godless spirit of the age, which is the spirit of Babylon that now permeates our culture.

I fear that today many believers are not heeding this call. They attempt to maintain dual citizenship in Jerusalem and Babylon, which Paul tells us is impossible: "For what fellowship has righteousness with lawlessness? And what communion has light with darkness? And what accord has Christ with Belial? Or what part has a believer with an unbeliever? And what agreement has the temple of God with idols? For you are the temple of the living God" (2 Cor. 6:14–16).

As God's temple, we must keep a clean house for Him to occupy. We must sweep out the contaminations of self-love, worldly pleasure, and materialistic ambition.

John warns us to get out of Babylon, "lest you share in her sins, and lest you receive of her plagues" (Rev. 18:4). The unholy attractions of Babylon are like bait in a trap, luring victims to share in the destruction reserved for that city and its diabolical system. Even before this plague of destruction descends, the security Babylon offers is a sham. Bank accounts, investments, economic expansion, and even gold and silver will prove to be unstable as a house of cards.

We find real security only in God. When we reject Babylon and remain in Jerusalem, we can share Paul's confidence in God's promise: "For I am persuaded that neither death nor life, nor angels nor principalities nor powers, nor things present nor things to come, nor height nor depth, nor any other created thing, shall be able to separate us from the love of God which is in Christ Jesus our Lord" (Rom. 8:38–39). Nothing—whether it's the growing instability of present culture or the persecution, famines, and distress of the coming Tribulation period—can separate us from God.

The world system is as precarious as the shifting tectonic plates beneath California. But God's promises never shift; they remain unshakeable and solid. We rightly grieve to see so many rushing headlong toward Babylon like lemmings to the sea. But it's right that we also celebrate the coming triumph of good over evil, removing for all eternity this perennial enemy of God that has inflicted so much misery on His people.

CHAPTER 5

AMERICA

When the sun rises over Washington, D.C., each morning, its rays fall on the eastern side of the city's tallest structure, the 555-foot-tall Washington Monument. The first part of that monument to reflect the rising sun is the eastern side of its aluminum capstone, on which the words *Laus Deo* are inscribed. That's Latin for "Praise be to God." This prayer of praise, visible to the eyes of heaven alone, is tacit recognition of our nation's unique acknowledgment of the place of God in its founding and its continuance.[1]

Were these words a grandiose but empty claim to national piety, or do they reflect a true reality? In *The Light and the Glory,* Peter Marshall and David Manuel ask a profound question:

What if Columbus' discovering of America had not been accidental at all? What if it were merely the opening curtain of an extraordinary drama? Did God have a special plan for America? . . . What if in particular He had a plan for those He would bring to America, a plan which saw this continent as a stage for a new era in the drama of mankind's redemption?[2]

President Ronald Reagan believed God had a plan for our nation. He wrote, "I have always believed that this anointed land was set apart in an uncommon way, that a divine plan placed this great continent here between the oceans to be found by people from every corner of the earth who had a special love of faith and freedom."[3]

AMERICA AND THE SOVEREIGNTY OF GOD

It seems clear that God does have a plan for America. It is true that we have no direct reference to that plan in the Old or New Testaments, but that does not discount the fact that God has a sovereign purpose for America in His redemptive plan.

As Marshall and Manuel suggest, God's hand on America began with its discoverer. In the rotunda of the Capitol Building is a great painting titled *The Landing of Columbus*, depicting his arrival on the shores of America. As Marshall asserts, when Columbus discovered the New World, God had His hand on the wheel of the ship and brought it here.

Looking back at our nation's history, we can see America's leaders turning to God for guidance. We see Washington kneeling in the snow of Valley Forge. We see our founding fathers on their knees at the first Continental Congress. We see Lincoln praying in the hour of national crisis. We see Woodrow Wilson reading his Bible at night by the White House lights. Washington summarized this national dependence on God when he said, "No People can be bound to acknowledge and adore the invisible hand, which conducts the Affairs of men more than the People of the United States."[4]

Clearly, America did not become the land of the free and the home of the brave by blind fate or a set of coincidences. A benevolent God has been hovering over this nation from its very conception.

Why has God blessed this nation above all other lands? Why has America in her short history outstripped the wealth, power, and influence of all ancient and modern civilizations? Can God have blessed a nation so richly without having a pivotal purpose? What is God's plan for America? What is its place in end-time prophecy?

To understand America's place in end-time prophecy, we must first explore the reasons for God's favor on America, and then we will show what this means in terms of coming events.

AMERICA HAS BEEN THE FORCE BEHIND WORLD MISSIONS

God has blessed America because we have been the launching pad of the world's great missionary movement. In the aftermath of World War II, Americans started 1,800 mission agencies and sent out more than 350,000 missionaries.[5] Even before the widespread use of the internet, scholars believed that "more than 95 percent of the population of the world—people from every culture and language and country—will have access to the gospel through some portion of Scripture in their language, through literature distribution, radio transmission, audio recordings, the JESUS film or simply through the message of an evangelist."[6]

These achievements are due largely to the missionary zeal of churches in the United States.

AMERICA HAS BEEN A FRIEND TO THE JEWISH PEOPLE

America's historic support of Israel is based not so much on efforts by Jewish lobbyists in Washington or the presence of Jewish groups in our society but on the Judeo-Christian heritage of our nation. President Truman's determination to recognize Israel as a modern state was fueled by his lifelong belief that, in the book of Deuteronomy, God gave the land of Israel to the Jewish people for all time.

At the founding of the modern state of Israel, surrounding Arab nations immediately declared war on the new nation. Few felt Israel could survive, and Western nations did not want to become embroiled in the conflict. Truman was under pressure not to intervene.

Jewish statesman Abba Eban flew to Paris to meet with an American delegation regarding recognition. Secretary of State George Marshall had to return home for medical treatment, and his deputy, John Foster Dulles, assumed leadership of the delegation.

Eban later wrote that Dulles held the key to the success of the talks. "Behind a dry manner, redolent of oak-paneled courtrooms in the United States, there was a curious strain of Protestant mysticism which led him to give the Israel questions a larger importance that its geo-political weight would indicate."[7]

What Eban called "a curious strain of Protestant mysticism" is the historic love that Christians have for the land and people of Israel, based upon their shared religious heritage and Scriptures. This, more than anything else, has cemented the friendship between America and Israel.

God promised to bless those who bless Israel (Gen. 12:3). He has amply fulfilled that promise. America has been abundantly blessed as a nation because we have blessed the Jews.

AMERICA HAS BEEN A FREE NATION

In my study of Scripture, I have observed that the principles of freedom are united with the tenets of Christianity. America today is the laboratory where those blended principles can develop and become an example to all the world. The Bible says, "You shall know the truth, and the truth shall make you free" (John 8:32).

Freedom can never be taken for granted in our world. As an independent watchdog organization, Freedom House studies the challenges to democracy and freedom around the world. In 2018, Freedom Houses' annual report indicated that only 45 percent of the world's population lives in nations categorized as "free"—meaning, nations that guarantee free and fair elections, the rights of minorities, freedom of the press, and the rule of law.[8] In fact, the tendency in a fallen world is always away from freedom and toward despotism and tyranny.

In his 1981 inaugural address, President Ronald Reagan spoke of our freedom in these stirring words: "No arsenal or no weapon in the arsenals of the world is so formidable as the will and moral courage of free men and women. It is a weapon our adversaries in today's world do not have. It is a weapon that we as Americans do have. Let that be understood by those who practice terrorism and prey upon their neighbors."[9]

America has learned what our repressive and terrorist adversaries do not understand: liberty without law is anarchy, liberty to defy law is rebellion, but liberty limited by law is the cornerstone of civilization. We Americans have tried to share what we have learned by exporting freedom wherever we have gone in the world. We have tried to help people understand that freedom is what creates the life God intended us to have from the beginning.

America has become the paradise of human liberty—a great oasis in a global desert of trouble, suffering, repression, and tyranny. Our nation is a dramatic exclamation point to the assertion that freedom works!

Today, our heritage of freedom is being challenged internally by the erosion of our culture. As long-held freedoms come under fire, some Americans, especially those with wealth, are deciding that the United States is no longer the best place to live. Sadly, if our culture continues to jettison the principles that made our nation great, we can hardly expect the blessing of almighty God to continue.

AMERICA WAS FOUNDED ON GOD AND HIS WORD

It is no mystery why America's founders insisted on the principle of freedom. Their dependence on the God of the Bible led them to subject themselves to Him as the ultimate authority for law rather than set themselves up as autocrats with the audacity to control the lives of their subjects. And because they submitted to God's authority, He has blessed this nation as none has ever been blessed. The psalmist wrote, "Blessed is the nation whose God is the Lord, the people He has chosen as His own inheritance" (Ps. 33:12). The book of Proverbs adds, "Righteousness exalts a nation, but sin is a reproach to any people" (14:34).

Dependence on God characterized our governmental philosophy through several generations and resulted in God's blessings on our nation.

Our leaders stabilized government with a lifeline between nation and God, with authority and blessing flowing downward as dependence and thanksgiving flowed upward.

George Washington set the tone for the nation's governmental authority when he said, "It is impossible to rightly govern the world without God and the Bible."[10] That philosophy remained intact through the time of Abraham Lincoln, who is quoted as saying, "It is my constant anxiety and prayer that both myself and this nation should be on the Lord's side."[11]

Benjamin Franklin explained why he requested that each day of the Constitutional Convention be opened in prayer: "The longer I live, the more convincing proofs I see of this Truth—that God governs in the Affairs of Men." He continued, "Without his concurring aid, we shall succeed in this political Building no better than the Builders of Babel."[12]

In 1911, President Woodrow Wilson said:

> The Bible . . . is the one supreme source of revelation of the meaning of life, the nature of God and spiritual nature and needs of men. It is the only guide of life which really leads the spirit in the way of peace and salvation. America was born a Christian nation. America was born to exemplify that devotion to the elements of righteousness which are derived from the revelations of Holy Scripture.[13]

Today, our heritage of national dependence on God is under fire. Forces within our nation threaten its divine lifeline. The attitude of many in our culture today seems symbolized by the legal tides trying to remove the words *under God* from the Pledge of Allegiance. Those two words were inserted into the pledge in 1954, partly to distinguish our nation from the atheistic communism of the Soviet Union. But while these words came late to the pledge, they certainly reflect what has been a part of America's heritage from the beginning.

Our leaders realized that once America failed to acknowledge that we were under God, our basis for freedom and equitable government would come crashing down. President Calvin Coolidge said it well: "The foundations of our society and our government rest so much on the teachings of the Bible that it would be difficult to support them if faith in these teachings would cease to be practically universal in our country."[14] In other words, when America turns from its position of being under God, we can no longer expect His blessings on this nation to continue.

THE SILENCE OF THE BIBLE ON THE FUTURE OF AMERICA

Dr. Tim LaHaye wrote, "One of the hardest things for American prophecy students to accept is that the United States is not clearly mentioned in Bible prophecy."[15] Indeed, no specific mention of the United States can be found in the Bible. One reason may be that in the grand scheme of history, the United States is a new kid on the block. Our nation is less than 250 years old—much younger than the nations featured in biblical prophecy. In fact, the Bible makes no mention of most nations in the modern world. The ancient prophets were primarily concerned with the Holy Land and its immediate neighbors. Most areas remote from Israel do not figure in Bible prophecy.

Dr. LaHaye went on to raise this question:

> "Does the United States have a place in end time prophecy?" My first response is no, there is nothing about the U.S. in prophecy! At least nothing that is specific. There is an allusion to a group of nations in Ezekiel 38:13 that could apply, but even that is not specific. The question is why? Why would the God of prophecy not refer to the supreme superpower nation in the end times in preparation for the One world government of the Antichrist?[16]

We can understand these issues better if we look at some of the best thinking that students of prophecy have given us on why America is absent from end-time prophecies. Here are some possible explanations for the Bible's silence on the future of America.

AMERICA WILL BE INCORPORATED
INTO THE EUROPEAN COALITION

Our first answer comes from prophecy expert John Walvoord, who wrote:

> Although the Scriptures do not give any clear word concerning the role of the United States in relation to the revived Roman Empire, it is clear this will be a consolidation of the power of the West. Unlike the coalitions led by the United States, this coalition will be led by others—the Group of Ten. . . . Most citizens of the United States of America have come from Europe, and their sympathies would more naturally be with a European alliance than with Russia . . . Asia, and Africa. . . . Europe and America may be in formal alliance with Israel in opposition to the radical Islamic countries of the Middle East.[17]

According to this theory, though America is not mentioned by name in prophecy, it will be in the mix of the political realignments that foreshadow the end of time. And we can see signs of such realignments taking place in recent years.

President George W. Bush welcomed EU Commission president Jos Barroso and the serving president of the European Council, German chancellor Angela Merkel, to the White House in April 2007. The president thanked the two for their part in "the trans-Atlantic economic integration plan that the three of us signed today. It is a statement of the importance of trade. It is a commitment to eliminating barriers to trade. It is a recognition that the closer that the United States and the EU become, the better off our people become."[18]

On the surface there seems to be nothing ominous about such an agreement; it appears to be simply about freeing up economic trade between nations. But agreements such as this have implications far beyond mere economic trade. What does this mean for America?

AMERICA WILL BE INVADED
BY OUTSIDE FORCES

Perhaps the silence of Scripture on the future of America indicates that by the time the Tribulation arrives, America will have lost her influence in the world and will no longer be a major player. America's thirst for oil and inability to close the gap between supply and demand could cripple our ability to defend our borders and protect our nation. Once again John Walvoord addresses the issue:

> Some maintain that the total absence of any scriptural reference to America in the end time is evidence that the United States will have been crippled by a nuclear attack, weapons of mass destruction, or some other major catastrophe. . . . In the post-9/11 world the detonation of a dirty bomb, nuclear device, or biological weapon on U.S. soil is a dreaded yet distinct possibility. Such an attack could kill millions of people, cripple the economy, and reduce the United States to a second-rate power overnight.[19]

Since the deployment of the first atomic bomb on Hiroshima in August 1945, America has enjoyed a certain fear-based aura of invincibility. Both friends and enemies knew we would use any and all weapons in our formidable arsenal to protect our nation. According to Ed Timperlake, who served in the Office of the Secretary of Defense, "Air Force and Navy personnel continue to stand vigilant 24 hours a day, seven days a week inside the strategic triad of bombers, land-based ICBMs and submarine 'boomers.'"[20]

In today's world, however, such power and vigilance may no longer deter enemies determined to attack the United States. In a column in the *Washington Times*, Timperlake observed that the political instability in Pakistan could lead to nuclear warheads falling into the hands of radical

Islamic jihadists. "It is certain," continued Timperlake, "that a nuclear weapon in the hands of fanatical jihadists will be used. The only current deterrence against its use is a worldwide hunt for the device before Israel, Paris, London, New York or D.C. disappears in a flash."[21] Timperlake went on to say that jihadists are not our only threat from a rogue nation armed with nuclear weapons. "What about the criminal state of North Korea or the vitriolic anti-Semitic nation of Iran?" he asked. "Either country for many perverse reasons can slip a device to a terrorist group."[22]

These enemies have different agendas, but they share a common disregard for human life and a burning hatred for the United States. While we would like to close our ears to predictions of impending disaster, experts such as Timperlake and others see a major attack on our country in the near future as virtually inevitable.

AMERICA WILL BE INFECTED WITH MORAL DECAY

The average lifespan of the world's greatest civilizations has been about two hundred years. During that two-century span, each of these nations progressed through the following sequence: from bondage to spiritual faith, from spiritual faith to courage, from courage to liberty, from liberty to abundance, from abundance to complacency, from complacency to apathy, from apathy to dependence, and from dependence back into bondage.[23]

At what point is America in this cycle? In 1947, forward-looking sociologist Dr. Carle Zimmerman wrote a text called *Family and Civilization*. He identified eleven "symptoms of final decay" observable in the fall of the Greek and Roman civilizations. See how many characterize our society:

- No-fault divorce
- "Birth Dearth"; increased disrespect for parenthood and parents
- Meaningless marriage rites/ceremonies
- Defamation of past national heroes

- Acceptance of alternative marriage forms
- Widespread attitudes of feminism, narcissism, hedonism
- Propagation of antifamily sentiment
- Acceptance of most forms of adultery
- Rebellious children
- Increased juvenile delinquency
- Common acceptance of all forms of sexual perversion[24]

One cannot read lists such as these and doubt that America is throwing away its treasured position as the most blessed nation. Remember, God blessed this country for a reason: our nation was founded on submission to Him. But now as the reasons for His blessings upon America are eroding, we can expect the blessings themselves to fade as well. It's a simple matter of cause and effect: remove the cause, and the effect ceases. Once, we invited God into our nation and made Him welcome as our most honored guest. But now our culture seems bent on shutting Him out.

Almost six decades ago, President Herbert Hoover wrote a warning that I fear America has not heeded. He stated, "Our greatest danger is not from invasion by foreign armies. Our dangers are that we may commit suicide from within by complaisance with evil."[25]

It saddens me to say it, but I believe the signs make it certain that America is now infected with the deadly disease of moral decay. And as that infection eats away at our foundations, we can expect the law of cause and effect to come into play. Scripture often warns us that even a long-suffering God will not forever strive with men. If we ignore divine directives, we cannot expect God's blessing. A limb that cuts itself off from the trunk will not continue to live.

AMERICA WILL BE IMPOTENT BECAUSE OF THE RAPTURE

If the Rapture were to happen today and all the true believers in Jesus Christ disappeared to heaven in a single moment, America as we know it could be obliterated. It is estimated that at the Rapture, America will lose millions of citizens.[26] Not only would the country lose much of her population, but she would also lose the very best, the "salt" and "light" of the nation. Who can imagine the chaos in our country when all the godly people disappear, leaving only those who have rejected God? It is not a pretty picture.

We who love Christ not only will know the joy of being with our beloved Lord but also will be spared the horrors that the world will suffer through the evil of people left in the wake of the Rapture. It's like a reverse surgical operation—one in which all the healthy cells are removed and only the cancerous ones are left to consume one another. Yet we cannot help but feel a sense of tension in our hearts. Yes, God will save us, but things we've never experienced are about to happen, and changes such as we've never imagined loom on the horizon. But in spite of the uneasiness, we approach with confidence the events we are anticipating because we know they were put into play by the Creator of the universe. He knows the end from the beginning, and because we are His friends, He is letting us in on the eternal secrets of His determined will.

In an article about the United States in prophecy, Herman A. Hoyt made a statement that is a fitting conclusion to this chapter. He wrote:

> Since the promise of Christ's coming for the Church has always been held out to His people as an event that could take place at any moment, surely the events of the present hour in relation to the United States ought to give new stimulus to watch momentarily for His coming. In these days of crisis, our trust should not rest in a nation that may shortly disappear, but in Him who works all things after the counsel of His own will.[27]

Dr. Hoyt is right; what do we have to worry about? Our trust has never been in governments, civilizations, or cultures. These institutions will be swept away by the winds of history. They are helpful while they are here, but they have never been worthy of our trust. We have always put our trust in the One who stands above institutions, above history, and even above time itself—the One by whose power and permission these things exist, and who knows their times and the ends of their days. Only He is worthy of our ultimate allegiance.

PART 2

CULTURAL SIGNS

As the story of the end continues to unfold, we encounter several cultural signs of what's to come—signs that are beginning to appear all around us even today.

Materialism is the most powerful "religion" of our day—an ample sign that we are nearing the last days Paul spoke of in his warning to Timothy, and that Daniel and Ezekiel predicted. The sign of moral decay is evident as well: the breakdown of family life; substance abuse, alcoholism, and runaway addictive disorders; gambling and gaming; cheating and bullying; and high crime rates and prison populations.

The rise of radical Islam is setting the stage for the events in Ezekiel 38–39, which prophesy an invasion of Israel in the end times by a vast coalition of nations, all of whom are Islamic today except Russia. The Bible also says that Christian persecution will increase and spiritual warfare will intensify as the end of the present age approaches. And, finally, there is perhaps the greatest cultural threat of all—apathetic Christians who simply don't care anymore about the signs of the time.

In this section, we'll explore these six important cultural signs of the end times.

CHAPTER 6

MATERIALISM

In March 2018, *Forbes* named investor and philanthropist Warren Buffett the third richest person in the world.[1] Yet this man of great means has chosen to live more frugally than you might imagine. Another article published a couple of months later tells us more:

> Buffett has long been admired for his dogged work ethic, staying close to his Nebraska roots and for maintaining a relatively modest lifestyle—at least for someone with a net worth exceeding $80 billion. He started out delivering newspapers seven decades ago in Washington, D.C., where he lived as a teenager for several years while his father served in the U.S. House. Today, Buffett lives in the same Omaha home he purchased in 1958. His emphasis on frugality and philanthropy has served as life lessons to those who follow him, every bit as much as the principles of value investing he has preached for decades as chairman and CEO of Berkshire Hathaway.[2]

Buffett, a self-described religious agnostic, might be in the business of making money, and perhaps he does love money. But his lifestyle doesn't lead observers to believe he's particularly materialistic.

If only that were true of everyone—including some Christians.

Money has a siren call that, if answered, is always destructive. Letting the love of money run amok inevitably leads to a lifestyle of materialism, which *Merriam-Webster* defines as "a preoccupation with or stress upon material rather than intellectual or spiritual things." That lifestyle can involve hoarding money and increasing what's in the bank at every opportunity. Or it can manifest as accumulating possessions, adding more and more belongings whenever possible. It can also mean constantly upgrading possessions because of a desire for not just more, but better.

Materialism comes with a cost that is sometimes subtle and sometimes all too obvious. For instance, materialism is the enemy of contentment. When a desire for more and better outweighs the desire for financial stability, it can lead to crippling debt. And the presence of discontent and debt can affect our general wellbeing and relationships for generations.

Far worse is how materialism can negatively affect our walk with God—and how rampant materialism is and will become in these last days. Pastor and speaker Dr. Mark Hitchcock pictures the inevitable culmination of this growing materialistic trend:

> During the coming Tribulation, the gulf between rich and poor will grow wider than ever before. Food will be so expensive that only the very wealthy will have enough. Famine will relentlessly hammer the middle class until the middle class disappears. The vast majority of people will wallow in misery, but the rich will continue to bask in the comfort of their luxurious lifestyle. The world will be radically divided among the elite "haves" and the mass of the "have-nots." . . . This will make the suffering of the have-nots even more unbearable as they watch the privileged few indulge themselves in the lap of luxury.[3]

In his unfolding vision of the end times, the apostle John describes the extreme scarcity of basic human needs that will occur during the Tribulation period:

When He opened the third seal, I heard the third living creature say, "Come and see." So I looked, and behold, a black horse, and he who sat on it had a pair of scales in his hand. And I heard a voice in the midst of the four living creatures saying, "A quart of wheat for a denarius, and three quarts of barley for a denarius; and do not harm the oil and the wine." (Rev. 6:5–6)

In John's day, a quart of wheat was the minimum daily survival need for one person. In the Tribulation period, this survival minimum will cost a full day's wages, which means common people will be forced to scrounge for cheaper, less nourishing food simply to avoid starvation. Salt, cooking oils, meat, or milk will be utterly unaffordable. The rich, on the other hand, will not suffer these shortages. They will thrive during the Tribulation, being able to afford ample food, the accoutrements to make their food palatable, and luxuries such as oil and wine.

CONSIDERING MATERIALISM

The Bible's warnings against loving money and possessions are stern, direct, and unambiguous. In His Sermon on the Mount, Jesus summed it up as an "either/or" choice: "No one can serve two masters; for either he will hate the one and love the other, or else he will be loyal to the one and despise the other. You cannot serve God and mammon" (Matt. 6:24).

Why is the love of money so terrible? Irish clergyman Donagh O'Shea gives us a penetrating explanation:

Money means a lot of different things; it is much more than it appears to be. It is God's greatest rival. . . . It is much more than the paper it seems to be, or the metal, or the plastic. It is our love of things; it is our escape from dependence on people; it is our security against death; it is our effort to control life. . . .

It is much easier to love things than to love people. Things are dead, so you can possess them easily. . . . If you can't love people you will begin to love money. It will never hurt your feelings or challenge your motives, but neither will it ever respond to you—because it is dead. . . . And after a while the problem will begin to show: you will begin to look dead yourself. . . . After a while you will be incapable of loving anyone, and then you might as well be dead. . . . [Money] is neutral. But an extreme attachment to it is not neutral; it is a kind of opposite religion. . . . The religion of God is the religion of love. The instinct of love is to share, to give away. But the instinct of Mammon is to accumulate.[4]

Please don't misunderstand the point, as many often do: money itself is not evil; it is merely a convenient medium of exchange. It's the *love* of money that's the problem. You can have money and still love God, but as Jesus said, you cannot love money and love God.

Money and possessions have always drawn people away from God, but in our present culture we see that problem running rampant and out of control. We can expect this headlong descent into deeper materialism to intensify as the end draws near. The apostle Paul clearly saw it coming:

In the last days perilous times will come: For men will be lovers of themselves, lovers of money, boasters, proud, blasphemers, disobedient to parents, unthankful, unholy, unloving, unforgiving, slanderers, without self-control, brutal, despisers of good, traitors, headstrong, haughty, lovers of pleasure rather than lovers of God, having a form of godliness but denying its power. (2 Tim. 3:1–5)

In this brief but prescient passage, Paul lists nineteen characteristics which will dominate society prior to the return of Christ. And he's not speaking merely of nonreligious people. As he points out, many professing believers will have "a form of godliness," but this "form" will have no power in their lives. They will claim to love God, but their lives will demonstrate that their real love is pleasure, power, and possessions. While it might be fruitful to examine all nineteen of these ungodly characteristics, we must limit our attention to the first two, which give us valuable insights into the subject of this chapter.

LOVERS OF SELF

When we disallow God His rightful place as supreme Lord of our lives, self moves in to replace Him. Self becomes our first love, and God no longer holds the supreme place in our lives. An old superstition claims that witches recite the Lord's Prayer backward, beginning with "Give us this day our daily bread" and ending with "Hallowed be Your name" and "Your will be done." While on the surface this may seem to be the same prayer, the inversion subtly alters its meaning. It places self first and God last, reflecting a complete reversal of priorities.

This simple inversion of a prayer demonstrates how subtly self-love can worm its way into the hearts of godly people and expand to the point that God is forced out. It can happen even while we convince ourselves that our Christianity is intact because we're still going through the motions, though in our hearts we have inverted our loyalties without realizing it. This inversion is clearly occurring in today's church. Many now warming the pews project a façade of godliness but live lives indistinguishable from atheists.

Self-love is more obvious, sometimes blatantly so, in the secular realm. The famous financial scammers of our generation—Bernie Madoff, Dennis Kozlowski, Martha Stewart, Kenneth Lay, and Bernard Ebbers—committed their frauds solely to benefit themselves. The same goes for the hackers who steal identities and drain private bank accounts, as well as phone scammers who con elderly people out of their life savings. They don't care who they hurt or how badly as long as they get what they want. They demonstrate the spirit of the age, which Paul identifies as an ominous sign that the end times are fast approaching.

LOVERS OF MONEY

It's as inevitable as night following day: those who are lovers of themselves will also be lovers of money. Why? Because money provides the means of pleasing oneself. This explains why Paul warned Timothy that as the last days approach, people will increasingly become "lovers of money." This growing, inordinate desire for money dominates today's society. It's the fuel that drives the engines of our rampant commercialism. It's the standard by which people's status, value, and success are judged.

Wilfred J. Hahn observes how the management of money dominates our culture: "Doesn't it seem unimaginable that an inanimate thing like money, which at one time served only as a medium of exchange, should become something so large and complex, requiring legions of people to manage the myriad arrangement of who owes it and who owns it? . . . This whole phenomenon is evidence of just how controlling the monetary system has become."[5]

British philosopher Simon Critchley unveils the truth about what money has become, calling it the dominant "religion" of our time: "In the seemingly godless world of global finance capitalism, money is the only thing in which we really must have faith. Money is the one, true God in which we all believe. . . . And when [it] breaks down . . . people experience something close to a crisis of faith."[6]

In a starkly revealing illustration, John Piper demonstrates the foolishness of putting unwarranted trust in the influence and prestige of wealth:

Picture 269 people entering eternity through a plane crash in the Sea of Japan. Before the crash, there are a noted politician, a millionaire corporate executive, a playboy and his playmate, and a missionary kid on the way back from visiting grandparents.

After the crash, they stand before God utterly stripped of Mastercards, checkbooks, credit lines, image clothes, how-to-succeed books, and Hilton reservations. Here are the politician, the executive, the playboy, and the missionary kid, all on level ground with nothing, absolutely nothing, in their hands, possessing only what they brought in their hearts. How absurd and tragic the lover of money will seem on that day—like a man who spends his whole life collecting train tickets and in the end is so weighed down by the collection that he misses the last train.[7]

COMBATTING MATERIALISM

According to the Bible, the antidote to materialism is generosity. Let's conclude by looking at four ways we can combat the ever-increasing human tendency toward loving money and possessions more than we love God and others. It all begins with how we view money.

CHANGE THE WAY YOU THINK ABOUT MONEY

From the day we hold that first paycheck in our hands, we wonder, *What will I buy for myself?* We think of our wages as "ours." We earn our pay through our work, so it must belong to us. We bristle at the amount withheld for taxes, health care, and even our own retirement. We look at what we actually take home and allocate it to rent, bills, and daily necessities. And what's left? We'll protect that with the ferocity of a lion guarding its kill.

And now we're expected to just give some away to people or organizations who didn't work for it? That's a hard pill to swallow.

The most vital step we can take toward overcoming materialism in our lives is turning the way we think about money on its head. When we remember that "every good gift and every perfect gift is from above" (James 1:17), we realize that nothing good is really ours to start with. It's God's, and He bestows it on us as a gift to be used to glorify Him. When we start thinking of money as just one of the countless good gifts from our Father who loves us, we can rest in the knowledge that He knows what we need, He promises to provide, and His storehouses are unending.

Think of it this way: you make a pie chart to see where your money's going. In this paradigm, the amount you have to work with is fixed, and each expenditure in every category takes away from the whole until you've used up the entire circle. It's a closed system. There's nothing for you outside that circle.

But God is infinite. He doesn't work in pie charts. He works in rivers. Rivers of blessings. And He never runs out.

If He is the one who supplies all our needs, and He never runs out of supplies, we can stop thinking about our money in terms of a pie being swiftly eaten up and start thinking of ourselves as conduits of His grace. What He gives to us, we can pass on to others without fear that there won't be enough left over for us.

BEFORE YOU DO THE BIG THINGS, DO THE LITTLE THINGS

We won't automatically become generous in a day. But we can begin to do little things we thought were unimportant.

- Consciously increase the amount you leave on the table for the waiter or waitress who serves you in restaurants.
- Carry some money with you specifically to give away to someone in need, and ask God to reveal ways to express love and generosity to the people you meet every day.
- Make a commitment to support your church and discover the joy and impact of tithing.

In 1981, Albert Lexie started working at the Children's Hospital of Pittsburgh, cleaning and polishing shoes for $5 a pair. Satisfied customers often tipped him, usually a dollar or two. One Christmas, a customer gave Albert $50 for shining one pair of shoes! Big tips like that were rare, of course, and over the years, as styles changed, Albert saw his business dwindle.

In 2013, Albert retired after thirty-two years on the job. There was a farewell party. Hospital staff and administrators spoke of how much he'd be missed. But when he walked out the door on his last day, his influence at that hospital continued.

Why? Because during all those years of shining shoes, Albert Lexie donated more than thirty percent of his earnings to the hospital's Free Care Fund, which helps cash-strapped parents pay for their children's medical care. And those tips? He gave every single one to the hospital, more than $200,000 dollars in all.[8]

We develop a habit of generosity in the same way we develop any good habit—through incremental adjustments we can maintain over the long haul. It's far better to start small and build up from there than to make one huge gift to a church or charity and fall into complacency because we've "done our part."

Generosity isn't a "one-and-done" situation. It's a lifestyle.

START GIVING MORE THAN YOU CAN AFFORD

The next step after giving a little is giving a lot. In one of his letters to the believers in Corinth, Paul reported on the generosity of Christians living in Macedonia:

> Now I want you to know, dear brothers and sisters, what God in his kindness has done through the churches in Macedonia. They are being tested by many troubles, and they are very poor. But they are also filled with abundant joy, which has overflowed in rich generosity. For I can testify that they gave not only what they could afford, but far more. And they did it of their own free will. They begged us again and again for the privilege of sharing in the gift for the believers in Jerusalem. (2 Cor. 8:1–4 NLT)

These believers gave not out of their abundance but out of their poverty. And they weren't content to give only a little. They wanted to give all that they had—and more.

At this point you might be asking, "Just how much should I give?"

Especially if you are someone who budgets and tracks your expenses, you may want a hard-and-fast rule, a percentage. You want to know how big a piece of the pie this generosity will require. In his best-known book, *Mere Christianity*, C. S. Lewis tried to answer that question:

> I do not believe one can settle how much we ought to give. I am afraid the only safe way is to give more than we can spare. In other words, if our expenditure on comforts, luxuries, amusements, etc., is up to the standard common among those with the same income as our own, we are probably giving away too little. If our charities do not at all pinch or hamper us, I should say [our expenditures] are too small. There ought to be things we should like to do and cannot do because our charities expenditure excludes them.[9]

The answer to the question "How much should I give?" is "More than you can afford." We all spend far more on things we don't need than on the causes that are truly close to God's heart, namely, the spread of the gospel and the care of the poor.

MAKE SURE YOU'RE MOVING
TOWARD YOUR TREASURE

Many people are familiar with the following words of Jesus: "Do not lay up for yourselves treasures on earth, where moth and rust destroy and where thieves break in and steal; but lay up for yourselves treasures in heaven, where neither moth nor rust destroys and where thieves do not break in and steal. For where your treasure is, there your heart will be also" (Matt. 6:19–21).

Far fewer of us are intimately familiar with these wise words from the apostle Paul:

> Teach those who are rich in this world not to be proud and not to trust in their money, which is so unreliable. Their trust should be in God, who richly gives us all we need for our enjoyment. Tell them to use their money

to do good. They should be rich in good works and generous to those in need, always being ready to share with others. By doing this they will be storing up their treasure as a good foundation for the future so that they may experience true life. (1 Tim. 6:17–19, NLT)

You may not think of yourself as rich, but you are. According to *Forbes*, "The typical person in the bottom 5 percent of the American income distribution is still richer than 68 percent of the world's inhabitants."[10]

No matter what your income, you are either moving away from your treasure or toward it. The Lord Jesus gives us a choice in the matter. Every heartbeat brings us one moment closer to eternity. If we selfishly spend our lives in the pursuit of wealth on earth, then we waste our lives. But if your treasure is in heaven, you are always moving toward it.

In many cultures throughout history, the dead were buried with items they might need in the next life. Think of the lavish tombs of the Egyptian pharaohs, stuffed with gold, precious jewels, weapons, and even food! Or the vast underground army of terracotta soldiers buried with Qin Shi Huang, China's first emperor, meant to protect him in the afterlife. But no matter who we are or how much we amass on this earth, none of it follows us when we die.

Bestselling author Stephen King shared these words with the 2001 graduating class at Vassar College:

A couple of years ago, I found out what "you can't take it with you" means. I found out while I was lying in a ditch at the side of a country road, covered with mud and blood and with the tibia of my right leg poking out the side of my jeans like a branch of a tree taken down in a thunderstorm. I had a MasterCard in my wallet, but when you're lying in the ditch with broken glass in your hair, no one accepts MasterCard.

We come in naked and broke. We may be dressed when we go out, but we're just as broke. Warren Buffet? Going to go out broke. Bill Gates? Going out broke. Tom Hanks? Going out broke. Steve King? Broke. Not a crying dime.

All the money you earn, all the stocks you buy, all the mutual funds you trade—all of that is mostly smoke and mirrors. It's still going to be a quarter-past getting late whether you tell the time on a Timex or a Rolex. . . .

So I want you to consider making your life one long gift to others. And why not? All you have is on loan, anyway. All that lasts is what you pass on. . . .

[This needy world is] not a pretty picture, but we have the power to help, the power to change. And why should we refuse? Because we're going to take it with us? Please. . . .

A life of giving—not just money, but time and spirit—repays. It helps us remember that we may be going out broke, but right now we're doing okay. Right now we have the power to do great good for others and for ourselves.

So I ask you to begin giving, and to continue as you begin. I think you'll find in the end that you got far more than you ever had, and did more good than you ever dreamed.[11]

Several years ago a video was posted online of a woman selling roses on a New York City subway train for $1 each. In the video, a man approaches her and asks how much for all the roses she has to sell. He gives her $140 for the entire bunch, but instead of taking his purchase with him, he asks the rose vendor to give them away to other people. When the train stops, he steps off, leaving the woman utterly stunned. She begins to sob.

Maria Lopez, the bystander who filmed the encounter, told the *Huffington Post*: "She started crying from the relief of someone actually being generous. This one little gesture of humanity is so huge. It's a testament to the lack of love and lack of generosity in the world. I think people are yearning for that."[12]

Yes, people are yearning for it. And when we hold the gifts of God in an open hand, rather than clenching our fists around them and holding on for dear life, we choose to show the world a better way to live, the way of love. In these last days, let's make the move from materialism to generosity as we use the resources we have to bless others and honor the Lord.

CHAPTER 7

IMMORALITY

On May 8, 2011, Tony Bennett walked across the stage of the Jacob Javits Center to sing a couple of ballads and open the program for a famous New York City charity. The full crowd before him was a glittering cosmos of New York's brightest celebrities. Bennett's timeless voice thrilled the house, and everyone marveled at the eighty-five-year-old crooner's enduring ability to charm an audience.

But later in the evening, it was Bennett himself who was charmed as he listened to a singer exactly sixty years his junior. He was swept off his feet by the clarion voice of Lady Gaga. Meeting her backstage, Bennett regaled her with stories of his favorite songwriter, Cole Porter, and impulsively asked her to sing on his 2011 album, Duets II.[1] A few years later, the two collaborated on another album, *Cheek to Cheek*, and the opening song was Porter's "Anything Goes."[2]

It was an apt choice. "Anything Goes" is a bouncy, toe-tapping number—you can't help but smile as you hum the melody—but its words, written in 1934, celebrated the moral free fall of the American twentieth century. The song boasts of how times have changed and claims the Puritans are in for a shock. The lyrics brag that profanity and nudity are in vogue. For all its toe-tapping trendiness, "Anything Goes" represents the moral relativism that has infected our culture, leaving the West on the brink of spiritual collapse.

Ironically, it is a philosophy that ruined Porter's own life. The famous composer grew up on an Indiana farm. His mother went to church, but her young son was not impressed. "I never felt religion was serious to her," he recalled. "It was of no importance. She went to show off her new hats."[3]

Porter learned to play the violin at age six and the piano at age eight. He wrote his first Broadway show tune in 1915 and went on to provide crooners, such as Tony Bennett and Frank Sinatra, with dozens of hits—"I've Got You Under My Skin," "Night and Day," "Just One of Those Things," "Don't Fence Me In," and "I Get a Kick Out of You."

His fans did not realize that his love songs were written for his boyfriends, that his marriage was a sham, or that his music financed an endless series of "anything goes" parties.

Porter lived as he sang—"anything goes." But after being injured in an equestrian accident, he never regained his health or happiness. He became reclusive and spent his last years depressed, diseased, drinking, and drugging. In 1964, Porter was wheeled into a California hospital for the last time. The nurse studied the patient, perhaps wondering how anyone so famous could look so cheerless. Clicking off the items on the questionnaire, the nurse came to the issue of the patient's religion.

"Put down none," replied Porter.

The nurse said, "Protestant?"

"Put down—none."

Shortly after, he sent someone to destroy his pornographic photographs. With that done, he died.

"He was terribly alone at the end," said a friend. "He really didn't have anything or anyone he was close to."[4]

His secretary lamented that her boss never found the strength that came from faith in God. "Without faith, one is like a stained glass window in the dark," she said. "How to reach his particular darkness," she added, "is an enigma."[5]

A similar darkness has descended on our world, and American culture now resembles that stained glass window through which no light is shining. We are living in a world where anything goes, but nothing satisfies.

THE EXPRESSION OF OUR MORAL DECLINE

The Bible anticipated that decadent times like our present age would come. In speaking of His second coming, the Lord Jesus said, "But as the days of Noah were, so also will the coming of the Son of Man be" (Matt. 24:37).

What were those "days of Noah" like? Genesis 6:5 tells us: "Then the LORD saw that the wickedness of man was great in the earth, and that every intent of the thoughts of his heart was only evil continually." This is a description of the society swept away by the Flood.

Perhaps America has not yet sunk to the lows of Noah's day. But, "Our moral compass seems no longer to have a 'true north.' The needle spins crazily, looking for a direction on which to settle."[6]

Second Timothy 3:1–5 says:

But know this, that in the last days perilous times will come: For men will be lovers of themselves, lovers of money, boasters, proud, blasphemers, disobedient to parents, unthankful, unholy, unloving, unforgiving, slanderers, without self-control, brutal, despisers of good, traitors, headstrong, haughty, lovers of pleasure rather than lovers of God, having a form of godliness but denying its power.

The description of Noah's generation and Paul's prediction of the generation that will introduce the last days summarize the depravity of man—yes, even the total depravity of man. I know that *total depravity* is a controversial term and certainly one that is often misunderstood.

Total depravity does not mean, as most people think, that human beings are as depraved as they could possibly be. This would, by necessity, mean that there is no good in humans at all. But we know this is not the case. Not all human beings are drunkards, felons, adulterers, or murderers. Many are noble, generous, self-sacrificing, highly moral, and loving. Total depravity defines the extent, not the degree, of our sinfulness. In other words, while our depravity does not make us as bad as we could be, it does affect us in every area of our being, corrupting every part of our humanness at varying degrees.

Charles Swindoll wrote:

> If depravity were blue, we'd be blue all over. Cut us anywhere and we'll bleed blue. Cut into our minds and you'll find blue thoughts. Cut into our vision and there are blue images full of greed and lust. Cut into our hearts and there are blue emotions of hatred, revenge, and blame. Cut into our wills and you'll find deep blue decisions and responses.[7]

This depravity, or godlessness, is the root cause of America's moral decline. We grasp for what feels good instead of what *is* good. In Noah's day, every thought and intent of the heart was continuously evil. Now we have the technology to take the most lurid fantasies of the human mind and project them onto a screen a child can hold in his or her hand. All this has led to the coarsening of Western culture. We have become a profane people, with fewer and fewer restraints on behavior and language and with a diminishing respect for human life.

In his book *Vanishing Grace*, Philip Yancey summarized the moral free fall of our nation:

> In my own lifetime the divorce rate has doubled, the rates of teen suicide and violent crime have both tripled, and births out of wedlock have sextupled. With less than 5 percent of the world's population, the US has almost a quarter of the world's prisoners (about the same number as Russia and China combined). We have become accustomed to homeless people sleeping in parks and under bridges, something virtually unknown in my childhood.

The leading causes of death are self-inflicted, the side-effects of tobacco, obesity, alcohol, sexually transmitted diseases, drugs, and violence.[8]

THE EXPLANATION FOR OUR MORAL DECLINE

It's time to ask the question: how did Western morality stray onto such a slippery slope? What happened to us? I can explain it in two ways: historically and biblically.

THE EXPLANATION FROM HISTORY

The historical explanation dates back to the eighteenth-century Enlightenment. Throughout the Middle Ages, the Western world, for all its darkness and depravity, at least had an understanding of objective truth. The existence of God was taken for granted, which provided a basis for belief in absolute values of right and wrong. The Reformation of the 1500s set this truth on fire. But hard on the heels of the Reformation, the secular thinking of the Enlightenment (or the Age of Reason) radiated from France like a force field across Europe and to the New World.

Many of the Enlightenment thinkers could not totally shake off belief in the existence of God, but they dispatched Him to insignificance by promoting a religion of deism—the teaching that the Creator, if He exists, is disinterested and uninvolved with the world. They believed humans were the true moral force in the universe.

Dave Breese, in his book *Seven Men Who Rule the World from the Grave*, wrote:

The early 1900s was the first era in which Darwin and his ideas had come to full flower. By that time, evolution was well on its way to capturing the world of academia and the thought processes of the average man. Virtually everyone believed that history was moving up from the gross and the animalistic into the sublime and even the angelic. . . . Social Darwinism was fast persuading society . . . that no problem was unsolvable, no difficulty unresolvable. Given enough time, all would be well. Humanity had within it a potential that would not be denied.[9]

The rising tide of humanistic secularism was shoehorned into America's educational system by John Dewey, a shy, bookish educator who hailed from Vermont. Dewey's core principle was the rejection of absolute, unchangeable truth. Final truth, he believed, was illusionary.[10] Breese explained, "This humanism, of which Dewey was a fountainhead . . . became pervasive in our American schools, especially on the graduate level. From that point on, the ruling point of view in American education was that there was no ruling point of view."[11]

Against this backdrop, moral relativism entered pop culture with a vengeance between the 1920s and 1960s, setting the stage for the sexual revolution of the 1960s through the 1980s. Hollywood jumped on the bandwagon, and America's moral values turned downward like the economic charts of the Great Depression.

In the meantime, secularism—the removal of theism or God-consciousness from public life—has become America's de facto religion. "A secular worldview," writes Ravi Zacharias, "is admittedly and designedly the underlying impetus that presently propels Western culture."[12]

Albert Mohler helpfully summarizes how we got where we are today. In the premodern age of antiquity and the medieval period, it was *impossible not to believe*. There was no intellectual alternative to belief in God. In the modern age, it became *possible not to believe* as philosophers began to posit alternatives. Nowadays secularists are asserting it is *impossible to believe*. The alternatives to God have become dominant. Christians have become "intellectual outlaws" in the secular world, says Mohler. "Secularism in America has been attended by a moral revolution without precedent and without end-game. . . . The story of the rise of secularism is a stunning intellectual and moral revolution."[13]

In short, there is no telling where a society will end up when "anything goes." Or rather, we do know where such a culture ends up. Sooner or later it circles around to the days of Noah.

THE EXPLANATION FROM THE BIBLE

If you really want to understand what is happening to Western morality today, trace the theological chain from the rejection of the Creator to total moral collapse as Paul described it in Romans 1:

> For the wrath of God is revealed from heaven against all ungodliness and unrighteousness of men, who suppress the truth in unrighteousness, because what may be known of God is manifest in them, for God has shown it to them. For since the creation of the world His invisible attributes are clearly seen, being understood by the things that are made, even His eternal power and Godhead, so that they are without excuse. (vv. 18–20)

Whether looking through a telescope or a microscope, I am amazed at the symmetry, the scope, and the systematic order of creation. As Psalm 19:1 tells us, the universe itself makes the existence of God too obvious to deny: "The heavens proclaim the glory of God. The skies display his craftmanship" (NLT).

The bottom-line reason for humanity's rejection of this obvious evidence is that the existence of a Creator implies His authority over all His creation. If we are subject to a Maker, we are not autonomous, for morality is intrinsically rooted in His holy character. We cannot live however we would like, nor should we. God's personal purity supplies a moral baseline for the universe and provides the guidelines by which we live healthy and holy lives.

To escape these implications, our society has chosen to believe the unbelievable—that everything came from nothing in an unexplainable explosion of dense matter with an inexplicable origin; that primordial sludge was jolted from death to life; that molecules developed from randomness into complexity; and that human beings are the resulting accidents—mere pieces of carbon destined to die as quickly as we arose, living in a universe without purpose and facing a future without ultimate hope. That is the foundation of secularism, and it leads downward in belief and behavior.

Here are the downward steps as the apostle Paul described them:

INGRATITUDE

Paul wrote, "Although they knew God, they did not glorify Him as God, nor were thankful, but became futile in their thoughts, and their foolish hearts were darkened" (Rom. 1:21).

IDOLATRY

"Professing to be wise, they became fools, and changed the glory of the incorruptible God into an image made like corruptible man—and birds and four-footed animals and creeping things" (1:22–23).

God created the human heart with a vacuum that can only be filled by the love of God. That hole demands to be filled with something, and when we reject the true God, we inevitably form other gods to fill it. That is called idolatry.

An idol is whatever comes first in your life. Anything that comes before Jesus Christ in your affections or priorities—that is your idol. In our materialistic age, millions of people are serving the god of money, possessions, and the accumulation of wealth. When our desire for financial success overshadows our love for God, it becomes just as idolatrous as bowing before a man-made image.

Make no mistake—when we reject the Creator-God of Scripture, we must find a substitute. When we reject God, we turn away from His love and provision and become our own god.

Donald Baillie helps us visualize what happens when we turn away from God's love. He pictured humanity standing in a circle facing God at the center:

In that circle we ought all to be standing, linked together with lovingly joined hands, facing towards the Light in the centre, which is God; seeing our fellow creatures all around the circle in the light of that central Love, which shines on them and beautifies their faces; and joining with them in the dance of God's great game, the rhythm of love universal. But instead of that, we have, each one, turned our backs upon God the circle of our fellows, and faced the other way, so that we can see neither the Light at the centre nor the faces on the circumference. And indeed in that position it is difficult even to join hands with our fellows! Therefore instead of playing God's game we play, each one, our own selfish little game. Each one of us wishes to be the centre, and there is blind confusion, and not even any true knowledge of God or of our neighbors. That is what is wrong.[14]

IMMORALITY

Paul continued in Romans 1:24–25 with this: "Therefore God also gave them up to uncleanness, in the lusts of their hearts, to dishonor their bodies among themselves, who exchanged the truth of God for the lie, and worshiped and served the creature rather than the Creator, who is blessed forever. Amen."

When we give up the true God of heaven, all other gods lead to an erosion of morality, to sensuality, to sexual sins, and to lust-driven lives. In fact, this passage says that God gives people up to this kind of depravity. How can a loving God give people up to the evils they choose? "He does not cause anyone's demise; the natural law of consequences does. He cannot abide in the presence of sin, which is why He abandoned His own Son at Calvary as Christ bore the sins of the world."[15]

How sad to follow this downward course when God offers us an upward path. But when we step off of His path, the steps keep descending toward the days of Noah.

INIQUITY

When a culture denies its Creator, worships its own gods, and succumbs to a lust-driven existence, it inevitably becomes overly sexualized. Paul put it plainly: "For this reason God gave them up to vile passions. For even their women exchanged the natural use for what is against nature. Likewise also the men, leaving the natural use of the woman, burned in their lust for one another, men with men committing what is shameful, and receiving in themselves the penalty of their error which was due" (1:26–27).

The headlines of recent years are simply our society's commentary on this passage. And this downward spiral of indecency leads to a total moral collapse. Dr. Donald Grey Barnhouse weighed in on these verses, marking the downward steps to their inevitable end:

> This is the description of mankind abandoned by God and the scene is a frightful one. The cause of the abandonment was the successive departure from God by the human soul in the successive steps of desertion that began with a failure to acknowledge God in worship and thanksgiving, and continued through the various stages of the deification of human reason to the ultimate folly of man in the most corrupt form of idolatrous practices. Having departed from God, man made a god in his own image.[16]

As appalling as this passage is, Dr. Martyn Lloyd-Jones says it is merely a preview of something even worse:

> Hell is just what is described here exaggerated and going on to all eternity. That is hell! Hell is a condition in which life is lived away from God and all the restraints of God's holiness. All that is described in this passage, exaggerated still more, and going on endlessly! In other words, hell is people living in all eternity the kind of life they are living now, only much worse! That is hell![17]

I know that some of you are thinking, *Do we really have to deal with all this? Why can't we just focus on the grace of God and get away from all this sin stuff?* But before we ignore sin and bask in the grace of God, we need to hear these words from theologian Cornelius Plantinga, Jr.:

To speak of grace without sin is . . . to trivialize the cross of Jesus Christ, to skate past all the struggling by good people down the ages to forgive, accept, and rehabilitate sinners, including themselves, and therefore to cheapen the grace of God that always comes to us with blood on it. What had we thought the ripping and the writhing on Golgotha were all about? To speak of grace without looking squarely at these realities, without painfully honest acknowledgment of our own sin and its effects, is to shrink grace to a mere embellishment of the music of creation, to shrink it down to a mere grace note. In short, for the Christian church (even in its recently popular seeker services) to ignore, euphemize, or otherwise mute the lethal reality of sin is to cut the nerve of the gospel. For the sober truth is that without full disclosure on sin, the gospel of grace becomes impertinent, unnecessary, and finally uninteresting.[18]

THE ESCAPE FROM OUR MORAL DECLINE

One of my most memorable moments as a teacher of the Word of God took place on Sunday night, April 28, 1995. I was just beginning to teach the book of Romans in our evening service, and my scheduled passage was Romans 1:29–32.

On this particular night, we were planning to observe the Lord's Table at the beginning of our service. But after studying these verses from Romans, I decided to teach first and observe Communion afterward.

I waded through the words Paul used to describe the corruption and depravity of man, and then we celebrated Communion. In that service something beautiful occurred in my heart, and I sensed that it was happening in the hearts of many of our people as well. I saw tears. I fought back my own!

On Monday morning, still somewhat mystified by what had happened the night before, I read these words in Plantinga's book *Not the Way It's Supposed to Be: A Breviary of Sin*:

Self-deception about our sin is a narcotic, a tranquilizing and disorienting suppression of our spiritual central nervous system. What's devastating about it is that when we lack an ear for wrong notes in our lives, we cannot play right ones or even recognize them in the performances of others. Eventually we make ourselves religiously so unmusical that we miss both the exposition and the recapitulation of the main themes God plays in human life. The music of creation and the still greater music of grace whistle right through our skulls, causing no catch of breath and leaving no residue. Moral beauty begins to bore us. The idea that the human race needs a Savior sounds quaint.[19]

I thought, *How many times has the "music of grace whistled right through our skulls" during our celebration of the Lord's Table?* But that Sunday night we all caught a fresh glimpse of our sinfulness and realized just how badly we needed a Savior. And then we were caught up in the fact that Jesus came, and through His death He washed all that ugliness and filthiness away from our souls. I don't ever remember being more thankful for grace and forgiveness than I was that night. Maybe for the first time I understood what Dr. Martyn Lloyd-Jones said about grace: "There is no more wonderful word than 'grace.' It means unmerited favor or kindness shown to one who is utterly undeserving. . . . It is not merely a free gift, but a free gift to those who deserve the exact opposite, and it is given to us while we are 'without hope and without God in the world.'"[20]

In Romans 1, we get a picture of what we would be apart from the grace of God and the death of Christ. No wonder Paul said that he was not ashamed of the gospel of Christ! It's the good news for you and for me that we can escape the moral decline in our world and in our hearts by trusting in the life, death, and resurrection of Jesus Christ.

Will you turn to Him?

CHAPTER 8

RADICAL ISLAM

Georges Sada was a general under Saddam Hussein. He was a military hero, Iraq's top air force pilot, and the man Saddam called on to hear the truth about military matters. In his book *Saddam's Secrets*, Sada speaks about the spreading impact of Islam around the world:

> I'm often asked about militant Islam and the threat of global terrorism. More than once I've been asked about the meaning of the Arabic words *Fatah* and *Jihad*. What I normally tell them is that to followers of the militant brand of Islam, these doctrines express the belief that Allah has commanded them to conquer the nations of the world both by cultural invasion and by the sword. In some cases this means moving thousands of Muslim families into a foreign land—by building mosques and changing the culture from the inside out, and by refusing to assimilate or adopt the beliefs or values of that nation—to conquer the land for Islam. This is an invidious doctrine, but it's . . . being carried out in some places today by followers of this type of Islam.[1]

Sada went on to warn Americans not to think that the Islamic revolution is a Middle Eastern or European problem. Their ultimate goal is conquest of the West and America:

[They] won't be stopped by appeasement. They are not interested in political solutions. They don't want welfare—their animosity is not caused by hunger or poverty or anything of the sort. They understand only one thing: total and complete conquest of the West and the destruction of anyone who does not bow to them and their dangerous and out-of-date ideology of hate and revenge.[2]

Americans do not seem to take the threat of Islam seriously. In fact, the Pew Research Center tells us that US citizens are essentially oblivious to the potential danger of radical Muslims. A recent poll indicated that "only 16 percent of the public report knowing a lot about the religious beliefs and practices of Muslims, while more than eight in ten say they know a little (57 percent) or nothing at all (26 percent)."[3]

According to Sada, Americans are particularly vulnerable to the spread of militant Islam because our enemies take advantage of traits that we consider socially positive:

One of the nicest things about the American people is that you are generous and friendly people, and because of this you are sometimes naïve and overly trusting. You want to be friendly, so you open up to people and then you're surprised when they stab you in the back. Many brave young soldiers have died in Iraq for this reason, but I think this is also a big part of the problem with the State Department and others in government who fail to understand the true nature of this enemy.[4]

The rise of radical Islam and the prevalence of terrorism has impacted the West in ways that cannot be overstated, especially since 9/11. We experience it every time we wait in an airport security line, every time we hear reports of another attack, and every time we turn on the news and hear commentators describe how Islamic culture is growing in our own land.

Yet radical Islam is more than a threat to our way of life. It's also a sign of the last days:

The rise of Islamic terror is setting the stage for the events in Ezekiel 38–39. These chapters prophesy an invasion of Israel in the end times by a vast coalition of nations, all of whom are Islamic today except Russia. Israel has said that a new "axis of terror"—Iran, Syria, and the Hamas-run Palestinian government—is sowing the seeds of the first world war of the twenty-first century. The rise of Islam, and especially radical Islamic terrorism, strikingly foreshadows Ezekiel's great prophecy.[5]

IS ISLAM MILITANT OR PEACEFUL?

Not long ago, Fox News aired a special called "Radical Islam: Terror in Its Own Words," which featured shocking clips from Islamic television showing clerics and political leaders advocating attacks on the United States and Israel. The documentary included programs shown on Islamic TV in which children sing of their desire to participate in violent jihad or to become suicide bombers. And it aired footage from a radical Islamic rally in California where the audience was told, "One day you will see the flag of Islam over the White House."[6]

In the face of such reports, one of the most unsettling puzzles about Islam is the contention by some Muslim leaders that they are a peace-loving people. Yet even as they make the claim, Islamic terrorists continue to brutally murder any person or group with whom they find fault. Former radical Shi'ite Muslim Reza F. Safa asked:

If Islam is a peaceful religion, then why did Muhammad engage in 47 battles? Why, in every campaign the Muslim armies have fought throughout history, have they slaughtered men, women and children who did not bow their knees to the lordship of Islam? The reign of terror of men such as Saddam, Khomeini, Ghadafi, Idi Amin and many other Muslim dictators are modern examples. If Islam is peaceful, why are there so many verses in the Koran about killing the infidels and those who resist Islam? If Islam is peaceful, why isn't there even one Muslim country that will allow freedom of religion and speech? Not one! If Islam is peaceful, who is imparting this awful violence to hundreds of Islamic groups throughout the world who kill innocent people in the name of Allah?[7]

To get a handle on these contradictory sides of Islam, it will help us to delve briefly into the history of how the religion came to be and what beliefs it holds today.

THE HISTORY OF ISLAM

The name Islam literally means "submission." A Muslim is "one who submits to God." There are about 1.8 billion Muslims in our world today. Approximately 3.45 million live in the United States, which is about 1.1 percent of the US adult population. While we usually associate Islam with the Middle East, the largest Muslim populations are actually in the Asia-Pacific region.[8]

According to Islamic tradition, the founder of Islam, Muhammad, was born in Mecca (in present-day Saudi Arabia) in AD 570. Mecca was a thriving center of religious pilgrimage, filled with temples and statues dedicated to the many gods the Arabian people worshiped at the time.

Muhammad's father died before the prophet was born, and his mother died when he was six years old. He was raised by his paternal grandfather, grew up to become a camel driver and then a merchant, and, at the age of twenty-six, married a wealthy caravan owner named Khadija. Khadija was forty years old and had been divorced four times. In spite of her age, she and Muhammad had six children together.

Muhammad worked in professions that brought him into contact with Christians and Jews who caused him to question the religion of his people. He was forty years old and meditating in a cave outside Mecca when he received his first revelation. From that moment on, according to his testimony, God occasionally revealed to him messages that he declared to the people. These messages, which Muhammad received throughout his life, form the verses of the Qu'ran, which Muslims regard as the divine word of God.

In the seventh-century Arabian world, the people worshiped more than 360 gods, one for each day of the lunar year. One of these was the moon god, the male counterpart to the female sun god. The moon god was called by various names, one of which was Allah, and it was the favorite god of Muhammad's family.

As Muhammad began to promote his new religion, he elevated the moon god, Allah, and declared him to be the one true God. His devotion to Allah was fierce. In establishing and spreading his religion of Islam, Muhammad slaughtered thousands of people who resisted conversion.[9]

Opposition in Mecca forced Muhammad and his followers to flee to Medina in AD 620, where he became the head of the first Muslim community. In AD 631, he returned to Mecca, where he died the following year. At his death, the Islamic community became bitterly divided over who would be Muhammad's successor. Even today that division survives in the two Islamic sects, now known as Shi'ite and Sunni. Conflict between these sects is one of the major stress points in Iraq and throughout the Islamic world.

At the death of Muhammad, the group we know as the Sunni followed the leadership of Muhammad's personally chosen successor, Abu Bakr. The Sunni now comprise about 90 percent of the Islamic world. They believe that Muhammad's spiritual gifts died with him and that their only authority today is the Qu'ran.

The Shi'ites, on the other hand, followed Muhammad's son-in-law Ali, believing Ali had inherited Muhammad's spiritual gifts. Winfried Corduan explains, "The Shi'ites believe that their leaders, the imams, have authority on par with the Qu'ran. It is the Shi'ites that believe that the Twelfth Imam went into concealment hundreds of years ago and continues to live there until he returns as the Mahdi . . . the Muslim Messiah!"[10]

Abu Bakr and his successors launched holy wars that spread Islam from northern Spain to India and threatened Christian Europe. Christians resisted the threat, and a series of wars followed that drove the Islamic invaders back into the Middle Eastern countries, where they still dominate. Their zeal to have their religion control the world has not diminished, however, and it remains a threat to all who do not maintain vigilance.

THE HABITS OF ISLAM

Sunni Muslims mandate five acts of worship, which are frequently referred to as the five pillars of Islam. Shi'ite Muslim worship comprises eight ritual practices, but these encompass the same five pillars of Islam as practiced by the Sunni. The five pillars are as follows:[11]

- To recite the *Shahadah*: The Shahadah is the Islamic creed, "There is no god but Allah, and Muhammad is his messenger." Its recitation is the duty of every Muslim.
- To pray (*salat*): Muslims pray while bowing toward Mecca five times each day: in the early morning, in the early and late afternoon, at sunset, and an hour after sunset.
- To give alms (*zakat*): Muslims are required to give 2.5 percent of their income to those in need. They may give more as a means of gaining further divine reward, but 2.5 percent is an obligatory minimum.
- To fast (*sawm*): Muslims refrain from food during the daylight hours throughout the lunar month of Ramadan. This month is to be given over to meditation and reflection, and it ends with a celebration.
- To make the pilgrimage (*hajj*): Those physically and financially able must visit Mecca at least once during their lifetime. The journey usually takes at least a week and includes many stops at other holy sites along the way.

THE HATRED OF ISLAM

No doubt the most frightening word associated with Islam is *jihad*. Sometimes called the "sixth pillar" of Islam, jihad means "struggle." The "Greater Jihad" is the inner struggle of each Muslim to submit to Allah. The "Lesser Jihad" is the outward struggle to defend the Islamic community. This is the jihad that strikes fear in the hearts of any who reject radical Islam. These Muslims take jihad to mean violent defense of Islam and expansion of the Islamic religion even by means of deadly aggression.

The hatred that the Muslims have for the Jews is well documented. But the settlement of Israel into her homeland in 1948 took this hatred to a level of murderous fury. Militants and radicals refer to Israel as "little Satan" and the United States as "big Satan," and they are determined to wipe both countries off the map.

While the majority of the world's Muslims attempt to live in peace with their neighbors, the number of radicals who preach violence and terror is mushrooming around the world.

Today, as I write these words, there is not a single predominantly Muslim nation on earth where Christians are not persecuted. As General Sada warned, we cannot afford to relax our vigilance in the name of tolerance and multiculturalism.

THE HOPES OF ISLAM

Radical Islam has a vision of its future that does not bode well for those who stand in the way. To gain a better understanding of this vision, we will look briefly at some of the goals the Islamic world hopes to achieve.

ISLAM HOPES TO RULE THE WORLD

It is one thing to read about Muslim determination to take over the world; it is quite another to watch it happening before our eyes, as it is in Europe. The most startling social migration of our age is the Islamification of Europe. Tony Blankley of the *Washington Times* sounded an alarm about this Islamic infiltration:

> The threat of the radical Islamists taking over Europe is every bit as great
> to the United States as was the threat of the Nazis taking over Europe in
> the 1940s. . . .

To point out the obvious, the resurgence of a militant Islam drove America to fight two wars in Muslim countries in two years, disrupted America's alliance with Europe, caused the largest reorganization of American government in half a century (with the creation of the Department of Homeland Security), changed election results in Europe, and threatened the stability of most of the governments in the Middle East.[12]

We can easily see and resist the effects of jihad in militant terrorism, but we have trouble seeing and resisting the subtler strategy that the Muslims call *fatah*. Fatah is infiltration, moving into a country in numbers large enough to insert the influence of Islam. In places where a military invasion will not succeed, the slow, systematic, and unrelenting methods of fatah are conquering entire nations. Two illustrations are instructive, the first concerning France:

What we're seeing in many places is a "demographic revolution." Some experts have projected that by the year 2040, 80 percent of the population of France will be Muslim. At that point the Muslim majority will control commerce, industry, education, and religion in that country. They will also, of course, control the government, as well, and occupy all the key positions in the French Parliament. And a Muslim will be president.[13]

Islamification is also happening in England, where Muslims are advancing their goal of dominance by taking advantage of the British policy of pluralistic tolerance. An example occurred in September 2006 when the British home secretary, John Reid, gave a speech to Muslim parents in east London, encouraging them to protect their children from becoming suicide bombers. A fundamentalist Muslim leader shouted the speaker down. He ranted, "How dare you come to a Muslim area? . . . I am absolutely furious—John Reid should not come to a Muslim area." Muslims are not only immigrating massively to Western countries but also claiming entitlement to keep their settlements off-limits to native citizens.[14]

In early 2008, England's archbishop of Canterbury, Rowan Williams, gave the world a stunning example of General Sada's claim of Western naiveté concerning Islamic intentions. Williams told a BBC correspondent that the growing Islamic population in Britain made it expedient to be accommodative. He said "the UK has to 'face up to the fact'" that it "seems unavoidable" that Islam's legal system, sharia law, will be incorporated into British law. His term for this blending of laws was "constructive accommodation."[15] Sharia law, derived from the Qu'ran and teachings of Muhammad, is the legal system by which Muslims are to live. In the West, the law is fairly benign and deals mainly with family and business. But in Muslim countries, it can include such things as honor killings in cases of suspected immorality.

You may hear other terms used to describe the Islamic goal of world domination. For example, "biological jihad" or "demographic jihad" describes the nonviolent strategy of Muslims moving into Europe and the West and having more babies than their hosts. Within several generations they hope to repopulate traditionally Christian cultures with their own people, and they are certainly on track to reach that goal. According to a Vatican report, the Roman Catholic Church understands this: "For the first time in history, we are no longer at the top: Muslims have overtaken us."[16]

ISLAM HOPES TO RETURN ITS MESSIAH

In 2005, Iranian president Mahmoud Ahmadinejad was called before the United Nations Security Council to explain his determination to develop nuclear weapons. He ended his speech with this prayer: "I pray to you to hasten the emergence of your last repository, the promised one, that perfect and pure human being, the one that will fill this world with justice and peace."[17] The "promised one" in Ahmadinejad's prayer was a reference to the Twelfth Imam, a figure in Shi'ite teaching that parallels the figure of Al-Mahdi in Sunni teaching. In essence, both of these titles refer to the Islamic messiah who is yet to come.

Shi'a Islam believes that the Twelfth Imam can appear only during a time of worldwide chaos. Even though the hope for an Islamic messiah is surely futile, the chaos that radical Islamic leaders are creating to bring about that hope is all too real. Many of the biblical prophecies concerning the end times will be brought about by the beliefs and actions of radical Islam. And we are beginning to feel the pressure of those impending events in the rapid spread of Islamic radicalism in our own time.

RESPONDING TO THE ISLAMIC THREAT

How are we responding to the rise of Islamic radicalism? Not too well, I fear. On the whole, those who shape our culture and policies are inadvertently accommodating the radical agenda of Islamic conquest. We must stop being deceived about this threat. We must stand our ground and affirm truths that many people seem all too willing to give up in the name of tolerance and accommodation.

Here are two truths on which I see much confusion today. It is critical that we affirm these truths to maintain a clear understanding of the vast chasm between Christianity and Islam.

"ALLAH" IS NOT ANOTHER NAME
FOR THE GOD OF THE BIBLE

In mid-August 2007, Dutch Catholic Bishop Muskens said that he "wants everyone to call God 'Allah.'" He explained during an interview on Dutch TV, "Allah is a very beautiful word for God. Shouldn't we all say that from now on, we will name God Allah?" A Roman Catholic news analyst disagreed with the bishop, stating, "Words and names mean things. Referring to God as Allah means something."[18]

Indeed they do! As Stan Goodenough reminded his *Jerusalem Newswire* readers, in the name of Allah, people hijack planes and use them to wreak unspeakable devastation, blow themselves up in crowded public venues to annihilate innocent people, and in the name of Allah, "millions of people pray for the destruction of Israel and the United States." Goodenough observed that when God introduced Himself to Moses, He gave His name as Jehovah. He went on to say, "He also has many other names describing aspects of His nature and character. 'Allah' is not one of them."[19]

Bishop Muskens surely knows the biblical names for God, so what was he thinking when he urged Christians to call God "Allah"? A statement on his diocese's website explained, "If Muslims and Christians address God with the same name, this contributes to harmonious living between both religions."[20] When Islamic leaders saw this, their mosques must have rung with the slaps of high fives. Their policy of fatah was working beautifully. And they must have been overjoyed when the spokesman for the Council on American-Islamic Relations embraced Muskens's proposal, saying, "It reinforces the fact that Muslims, Christians and Jews all worship the same God."[21]

We hear this appalling claim often these days, but nothing could be further from the truth. Allah and God are emphatically not the same! The God of the Bible is knowable. According to the Qu'ran, Allah is so exalted that he cannot be known. The God of the Bible is a personal being with intellect, emotion, and will. Muslim theology tells us Allah is not to be understood as a person. The God of the Bible is one God in three persons. The Qu'ran denies the Trinity and views it as a heresy. The God of the Bible is a God of love. Allah does not have emotional feelings toward humanity. The God of the Bible is a God of grace. According to the Qu'ran, there is no Savior. Clearly, the God of the Bible and Allah are not at all the same and should never be equated with each other.[22]

THE QU'RAN IS NOT A DIVINE BOOK ON PAR WITH THE BIBLE

Many people also say that we should consider the Qu'ran to be on the same level as the Bible. A comparison of the two books shows the absurdity of such a claim. The Bible is a masterpiece of cohesion, depth, and consistency. God inspired more than forty men over a period of fourteen hundred years to write the God-breathed words that carry His unified message from Genesis to Revelation (2 Tim. 3:16).

The Qu'ran, on the other hand, is a self-contradicting book supposedly given by the angel Gabriel to Muhammad. Since Muhammad could neither read nor write, the sayings were translated and collected from the memories of those who had heard him.

Objective readers who have read both the Bible and the Qu'ran are immediately able to tell the difference between the quality and comprehensibility of the two books. Historian Edward Gibbon is an example of such a reader. Gibbon could hardly be accused of being a Christian, yet he described the Qu'ran as "an incoherent rhapsody of fable, and precept, and declamation, which sometimes crawls in the dust, and sometimes is lost in the clouds."[23]

MUSLIMS ARE WITHIN THE REACH OF GOD'S GRACE

We may find it hard to pray for avowed enemies who threaten our destruction, but Jesus commands us to "love your enemies, bless those who curse you, do good to those who hate you, and pray for those who spitefully use you and persecute you" (Matt. 5:44). I believe that includes radical Islamic terrorists.

We have good evidence that such prayers are effective. Our weekly television program, *Turning Point*, is available in many Arab countries. We routinely get correspondence from individuals who have come to Christ through the ministry of God's Word via satellite TV. Recently, we received a letter from an Arab country in which the writer told us he had accepted Christ. A postscript pleaded with us not to send any materials to his address—a sobering reminder of the courage it takes for a Muslim in an Islamic country to confess Christ as Savior.

God is at work in the Islamic world. Many Muslims are being confronted with the gospel in their dreams. One Saudi Arabian had a terrifying nightmare in which he was being taken into hell. This vivid and horrifying dream destroyed the man's peace night after night. One evening, Jesus appeared in his dream and said, "Son, I am the way, the truth, and the life. And if you would give your life to Me, I would save you from the hell that you have seen."

This young man knew something of Jesus from the distorted teachings of the Qu'ran, but he didn't know the Jesus of the New Testament. So he began searching for a Christian who could help him. Christianity is banned in Saudi Arabia, and a Christian caught witnessing to a Muslim could be beheaded, so the young man's search took time. But the Lord eventually led him to an Egyptian Christian who gave him a Bible. He began reading, and when he got to the New Testament, he was moved to give his life to Jesus Christ.

Soon afterward, an opponent of the young man discovered his conversion. The authorities arrested and imprisoned him. In jail, he was tortured and sentenced to death by beheading. But on the morning of his scheduled execution, no one showed up to escort him from the cell. Two days later, the authorities threw open his cell door and screamed at him, "You demon! Get out of this place!"[24]

The man learned later that his execution had not occurred because on the very day he was to be beheaded, the son of his accuser had mysteriously died. The new Christian is now quietly working to bring other Muslims to faith in Christ.

Abraham Lincoln once said, "The best way to destroy an enemy is to make him a friend." The best way to counter the threat of Islam is to make Christians out of Muslims. This won't turn away prophecies of events sure to come, but it does give you a role in the drama to be played. Our prayers, our testimonies, and our love for our Islamic neighbors may not turn the inevitable tide for the world, but they can turn the tide for individuals and allow them to escape the wrath to come. And that is definitely worth doing.

CHAPTER 9

PERSECUTION

Kelvin Cochran quickly rose through the ranks to become Shreveport's first African American fire chief. Eight years later, Cochran was invited to head Atlanta's fire department, making it one of only sixty US departments to receive a Class 1 rating.

Although Cochran is a committed Christian, he carefully observed workplace rules about faith, discussing religion only with those who approached him first. He led Bible studies in his church and formed a study group for men, which led him to write a privately published book on authentic manhood. He gave the book only to people with whom he had shared his faith and, as a courtesy, to Atlanta's mayor and a handful of civic leaders.

Almost a year after the book's publication, Councilmember Alex Wan read the few pages outlining the biblical approach to sexuality—that sex outside of male–female marriage is contrary to God's will. That's when the trouble began. Meetings among Atlanta's top officials followed, and as the *National Review* reported, "On January 6, 2015, the City of Atlanta fired Cochran—without providing him the proper process prescribed by city codes and, he claims, without providing him an opportunity to respond to either his suspension or his termination. At no point did any employee of the fire department complain of mistreatment or discrimination."

Wan, however, made the reason for Cochran's dismissal clear: "When you're a city employee, and [your] thoughts, beliefs, and opinions are different from the city's, you have to check them at the door."[1]

This incident is merely one of many similar ones revealing that American culture is growing increasingly hostile toward Christianity. We are in the first stages of repression of Christian speech and actions, and even stronger measures may well follow.

America was founded on Christian principles. The Declaration of Independence recognizes that God is the source of human rights and freedom: "We hold these truths to be self-evident, that all men are created equal, that they are endowed by their Creator with certain unalienable Rights."

This foundational premise began to erode in the mid-twentieth century with the post–World War II economic boom and the protest culture of the 1960s. Today, the concept of freedom has degenerated into the elimination of virtually all moral restraints. Christianity is being edged out because its adherence to biblical morality is at odds with the philosophy of unrestricted freedom that now dominates America's cultural landscape.

As Dr. Paul Nyquist noted, "We're witnessing an epic change in our culture—a spiritual climate shift threatening to reshape life as we know it. Hostility and intolerance are replacing toleration. Rejection and even hatred are pushing aside acceptance."[2]

It is no secret that Christianity is declining in America. The government, the educational system, the entertainment industry, and the media no longer share biblical values, which means Christianity is now a religious subculture, increasingly ridiculed and marginalized.

"Get ready," Dr. Nyquist urges. "As cultural changes sweep our country, we'll soon be challenged to live out what the Bible says about confronting and responding to persecution."[3]

THE SUBSTANCE OF CHRISTIAN PERSECUTION

You may wonder whether *persecution* is too strong a word to describe what is happening to Christians in America today. But *Christianity Today* reminds us that "most persecution is not violence. Instead, it's a 'squeeze' of Christians in five spheres of life: private, family, community, national, and church."[4]

We should not assume, however, that everything bad that happens to us is persecution. Persecution is only trouble that occurs "for righteousness' sake" (Matt. 5:10). Sometimes our own stress, sin, or bad choices bring difficulties into our lives (1 Peter 4:15). To be persecuted for righteousness' sake means that we are opposed or suffer solely for following Christ.

THE STAGES OF CHRISTIAN PERSECUTION

To show the extent of the persecution problem, let's look at five stages of religious suppression occurring in our nation.

STAGE 1: STEREOTYPING

Today Christians are often stereotyped as ignorant, uneducated, inhibited, homophobic, and intolerant. Movies and television usually feature a Christian as the antagonist, a holier-than-thou bigot who judges others harshly. Or he is portrayed as a hypocrite who doesn't live what he professes to believe, like the prison warden in *The Shawshank Redemption* who recites the Bible but abuses inmates.

While it is true that some professed Christians represent the faith poorly, these stereotypes do not reflect the reality of authentic Christianity; they grow out of the rising cultural prejudice against the Christian faith. Our duty is to live our convictions in a way that shows these slanderous depictions to be gross distortions of the truth.

STAGE 2: MARGINALIZING

Many secularists want Christianity to be displaced from the center of American life. If the church must be allowed to exist, they want it confined to the realm of personal privacy. That is why public prayer must be forbidden, Christian influence in public policy eliminated, and Christian holidays secularized. Christians must be excluded from positions of power and influence, which includes politics, academia, entertainment, and the media.

As former MSNBC personality Chris Matthews tweeted, "If you're a politician and believe in God first, that's all good. Just don't run for government office, run for church office."[5]

STAGE 3: THREATENING

Banning religious expression within academic, institutional, corporate, or public arenas is not enough for many secularists. They are determined to make Christians pay the price even when privately performing actions that conflict with the progressive agenda.

For example, an intern at California State University Long Beach was terminated for discussing her faith with coworkers, even though she did it only in her off hours.[6] A manager in a national insurance firm was fired for expressing his opposition to gay marriage in a post he wrote online from his home computer.[7] Brendan Eich, chief executive of Mozilla, was forced to resign when it was discovered he had personally contributed $1,000 to support California's Proposition 8, which defined marriage as the union of a man and a woman.[8]

STAGE 4: INTIMIDATING

In 2013, the American Civil Liberties Union (ACLU) sued Mercy Health Partners, a Catholic hospital, because it did not offer abortion services to a client experiencing a difficult pregnancy. As noted in *National Review*, "The issue is not whether those who wish to avail themselves of certain services will be able to, but that those who object to them must be forced to participate."[9]

In 2014, several Houston pastors encouraged Christians to sign a petition calling for a referendum on an ordinance that allowed men and women to use one another's restrooms. The Houston city government, under mayor Annise Parker, ordered five of the pastors to turn over all sermons, text messages, and emails addressing homosexuality or gender issues. Refusal to comply would mean contempt of court and jail. Mayor Parker later rescinded the subpoenas in the wake of nationwide negative reaction.[10]

STAGE 5: LITIGATING

A growing number of Christians are being taken to court for refusing to compromise their Christian convictions. At the frontline of the battle are small businesses that provide wedding services. One of the most outrageous of these incidents was the $135,000 fine levied against an Oregon bakery owned by a Christian couple who declined to bake a wedding cake for a lesbian couple.[11] Many Christians have paid heavily for standing by their convictions. Some lost their life's savings, others were forced out of business or into bankruptcy, and several even received death threats from activists. Unless there is a major turnaround, we can expect lawsuits and court judgments against Christians who practice their faith to escalate.

I think America is a long way from the kind of persecution that involves torture and death, as Christians endured in the New Testament and now endure in other countries. But one never knows what may lurk around the corner.

THE STORY OF CHRISTIAN PERSECUTION

Christianity has suffered severe opposition from its inception, beginning with Christ Himself. He was plotted against, arrested, convicted in a rigged trial, scourged, and crucified. He warned that following Him would mean similar persecution. Consider His words to His disciples in Matthew 10:

"Behold, I send you out as sheep in the midst of wolves. . . . They will deliver you up to councils and scourge you in their synagogues. You will be brought before governors and kings for My sake. . . . Brother will deliver up brother to death, and a father his child; and children will rise up against parents and cause them to be put to death. And you will be hated by all for My name's sake" (vv. 16, 17–18, 21–22).

Eugene Peterson wrote, "God's revelation of himself is rejected far more often than it is accepted, is dismissed by far more people than embrace it, and has been either attacked or ignored by every major culture or civilization in which it has given its witness."[12]

Why does the gift of salvation encounter such persistent opposition? It's because along with salvation comes submission to God. But since humanity's fall, people have resisted submission to any power outside self. They demand freedom to define right and wrong for themselves.

Christian behavior angers non-Christians because it makes them feel judged. It resurrects the moral accountability that God planted in every human heart. But as Paul wrote, the existence of God and the tenets of natural law are too obvious to be suppressed: "Since the creation of the world His invisible attributes are clearly seen, being understood by the things that are made . . . so that they are without excuse" (Rom. 1:20).

When Christianity arouses the consciences of non-Christians, their response is seldom to accept the message but rather to silence the messenger. This is why persecution has been a persistent counterpoint to Christianity.

PERSECUTION OF CHRISTIANS IN THE BIBLE

Persecution in the New Testament begins shortly after Christ's birth and does not end until the final chapters of Revelation. Here are a few of the most notable examples:

- King Herod, fearful of reports that a prophesied king had been born in Bethlehem, tried to protect his dynasty by killing all the male babies born there within the prophetic time frame (Matt. 2:1–16).

- John the Baptist, the first public proclaimer of Christ, was beheaded by Herod's son, Herod Antipas (Mark 6:25–29).
- The Jewish people, angered over Jesus' message, tried to kill Him before their successful crucifixion plot (Luke 4:28–30; 13:31; John 5:16, 18; 7:1, 19, 25, 44; 8:37, 40; 11:53).
- Peter and other apostles were arrested, beaten, and imprisoned for preaching Christ (Acts 4:1–3; 5:17–18, 22–40; 12:1–4).
- Stephen was stoned to death for preaching Christ (7:54–60).
- The first Christian converts living in Jerusalem fled persecution by the Jewish leaders (8:1).
- All the apostles died violent deaths at the hands of their persecutors except John, who was exiled to the island of Patmos (Rev. 1:9).
- Paul was imprisoned, stoned almost to death, five times beaten with thirty-nine stripes, three times beaten with rods, run out of town, and often hungry, cold, and without adequate clothing (2 Cor. 11:22–29).

Soon after Pentecost, many Christians were forced to leave their homes and faced imprisonment or death. Did this make them bitter, unhappy, or regretful? Hardly! Instead of bemoaning their fate, Luke tells us that they formed a flourishing, supportive community: "The multitude of those who believed were of one heart and one soul; neither did anyone say that any of the things he possessed was his own, but they had all things in common. And with great power the apostles gave witness to the resurrection of the Lord Jesus. And great grace was upon them all" (Acts 4:32–33)

When Peter and John reported how they had been arrested, jailed, and warned never again to preach about Jesus, they prayed, "Lord, look on their threats, and grant to Your servants that with all boldness they may speak Your word, by stretching out Your hand to heal, and that signs and wonders may be done through the name of Your holy Servant Jesus" (vv. 29–30).

Persecution increased their dedication and made them bolder in proclaiming the truth. It is an inspiring example for us today.

PERSECUTION OF CHRISTIANS IN HISTORY

In the first century, Romans under Nero burned Christians on stakes and fed them to lions for arena entertainment. Later, the Roman emperor Domitian declared himself to be "Lord and God" and executed Christians who refused to worship him.[13]

Other empires, nations, and religions also have taken up the sword against Christians:

- Seventeenth-century Japan made Christianity illegal, expelled missionaries, and executed converts.
- Eighteenth-century China made Christianity illegal and persecuted Christians severely.
- The French Revolution of 1789 outlawed Christianity. Clergy were banished or killed. Churches were desecrated, and all semblances of Christianity were removed.[14]
- The Ottoman Empire has a long history of persecuting Christians. Estimates of Christian deaths during the history of the empire run as high as 50 million.[15]
- After the Russian Revolution of 1917, churches and Christian teaching were made illegal. The state confiscated all church property. Millions of dissenters were executed.[16]

PERSECUTION OF CHRISTIANS IN TODAY'S WORLD

During just one month in the fall of 2018, these startling headlines screamed the news:

- "At Least 7 Killed in Attack on Christians in Egypt"
- "A Handful of Rotten Corn—a Day in the Life of 50,000 Christians in North Korean Prison Camps"
- "80 Lashes and Other Brutal Sentencing of Christians in Iran"
- "China Shutters 6 More Christian Churches and Tears Down Crosses"[17]

These are not isolated events. Every month in our modern world:

- 255 Christians are killed.
- 104 Christians are abducted.
- 180 Christian women are raped, sexually harassed, or forced into marriage.
- 66 churches are attacked.
- 160 Christians are detained without trial and imprisoned.[18]

Unfortunately, statistics like these fail to get the attention of most Christians in America. They seem in stark contrast to the life of a believer in the United States. As modern-day Americans who have never lived in oppression, we're prone to take our freedoms for granted. We don't face isolation from our families and friends; we aren't denied access to basic needs such as water, food, and health care, and we are not violently abused, imprisoned, and killed.

Yet, when Jesus was asked by His disciples about the end times and the sign of His coming, He prophesied that there would not only be wars, famine, and earthquakes, but that persecution would increase, especially as His return approached (Matt. 24). That is certainly happening on a global scale, and it appears as if the seeds of Christian persecution are being planted in America as well.

THE SIDE EFFECTS OF CHRISTIAN PERSECUTION

How should Christians in the United States react to persecution? Our first response might naturally be anger. But the New Testament gives us a more constructive response. The early Christians suffered severe persecution, but we don't find them responding in anger. On the contrary, they found positive benefits in suffering.

Paul told the Philippian church, "To you it has been granted on behalf of Christ, not only to believe in Him, but also to suffer for His sake" (Phil. 1:29). Paul made suffering sound like a gift. Really? The natural impulse is to say we'd like to return it. But to reject suffering is to miss out on enormous blessings. Let's explore just what this means.

SUFFERING PROMOTES CHARACTER

A man came to his pastor and said, "Pastor, would you please pray that God will give me patience?"

Two weeks later, he returned and said, "Good grief, Pastor! Terrible things are happening to me. My life's coming unglued."

"Well," replied the pastor, "you wanted patience. The Bible says, 'Tribulation works patience,' so I prayed for tribulation. God must be answering my prayer."

Although persecution is inflicted by enemies of God, He can use it to mold us into greater Christlikeness. As Paul told us, "We also glory in tribulations, knowing that tribulation produces perseverance; and perseverance, character; and character, hope" (Rom. 5:3–4).

Contrary to what we often hear, the call to follow Christ is not a call to an easy life. As John Ortberg put it, "God isn't at work producing the circumstances I want. God is at work in bad circumstances to produce the me he wants."[19]

SUFFERING PROVOKES COURAGE

Courage reflects Christ's character in adverse circumstances. It is the crucial virtue that Christians must deploy when facing cultural demands that conflict with biblical teaching.

The apostles Peter and John faced such a demand when the Jewish leaders hauled them into court and told them to cease preaching Christ. Peter and John replied, "Whether it is right in the sight of God to listen to you more than to God, you judge. For we cannot but speak the things which we have seen and heard" (Acts 4:19–20).

After Paul's conversion, his life became a sterling example of this kind of courage. As he wrote to the Philippians, "I eagerly expect and hope that I will in no way be ashamed, but will have sufficient courage so that now as always Christ will be exalted in my body, whether by life or by death. For to me, to live is Christ and to die is gain" (Phil. 1:20–21 NIV).

SUFFERING PROVES GODLINESS

A. W. Tozer wrote, "To be right with God has often meant to be in trouble with men."[20] As Paul put it, "All who desire to live godly in Christ Jesus will suffer persecution" (2 Tim. 3:12). It's a matter of simple logic: Why would the enemies of Christianity bother anyone who is not displaying the nature of Christ?

The writer of Hebrews said, "Whom the LORD loves He chastens" (Heb. 12:6). D. Martyn Lloyd-Jones wrote, "If you are suffering as a Christian, and because you are a Christian, it is one of the surest proofs you can ever have of the fact that you are a child of God."[21]

SUFFERING PRODUCES JOY

When we realize the purpose and positive results of suffering persecution, it can become a source of joy, as it was for Paul and Silas when they encountered opposition. In Acts 16:22–24, they were arrested, beaten, and thrown into prison. Then we read, "At midnight Paul and Silas were praying and singing hymns to God, and the prisoners were listening to them" (v. 25).

These disciples, beaten and imprisoned without a trial, were so joyful they burst into song! This tells us that the source of joy is our relationship with God, and that relationship is affirmed when we courageously endure persecution.

SUFFERING PROVIDES REWARDS

The Scriptures abound with promises of rewards for those who endure suffering. Often we allow these future rewards to be obscured by immediate gratifications. Moses could easily have allowed the immediate to obscure the distant. Raised as a prince in Egypt's royal palace, he had access to riches, pleasure, status, and power. But the Bible tells us, "By faith Moses . . . refused to be called the son of Pharaoh's daughter, choosing rather to suffer affliction with the people of God than to enjoy the passing pleasures of sin, esteeming the reproach of Christ greater riches than the treasures in Egypt; for he looked to the reward" (Heb. 11:24–26).

Moses was willing not only to turn his back on immediate pleasure, position, and power but also to suffer affliction in order to receive the promised eternal reward.

What are some of the rewards promised to those who endure persecution?

- They will be avenged (Rev. 6:9–11; 16:5–7; 18:20; 19:2).
- They will be given perfect and abundant lives free of sorrow (Rev. 7:14–17).
- They will find eternal rest (Rev. 14:13).
- They will receive the crown of eternal life (James 1:12).
- They will have no more death to fear (1 Cor. 15:54; Rev. 20:14).

These are just a few of the rewards that await those who suffer persecution for Christ's sake. Paul wrote, "I consider that the sufferings of this present time are not worthy to be compared with the glory which shall be revealed in us" (Rom. 8:18).

THE STRENGTH TO FACE CHRISTIAN PERSECUTION

Many Christians have not yet faced serious opposition for their beliefs. When we are untested, we wonder just how strong we will be when it is our freedom, our job, or our pocketbook on the line.

Paul knew the importance of preparing his converts for suffering. He said to the believers in Thessalonica: "[We] sent Timothy . . . to establish you and encourage you concerning your faith, that no one should be shaken by these afflictions . . . For, in fact, we told you before when we were with you that we would suffer tribulation, just as it happened" (1 Thess. 3:2–4).

Richard Wurmbrand "was a Romanian evangelical minister and a Jew who spent fourteen years in Communist imprisonment and torture in his homeland of Romania."[22] His experience led him to help others prepare for suffering. He said, "We have to make the preparation now, before we are imprisoned. In prison you lose everything. . . . Nothing of what makes life pleasant remains. Nobody resists who has not renounced the pleasures of life beforehand."[23]

Let's look at three things we can do to prepare for that moment when persecution comes.

DETERMINE TO STAND FOR TRUTH

To live worthy of the gospel is to stand for God's truth without bending. As Paul urged the Corinthians, we are to "watch, stand fast in the faith, be brave, be strong. Let all that you do be done with love" (1 Cor. 16:13–14).

Wherever we are, we are called to be God's agents at that time and place. Whatever the situation, our task is simple: Don't think about the cost or the result; just think about what you decided in advance that you would do when you are tested.

We naturally seek the approval of our peer groups, but peer acceptance is one of the things we may be called to sacrifice. This means willingness to be labeled a prude for avoiding entertainment, speech, and activities that promote immorality, sacrilege, or ungodly values. It means willingness to be labeled stupid for believing in creation, homophobic for rejecting homosexuality, anti-feminist for rejecting abortion, and intolerant for professing the exclusivity of Christ. As Paul put it, we must be willing to be "fools for Christ's sake" (4:10).

It is our duty to speak out for biblical truth when it is attacked. But it is also our duty to confront with love, taking care that we do not justify the labels of hate and intolerance. Paul gave us our rules of engagement: "Being reviled, we bless; being persecuted, we endure; being defamed, we entreat" (4:12–13). When faced with persecution, we must defend our faith with reason and civility: "Always be ready to give a defense to everyone who asks you a reason for the hope that is in you, with meekness and fear; having a good conscience, that when they defame you as evildoers, those who revile your good conduct in Christ may be ashamed" (1 Peter 3:15–16).

DRAW SUPPORT FROM ONE ANOTHER

When we are under attack, having a supportive group of people who share our beliefs makes resisting progressivism easier. This is why regular church attendance is critical to a healthy Christian lifestyle. By attendance, I mean more than just showing up on Sunday morning. Attend classes, serve others, become involved in outreach, and participate in fellowship. The church needs you, and you need the church.

As the writer of Hebrews put it, "Let us consider one another in order to stir up love and good works, not forsaking the assembling of ourselves together, as is the manner of some, but exhorting one another, and so much the more as you see the Day approaching" (10:24–25). We need other Christians with whom we can share encouragement, struggles, and victories.

DERIVE YOUR SECURITY FROM THE LORD

The key to standing firm in the face of persecution is to remember that we belong to Christ, and He secures us in His hand. Thus, we need not fear danger to our reputations, our jobs, our finances, or even our physical lives. As Jesus said, "Whoever desires to save his life will lose it, but whoever loses his life for My sake will find it" (Matt. 16:25). We also draw courage from knowing the glory that awaits us: "Our citizenship is in heaven. And we eagerly await a Savior from there, the Lord Jesus Christ" (Phil. 3:20 NIV).

John Chrysostom, the archbishop of Constantinople, ran afoul of

Byzantine Empress Eudoxia for preaching against the court's misuse of wealth, the neglect of the poor, and immoral indulgences. False charges of heresy were brought against Chrysostom, and he was brought before the empress for trial. When he refused to bend, the story is told that the empress threatened to banish him.

"You cannot banish me," Chrysostom replied. "For this world is my Father's house."

"But I will kill you," said Eudoxia.

"No, you cannot, for my life is hidden with Christ in God."

"I will take away your treasures."

"No, you cannot, for my treasure is in heaven and my heart is there."

"But I will drive you away from your friends," said Eudoxia.

"No, you cannot, for I have a Friend in heaven from whom you cannot separate me. There is nothing you can do to harm me."

What do you do with a man like that? Eudoxia finally exiled Chrysostom to hostile conditions that brought about his death.[24]

We, like Chrysostom, must realize that our persecutors can take nothing from us that we don't already have securely fixed in Christ. That is the key to standing up to persecution.

It is not likely that Christians in America will soon face martyrdom. But we can draw courage from martyrs throughout the centuries and Christians who are now enduring severe persecution in other countries. If they can stand strong in the face of torture and death, we should be willing to stand strong in the face of the Christian repression that is rising in our nation today.

CHAPTER 10

SPIRITUAL WARFARE

The vast majority of books on military strategy appeal to a limited audience—namely, those people who are involved in military strategy. But there's one book that has a much broader appeal.

This book is recommended reading for every officer in the Central Intelligence Agency and has been listed in the US Marine Corps Professional Reading Program for years, as you might expect. But this book is also read and referenced today by leaders in business, entertainment, education, sports, politics, and many other fields. Such broad appeal is all the more surprising because this book was written twenty-six hundred years ago in ancient China.

That book is *The Art of War* by Sun Tzu. If you read it, you'll find dozens of principles spread out over thirteen chapters. But it's principle eighteen, the last principle in chapter 3, that I believe is critical information for members of the church:

> Hence the saying: If you know the enemy and know yourself, you need not fear the result of a hundred battles. If you know yourself but not the enemy, for every victory gained you will also suffer a defeat. If you know neither the enemy nor yourself, you will succumb in every battle.[1]

It's because of this paragraph that Sun Tzu is often credited with coining the phrase, "Know your enemy." But this commonsense idea is even older than Sun Tzu. Moses knew the value of this principle, which is why he sent the twelve spies from Kadesh into Canaan to "see . . . whether the people who dwell in it are strong or weak, few or many" (Num. 13:18). Joshua did the same from the east bank of the Jordan River before entering Canaan, sending spies to assess the strength of Jericho (Josh. 2:1). Even Jesus Christ taught the importance of knowing your enemy: "What king, going to make war against another king, does not sit down first and consider whether he is able with ten thousand to meet him who comes against him with twenty thousand?" (Luke 14:31).

Maybe you're wondering, *Why do I need to hear about knowing my enemy? I'm not a soldier. I'm not involved in a war.*

But that's not correct. If you are a disciple of Jesus, then you *are* in a war. A spiritual war. And if the idea of knowing one's enemy makes sense in a conventional battle, it makes even more sense in our spiritual battle because our enemy is stronger and the stakes are higher. What's more, as the end of the present age approaches, we can be sure that satanic activity will increase: "The Spirit expressly says that in latter times some will depart from the faith, giving heed to deceiving spirits and doctrines of demons" (1 Tim. 4:1).

The biblical writers spared no effort in giving us intelligence on the nature of our spiritual enemy, Satan himself. Indeed, they covered both of Sun Tzu's requirements for victory: know yourself and know your enemy. Our task is to embrace what the Bible tells us and be prepared for the battle we most certainly will face.

So, let's begin our study of this important topic by acknowledging the reality and the nature of our enemy.

SPIRITUAL WARFARE IS REAL

God's Word tells us Satan is a fallen angel, originally named Lucifer (Isa. 14:12). It also traces his presence in our world from Genesis to Revelation.

Genesis tells us how the Devil went to Eve as a serpent, convincing her she could be like God if she would only eat of the Tree of Knowledge of Good and Evil (Gen. 3). In the book of Revelation, we see that in the end God will banish Satan, among others: "The devil, who deceived them, was cast into the lake of fire and brimstone where the beast and the false prophet are. And they will be tormented day and night forever and ever" (Rev. 20:10). That's good news for the future.

But between the first human sin in the garden of Eden and God casting out Satan in the final days, the Bible clearly warns us to be aware of the Devil, his power, and his intentions. Ephesians 6:12 says, "We do not wrestle against flesh and blood, but against principalities, against powers, against the rulers of the darkness of this age, against spiritual hosts of wickedness in the heavenly places."

That's our reality.

And we need to remember that reality because it reminds us that other people aren't our true enemies. We often blame those who lie, deceive, divide, and destroy for everything wrong in this world. Yes, the people who do those things must be held accountable—and God will do that in His time. But our true enemy is Satan, who uses people for many of his evil actions.

In a commentary on the books of Ephesians and Philippians, John Phillips wrote:

> Satan may use people to persecute us, lie to us, cheat us, hurt us, or even kill us. But our real enemy lurks in the shadows of the unseen world, moving people as pawns on the chessboard of time. As long as we see people as enemies and wrestle against them, we will spend our strength in vain.[2]

Satan uses people to do his dirty work, yet the tragedy is we fight against those people instead of fighting against him. We must concentrate our efforts against the being who disguises himself as an angel of light instead of the destroyer he is (2 Cor. 11:14).

The Bible tells us Satan has a strategic plan that is very well thought through: "Put on the whole armor of God, that you may be able to stand against the wiles of the devil" (Eph. 6:11). The word *wiles* comes from the Greek word *methodia*, from which we get our word *method*. Did you know Satan has a strategy for you and for me and for every other person on this planet? It's not a strategy for good; it's a strategy for evil.

Before we can learn how to fight him with the provisions God grants us, we need to learn how to recognize his strategy. Let's look at three common ways Satan wages war: deception, division, and destruction.

SATAN DECEIVES

John 8:44 says Satan "does not stand in the truth, because there is no truth in him. When he speaks a lie, he speaks from his own resources, for he is a liar and the father of it." In some translations of this verse, he's called the "father of lies" (NIV).

The late evangelist Billy Graham said:

> The Devil can be very convincing! After all, he doesn't usually come to us and say, "Listen! What I'm about to tempt you to do is a lie, and will lead you down the path to destruction!" No, he is very clever, and he will do everything in his power to convince us that his way is best—and God's way is wrong.[3]

Revelation 12:9 says Satan "deceives the whole world." In the last days he will bring us the Antichrist, whose deception will inflict untold damage: "That Day [of Christ] will not come unless the falling away comes first, and the man of sin is revealed, the son of perdition, who opposes and exalts himself above all that is called God or that is worshiped, so that he sits as God in the temple of God, showing himself that he is God" (2 Thess. 2:3–4). We need to be armed against this deception.

SATAN DIVIDES

One of Satan's methods of attack against God's kingdom is to divide us so we don't benefit from the unity Christ desires for us. Paul implored the church at Corinth to remember the value and necessity of unity after he'd heard they were having problems with one another: "Now I plead with you, brethren, by the name of our Lord Jesus Christ, that you all speak the same thing, and that there be no divisions among you, but that you be perfectly joined together in the same mind and in the same judgment" (1 Cor. 1:10).

Although it feels like there's plenty of blame to go around, who do you think is truly responsible for the increased division and polarization in our country today? In our world? And what about our churches, where petty arguments and bullheadedness often lead to division and splits, which are a terrible witness to those watching from the outside? The answer to each of these questions is Satan, the ultimate divider.

Paul said to the Romans, "Watch out for those who cause divisions and create obstacles contrary to the doctrine that you have been taught; avoid them. For such persons do not serve our Lord Christ, but their own appetites, and by smooth talk and flattery they deceive the hearts of the naive" (Rom. 16:17–18 ESV).

SATAN DESTROYS

During the Tribulation, demons will be allowed to leave hell and invade our world to kill and destroy. We're told this about the one who will be leading them: his "name in Hebrew is Abaddon, but in Greek he has the name Apollyon" (Rev. 9:11). *Abaddon* and *Apollyon* both mean "Destroyer."

In John 10:10, Jesus also calls Satan a thief. He says, "The thief does not come except to steal, and to kill, and to destroy." Yet in that same verse Jesus said, "I have come that they may have life, and that they may have it more abundantly." Satan's intent is nothing like Christ's. He doesn't give; he takes. He doesn't preserve; he destroys. He doesn't increase; he lessens. He doesn't give life; he sucks it out of us.

While we must study Satan's strategies, the good news is we don't need to fear him or assign to him more power than he actually has. Author Randy Alcorn explains: "When asked to name the opposite of God, people often answer, 'Satan.' But that's false. Michael, the righteous archangel, is Satan's opposite. Satan is finite; God is infinite. God has no equal."[4]

Thankfully, we are not alone in our efforts to resist the Devil. God offers us His power in our struggle against Satan. When we, by faith, put on the Lord Jesus Christ (Rom. 13:14), we clothe ourselves with His strength, and we turn the tables on our enemy because "He [Christ] who is in you is greater than he [Satan] who is in the world" (1 John 4:4).

SPIRITUAL WEAPONS ARE REQUIRED

Now that we understand the nature of our enemy, let's get to know the spiritual weapons that will help us stand strong in the battle. In Ephesians 6, we are told that our armor consists of five defensive pieces—the girdle of truth, the breastplate of righteousness, the shoes of the preparation of the gospel of peace, the shield of faith, the helmet of salvation—and one offensive piece, "the sword of the Spirit, which is the word of God" (vv. 14–17). With the defensive armor, we are able to resist Satan's attacks. And with the offensive weapon of the Word, we are ensured that Satan must flee from the authority of God's truth.

Let's look at each of these weapons one at a time.

THE BELT OF TRUTH

Paul's first instruction is to "stand therefore, having girded your waist with truth" (v. 14). The belt had a central function in Paul's day that was vital to most of the soldier's armor and weapons.

The soldier's basic attire was a tunic—a shirt-like garment that draped from shoulder to knee. Over this he wore metal torso armor and long, protective leather strips that hung from his waist to his lower thighs around his entire body. His belt was a band of wide, thick leather with loops and slots that clamped over these items. From it hung a sword, rope, ration sack, money sack, and darts.

Everything the soldier needed in hand-to-hand combat was on his belt, right there at his fingertips. When running, the soldier pulled up his tunic and tucked it in his belt, freeing his legs for speed and maneuverability. This was known as "girding one's loins." And while the belt had no offensive function of its own, it was the piece of equipment that essentially held everything else together, keeping the soldier ready for anything he might face.

Here's what this means for us today: truth is what fits us for the life of a Christian. Truth holds everything together and makes us ready. At the center of our lives, we place "the truth [that] is in Jesus" (4:21).

Why is truth to be our primary concern? Because the weapons of Satan's major attacks against believers are falsehood and deception. He is the great deceiver! This is how the Bible describes the Devil: "When he speaks a lie, he speaks from his own resources, for he is a liar and the father of it" (John 8:44).

THE BREASTPLATE OF RIGHTEOUSNESS

The breastplate of the common Roman soldier was a piece of armor made of hardened, reinforced leather. For an officer, the leather was covered with metal plating for extra protection. The breastplate covered the torso and protected the soldier's vital organs—especially his heart. A warrior without his breastplate was vulnerable and dangerously exposed to the enemy.

In his letter, Paul used this literal breastplate that protected the physical heart as a metaphor. Righteousness, he inferred, acts as a "breastplate" to protect the figurative, spiritual heart of the Christian—the spiritual center of one's life.

How do we put on the breastplate of righteousness? Pastor Erwin Lutzer has given us a good illustration:

Imagine a book entitled *The Life and Times of Jesus Christ*. It contains all the perfections of Christ: the works He did, His holy obedience, His purity, His right motives. A beautiful book indeed.

131

Then imagine another book, *The Life and Times of [insert your name]*. It contains all of [your] sins, immorality, broken promises, and betrayal of friends. It would contain sinful thoughts, mixed motives, and acts of disobedience.

Finally, imagine Christ taking both books and stripping them of their covers. Then He takes the contents of His own book and slips it between the covers of [your] book. We pick up the book to examine it. The title reads, *The Life and Times of [insert your name]*. We open the book and turn the pages and find no sins listed. All that we see is a long list of perfections, obedience, moral purity, and perfect love. The book is so beautiful that even God adores it.[5]

Having received the righteousness of Christ by faith, we can now put on His righteousness in practice. We can take on the obligation and determination to live as closely to God's Word, and as closely to Jesus' example, as we are able.

THE SHOES OF THE GOSPEL OF PEACE

Paul describes the third implement of warfare in Ephesians 6:15: "Stand therefore . . . having shod your feet with the preparation of the gospel of peace" (vv. 14–15). The New Living Translation renders this verse: "For shoes, put on the peace that comes from the Good News so that you will be fully prepared."

The shoes Paul used for his illustration were not the average person's shoes; they were the open-toed leather boots worn by Roman soldiers. Made with nail-studded soles designed to grip the ground, they resembled our modern cleated football shoes. These boots were not made for running or even for marching. Instead, they were specifically designed for one primary purpose: to give the soldier stability in hand-to-hand combat against the enemy.

The Christians of that day would have understood what this meant: in hand-to-hand combat, the first to accidentally lose his footing is the first to fall! Just as the Roman soldier's studded shoes anchored him firmly to the ground as he faced his opponent, peace anchors us firmly to God as we face the troubles and uncertainties that assail us in this fallen world.

THE SHIELD OF FAITH

Now we come to the fourth military implement listed in the closing verses of Ephesians 6: "Above all, taking the shield of faith with which you will be able to quench all the fiery darts of the wicked one" (v. 16).

Paul was describing the large shield Roman infantry used to protect their whole bodies. These shields were four feet tall and two-and-a-half feet wide. Made of leather stretched over wood, they were reinforced with metal at the top and bottom.

In ancient times, enemy soldiers would dip the tips of their darts or arrows into a solution of lethal poison. Even if those darts only grazed a soldier's skin, the poison would spread through his bloodstream, producing a swift and painful death. On other occasions the enemy would dip their darts in pitch and ignite them before shooting them into the Roman camp, setting it on fire.

Of all the implements of warfare included in Paul's description of the Roman soldier, this is the only piece that is given a plainly specified purpose. Paul tells us that the purpose of the shield of faith is to protect us from "all the fiery darts of the wicked one."

According to New Testament scholar Peter O'Brien, these fiery darts represent "every kind of attack launched by the Devil and his hosts against the people of God. They are as wide-ranging as the 'insidious wiles' that promote them, and include not only every kind of temptation to ungodly behavior, doubt, and despair, but also external assaults, such as persecution or false teaching."[6]

THE HELMET OF SALVATION

Crisscrossing the nations of the Roman Empire throughout his ministry, Paul saw the helmets of Roman soldiers everywhere.

In the Roman army, helmets of common soldiers were made of hardened leather. Officers' helmets could be augmented with metal; senior officers' helmets were topped by plumed crests. All served the same purpose as today's counterparts: to protect the skull and brain from blows inflicted by the enemy.

The helmet first became a metaphor for salvation in Isaiah 59:17, where it referred to the salvation Christ would bring to humanity. In Ephesians 6:17, Paul picked up this metaphor when he said to Christians, "And take the helmet of salvation."

In Ephesians, Paul was writing to believers—people who'd already received salvation. So the purpose of the spiritual helmet was not to impart salvation but to protect the believer's assurance of it. This assurance gives believers courage to fight their spiritual battles against mankind's great deceiver. This idea is reinforced in 1 Thessalonians 5:8, where Paul called the helmet "the hope of salvation."

Just as a physical helmet protects a soldier's brain, the spiritual helmet protects your mind from the assaults of Satan's lies, corrupt philosophies, and confusion of thought—the weapons he uses to undermine your commitment and conviction of security in Christ.

More specifically, the helmet is a metaphor for the mind of Christ. Paul called Christ "the wisdom of God" (1 Cor. 1:24) and "wisdom from God" (v. 30). When you put on this helmet, you put on the assurance of your own salvation, and you protect your mind from Satan's deceptions with the wisdom of God. This wisdom comes to you through the person of Jesus Christ.

THE SWORD OF THE SPIRIT

The sword "refers to a dagger anywhere from six to eighteen inches long. It was carried in a sheath or scabbard at the soldier's side and used in hand-to-hand combat. The sword of the Spirit is not a broadsword you swing or flail around, hoping to do damage. It's incisive; it must hit a vulnerable spot or it won't be effective."[7]

Ephesians 6:17 leaves no ambiguity as to what the sword metaphor means for the Christian. Paul tells us plainly that "the sword of the Spirit . . . is the word of God." But there are two Greek terms commonly translated into English as "word." The first is *logos*, the more common of the two. It's used to describe the overarching revelation of God that we have in the Bible. It's an all-encompassing term denoting the whole of the Bible—what we often call God's Word. The Bible in its totality is the logos of God, as in: "Remember those who rule over you, who have spoken the word [logos] of God to you" (Heb. 13:7).

But *logos* is not the word we find in Ephesians 6:17.

The Greek term for "word" in Ephesians 6:17 is *rhema*. The rhema of God means "a saying of God." We could translate the verse this way: "Take the sword of the Spirit, which is a saying of God."

The difference between the *logos* of God and the *rhema* of God is critical to our understanding of this offensive weapon. *Logos* refers to the complete revelation of what God has said in the Bible. But *rhema* means a specific saying of God—a passage or verse drawn from the whole that has special application to an immediate situation.

Ray Stedman has a helpful word concerning the way the sword of the Spirit works in our lives:

> Sometimes when you are reading a passage of Scripture, the words seem suddenly to come alive, take on flesh and bones, and leap off the page at you, or grow eyes that follow you around everywhere you go, or develop a voice that echoes in your ears until you can't get away from it. This is the rhema of God, the sayings of God that strike home like arrows to the heart. This is the sword of the Spirit which is the word of God.[8]

PRAYER

There is another spiritual weapon we have at our disposal in the war against evil: prayer.

In Ephesians 6:10–18, Paul instructed us to put on the armor of the Lord so that we might stand against the wiles and strategies of the enemy.

Now we come to the postscript of this famous section of Scripture: "Praying always with all prayer and supplication in the Spirit, being watchful to this end with all perseverance and supplication for all the saints" (v. 18).

As someone once said, "praying always" means the telephone line to heaven is always open. That doesn't mean you're talking on it every second of the day, but it does mean it's an open line ready to be used. "Praying always" is the same as Paul's words, "Pray without ceasing" in 1 Thessalonians 5:17. Or Jesus' words in Luke 18:1—"that men always ought to pray." It doesn't mean a continual stream of mumbling prayers under your breath to God. Think of it more as a continuing conversation in which one commits to God all the concerns of the day—as well as words of thanks and praise— with all kinds of prayers on an ongoing basis.

Professor Donald Whitney of the Southern Baptist Theological Seminary offers excellent advice: "If you've ever learned a foreign language, you know that you learn it best when you actually have to speak it. The same is true with the 'foreign language' of prayer. There are many good resources for learning how to pray, but the best way to learn how to pray is to pray."[9]

Pastor and author Jack Taylor describes for us one practical way we can put on Christ's armor—through this prayer, which he prays each morning as he prepares for the day ahead:

> I choose now to be strong in the Lord and in the power of His might. I confess that I am in the Lord and thus, am located in the power of His might.
>
> I choose to put on the whole armor that God has provided me, in order that I might stand against the methods of the enemy. I know that the battle is not with flesh and blood but against principalities, powers, rulers of darkness, and spiritual wickedness in high places.
>
> Therefore I stand to accept the armor, which is mine in Jesus . . .
>
> I put on the breastplate of righteousness, the Lord Jesus Christ. He is made unto me righteousness. I am made righteous in Him.
>
> I put on the girdle of truth. I accept the fact that Jesus is Truth and that Truth has made me free. I refuse deception and I accept the truth.

I slip into the footwear of preparation in the Gospel. I am now ready to walk with Him.

I put on the helmet of salvation. The certainty of my salvation covers and protects my mind and my outlook. I stand in that certainty now!

I take up the shield of faith. I now trust in the trustworthiness of God! I am covered from head to toe so that Satan's fiery darts cannot touch me . . .

I now take my offensive weapon, the Word of God . . . declaring it to be true without error, reliable, powerful, and alive—God's word to me!

And now I am dressed from head to foot for battle.[10]

MORE THAN CONQUERORS

When you look back at the major wars that have been fought throughout history, there is almost always a single battle or event that served as the turning point—a specific, decisive moment that ultimately led to victory or defeat. For example, most historians agree the Battle of Gettysburg was the turning point in the American Civil War; the North's victory in that battle was the key to victory in the war. Similarly, the Allied forces' surprise invasion of Normandy on D-Day was the beginning of the end of World War II.

As members of God's kingdom, we have the comfort of knowing that a similar turning point has already taken place in the war between Satan and God. That turning point was the death and resurrection of Jesus Christ. Ever since that moment, God's victory has been assured—and Satan knows it.

I remember hearing a story about Napoleon Bonaparte during his attempt to conquer every civilization in the known world. While meeting with his various lieutenants, he spread out a large map of the world and pointed to a single spot. "Sirs," he said, "if it were not for that red spot, I could conquer the world." That red spot represented Great Britain—the same nation whose armies ultimately defeated Napoleon at the Battle of Waterloo.

In a similar way, I can imagine Satan surrounded by his minions and talking about his plans for spiritual domination. I can see our enemy pointing to the hilltop of Calvary where Jesus' blood was spilled, and I can hear him say: "If it were not for that red spot, I could rule the world!"

That red spot is what has made all the difference in our spiritual struggle against evil. The truth is that we don't have to live in fear of Satan, our enemy. Nor do we have to live in fear of the demons at his command. All we must do as soldiers in God's army is take our place in the spiritual battle to which we have been called—and stand. And that's the wonderful news: we *can* stand because we've been armed with the truth that God's ultimate victory over Satan has already been won.

Right now, you and I are "more than conquerors through Him who loved us" (Rom. 8:37). And to that I say, "Thanks be to God, who gives us the victory through our Lord Jesus Christ" (1 Cor. 15:57).

CHAPTER 11

APATHY

The late A. W. Tozer wrote about what he called "the decline of apoca-lyptic expectation" in the contemporary church. Tozer felt that believers were forgetting the importance of Christ's approaching return, and he com-pared that attitude to the generation just prior to his own:

> There was a feeling among gospel Christians that the end of the age was near, and many were breathless with anticipation of a new world order about to emerge.
>
> This new order was to be preceded by a silent return of Christ to earth, not to remain, but to raise the righteous dead to immortality and to glorify the living saints in the twinkling of an eye. These He would catch away to the marriage supper of the Lamb, while the earth mean-while plunged into its baptism of fire and blood in the Great Tribulation. This would be relatively brief, ending dramatically with the battle of Armageddon and the triumphant return of Christ with His Bride to reign a thousand years.[1]

In recent years, however, the church has forgotten this truth. Christians, rather than being distinct from the world around them and living in expectation of their Lord's return, have become so much like the world that sometimes you can scarcely tell the difference between the two. Many churches reflect an apathetic, rather than serious, attitude toward the coming of the Lord.

Apathy, according to Webster's, is "the feeling of not having much emotion or interest." An apathetic Christian is a cynical one—a person who simply doesn't care anymore about the signs of the time.

This is not to say that we who are believers should be walking around with our heads down in some sort of doomsday mentality. That's not what the Bible is all about. The coming of Christ is not a negative subject; it is the brightest, most radiant star on the horizon. But it is also a teaching attended by stern biblical warnings. As God's people, we cannot allow those truths to be shunted off to one side.

In over fifty years of gospel ministry, I have watched evangelical preachers gradually change their attitudes about declaring the return of Christ. More and more, I'm hearing that the subject is "not relevant enough" to occupy a Sunday morning message. If you're going to talk about the return of Christ, it's being said, let it be in a seminary classroom or in a weekday Bible study. But please don't spend an hour teaching "end time" matters on Sunday mornings to people with family struggles, business failures, and a host of other emotional and physical problems. That is so irrelevant!

Irrelevant?

I can promise you one thing with a strong degree of assurance: One minute after the Rapture, the subject won't be "irrelevant" at all. It will be the very definition of *relevant*.

A DOMINANT THEME

One of the positive aspects of being an expository preacher is that you have some built-in protection to keep you from getting off on special-interest areas or lingering on favorite topics. If you teach the Word of God systematically and you are true to the text, you have to deal with God's priorities as they surface in the Scriptures from week to week.

And if you happen to be teaching through the Gospels, you will come to Matthew 24 and 25 and find yourself headlong in the second coming of our Lord. Beginning at verse 36 in chapter 24, we read these words:

> But of that day and hour no one knows, no, not even the angels of heaven, but My Father only. But as the days of Noah were, so also will the coming of the Son of Man be. For as in the days before the flood, they were eating and drinking, marrying and giving in marriage, until the day that Noah entered the ark, and did not know until the flood came and took them all away, so also will the coming of the Son of Man be. Then two men will be in the field: one will be taken and the other left. Two women will be grinding at the mill: one will be taken and the other left. Watch therefore, for you do not know what hour your Lord is coming. But know this, that if the master of the house had known what hour the thief would come, he would have watched and not allowed his house to be broken into. Therefore you also be ready, for the Son of Man is coming at an hour you do not expect. (vv. 36–44)

The disciples, you might remember, had asked the Lord three specific questions regarding future events. His answer in the passage above came in response to the last question: "Lord, when will these things happen?" He had told them about the cataclysmic events that would occur at the end of the age. And the disciples were just as curious as we are. "When, Lord, *when*? When will all this take place?"

The Lord answered them but didn't give them everything they wanted to know. Instead, He gave them what they *needed* to know. Someone said that good preaching is giving people what they need disguised as what they want. Master preacher that He was, the Lord Jesus gave His hearers just what they needed—and they were all ears.

The information contained in these two chapters of Matthew is primarily addressed to those who will be alive during the generation of the Tribulation. But believers today need to heed the voice of the Lord as well; He will come for us at the Rapture of the church, which will also be at an unknown day and hour.

So why should we concern ourselves? "After all," someone might reason, "if you can't know the when and the where, why even worry about it?" It reminds me of a question-and-answer sequence I heard some time ago:

Q: What's the difference between ignorance and apathy?
A: I don't know and I don't care.

That's the way a lot of people feel about the Rapture. They don't know and they don't really care.

Yet Scripture keeps repeating the theme of His coming over and over, like the clear tolling of a great bell on a frosty morning, "Be prepared! Be ready! He's coming soon!"

Some have tuned out the sound of that bell. They've grown used to it, in the way people become accustomed to the familiar chiming of a grandfather clock in the den.

Can you hear it as you turn the pages of your Bible?

Hear it in Paul's great rallying cry to the Romans:

And do this, understanding the present time: The hour has already come for you to wake up from your slumber, because our salvation is nearer now than when we first believed. The night is nearly over; the day is almost here. So let us put aside the deeds of darkness and put on the armor of light. Let us behave decently, as in the daytime, not in carousing and drunkenness, not in sexual immorality and debauchery, not in dissension and jealousy. Rather, clothe yourselves with the Lord Jesus Christ, and do not think about how to gratify the desires of the flesh. (Rom. 13:11–14 NIV)

Hear it in the apostle's strong commendation of the first-generation church in Corinth: "You come short in no gift, eagerly waiting for the revelation of our Lord Jesus Christ" (1 Cor. 1:7).

Hear it again from his prison cell, when he penned timely encouragement to the Philippians: "For our citizenship is in heaven, from which we also eagerly wait for the Savior, the Lord Jesus Christ" (Phil. 3:20).

Hear it from the writer of the book of Hebrews, who urged his readers: "And let us consider how we may spur one another on toward love and good deeds, not giving up meeting together, as some are in the habit of doing, but encouraging one another—and all the more as you see the Day approaching" (Heb. 10:24–25 NIV).

Hear it from James as he wrote: "You too be patient; strengthen your hearts, for the coming of the Lord is near" (James 5:8 NASB).

Hear it from Peter: "The end of all things is near. Therefore be alert and of sober mind so that you may pray" (1 Pet. 4:7 NIV).

Hear it from the elderly apostle John: "Little children, it is the last hour; and as you have heard that the Antichrist is coming, even now many antichrists have come, by which we know that it is the last hour" (1 John 2:18).

Hear the echo of that great bell in the concluding words of the Bible: "He who testifies to these things says, 'Surely I am coming quickly.' Amen. Even so, come, Lord Jesus!" (Rev. 22:20).

What do you do with biblical emphases like these? Ignore them? Shelve them? Skip over them? Set them aside to deal with "more relevant personal matters"?

We practice such neglect, I believe, at our own spiritual peril.

If you go back through all those passages, you will find that in almost every one, the *future* truth impacts some *present* responsibility. It is the knowledge of His imminent return that puts urgency in our walks, determination in our service, and gravity in our decisions and conversations. "Work, for the night comes!"

Some Christians tell themselves they have a lot of time to win friends and family to Christ. We think in terms of seasons and years, but we may not have seasons and years. We may not have the luxury of waiting for that ideal moment when everything falls into place and the door swings wide open. Why not? Because Jesus may come tomorrow morning! Jesus may come tonight at the stroke of midnight! And then it will be too late—forever, eternally too late: "The harvest is past, the summer is ended, and we are not saved!" (Jer. 8:20).

Yes, it is common to hear people speak of "prophecy buffs" and smile indulgently at their preoccupations. Yet the truth is, the prophetic teaching of Scripture is some of the most practical truth in all the Word of God. We must not compartmentalize these great teachings into some obscure "curiosity corner" out of the mainstream of our daily lives. We must not shrug off prophetic issues, saying, "The scholars will deal with that stuff. I'm just going to worry about raising my children and taking care of daily life."

Don't do that, friend! Because "the blessed hope" of His coming will impact your daily life like nothing else! In the remaining pages of this chapter, I want to identify three attitudes that our Lord warned against in Matthew 24.

JESUS WARNED AGAINST A CAVALIER ATTITUDE

As I mentioned earlier in this chapter, in Matthew 24:37–39 Jesus used an illustration that would have sparked immediate recognition in every one of His listeners:

> But as the days of Noah were, so also will the coming of the Son of Man be. For as in the days before the flood, they were eating and drinking, marrying and giving in marriage, until the day that Noah entered the ark, and did not know until the flood came and took them all away, so also will the coming of the Son of Man be.

Jesus said that when the Son of Man returns, it will be the way it was before the Flood. What was it like then? Genesis 6:5 tells us that when the Lord looked down upon His creation He "saw that the wickedness of man was great in the earth, and that every intent of the thoughts of his heart was only evil continually."

Now, today's culture may not be quite there, but who can deny we're headed in that direction? Contrary to the fondest hopes of the evolutionist, this world is not growing better and better. In fact, it is precisely the opposite.

And the thoughts of men's minds? You wonder sometimes when you see the vile stuff reported in the news. How could anyone ever think up something so evil? That's the way it was just before the Flood.

I want you to understand that the growing evil on this planet is *not* what the Lord was talking about when He spoke of the "eating and drinking" that went on before the Flood. I've heard preachers say, "You see how terrible it was? They were out gorging themselves with food and drinking themselves under the table. Gluttony! Drunkenness!"

Well then, what are you going to do with the rest of it? What about the phrase that says they were "marrying and giving in marriage"? That sounds almost wholesome.

No, Jesus is not speaking primarily of humanity's evil activities in this passage; His message is rather that people across the world in that day were all caught up in doing ordinary things. They were cooking meals. They were drawing water from their wells. They were celebrating weddings. They were taking life as it was, day by day.

And they were completely ignoring the warnings of Noah.

Life went on, and that fanatic kept building a ship the size of a football field and talking about "rain"—whatever that was. So, they didn't pay any attention.

How long did Noah preach to these people about the coming flood? Do you remember? One hundred twenty years! That's a long time to preach one message. How many different ways can you say, "It's going to rain"? But that's the message he brought. Faithfully. Repeatedly. Passionately. That's what this "preacher of righteousness" did.

And everybody passed it off with a smile, a shrug of the shoulders, and a shaking of the head.

Noah's neighbors might have said of his preaching: "You're not relevant, Noah. If you must preach, talk to us about the real stuff of life. Talk to us about marriage and raising kids and earning a living. Don't keep harping on some future 'judgment' that nobody believes in anyway. Get a life, Preacher!"

Eating. Drinking. Marrying. Having kids. Working nine to five. Kicking back on the weekends. Life goes on. And rather than turning to God in repentance, the population didn't do anything; men and women drifted along with the prevailing culture, the prevalent attitudes. And the Bible tells us that is the way it will be before Jesus comes again.

It sounds a lot like our world today, doesn't it? Nobody has time for prophecy. Nobody wants to talk about the Second Coming. "Hey, I've got to go to a wedding this afternoon"; "We're having a dinner at our house tonight"; "We're going for a few drinks after work"; "We're having a baby in March"; "I'm taking the grandkids to the zoo"; "I finally made manager; my career's finally startin' to hum."

So, just as in Noah's day, people move through life in a cavalier, heedless sort of way. They look forward to the future and take no heed of God's warnings. They live in the same way they have always lived.

The people of Noah's day ignored and even ridiculed his warnings. He preached for 120 years, and not one individual outside his immediate family believed him. He preached and preached and preached. He gave invitation after invitation. And then the last day of opportunity passed by, and someone, somewhere, felt the first raindrop that ever fell. Then the heavens opened up and the fountains of the great deep broke loose, and God closed the door to the ark.

Peter the apostle has a word to say about this. Notice the startling parallels with today's world:

Above all, you must understand that in the last days scoffers will come, scoffing and following their own evil desires. [And what will they say? Just listen!] They will say, "Where is this 'coming' he promised? Ever since our ancestors died, everything goes on as it has since the beginning of creation." [Doesn't that sound familiar?] But they deliberately forget that long ago by God's word the heavens came into being and the earth was formed out of water and by water. By these waters also the world of that time was deluged and destroyed. (2 Pet. 3:3–6 NIV).

What is Peter saying? He's saying the time immediately before Christ's return will be just as it was during Noah's day. The public grew bored with Noah's preaching. The old man was politically incorrect. He kept saying what people didn't want to hear. For as long as most people could remember, he'd been hammering away about "judgment" and an approaching "flood." But where was it? Where was the water? Where was the rain?

And because God's judgment didn't appear on their monthly calendars, these people assumed it couldn't be real.

Jesus warned against a cavalier attitude. You may have such an attitude yourself. You may say: "Oh, here we go again. Jeremiah's off on another prophecy trip. What's this? His second book on this stuff? Or his third? Doesn't he have anything else to say?"

I have written some books about this subject because it is important. And people who refuse to believe that's true will one day take notice of their surroundings with a different attitude. Members of their immediate family will be missing. They'll knock at the door of a friend's house and no one will answer. The car will be in the driveway and the lights will be on inside, but nobody will be home. And they will begin to wonder, as panic grips their throats, *Why didn't I listen when they were talking to me about the Lord's return?*

Jesus gave a second warning.

JESUS WARNED AGAINST A CARELESS ATTITUDE

As we read earlier, the Lord tells a little story in Matthew 24:42–44:

> Watch therefore, for you do not know what hour your Lord is coming. But know this, that if the master of the house had known what hour the thief would come, he would have watched and not allowed his house to be broken into. Therefore you also be ready, for the Son of Man is coming at an hour you do not expect.

Jesus does not say that He is like a thief. But He uses the modus operandi of a thief as an illustration to make His point. In fact, the Bible uses that word picture a number of times.

Notice Luke 12:39: "Know this, that if the master of the house had known what hour the thief would come, he would have watched and not allowed his house to be broken into." And 1 Thessalonians 5:2: "For you yourselves know perfectly that the day of the Lord so comes as a thief in the night."

It's also in 2 Peter 3:10: "But the day of the Lord will come as a thief in the night, in which the heavens will pass away with a great noise, and the elements will melt with fervent heat; both the earth and the works that are in it will be burned up." Revelation 3:3 says: "Remember therefore how you have received and heard; hold fast and repent. Therefore if you will not watch, I will come upon you as a thief, and you will not know what hour I will come upon you." Revelation 16:15 adds: "Behold, I am coming as a thief. Blessed is he who watches, and keeps his garments, lest he walk naked and they see his shame."

What was Jesus saying? I believe the message was simply this: "Just because you don't see this taking place right under your nose, don't become careless in your attitude." Jesus warned against an approach that says, "I haven't been robbed this year, so I'm turning off my alarm. I'm leaving my doors unlocked. I'm not collecting the newspapers from the driveway.

Nobody has ever robbed me. Nobody has ever robbed my neighbors. It won't happen to me."

Perhaps you could testify that real people do get robbed. Maybe you became careless or heedless, and the thing you thought would never happen, *did* happen.

That's what Jesus was saying. He was warning against a careless, reckless, self-deceptive attitude that keeps insisting, "It can't happen to me."

Yes, it can! Jesus Christ will return without any announcement. One day God will say, "That's enough," and His judgment will fall upon the earth and upon all who have rejected His Son.

But there is also a third warning.

JESUS WARNED AGAINST A CALLOUS ATTITUDE

Jesus told yet another story to make His point clear:

> Who then is a faithful and wise servant, whom his master made ruler over his household, to give them food in due season? Blessed is that servant whom his master, when he comes, will find so doing. Assuredly, I say to you that he will make him ruler over all his goods. But if that evil servant says in his heart, "My master is delaying his coming," and begins to beat his fellow servants, and to eat and drink with the drunkards, the master of that servant will come on a day when he is not looking for him and at an hour that he is not aware of, and will cut him in two and appoint him his portion with the hypocrites. There shall be weeping and gnashing of teeth. (Matt. 24:45–51)

Here, Jesus described two servants who work for an absentee master. One servant is good and faithful, the other evil and faithless. The first servant represents believers who will be on the earth before the Lord's return, while the evil servant represents the nonbelievers. The Lord declared that every person in the world holds his life, his possessions, and his abilities in trust from God, and every individual will be held accountable to the Lord for what he has done with that trust.

This evil servant displays the dominant attitude of callous procrastination. He doesn't really believe the master will come back anytime soon, so he has no motivation to cease doing all the evil things he has become accustomed to doing. Christ's word of warning to him was that he had better be careful because he doesn't know heaven's timetable.

Even as a pastor, I hear people say things like the following: "Yeah, I believe in the coming of the Lord. But I've got some wild oats to sow and some crazy things I want to do. I've got this all figured out. When I first begin to see anything that looks like the Second Coming, then I'll pull my life together and I'll be ready to go up."

First of all, I question the sincere faith of anybody who reasons like that. That's not the way a real Christian reasons. But even if you could reason like that, how foolish! What folly to do such a thing, for "in such an hour as ye think not," He comes! (v. 44 KJV)

Not long ago I was talking to a man about the Lord. He wanted to become a Christian, he told me, but it "wasn't convenient" for him at that time. So he put it off. I wouldn't want to be in that man's shoes if he continues to procrastinate and one day has to stand before the throne of judgment. Can you hear him mumbling as he stands before the Lord of the universe, saying, "Well, Lord, I was going to accept You and follow You, but—well, it just wasn't convenient."

The hard truth is, it won't be "convenient" for God to allow you into heaven—because it wasn't "convenient" for you to accept His provision for your sins.

William Barclay, one of the great historic commentators on the Scripture, relates a fable in which three of the Devil's apprentices were coming to this earth to finish up their apprenticeships. They were talking to Satan, the chief of devils, about their plans to tempt and ruin man. The first devil said, "I know what I'll do. I'll tell them there is no God."

Satan said, "That won't delude anybody. They know there is a God."

The second one said, "I'll tell them there is no hell."

"You will deceive no one that way," Satan replied, "because men know deep down in their hearts that there is a place called hell and a punishment for sin."

The third said, "I know what I'll do. I'll tell them there is no hurry."

And Satan said, "You will ruin men by the thousands. The most dangerous of all delusions is that there is plenty of time."[2]

In the mid-eighties I was working on a project about the book of Revelation called *Before It's Too Late*. I came across a story about a time when the Pacific Northwest of the United States witnessed a cataclysm unlike anything our nation had seen for generations.

Old Harry was a stubborn man. He had become a legend in the Pacific Northwest. Though he was warned repeatedly that his life was in jeopardy, he just laughed. Red flags and danger signs are often ignored, and Harry, well, he was just a picture of that kind of person. He lived at the foot of a quiet mountain.

At least, the mountain had been quiet for 123 years. Sometimes she stirred to spit cinder and ash or drool lava from her cavernous crater. Occasionally she looked down steep snow fields and rumbled a muted threat to the people who explored the lush forest and mountain meadows below. Some thought Bigfoot, the legendary giant beast, stalked her slopes. But Mount Saint Helens was seething inside, ready to unleash her force upon unbelieving admirers. She was awesome and mysterious, but only threatening to the few who understood her power.

In March 1980, an earthquake measuring 4.1 on the Richter scale registered near Mount Saint Helens in southwestern Washington state. Forest rangers were advised of possible dangers from avalanches which could trap skiers or climbers. Most folks were unconcerned. The mountain setting was tranquil as people anticipated a time for renewal. The earth was singing with new warmth.

Then on March 27 a ranger heard what he thought was a sonic boom.

The mountain had erupted. Scientists rushed to assess the explosive potential of the mountain. They painted a frightening scenario of future destruction. People listened, but many could not comprehend a disaster of such magnitude. Old Harry probably read the news stories while he ate a solitary breakfast and fed scraps to his sixteen cats. "Nobody knows more about this mountain than Harry, and it don't dare blow up on him," he bragged.

Days and weeks passed. Some became impatient with the geologists' negative reports. People lost their concern of anything ever happening and wanted to get back to business as usual. Everybody heard the geologists say what they wanted to hear them say. They weren't really listening to them at all.[3]

When sheriffs' deputies ordered all residents on the shores of Spirit Lake at the base of the mountain to leave for safety, Harry said, "I'm . . . living my life alone. I'm king of all I survey. I've got plenty of whiskey. I've got food for fifteen years, and I'm sitting high on the hog."[4] Sunday morning, May 18, 1980, the mountain exploded and hurled pulverized rock and ash almost fourteen miles high. The force of the blast flattened trees, uprooting and smashing them like millions of dominoes spreading out from the crater. Steam, ash, and gases spouted from the incinerated vegetation. Mud flows flooded the rivers and transformed the beautiful mountain lands into a ghastly, charred landscape. The mountain's vengeance was five hundred times greater than the nuclear bomb that leveled Hiroshima.

The warnings were over. There was no longer any time to run. No one ever saw Harry again.

A scary story? Yes—and more. It is also a true picture of how people stubbornly refuse to listen to the truth, because their minds become filled with other things.

Don't be one of those people.

The mountain may not be erupting at just this moment—but can you feel the earth trembling?

PART 3

HEAVENLY SIGNS

With act three, we reach the middle of the story—and a glimmer of hope arrives.

It all starts with the Rapture of the church as described by the apostle Paul in 1 Thessalonians 4:16: "For the Lord Himself will descend from heaven with a shout, with the voice of an archangel, and with the trumpet of God." Can you imagine how stunning, splendid, and sensational the sight of Christ descending from heaven will be?

But that's only the beginning. The Rapture will immediately encompass the resurrection of dead believers and the transformation of living believers, all of whom will be changed "in the twinkling of an eye." Jesus will then escort them to heaven—a heaven even more amazing than you and I could ever imagine. There, believers will experience the judgment seat of Christ where rewards for faithful service will be handed out and where a praise and worship celebration unlike anything witnessed on earth will begin.

Let's continue our study of the thirty-one undeniable signs of the Apocalypse by looking together at six heavenly signs designed to give us confidence in a chaotic world.

CHAPTER 12

RAPTURE

In October 2007, I personally witnessed what was at that time the largest evacuation of homes in California history, and the largest evacuation for fire in United States history. Emergency personnel evacuated 350,000 homes, displacing almost one million Californians as sixteen simultaneous fires swept through our community.[1]

Imagine a person who missed the call to evacuate, waking up after everyone else was gone and stumbling through the acrid smoke and empty streets, confused and amazed, wondering why he had been left behind. That person's reaction would be nothing compared to the shock of those who witness the coming worldwide evacuation known as the Rapture.

The Bible tells us that on that day, millions of people will disappear from the face of the earth in less than a millisecond. And the purpose of that evacuation is similar to that of the emergency evacuation of Southern Californians: to avoid horrific devastation. This evacuation will remove God's people from the disastrous effects of coming earthquakes, fire, and global chaos.

The Rapture is the event in which all who have put their trust in Jesus Christ will be suddenly caught up from the earth and taken into heaven by Him. It is set to occur at an unspecified time in the future.

The word *rapture* is a translation of the Greek word *harpazo*. It occurs fourteen times in the New Testament, and it means "to carry off by force." Satan and his demonic cohorts will do everything in their power to keep the saints here on earth. But Christ's angelic forces will overpower them and carry the believers away by force, delivering them to heaven by the omnipotent power at His command. The Devil is mighty; the Lord is almighty.

My study of Scripture convinces me that the two most important events in world history are the first and second comings of the Lord Jesus Christ. We give great attention to His first coming, as we should, but His second coming deserves no less. In fact, I could make a strong case for an even greater emphasis on the second coming than on the first. For every prophecy in the Bible about the birth of Christ—His first coming—there are eight about His second coming. The 260 chapters of the New Testament contain 318 references to the second coming of Christ.[2]

I believe there will be two stages to the second coming of Christ. First, He will come suddenly in the air to snatch up His own. This is the Rapture, the "catching up" of the church, which will occur at the beginning of the Tribulation that is coming upon the earth.

The Tribulation will be an extended time of horror, agony, and devastation like nothing ever before seen or imagined. The Rapture is God's provision for His saints to escape the Tribulation. Jesus will return immediately before this time of world judgment to remove completely all those who have put their trust in Him. As He told the church in Philadelphia, "Because you have kept My command to persevere, I also will keep you from the hour of trial which shall come upon the whole world" (Rev. 3:10).

UNDERSTANDING THE RAPTURE

While 1 Corinthians 15 and John 14 provide some information about the Rapture, it is Paul's letter to the Thessalonians that presents the most concise and logical truth about this coming event:

I do not want you to be ignorant, brethren, concerning those who have fallen asleep, lest you sorrow as others who have no hope. For if we believe that Jesus died and rose again, even so God will bring with Him those who sleep in Jesus.

For this we say to you by the word of the Lord, that we who are alive and remain until the coming of the Lord will by no means precede those who are asleep. For the Lord Himself will descend from heaven with a shout, with the voice of an archangel, and with the trumpet of God. And the dead in Christ will rise first. Then we who are alive and remain shall be caught up together with them in the clouds to meet the Lord in the air. And thus we shall always be with the Lord. Therefore comfort one another with these words. (1 Thess. 4:13–18)

From Paul's letter to the church in Thessalonica, here are seven important truths we can know about the Rapture.

THE RAPTURE IS A "SIGN-LESS" EVENT

Matthew 24–25 give us many signs that point to the second coming of the Lord. They include all the deception, war, famine, pestilences, and earthquakes of the Tribulation. But it is important to realize that none of these signs point to the first stage of His coming. No signs will be given to prepare us for the arrival of the Rapture. It can occur at any moment—possibly before you finish reading this chapter.

The "at-any-moment" timing of the return of Christ is called the doctrine of *imminency*. In his definitive book on the Rapture, Renald Showers gave us an in-depth exploration of the word *imminent*:

The English word *imminent* means "hanging over one's head, ready to befall or overtake one; close at hand in its incidence." Thus, an imminent event is one that is always hanging overhead, is constantly ready to befall or overtake a person, is always close at hand in the sense that it could happen at any moment. Other things *may* happen before the imminent event, but nothing else *must* take place before it happens. If something else must take place before an event can happen, that event is not imminent.[3]

Without any sign, without any warning, Jesus Christ will return to rapture His saints and take them to heaven. Paul understood the implications of this sign-less event. It means that we must be ready for the Lord's return at any time and at all times. Thus, he urged Titus to be always "looking for the blessed hope and glorious appearing of our great God and Savior Jesus Christ" (Titus 2:13).

THE RAPTURE IS A SURPRISE EVENT

The apostle Paul wrote, "Concerning the times and the seasons, brethren, you have no need that I write to you. For you yourselves know perfectly that the day of the Lord so comes as a thief in the night" (1 Thess. 5:1–2).

If you hear or read of someone who says he or she knows when Jesus is coming back, you should make it your purpose to stay away from that person both in thought and in deed. To claim knowledge of the exact time of our Lord's return is to know what even the angels do not know and what our Lord did not know while He was on this earth: "But of that day and hour no one knows, not even the angels of heaven, but My Father only" (Matt. 24:36).

The Bible does not give us specific information on the date of the Lord's return for the very reason we noted above: awareness that He could return at any time encourages us to be ready at all times. "Therefore you also be ready, for the Son of Man is coming at an hour you do not expect" (v. 44).

As Saint Augustine said, "The last day is hidden that every day may be regarded."

THE RAPTURE IS A SUDDEN EVENT

The apostle Paul emphasized the suddenness of the Rapture when he said it will happen "in a moment, in the twinkling of an eye" (1 Cor. 15:52).

Paul's reference to "the twinkling of an eye" naturally conjures up the image of an eye blinking, which is a reasonably good metaphor for suddenness. But Paul's "twinkling" probably does not mean "blinking"; rather, it likely refers to the amount of time it takes for light, traveling at 186,000 miles per second, to be reflected on the retina in one's eye. The whole idea is that this event will occur suddenly—at the speed of light. In less than a nanosecond, the Lord will call all believers to Himself to share His glory.

THE RAPTURE IS A SELECTIVE EVENT

All three of the major passages that teach about the Rapture make it clear that it involves believers only.

In John 14:1–3, Jesus addressed His disciples as believers in God and in Him, indicating that what He was about to tell them was for believers only. He went on to say that He would soon leave to prepare for them a place in His Father's house—a place reserved for family members only. Then He said, "I will come again and receive you to Myself; that where I am, there you may be also" (v. 3). That coming again is the moment of the Rapture. The entire passage speaks of the Rapture as a family affair reserved solely for those who have put their faith in Jesus Christ.

Paul affirmed the selective nature of the Rapture in 1 Corinthians 15:23, where he described its participants as "those who are Christ's at His coming." Furthermore, in the first verse of that chapter, he identified his readers as "brethren," a term used in the New Testament almost exclusively to describe believers. As if intentionally removing all possibility of misunderstanding, Paul concluded this passage on the Rapture with encouragement directed specifically to the church: "Therefore, my beloved brethren, be steadfast, immovable, always abounding in the work of the Lord, knowing that your labor is not in vain in the Lord" (v. 58).

Finally, in 1 Thessalonians 4:13–18—Paul's main passage on the Rapture—he affirmed its selectivity in triplicate. First, he opened his description of the event by referring to his readers as "brethren." Second, he identified them in verse 14 as those who "believe that Jesus died and rose again." Third, in verse 16, he described the deceased family members of the Thessalonian church as dead "in Christ."

These passages leave no doubt that the Rapture is restricted exclusively to believers. Only those who are followers of Christ will be taken up into heaven when He returns.

THE RAPTURE IS A SPECTACULAR EVENT

No scene described in the Bible is more glorious, stunning, or sensational than the second coming of Christ. But it is usually the second stage of His coming at the end of the Tribulation that draws the spotlight. And for good reason. The apostle John's graphic description of the event is unrivaled by anything else recorded in the Bible (Rev. 19:11–16).

Not only is the final stage of the second coming a glorious spectacle, it is a worldwide event that will impact every person alive on the planet at the time. The Rapture, on the other hand, is a limited, family event that will affect only believers.

But I want to present to you my case for the spectacular nature of the Rapture. Take your seat in the jury box and judge whether I succeed. I call as my primary witness the great apostle Paul, who by the inspiration of the Holy Spirit recorded the preeminent description of the event in 1 Thessalonians 4. As exhibit A, I direct your attention to verse 16: "For the Lord Himself will descend from heaven with a shout, with the voice of an archangel, and with the trumpet of God."

As you read these words, the Lord Jesus Christ is seated in the heavens at the right hand of the almighty Father. But when the right moment comes, He will initiate the Rapture by literally and physically rising from the throne, stepping into the corridors of light, and actually descending into the atmosphere of planet Earth from which He rose into the heavens over the Mount of Olives two thousand years ago. It is not the angels or the Holy Spirit but the Lord Himself who is coming to draw believers into the heavens in the Rapture.

The details of this passage paint an amazingly complete sensory picture of the Rapture. Paul even gave the sounds that will be heard—a shout, the voice of an archangel, and the trumpet of God. These three allusions to sounds are not to be taken as coordinate but rather as subordinate. Paul was not describing three separate sounds; he was describing only one sound in three different ways. This sound will be like a shout, ringing with commanding authority like the voice of an archangel.

It will also be like the blare of a trumpet in its volume and clarity. And the sound will be exclusively directed—heard only by those who have placed their trust in Christ. When Jesus raised Lazarus from the dead, He shouted "Lazarus, come forth!" (John 11:43). I've heard Bible students speculate as to what might have happened had Jesus forgotten to mention Lazarus's name. Would all the dead within the range of His voice have emerged from their graves? At the Rapture that is exactly what will happen. His shout of "Come forth!" will not name a single individual, but it will be heard by every believer in every grave around the world. All those tombs will empty, and the resurrected believers will fly skyward.

This arising from the grave was the hope that Winston Churchill movingly expressed in the planning of his own funeral. Following the prayer by the archbishop of Canterbury and the singing of "God Save the Queen," a trumpeter perched in the highest reaches of the dome of Saint Paul's Cathedral sounded "The Last Post" (or "Taps" as we know it). As the last sorrowful note faded, "high in another gallery, sounded the stronger blaring 'Reveille.'"[4] The call to sleep was followed by a call to arise.

All the evidence clearly shows that the Rapture of the saints will be a cosmic spectacle like nothing humans have ever seen or heard.

THE RAPTURE IS A SEQUENTIAL EVENT

In 1 Thessalonians 4, Paul identified five major aspects of the Rapture in their sequential order.

THE RETURN

"The Lord Himself will descend from heaven with a shout, with the voice of an archangel, and with the trumpet of God" (1 Thess. 4:16).

In the Rapture, it is the Lord Himself who is coming. This is in keeping with the words of the two angels who spoke to the disciples at the time of Jesus' ascension: "Men of Galilee, why do you stand gazing up into heaven? This same Jesus, who was taken up from you into heaven, will so come in like manner as you saw Him go into heaven" (Acts 1:11). If Jesus is to descend in the same manner in which He ascended, then we can certainly expect His coming to be personal and physical.

And when the Lord returns, He will bring with Him all the souls of those who have died as believers. Here is what Paul wrote about that: "God will bring with Him those who sleep in Jesus" (1 Thess. 4:14).

THE RESURRECTION

When Christ descends from heaven with a shout, He will begin by summoning to Himself "those who are asleep" (v. 15). The word used to describe that state has great significance for every believer today. Paul said they had fallen asleep. For the word translated *asleep*, he used the Greek word *koimao*, which has as one of its meanings, "to sleep in death." The same word is used to describe the deaths of Lazarus (John 11:11), Stephen (Acts 7:60), David (Acts 13:36), and Jesus Christ (1 Cor. 15:20).

This concept of death is emphasized in the wonderful word early Christians adopted for the burying places of their loved ones. It was the Greek word *koimeterion*, which means "a rest house for strangers, a sleeping place." It is the word from which we get our English word *cemetery*. In Paul's day, this word was used for inns or what we would call a hotel or motel. We check in at a Hilton Hotel or a Ramada Inn, expecting to spend the night in sleep before we wake up in the morning refreshed and raring to go. That is exactly the thought Paul expressed in words such as *koimao* and *koimeterion*. When Christians die, it's as if they are slumbering peacefully in a place of rest, ready to be awakened at the return of the Lord. The words have great import, for they convey the Christian concept of death not as a tragic finality, but as a temporary sleep.

The Bible teaches that those who are sleeping in Jesus will not be left out of the Rapture. In fact, they will have the prominent place when Jesus comes in the skies: "We who are alive and remain until the coming of the Lord will by no means precede those who are asleep. . . . The dead in Christ will rise first" (1 Thess. 4:15–16).

THE REDEMPTION

Not only will those who have died as believers be changed as part of the resurrection, but Paul spoke of those "who are alive and remain" (v. 15). They will also be changed. That comes to us at the sure word of Paul, who wrote to his Corinthian friends: "We shall not all sleep, be we shall all be changed" (1 Cor. 15:51).

In his letter to the Romans, Paul wrote of this change as "the redemption of our body" (Rom. 8:23). In his letter to the Philippians, he described it as the moment when the Lord Jesus Christ will "transform our lowly body that it may be conformed to His glorious body" (Phil. 3:21). The apostle John said it this way: "We know that when He is revealed, we shall be like Him, for we shall see Him as He is" (1 John 3:2).

What will those bodies be like? Dr. Arnold Fruchtenbaum wrote:

It is possible that information as to the nature of the new body may be gleaned from a study of the nature of the resurrected body of Jesus. . . . We know that His voice was recognized as being the same as the one He had before His death and resurrection (Jn. 20:16). Also, His physical features were recognized, though not always immediately (Jn. 20:26–29; 21:7). It was a very real body of flesh and bone and not a mere phantom body, since it was embraceable (Jn. 20:17, 27). The resurrected Messiah was able to suddenly disappear (Lk. 24:31) and go through walls (Jn. 20:19). It was a body that was able to eat food (Lk. 24:41–43).[5]

THE RAPTURE

While raptures are extremely rare, they have happened before, and they will happen again. There are six raptures recorded and described in the Bible. Four of those raptures have already taken place, and two are yet to come.

The four raptures that have already occurred were experienced by Enoch (Heb. 11:5), Elijah (2 Kings 2:11), Paul (2 Cor. 12:2–4), and Jesus Christ (Acts 1:10–11). The two raptures that are yet to happen are the rapture of the church, which is the discussion of this chapter, and the rapture of the two witnesses as prophesied in Revelation 11:12.

These records affirm the utter reality of the Rapture by providing us with prototypes of sorts to show that God can accomplish this coming event He promises to His people.

So here is a summary of what happens: The Lord Jesus Christ returns from heaven, bringing the souls of those who have already died with Him. The bodies of those dead saints are resurrected and changed, and then the bodies of those Christians who are alive and remain at His coming are also changed.

When this happens, God is going to hover over this universe, and all who have accepted Jesus Christ as Savior, those who have been resurrected and those who have never died, are going to be snatched up like particles of iron drawn upward by a magnet, pulled right out of the population, suctioned off the planet. It is going to happen instantly. No time to get ready. No prelude. No preliminaries.

THE REUNION

The Rapture sets up a delightful series of meetings or reunions. Paul wrote, "Then we who are alive and remain shall be caught up together with them in the clouds to meet the Lord in the air. And thus we shall always be with the Lord" (1 Thess. 4:17). Note that Paul began here with the word then, which is an adverb indicating sequence. It connects the previous events of the Rapture that we have already considered with this final event in a definite order of sequential reunions as follows:

- Dead bodies reunited with their spirits
- Resurrected believers reunited with living believers
- Resurrected believers and raptured believers meet the Lord

As Paul pointed out, the ultimate consequence of this reunion with the Lord is that there will be no subsequent parting. After His return, our union and communion with Him will be uninterrupted and eternal. This glorious fact alone shows us why the word *Rapture* is an altogether appropriate term for this event.

THE RAPTURE IS A STRENGTHENING EVENT

After completing his description of the Rapture to the Thessalonians, Paul wrapped up the passage with this practical admonition: "Therefore comfort one another with these words" (1 Thess. 4:18).

Here the apostle was telling both the Thessalonians and believers today that it's not enough to passively understand what was just explained about the Rapture, Christian death, and the resurrection. Our understanding should spur us toward a certain action—to "comfort one another." And in the preceding verses he gave exactly the kind of information that makes true comfort possible. When believers suffer the loss of family members or dearly loved friends, we have in Paul's descriptions of Christian death and resurrection all that is needed to comfort each other in these losses. Christian death is not permanent; it is merely a sleep. A time is coming when we and our loved ones will be reunited in a rapturous meeting, when Christ Himself calls us out of this world or out of our graves to be with Him forever in an ecstatic relationship of eternal love.

Nineteenth-century Bible teacher A. T. Pierson made this interesting observation about these things:

> It is a remarkable fact that in the New Testament, so far as I remember, it is never once said, after Christ's resurrection, that a disciple died— that is, without some qualification: Stephen *fell asleep*. David, after he had served his own generation by the will of God *fell asleep and was laid with his father*. Peter says, "Knowing that I must shortly *put off this my tabernacle* as the Lord showed me." Paul says, "*the time of my departure is at hand*." (The figure here is taken from a vessel that, as she leaves a dock, throws the cables off the fastenings, and opens her sails to the wind to depart for the haven) . . . The only time where the word "dead" is used, it is with qualification: "the *dead in Christ*," "the *dead which die in the Lord*."[6]

As Pierson implies, Christ abolished death so completely that even the term *death* is no longer appropriate for believers. That is why Paul wrote that we should comfort one another with reminders that for Christians, what we call death is nothing more than a temporary sleep before we are called into our uninterrupted relationship with Christ forever.

At the beginning of this chapter I told you about the wildfires that swept down upon us in San Diego in 2007. Two years before those wildfires, San Diego regional authorities had installed Reverse 911. Citizens who lived in fire zones were asked to register their phone numbers with the agency so that when future fires put them in harm's way, one simple warning call could go out to all who were on the list. This early warning system was first used to warn residents of the approaching wildfires of 2007. Homeowners who did not register did not receive a call. Some had phone systems that screened out the warning call as an unrecognized number. Others received the call but chose to ignore it. Some of those who did not hear the warning did not vacate their homes and, as a result, lost their lives.[7]

God has sounded the warnings loudly and clearly. They have come through His prophets in the Old Testament, through New Testament writers, and even through Jesus Himself. The firestorm is coming in the form of the seven years of tribulation, when no Christian influence will temper the evil that will plunge the earth into a cauldron of misery and devastation. But you can avoid the destruction and be evacuated. You can enter your name on the list of those who will hear the trumpet call of the Rapture by turning to Christ and beginning to live the pure and holy life that characterizes those who will enter heaven. As the apostle John wrote: "There shall by no means enter it [the heavenly city of God] anything that defiles, or causes an abomination or a lie, but only those who are written in the Lamb's Book of Life" (Rev. 21:27).

If your name is not in that book, when the Rapture occurs you will be left behind to experience horrors worse than anything the world has yet seen. I hope you will not wait another day; turn to Jesus Christ now, before it is too late, and become one of those who will hear His call on that great and terrible day.

CHAPTER 13

RESURRECTION

A remarkable new clinical drug trial is currently under way across America with the potential of vastly increasing our life spans. Approved by the US Food and Drug Administration, this study has targeted three thousand people between the ages of seventy and eighty to see if certain medications can halt or slow down human aging. The most promising known anti-aging drug is Metformin, the world's most widely used diabetes drug, and one that is readily available and relatively inexpensive.

Some years ago, researchers in Belgium began testing Metformin on roundworms, and the results were surprising. The tiny worms aged more slowly, didn't develop wrinkles, and stayed healthier longer. When doctors subsequently gave the drug to laboratory mice, the results were similar. It increased the animals' longevity by nearly 40 percent and improved the durability of their bones. In this new trial, medical researchers are now testing this drug on humans. If successful, the researchers claim, it could make seventy-year-olds as biologically healthy as fifty-year-olds and allow people to live well into their 110s or 120s.[1]

The advancement of medicine and technology has created a host of ethical challenges, and it's a little frightening to see science fiction coming to life all around us. Yet if it weren't for medical science, many of us wouldn't be alive to read this book—or to write it. I'm grateful for the medical professionals who, by God's grace, have helped us so much.

But let's keep things in context. After the flood, lifespans dropped drastically. According to Psalm 90, people could still hope to live seventy or eighty years, but because of disease and infant mortality the average lifespan for much of history dipped as low as thirty-five before the advent of modern medicine in the late 1800s. By 1990, the average lifespan was seventy-six. Today it's a bit higher; but even if scientists get the number over the century mark, it's still only the flash of a moment in view of eternity.[2] Technology can never give us a truly indestructible or imperishable body or enable us to live forever. For that, we need the resurrection.

The Bible consistently teaches the reality of the resurrection, for God created us with eternity in our hearts. We're made for something more than planet earth. We're made for heaven, and we aren't going to exist there in a disembodied form. When we die in Christ, our bodies fall asleep and are buried, and our souls go to be with Christ in paradise where we receive temporary bodies until the moment of resurrection. But what then? What will the resurrection be like? What will our resurrection bodies look like and how will they function?

The most extensive passage on this subject is 1 Corinthians 15, which we commonly call the resurrection chapter of the Bible. Here the apostle Paul, writing under the inspiration of the Holy Spirit, answered two questions posed to him by some of the Christians in the city of Corinth: "How are the dead raised up? And with what body do they come?" (1 Cor. 15:35).

When we die, our bodies are buried and go into the ground. On the day of resurrection, they are going to come out of the ground, but they're going to be different from when they went in. It will still be the same in essence—we will still be humans and you will still be you. But our bodies now are inferior to what we need for everlasting life. I'm reminded every day when I go to the gym that the older we get, the harder we have to work to maintain the same level of fitness we had earlier in life. But our resurrection bodies will be perfectly suited for eternity.

OUR NEW BODIES WILL
BE INDESTRUCTIBLE

First, our new bodies will be indestructible. First Corinthians 15:42 says, "So also is the resurrection of the dead. The body is sown in corruption, it is raised in incorruption." Throughout the history of time as we know it, there has only been one body not subject to corruption—the body of the Lord Jesus. Psalm 16:10 says prophetically of Him, "You will not leave my soul in Sheol, nor will You allow Your Holy One to see corruption." Jesus was buried, but on the third day He came out of the grave. His body incurred no corruption.

Our present bodies wear out and grow old, but our resurrection bodies will never wear out or grow old. They will have no capacity for deterioration or decay. Your new body will be designed for eternity. It will not be subject to accident, disease, aging, or death. It will be pain-free and disease-free. It will never wear out and never die; it will outlive the stars.

The exclamation point to this truth is found in Romans 6:8–9, where the resurrection body of Jesus is described: "Now if we died with Christ, we believe that we will also live with him. For we know that since Christ was raised from the dead, he cannot die again; death no longer has mastery over him" (NIV).

Notice those words about Jesus: *He cannot die again.*

From the moment He arose from the tomb of Joseph of Arimathea on Easter Sunday, there is one thing Jesus Christ cannot do. He did it once, but He can never repeat the action. It is impossible for Him to die again. His glorified body is imperishable and indestructible. And His glorified body is the pattern for our own resurrection bodies. Hebrews 9:27 says, "It is appointed for men to die *once*" (emphasis added).

I think of that when I get on my bicycle or go for a long walk. Sometimes my body feels its age, and I struggle to finish my uphill ride or my exercise routine. But I've learned to use those occasions to remind myself that one day I will have a perfect, indestructible body that can never wear down or wear out. When we get to heaven, coming back from a long bicycle ride or running a marathon will be just as easy as going out to meet with a friend because of our indestructible bodies.

OUR NEW BODIES WILL BE IDENTIFIABLE

First Corinthians 15:43 indicates our resurrection bodies will be glorious and identifiable. Paul wrote, "It is sown in dishonor, it is raised in glory." We could accurately translate the word *glory* as "brilliance." Our new bodies may actually have a luminescent quality to them. In Exodus 34:29, Moses spent time with the Lord and something unusual happened to him. His face became radiant and began to shine. The same thing happened to Jesus on the Mount of Transfiguration (Luke 9:28–30). In Revelation 21, we're told the entire city of New Jerusalem will be luminescent, brightly illumined by the light that radiates from the glory of God. Matthew 13:43 says, "Then the righteous will shine forth as the sun in the kingdom of their Father."

The glory the Lord Jesus had in His glorious body is a pattern for the glory we will have in our own bodies when we're resurrected from the grave. This is the essence of our teaching about the resurrection. As several Scriptures tell us, the Lord Jesus Christ, in His own resurrection, provided the payment, the proof, and the pattern for our own resurrection. The Bible says:

- "Our citizenship is in heaven, from which we also eagerly wait for the Savior, the Lord Jesus Christ, who will transform our lowly body that it may be conformed to His glorious body, according to the working by which He is able even to subdue all things to Himself" (Phil. 3:20–21).
- "Beloved, now we are children of God; and it has not yet been revealed what we shall be, but we know that when He is revealed, we shall be like Him, for we shall see Him as He is" (1 John 3:2).

- "As we have borne the image of the man of dust, we shall also bear the image of the heavenly Man" (1 Cor. 15:49).

The heavenly Man is Jesus. Just as we now bear the image of old Adam in our current bodies, we will bear the image of the Man of heaven—Jesus—in our resurrection bodies. Our new bodies will be glorious.

The Bible gives us a few glimpses of our Lord's resurrection body by telling us some of the things that happened during the forty days between His resurrection and ascension. From what we know in the New Testament, Jesus appeared perhaps ten or twelve times during this period; and when we look at those passages we see our Lord with His glorified body.

The most important thing about His body—and He emphasized this repeatedly—is that it was real, literal, physical, and tangible. It was the very body that had been crucified. On one occasion when Jesus appeared to His disciples, He told them, "Behold My hands and My feet, that it is I Myself. Handle Me and see, for a spirit does not have flesh and bones as you see I have" (Luke 24:39).

This tells us we aren't going to be some kind of ghost—like a phantom that floats around forever. We're going to have our same literal, physical bodies, but they will be risen, resurrected, and glorified—equipped for eternity.

During two of His post-resurrection appearances, Jesus ate with His disciples, which shows us our glorified bodies will be capable of eating. I consider that good news, don't you? People seem to be curious about this because I've often been asked if we will need to eat in heaven. Well, I don't know if we will *need* to eat, but we certainly will enjoy eating and drinking since Jesus did. Two other passages emphasize this.

- "He showed them His hands and His feet. But while they still did not believe for joy, and marveled, He said to them, 'Have you any food here?' So they gave Him a piece of a broiled fish and some honey-comb. And He took it and ate in their presence" (Luke 24:40–43).

- "Jesus said to them, 'Come and eat breakfast.' Yet none of the disciples dared ask Him, 'Who are You?'—knowing that it was the Lord. Jesus then came and took the bread and gave it to them, and likewise the fish" (John 21:12–13).

In Luke 24, Jesus clearly ate with His disciples; and in John 21, there is a strong suggestion He did, for He prepared breakfast for everyone. Imagine! Being able to eat all we want without gaining weight or getting an upset stomach. Imagine tasting foods we've never had before. Perhaps we'll be able to sample manna in heaven. Psalm 78:25 says about the children of Israel in the desert: "Men ate angels' food." I don't want to become speculative, but imagine the joy of eating a feast prepared by angelic chefs!

The body of Christ was also touchable. It could be held. In John 20:27, Jesus told Thomas, who had a hard time believing that Jesus had really risen from the dead, "Reach your finger here, and look at My hands; and reach your hand here, and put it into My side. Do not be unbelieving, but believing."

In John 20:17, Jesus had to tell Mary to quit clinging to Him. "Do not cling to Me," He said, "for I have not yet ascended to My Father." That implies His body was tangible, touchable, and capable of being held and hugged.

Many people ask me, "In my new resurrection body, will people know me? Will they recognize me? And will I know others?" After the Resurrection, Jesus knew His disciples and they knew Him. They recognized the glorified Jesus as the very same One they had known before His death. They were so convinced of the identity of the risen Christ that they all went to their death proclaiming the reality of the message of everlasting life.

When you get to heaven, you're going to know all the people you met down here and they will know you. It is unthinkable to me that in heaven we will know less than we do here. The Bible says, "Now we see in a mirror, dimly, but then face to face. Now I know in part, but then I shall know just as I also am known" (1 Cor. 13:12).

We will have a greater sense of recognition in heaven than we've ever had here on this earth. When Moses and Elijah appeared out of heaven to stand with Christ on the Mount of Transfiguration, the disciples instinctively recognized Moses and Elijah as real people. They knew them. When Jesus described heaven in Matthew 8:11, He said, "I say to you that many will come from east and west, and sit down with Abraham, Isaac, and Jacob in the kingdom of heaven."

Missionary Amy Carmichael wrote about this, saying:

> Will we know one another in heaven? Will we love and remember? I do not think anyone need wonder about this or doubt for a single moment. . . . For if we think for a minute, we know. Would you be yourself if you did not love and remember? . . . We are told that we shall be like our Lord Jesus. . . . And does not He know and love and remember? He would not be Himself if He did not, and we would not be ourselves if we did not.[3]

OUR NEW BODIES WILL BE INCREDIBLE

The resurrection body, then, will be indestructible. It will be identifiable. It will also be incredible. The apostle Paul went on to write in 1 Corinthians 15:43, "It is sown in weakness, it is raised in power."

We will be buried in weakness. That's absolutely true, isn't it? A dead body has no strength or power. It cannot lift a finger. But when we come out of the grave, we'll have so much energy we'll think a lightning bolt has supercharged us with electricity.

It doesn't take a lot of work here on earth to exhaust us. Some time ago, I went with a group to Africa for missions and humanitarian work. We planted gardens all day in the sweltering heat of what was then Swaziland, and every day we grew more tired. The heat and labor drained us. I noticed I had a little less energy with every passing day.

Our resurrection bodies won't present the same problems. They will be incredible, full of energy, always full of enthusiastic power, and perhaps capable of extraordinary functions. When you read about the Lord Jesus after His resurrection, He could enter sealed rooms without going through the door. John 20:19 says, "Then, the same day at evening, being the first day of the week, when the doors were shut where the disciples were assembled, for fear of the Jews, Jesus came and stood in the midst, and said to them, 'Peace be with you.'"

If the glorified body of Christ could pass through walls and travel by impulses of thought, perhaps the same will be true for us. Without being dogmatic on the specifics, I'm convinced our glorified bodies will not have the same limitations we have today. We will certainly be mobile and able to move, which means we can travel from place to place. In the aforementioned trip to Africa, one of the hardest parts was getting there and back. The flights were tiresome. How wonderful to contemplate traveling around the new earth without the fatigue or stress of airport security and seats made for tiny people.

At His ascension, Jesus rose into the sky and disappeared into the clouds. We shouldn't become over-speculative, but it's not hard to visualize the possibilities of traveling through the new heaven, the new earth, and the city of New Jerusalem with wide-eyed wonder and joyful excursion.

OUR NEW BODIES WILL BE INFINITE

Our bodies will be indestructible, identifiable, incredible—and also infinite. First Corinthians 15:44–45 says, "It is sown a natural body, it is raised a spiritual body. There is a natural body, and there is a spiritual body. And so it is written, 'The first man Adam became a living being.' The last Adam became a life-giving spirit."

What did Paul mean by a "spiritual" body? I've already indicated my firm belief that our heavenly bodies will be literal, physical, touchable, identifiable, and powerful. I do not believe the word *spiritual* in verse 44 implies that our bodies will be incorporeal or mere apparitions. Jesus rose from the dead with the same physical body that was crucified. The apostle John began his first epistle by saying, "That which was from the beginning, which we have heard, which we have seen with our eyes, which we have looked upon, and our hands have handled, concerning the Word of life—the life was manifested, and we have seen, and bear witness, and declare to you that eternal life which was with the Father and was manifested" (1 John 1:1–2).

Jesus had a material body and we're going to have bodies just like Him—so we are not going to have ghostlike, specter bodies. In 1 Corinthians 15, Paul was talking about a real body. Our new bodies will exist on a higher plain. Instead of being governed by our appetites, they will be governed by the Holy Spirit. That's what a spiritual body is. The basic difference between a natural body and a spiritual body is that the former is suited for life on earth, and our spiritual bodies will be suited for life in heaven for eternity with God. In our current bodies, we couldn't function in the realm of heaven. But God is going to give us new real bodies like the ones we have now, only completely transformed.

Think of it this way. Have you ever had one hour, or maybe even fifteen minutes, when you sensed the Holy Spirit was in total control of who you were and what you did? It is the most glorious thing to have consciousness of that.

Marie Monsen, a Norwegian missionary in China during the first decades of the twentieth century, lived in constant danger, especially from the gangs of outlaws and rebel soldiers who terrorized the interior of China in those days. On one occasion she was with three other Norwegian missionaries engaged in a series of gospel meetings in a certain town. News came that a local militia had been defeated in battle and was heading toward town intent on revenge. They were killing everyone they met. Even women and children in the fields were being shot. The missionaries gathered the local Christians into a house and reminded them of God's promises, such as 1 Peter 5:7, which says that God cares for us. As the night wore on, Marie suggested they go to bed and get whatever rest they could, even if sleep was impossible. Marie lay down and repeated the promises of God to herself throughout the night.

Early the next morning, the butt-end of a gun battered on the gate, and Marie ran and opened it to find a solitary soldier. She let him in and barred the gate behind him. He was astonished to find a small group of smiling people who invited him to have a cup of tea. "You probably don't get much time for food, do you?" Marie asked him. The man sighed deeply and said it would be good to sit down for a moment of quietness and have something to eat and drink. He asked who they were and what they were doing in the city, and they told him about the Lord.

Leaving, the soldier said no one else would bother them. The looting soldiers left town twenty-four hours later, leaving trauma in their wake. But in that little house, the Christians had focused all their energy on the promises of God, who kept His words to them.

In finishing the story, Marie said something wonderful: "It was unutterably marvelous to experience over and over again the peace Jesus spoke of, which the world cannot give. In the midst of confusion and distress, one found oneself steadied by such wonderful restfulness of mind, that one did not recognize oneself."[4]

I believe Marie Monsen experienced a little bit of heaven on the way to heaven. When we arrive there, we're going to be in such a state of Spirit-controlled restfulness of mind that we will hardly recognize ourselves. According to Scripture, when our resurrection bodies come out of the grave we're going to be totally in the Spirit. We'll have the peace of the Spirit, the joy of the Spirit, the love of the Spirit. We're going to be spiritual people. We will do only those things that please the Lord, and our struggle with the flesh and with the sinful nature will be remembered no more. No more temptation. No more defeat. No more sin. No more downward pull of immoral attractions. No more Satan to beguile us.

Exactly when and how and where will that happen? First Corinthians 15 ends with a grand finale of truth about the moment of our resurrection.

Behold, I tell you a mystery: We shall not all sleep, but we shall all be changed—in a moment, in the twinkling of an eye, at the last trumpet. For the trumpet will sound, and the dead will be raised incorruptible, and we shall be changed. For this corruptible must put on incorruption, and this mortal must put on immortality. . . . Then shall be brought to pass the saying that is written: "Death is swallowed up in victory." . . . But thanks be to God, who gives us the victory through our Lord Jesus Christ (vv. 51–54, 57).

When we compare this to a similar passage in 1 Thessalonians 4:13–18, we can say that Jesus will return one day very soon, in the air. He will shout. The voice of an archangel will ring out. A trumpet will blast. Those who have died in Christ will come out of the ground and out of the sea, and somehow God will reassemble and transform their bodies instantly, giving them eternal, resurrected, incorruptible bodies. Then every Christian who is still alive at that moment will be snatched up with them in the air, and their bodies will likewise be instantaneously transformed. All of us will be ushered into heaven by the Lord Himself with glorified bodies patterned after our risen and glorified Christ.

I've often said I believe I'm going to be alive when that happens, and I think every Christian should have that hope in their hearts. Perhaps as you're reading this, you're thinking of issues you're currently having with your own body. Perhaps you've been injured. Perhaps your body is diseased or disabled. Let me quote from Joni Eareckson Tada because her unique perspective has been formed by her years being a quadriplegic in a wheelchair, paralyzed from a diving accident. In one of her books she wrote:

I still can hardly believe it. I, with shriveled, bent fingers, atrophied muscles, gnarled knees, and no feeling from the shoulders down, will one day have a new body, light, bright, and clothed in righteousness—powerful and dazzling. Can you imagine the hope this gives someone spinal cord-injured like me? Or someone who is cerebral palsied, brain-injured, or who has multiple sclerosis? Imagine the hope this gives someone who is manic-depressive. No other religion, no other philosophy promises new bodies, hearts, and minds. Only in the Gospel of Christ do hurting people find such incredible hope.[5]

No wonder Paul said that if in this life only we have hope, we are most miserable (1 Cor. 15:19). But we do have hope; we have hope beyond this life, and it is a sure and certain hope, guaranteed by the resurrection of Jesus of Nazareth. One day all the pains and aches and deficiencies of our earthly bodies will fall away, replaced by an indestructible and indescribable body modeled after that of Jesus. This is why I'm so passionate about trying to take people to heaven with me. I don't want anyone to miss what God has planned for His children.

Jack Welch, who led General Electric through some of its most successful days, wrote a book called *Winning*, which is essentially a question-and-answer book. Taking questions people had asked him, he compiled his answers into a book of business and management principles. As I skimmed the book, I was surprised at one of the questions. Someone had asked Jack Welch, "Do you think that you will go to heaven when you die?"

Of course, I was interested in his answer. Jack began by describing some of the mistakes he had made in business and in life, including two failed marriages. Then he said, "So as far as heaven, who knows? I'm sure not perfect, but if there are any points given out for caring for people with every fiber of your being and giving life all you've got every day, then I suppose I have a shot."[6]

Oh, Jack, I want to tell you heaven's not about having a shot! It's not even about caring for people or giving life everything you've got every day. Heaven is about putting your trust in Jesus Christ and in Him alone.

Perhaps that's harder for a successful businessman to understand than anyone else because his own energy, drive, and vision have helped him achieve success. But when it comes to heaven, those rules are thrown out. Heaven is not something that you earn. It is a gift. The Bible says, "The wages of sin is death, but the gift of God is eternal life in Christ Jesus our Lord" (Rom. 6:23).

The way to get to heaven is to humble yourself as a little child and acknowledge you cannot do enough good things to get to heaven; you can never make it to heaven on your own. You cannot buy a glorified supernatural body. The Lord wants to give it to you for free, by grace and through faith.

Life on earth is fragile and uncertain, but we have a Savior who died for our sins according to the Scriptures and was buried and raised on the third day according to Scriptures. And by the grace of God we await that wonderful day when we'll be raised incorruptible and given our new supernatural bodies, made by Christ. This will not be a hard thing for God to do. The Bible says, "Why should any of you consider it incredible that God raises the dead?" (Acts 26:8 NIV).

Commentator Matthew Henry wrote: "And why should it not be as much in the power of God to raise incorruptible, glorious, lively, spiritual bodies, out of the ruins of those vile, corruptible, lifeless . . . ones, as first to make matter out of nothing? . . . To God all things are possible."[7]

And to that we say, "Hallelujah!"

CHAPTER 14

HEAVEN

One December, Suzanne Edwards found a deflated, blue helium balloon in the backyard of her home in Monroe, Georgia. Attached to it was a tender picture of a man, woman, and little boy, who all seemed very happy. Also attached, a note scribbled in childlike printing. As she read the note, Suzanne began to cry.

It said:

> Dad, I wish you were here so we could have fun together. I wish you a Merry Christmas. I hope you tell God to give me those presents.
> I hope you are happy in heaven. If you are OK then tell me. I love you,
> Alejandro

The author of those plaintive words, as Suzanne learned later, was seven-year-old Alejandro Garcia-Herreros, whose home was about twenty miles away. Three years before, Alejandro had been living with his parents in Cúcuta, Colombia, where his father, Carlos, was a law professor known for his pro-law-enforcement views. On December 4, 2013, Carlos was murdered in the street. He was shot to death in front of Alejandro.

Alejandro's mother subsequently moved with him to the United States, but Christmas remained a poignant and painful season for the boy. Toward the end of each year he composed a letter to his dad and sent it upward in a helium balloon, with the belief the balloon would ascend to heaven and take the message to his dad.

Using social media, Suzanne attempted to get in touch with Alejandro's mother by saying, "A helium balloon floated into my yard today and landed on my heart!" Writing a message to be passed on to the boy, Suzanne also told him: "I want you to know that heaven is a wonderful place, more amazing than you or I can even imagine. It is a place where there is no pain and no worries. I am certain your daddy didn't want to leave you or cause you to feel lonely or sad. . . . He will always love you and I am sure that you make him proud! Have a Merry Christmas!!"

When his mother relayed the message to him, Alejandro cried—and so did millions of other people when the story was discovered and picked up by major media outlets around the globe.[1]

It touched my heart too. While I'm pretty sure a blue helium balloon will not make it all the way up to the heaven of heavens, I do believe God sees every sparrow that flies and falls. He knows the rising and falling of our spirits. He knows the heartaches and hopes of every child. He who directs the planets in their orbits can certainly send reminders of heaven to those of us on earth who need it.

And we all need these reminders. We need the comfort that comes from knowing the true biblical doctrine of heaven—that wonderful place, which has been a sign of God's love for his creation from Genesis to Revelation and is more amazing than you and I could ever imagine. God created us for heaven. That's our true home. That's our country. That's our destination. And when we set our minds on things above, we can experience a supernatural peace even when the world around us is falling apart.

At the rapture of the church, Jesus will escort believers to heaven to live with Him there forever. And as we'll discover in future chapters, amazing new experiences are in store for believers in heaven while the Tribulation unfolds on earth. In this chapter, I want to explore what the Bible teaches us about the nature of heaven, tracing what it's like now and what it will be like in the future.

THE PROMINENCE OF HEAVEN

Let's begin with some foundational truths about heaven. The word *heaven* is mentioned almost seven hundred times in the Bible. Thirty-three of the thirty-nine Old Testament books talk about heaven, along with twenty-one books in the New Testament. The word *heaven* refers to something that is raised up, or lofty. So the language of the Bible speaks of heaven as a place that is high, lofty, and lifted up.

Heaven plays such a prominent role in Scripture that if you delete all references to it from the Word of God, the text of the Bible would fall apart in key places and turn to mishmash.

THE PLURALITY OF HEAVEN

As you work your way through the hundreds of mentions of the word *heaven* in the Bible, you soon realize there is a plurality of heavens. In fact, the Bible specifically speaks of three distinct heavens. When the apostle Paul wrote to the Corinthians about his visions and revelations, he told them of a time when he was "caught up to the third heaven" (2 Cor. 12:2). That clearly implies there is also a first and second heaven.

THE FIRST HEAVEN

The first heaven is the atmospheric heaven—the sky, with its clouds, birds, and life-giving oxygen. Isaiah 55:10–11 says, "For as the rain comes down, and the snow from heaven, and do not return there, but water the earth, and make it bring forth and bud, that it may give seed to the sower and bread to the eater, so shall My word be." In this passage, the word *heaven* refers to the atmosphere that yields its rain and snow to the earth.

We live on a privileged planet, surrounded by a thin layer of gasses—mainly nitrogen and oxygen—that make life possible. Traces of the earth's atmosphere stretch three hundred miles into space, but it doesn't abruptly end. It simply tapers off gradually. The most vital resources of our atmosphere are within ten miles of the surface of the earth, and God custom designed them to sustain life. No other known planet in the entire universe has an atmosphere like ours, and this is the first heaven.

THE SECOND HEAVEN

The second heaven is the vast universe in which we live, filled with billions of stars, planets, dust clouds, meteors, and galaxies. The story of the creation of the second heaven is told in Genesis 1:14–17:

> Then God said, "Let there be lights in the firmament of the heavens to divide the day from the night; and let them be for signs and seasons, and for days and years; and let them be for lights in the firmament of the heavens to give light on the earth"; and it was so. Then God made two great lights: the greater light to rule the day, and the lesser light to rule the night. He made the stars also. God set them in the firmament of the heavens to give light on the earth.

The psalmist referred to this second heaven when he wrote, "The heavens declare the glory of God; and the firmament shows His handiwork" (Ps. 19:1). Jesus said that at the very end of time, "The sun will be darkened, and the moon will not give its light; the stars will fall from heaven" (Matt. 24:29). These are all references to the second heaven, the stellar skies.

THE THIRD HEAVEN

The third heaven is the one Paul had in mind when he wrote:

I know a man in Christ who fourteen years ago—whether in the body I do not know, or whether out of the body I do not know, God knows—such a one was caught up to the third heaven. And I know such a man—whether in the body or out of the body I do not know, God knows—how he was caught up into Paradise and heard inexpressible words, which it is not lawful for a man to utter. (2 Cor. 12:2–4)

Paul was not referring to the atmospheric heaven or to the stellar heaven. He was referring to the highest heaven, the very dwelling place of God. King Solomon had a different name for this place in 1 Kings 8:27, when he said, "Will God indeed dwell on the earth? Behold, heaven and the heaven of heavens cannot contain You. How much less this temple which I have built!" Moses called this the "highest heavens" in Deuteronomy 10:14.

Jesus was referring to this heaven when He taught us to pray, "Our Father in heaven" (Matt. 6:9). The psalmist said, "The LORD is in His holy temple, the LORD's throne is in heaven" (Ps. 11:4). Psalm 103:19 says, "The LORD has established His throne in heaven, and His kingdom rules over all."

This heaven—the heaven of heavens, the highest heaven—is the locale of the throne and the dwelling place of God. It is paradise. It is our eternal home. This is where we will soon live side by side with God and with the angels and with the redeemed of all the ages.

THE PLACE CALLED HEAVEN

It's important for us to realize the third heaven is just as real and just as literal as the other two heavens. The Bible refers to it as a *place*, a word that implies a specific, literal location. In John 14:1–3, Jesus said, "Let not your heart be troubled; you believe in God, believe also in Me. In My Father's house are many mansions; if it were not so, I would have told you. I go to prepare a *place* for you. And if I go and prepare a *place* for you, I will come again and receive you to Myself; that where I am, there you may be also" (emphasis added).

Jesus spoke those words in the Upper Room on the night before His death. He had just told His disciples He would die for them on the cross. He explained He would be buried and resurrected and that He would return to heaven. They were confused by this and filled with sorrow. But Jesus told them they shouldn't be troubled. He said, "I go to prepare a place for you." The Greek word used in John 14:3 is *topos*, which strictly refers to a place that can be located—a real place.

The apostle Paul spoke of Christ as ascending to heaven to sit at God's right hand "in the heavenly *places*" (Eph. 1:20, emphasis added).

Jesus doesn't intend for us to live in a vapory nether-land, in a disembodied haze, or in a blissful but intangible state of mind. No, the Bible refers to heaven as a specific place.

Sometimes the Bible refers to heaven as a country, which implies vastness of territory. Sometimes it's referred to as the celestial city, which brings to mind buildings, streets, residents, and activity. Sometimes heaven is referred to as a kingdom, which speaks of organization and government. In the passage I quoted from John 14, Jesus referred to heaven as "My Father's house."

There's something intimate, sweet, and personal about heaven when we talk about it as "My Father's house." It's no longer an empty space. In our mind's eye, we see a home. Jesus promised that if we put our trust in Him, He will prepare a place for us in our Father's house that will serve as our heavenly home. There is nothing imaginary, hypothetical, or intangible about that.

Where is this place? The Bible doesn't give us exact coordinates of latitude and longitude, but the Bible does give us one important clue.

Heaven is up!

In Mark 6:41, Jesus took the boy's loaves and fish and "He looked up to heaven, blessed and broke the loaves, and gave them to His disciples."

At the very end of His earthly ministry, Jesus led His disciples to the Mount of Olives and, the Bible says, "He lifted His hands and blessed them.

Now it came to pass, while He blessed them, that He was parted from them and carried up into heaven" (Luke 24:50–51).

Ephesians 4:10 says, "He who descended is also the One who ascended far above all the heavens, that He might fill all things." This kind of language permeates the Scripture, as heaven is continually viewed as being up, above the earth; and the earth is described as down, below the heavens of God.

Where, then, is heaven? Heaven is up. But which way is up? That's not an easy question to answer. It depends on our location on the surface of the earth. Suppose America and China both launched a missile at the same time, each programmed to travel into space at a right angle from the location of its launch. Both missiles would go up, but they would be traveling through the solar system in opposite directions. *Up* is a helpful word, but it isn't very specific in terms of location.

Let's narrow down the location of heaven a bit more. We find a fascinating reference to heaven in Isaiah 14:13, in the passage that speaks of the moment Lucifer was evicted from heaven following his rebellion against God. Notice the terminology. The Lord told the Devil, "You have said in your heart: 'I will ascend into heaven, I will exalt my throne above the stars of God; I will also sit on the mount of the congregation on the farthest sides of the north.'"

That last phrase is a reference to the third heaven—"the farthest sides of the north."

No matter where you are on earth, north will always be up. So it would seem reasonable to conclude that heaven is somewhere in the northern universe beyond the reach of astronomers' telescopes. And when I read scientists' reports that a place exists in the northern heavens that seems strangely vacant of stars and galaxies, it validates that conclusion. Astronomers in Hawaii have found a huge hole in the universe that dwarfs anything else of its kind. One report tells us, "The 'supervoid,' which is 1.8 billion light-years across, is the largest known structure ever discovered in the universe but scientists are baffled about what it is."[2]

Without the Scriptures, which are inspired by the Holy Spirit, we would have no idea of heaven's existence or description. But God has revealed to us what heaven is like. Granted, even with the biblical data we can't fully visualize heaven or appreciate all its glories. But we can form a very biblical concept of what heaven is like, and we can visualize it within the parameters of biblical revelation. God desires we do so.

THE PRECIOUSNESS OF HEAVEN

Everything that is near and dear to you and me, everything that is important to Christ followers, is in heaven. Everything!

OUR REDEEMER IS IN HEAVEN

First of all, our Redeemer is in heaven. Hebrews 9:24 says, "Christ has not entered the holy places made with hands, which are copies of the true, but into heaven itself, now to appear in the presence of God for us."

Just imagine the moment we get to heaven and we see Jesus! Right now we don't see Him with our visual eyesight. The Bible says, "whom having not seen you love. Though now you do not see Him, yet believing, you rejoice with joy inexpressible and full of glory" (1 Pet. 1:8).

If we rejoice with joy inexpressible and full of glory now, when we cannot see Him with visible eyesight, think of our joy and glory when we can! Everything else will pale into insignificance. Revelation 22:3–4 says about heaven: "The throne of God and of the Lamb shall be in it, and His servants shall serve Him. They shall see His face."

OUR RELATIONSHIPS ARE IN HEAVEN

Second, heaven is precious because our relationships continue there. Our loved ones who have died in Christ are all in heaven. My father told me toward the end of his life, "You know, David, one of the things about getting old is this. One day you begin to realize you have more friends in heaven than you have on earth." He was right about that. It happens gradually but surely as we age.

OUR RESOURCES ARE IN HEAVEN

Third, our resources are in heaven. The Bible says, "Blessed be the God and Father of our Lord Jesus Christ, who according to His abundant mercy has begotten us again to a living hope through the resurrection of Jesus Christ from the dead, to an inheritance incorruptible and undefiled and that does not fade away, reserved in heaven for you" (1 Pet. 1:3–4).

When you became a Christian, God became your Father and He made you an heir. We are heirs of God, and the Bible is full of information about our inheritance. The book of Ephesians says, "In Him also we have obtained an inheritance" (1:11). Colossians 1:12 says we are qualified in Christ "to be partakers of the inheritance of the saints in the light." Hebrews 9:15 says we are called in Christ to "receive the promise of the eternal inheritance." Revelation 21:7 says about the glories of heaven, "He who overcomes shall inherit all things."

You have an inheritance in Christ that will never be touched by inflation. It won't be lost in an economic crash. Its value will never decline or decrease, and it is both reserved and preserved for you. Your name is on it, and your eternal resources are there.

OUR RESIDENCE IS IN HEAVEN

Heaven is also precious to us because our residence is there. I'm not just talking about where we will live; I'm talking about our citizenship. When we become Christ followers, we become residents of heaven. Philippians 3:20 says, "Our citizenship is in heaven, from which we also eagerly wait for the Savior, the Lord Jesus Christ." We are not citizens of earth who are going to heaven; we are citizens of heaven who are traveling through earth.

When you apply for a passport, you have to state where you were born, where you currently live, your birthdate, and so forth; and, if approved, the government issues you a passport to let other governments know you are a citizen of the United States, Germany, Mexico, or wherever. I was born in Toledo, Ohio, and I live in Southern California. I have a United States passport. But my real residence is in heaven, I'm a citizen of that land, and

I'm currently here on earth as an ambassador. That's true of every believer. The apostle Paul said, "Our citizenship is in heaven. . . . Now then, we are ambassadors for Christ" (Phil. 3:20; 2 Cor. 5:20).

OUR REWARD IS IN HEAVEN

Our Redeemer, our relationships, our resources, and our residence are in heaven—and so are our rewards. Jesus told His followers amid persecution, "Rejoice and be exceedingly glad, for great is your reward in heaven, for so they persecuted the prophets who were before you" (Matt. 5:12).

Chapter 16 of this book is devoted entirely to what the Bible says about the rewards awaiting us in heaven.

OUR RICHES ARE IN HEAVEN

Heaven is also precious to us because it is where our riches are. Matthew 6:19–21 says, "Do not lay up for yourselves treasures on earth, where moth and rust destroy and where thieves break in and steal; but lay up for yourselves treasures in heaven, where neither moth nor rust destroys and where thieves do not break in and steal. For where your treasure is, there your heart will be also."

What a statement! How can we lay up for ourselves riches in heaven? The only way we can get our treasures from here to there is by investing in God's work. We can't take our money with us to heaven, or our homes, cars, boats, or articles of clothing. But we can take other people with us by investing our lives and resources in the spreading of God's kingdom. The only things going from earth to heaven are human souls and the Word of God. So if you're trying to build equity in heaven, invest your time, talents, and treasure in the Word of God and the souls of men and women who need the message of Jesus Christ.

OUR RESERVATION IS IN HEAVEN

Finally, heaven is precious because our reservation is there. There is a book in heaven, a registry, called the Lamb's Book of Life, in which the names of all who will be in heaven are recorded. Jesus said to His disciples on one occasion after they had reported great success in their ministries, "Nevertheless do not rejoice in this, that the spirits are subject to you, but rather rejoice because your names are written in heaven" (Luke 10:20).

Is your name written in heaven? Do you have a reservation there? One day you'll stand before God and He will say to you, "Why should I let you into My heaven?" You must be able to say, "My name is in the Lamb's Book of Life. I have a reservation. I have put my trust in Jesus Christ as my Savior, and therefore I qualify to come in through His shed blood."

Ruthanna Metzgar is a professional singer who told a story that illustrates the importance of this. Several years ago, Ruthanna was asked to sing at a wedding in Seattle, where she lives. It was a very upscale wedding. A member of one of the wealthiest families in the city was getting married, and Ruthanna considered it a great honor to be chosen as the soloist. She was particularly excited because the wedding reception was to be held on the top two floors of the Columbia Center, the tallest building in the Northwest. It was very exclusive, and Ruthanna couldn't help thinking about how fun it would be to go there with her husband, Roy.

After the wedding, Ruthanna and Roy drove to the beautiful facility and approached the reception desk. They saw how the maître d', who was decked out in a splendid tuxedo, admitted and introduced the guests and ushered them toward luscious hors d'oeuvres and exotic beverages. About that time, the bride and groom approached a beautiful glass and brass staircase leading to the top floor, and someone ceremoniously cut a satin ribbon draped across the bottom of the stairs and announced that the wedding feast was about to begin.

As Roy and Ruthanna approached the top of the stairs, the maître d' asked them, "May I have your name please?" Before him was a bound book.

"I am Ruthanna Metzgar and this is my husband, Roy."

The maître d' searched through the listings in the book, and then he looked again. He asked Ruthanna to spell her name, and he searched again. Finally he looked up and said, "I'm sorry, but your name isn't here."

"Oh, there must be some mistake," Ruthanna said. "I am the singer. I sang for this wedding!"

"It doesn't matter who you are or what you did," said the man. "Without your name in the book you cannot attend this banquet." He motioned to a waiter and said, "Show these people to the service elevator please."

The Metzgars were unceremoniously ushered past beautifully decorated tables laden with shrimp, whole smoked salmon, and magnificent carved ice sculptures. They passed the orchestra, preparing to perform. All the musicians were resplendent in white tuxedos. The Metzgars were led past the guests enjoying the food, the fellowship, the views, and the opulence of the moment.

The waiter took Ruthanna and Roy to the service elevator, ushered them in, and pushed G for the parking garage. The Metzgars were stunned to find themselves out on the street, driving home in silence. Somewhere along the way, Roy looked over and asked, "Sweetheart, what happened?"

She said, "When the invitation arrived for the reception I was very busy and I never bothered to return the RSVP. Besides, I was the singer, surely I could go to the reception without returning the RSVP!"

Then, as Ruthanna later recalled, she started to cry—not only because she had "missed the most lavish banquet" she'd ever been invited to but also because she suddenly had a small taste of what it will be like someday for people as they stand before Christ and find their names missing from the Lamb's Book of Life.[3]

Almighty God is inviting you to the banquet, but you need to reserve your place. You must respond to His RSVP.

If you're reading these words and aren't sure your reservation is secure, I urge you to pray about it right now. Confess your sins. Acknowledge Jesus Christ as your Lord and Savior. Do it now. Turn your life over to His control and accept His free offer of the gift of eternal life. "For God so loved the world that He gave His only begotten Son, that whoever believes in Him should not perish but have everlasting life" (John 3:16).

CHAPTER 15

JUDGMENT SEAT OF CHRIST

Cotton Fitzsimmons was a famous NBA basketball coach who was brilliant at motivating his teams. On one occasion when his team was playing the great Boston Celtics in a game they were not expected to win, Fitzsimmons hit on an idea that he thought would help motivate his players. His pre-game speech went something like this:

> "Gentlemen, when you go out there tonight, instead of remembering that we are in last place, pretend we are in first place; instead of being in a losing streak, pretend we are in a winning streak; instead of this being a regular game, pretend this is a playoff game!"
>
> With that, the team went onto the basketball court and were soundly beaten by the Boston Celtics. Coach Fitzsimmons was upset about the loss. But one of the players slapped him on the back and said, "Cheer up, Coach! *Pretend* we won!"[1]

I don't know if you have noticed, but there is an awful lot of pretending going on. Many people love to pretend they are Christians when deep down in their hearts they know better. They have never truly had a life-changing experience of salvation.

Christians also play this pretend game—pretending to really love the Lord and even going through the motions of serving Him—but it's not real and they know it.

What is to become of all this pretending? The Bible clearly teaches that one day, all this make-believe will be unmasked.

Almost all Christians have some idea about a future judgment when everyone will stand before God. A final judgment is coming—of that we can be certain: "It is appointed for men to die once, but after this the judgment" (Heb. 9:27).

But few Christians realize that there will be not one, but two days of judgment—first the judgment seat of Christ, and second the Great White Throne Judgment. Our relationship with Christ will determine which court will try our case.

Let's start with the second judgment, which is usually referred to as the Great White Throne Judgment. There unbelievers and those who pretend to be Christians will stand before God (Rev. 20:5, 11–15). There they will face the consequences of rejecting Jesus Christ as Savior and Lord. This judgment is the final bar of justice in God's plan for the inhabitants of planet Earth, and there will be no grading on a curve. The accused will be judged by the standard of absolute truth.

According to Warren W. Wiersbe: "The White Throne Judgment will be nothing like our modern court cases. At the White Throne, there will be a Judge but no jury, a prosecution but no defense, a sentence but no appeal. No one will be able to defend himself or accuse God of unrighteousness."[2]

The first judgment—the judgment seat of Christ—occurs more than one thousand years before the Great White Throne Judgment. This first judgment occurs immediately after the Rapture of the church to heaven.

The purpose of this judgment is not to pronounce condemnation. No one judged at this court will be condemned, for all will be followers of Christ who have submitted their lives to Him. The purpose of this judgment is for Christ to assess every believer's earthly works to determine what rewards are to be received: "We must all appear before the judgment seat of Christ, that each one may receive the things done in the body, according to what he has done, whether good or bad" (2 Cor. 5:10).

The judgment seat of Christ is the subject of this chapter. This biblical truth is almost never preached in our churches today, but it may be one of the most important and motivating doctrines in the Bible.

The New Testament (Greek) word for "judgment seat" is *bema*. This word can also be translated as "throne," "tribunal," "platform," or "raised place" depending on the context. In each case, whether referring to Christ or a public official of some sort, the implication is always the same: the *bema* was a place of authority from which one made announcements, declarations, speeches, or judgments. In Paul's use of the word in relationship to the judgment seat, he is always referring to the *bema* seat in an Olympic arena.

According to twentieth-century theologian Leonard Sale-Harrison: "In Grecian games in Athens, the old arena contained a raised platform on which the president or umpire of the arena sat. From here he rewarded all the contestants; and here he rewarded all winners. It was called the 'bema' or 'reward seat.'"[3]

From this high and exalted seat, the judges of the Greek Olympic Games reviewed the preparation and training of each of the contestants and rewarded the winners who had kept the rules.

As we examine the important topic of the judgment seat of Christ, we will look at three distinct categories: the Judge, the judged, and the judgment.

THE JUDGE

The God of the Bible is a God who makes judgments.

Ever since the garden of Eden when Adam and Eve were judged for their disobedience, judgment is a thread that runs from the beginning (Gen. 3) to the end (Rev. 22) of God's redemptive story.

- Solomon wrote, "God will bring every work into judgment, including every secret thing, whether good or evil" (Eccl. 12:14).

- Jesus said, "Nothing is secret that will not be revealed, nor anything hidden that will not be known and come to light" (Luke 8:17).
- Paul declared, "God will judge the secrets of men by Jesus Christ" (Rom. 2:16).
- And the writer of Hebrews added, "There is no creature hidden from His sight, but all things are naked and open to the eyes of Him to whom we must give account" (Heb. 4:13).

As British scholar J. I. Packer wrote, "There are few things stressed more strongly in the Bible than the reality of God's work as Judge."[4]

On this awesome day of reckoning, only God Himself is qualified to be seated at the judgment seat.

John 5:22 and 27 say God "has committed all judgment to the Son . . . and has given Him authority to execute judgment" (see also Acts 17:31; 2 Tim. 4:1; 1 Peter 4:5). Acts 10:42 says that Christ was "ordained by God to be the Judge of the living and the dead."

In one of the central verses on this subject, 2 Corinthians 5:10, we are told that we must all "appear" before the judgment seat of Christ. The word *appear* is better translated "made manifest." In other words, we are not going to just show up. Our lives are going to be revealed for what they really are. There will be no pretending at this tribunal.

George Sweeting, the former president of Moody Bible Institute, writes:

God gives Jesus Christ the right to judge all men because of who He is. Jesus is uniquely qualified to judge because He is God and has existed from eternity (John 1:1). As God, He knows everything, can be everywhere at once, and has unlimited power and authority. He knows everything we think and sees everything we do. Thus He can judge perfectly, and with wisdom and full understanding and without error or partiality. Christ is also uniquely qualified to judge because of what He has done. He demonstrated perfect love for all men. Thus, when He judges, His perfect righteousness is balanced by His perfect love.[5]

Mark Hitchcock uses this lighter illustration to underscore the completeness of God's judgment:

A group of children was lined up in the cafeteria of a Catholic elementary school for lunch. At the head of the table was a large pile of apples. A nun posted a note on the apple tray: "Take only one. Remember, God is watching." Moving further along the lunch line, at the other end of the table was a large pile of chocolate chip cookies. A child had written a note, "Take all you want. God is watching the apples." The truth is—God is watching the apples and the cookies.[6]

THE JUDGED

The judgment seat of Christ is for believers only. At this tribunal everyone who has accepted Christ as their personal Savior, from the time of Pentecost until the Rapture, will give an account of themselves before the Lord. No unsaved person will appear at the judgment seat of Christ. But every believer will make an appearance. Here are the three central passages on this future event:

- Why do *you* judge *your* brother? Or why do *you* show contempt for *your* brother? For *we* shall all stand before the judgment seat of Christ. . . . So then *each of us* shall give account of *himself* to God. (Rom. 14:10, 12, emphasis added)
- For no other foundation can anyone lay than that which is laid, which is Jesus Christ. Now if *anyone* builds on this foundation with gold, silver, precious stones, wood, hay, straw, *each one's* work will become clear; for the Day will declare it, because it will be revealed by fire; and the fire will test *each one's* work, of what sort it is. If *anyone's* work which *he* has built on it endures, *he* will receive a reward. If *anyone's* work is burned, *he* will suffer loss; but *he himself* will be saved, yet so as through fire. (1 Cor. 3:11–15, emphasis added)

- *We* must all appear before the judgment seat of Christ, that *each one* may receive the things done in the body, according to what *he* has done, whether good or bad. (2 Cor. 5:10, emphasis added).

I have emphasized particular pronouns in these critical verses because this event is not a community affair or even a church gathering. This is a one-on-one examination by the Son of the living God.

THE JUDGMENT

Here are four additional truths Christians should know and remember about the judgment seat of Christ.

THE CONFUSION ABOUT THIS JUDGMENT

One erroneous idea that has grown up around the judgment seat of Christ is that it is a judgment that takes place in heaven, at the time of death, to determine whether a person is permitted to enter heaven. Here, in the words of prophecy scholar J. Dwight Pentecost, is the definitive answer to that false assumption:

> The only judgment to which a believer will ever have been subjected is the judgment on the cross. He was judged in the person of Christ. Jesus Christ has borne his judgment, and there need not be any examination to see whether a child of God is permitted into glory, because the presence of the Holy Spirit in that believer is the believer's right to enter in without judgment or examination.[7]

Some also believe that the judgment seat of Christ is for the purpose of giving an account of all the sins a believer commits after he becomes a believer. But the Scriptures make this impossible: "There is therefore now no condemnation to those who are in Christ Jesus" (Rom. 8:1).

It is not logical to think that Jesus took care of all the sins I committed before I became a Christian, but that I am responsible for all those sins I have committed after I was born again. All my sins were future when Jesus died for them. He paid the penalty at the cross for all the sins I would ever commit.

In the days of the pioneers, when men saw that a prairie fire was coming, they would take a match and burn the designated area around them. Then they would take their stand in the burned area and be safe from the threatening fire. Even as the rush of fire surged around them there was no fear, because fire had already passed over the place where they stood.

When the judgment of God comes to sweep men into hell for eternity, one spot will be safe. Nearly two thousand years ago the wrath of God was poured out on Calvary. There, the Son of God took the wrath that should have fallen on us. Now if we take our stand by the cross, we are safe for time and eternity. The judgment has fallen and it never need fall again.

THE CHRONOLOGY OF THIS JUDGMENT

The judgment seat of Christ is an event that will take place immediately after the Rapture of the church. This sequence of events is reflected in the words of Paul to the Corinthians: "Judge nothing before the time, until the Lord comes, who will both bring to light the hidden things of darkness and reveal the counsels of the hearts. Then each one's praise will come from God" (1 Cor. 4:5).

James is on the same page, as the following verse reveals: "Do not grumble against one another, brethren, lest you be condemned. Behold, the Judge is standing at the door!" (James 5:9).

Jesus said it the best: "Behold, I am coming quickly, and My reward is with Me, to give to every one according to his work" (Rev. 22:12).

THE CRITERIA FOR THIS JUDGMENT

On what basis will we be judged when we stand before the Lord at the judgment seat? To make the answer to this question crystal clear, Paul uses an illustration that has been relevant to every generation from the time it was given to this very day. That illustration is found in 1 Corinthians 3:11–15:

> For no other foundation can anyone lay than that which is laid, which is Jesus Christ. Now if anyone builds on this foundation with gold, silver, precious stones, wood, hay, straw, each one's work will become clear; for the Day will declare it, because it will be revealed by fire; and the fire will test each one's work, of what sort it is. If anyone's work which he has built on it endures, he will receive a reward. If anyone's work is burned, he will suffer loss; but he himself will be saved, yet so as through fire.

The apostle Paul uses the construction of a building to illustrate what will happen to believers at the judgment seat of Christ. The Builder, Jesus Christ, is going to evaluate the work that the builders of His church have accomplished.

According to Paul, just as there are two contrasting ways to build a building, there are two different ways to build a life. Some will construct their lives out of gold, silver, and precious stones, while others will build with wood, hay, and straw.

But what constitutes gold, silver, and costly stones or wood, hay, and straw? Here is one of the best answers to that often-asked question:

> I observe that gold, silver, and costly stones are those things which God Himself creates and plants in the earth, and man can do no more than reap the bounty of the provision of God. The wood, the hay, and the stubble are those things that man plants, cultivates, harvests, manufactures, and uses according to his will. And so the suggestion we make is that which God is permitted to do in and through the child of God is that which is gold, silver and costly stones, and that which the individual does by his own power, for his own glory, because it suits his own will, because it promotes his own purpose, is the wood and the stubble.[8]

In Paul's illustration, there is a fire in the building and the nature of the materials that were used to build the building are made manifest or revealed.

Even today, this illustration holds true. We have all read of buildings that have been destroyed by fire simply because the builders used inferior materials and they covered it up, thinking that no one would ever know. But then the fire came and it was all exposed—and they, too, were exposed for being unfaithful builders. That is what Paul is talking about here. That is his illustration.

What does the fire represent for those who are building their lives? I believe it is the fire of Christ's omniscient gaze (Rev. 1:14). That fire will burn up all work that has not been done for Him in a spirit of faithfulness, unity, and love for Christ, His church, and for others.

"Fire" is a well-known biblical image of testing and refining (Prov. 27:21; Isa. 47:14; Zech. 13:9), and it is the same image Paul uses to describe the effects of Christ's evaluation of our works at His judgment seat.

THE CONCLUSION OF THIS JUDGMENT

In Paul's letter to the Corinthians, he tells them of two possible outcomes from the judgment seat of Christ: the loss of rewards and the reception of rewards.

First, the loss of rewards. As we have explained above, those things done in the energy of the flesh and for the glory of the individual will be examined, and for those things there will be no reward.

In His introduction to the disciples' prayer, Jesus gives us two examples of the kind of religious activity that will result in the loss of rewards:

- "Take heed that you do not do your charitable deeds before men, to be seen by them. Otherwise you have no reward from your Father in heaven" (Matt. 6:1).
- "When you pray, you shall not be like the hypocrites. For they love to pray standing in the synagogues and on the corners of the streets,

that they may be seen by men. Assuredly, I say to you, they have their reward" (Matt. 6:5).

When Jesus told His famous story of the nobleman, He did not mention the judgment seat, but He did give us another illustration that helps us understand the loss of rewards. In that story, found in Luke 19:11–27, the nobleman returns to his property after a long trip. In his absence he had placed three of his servants in charge. One of his servants has worked hard and managed well, and he is rewarded with a great reward. The second servant has not been a bad steward, but he was not a good one either, and so he receives a moderate reward. But the third servant has been unfaithful and lazy, and he not only does not receive a reward but the Master takes what he already has and gives it to another. He loses his reward.

Paul, in his first letter to the Corinthians, expresses his fear of losing his reward: "I discipline my body and bring it into subjection, lest, when I have preached to others, I myself should become disqualified" (1 Cor. 9:27).

When the apostle used the word translated *disqualified* he was not talking about losing his salvation. The word *disqualified* comes from the Greek word *adokimos*, which means "to reject something on the basis of an examination." Paul feared that his service for the Lord would be "weighed in the balances, and found wanting," and he disciplined his life so in that final day of reckoning he would not suffer the loss of his reward.

But listen carefully: Paul was never concerned about the loss of his salvation. In his explanation of the examination at the judgment seat, this is what he wrote: "If anyone's work which he has built on it endures, he will receive a reward. If anyone's work is burned, he will suffer loss; but he himself will be saved, yet so as through fire" (1 Cor. 3:14–15).

The judgment seat of Christ is a sobering reminder to every Christian that a day of testing is coming and the day of pretending will be over.

Peter tells us to take this judgment of God in our lives very seriously, and he explains that if we do that it will change the way we live: "If you call on the

Father, who without partiality judges according to each one's work, conduct yourselves throughout the time of your stay here in fear" (1 Pet. 1:17).

Next, the reception of rewards. This moment of judgment will not be entirely negative. Indeed, this judgment will also be a time of rewards. We'll develop this in more detail in the next chapter, but the New Testament mentions five rewards, typically labeled as "crowns," available to the believer:

1. The Victor's Crown (1 Cor. 9:25–27)
2. The Crown of Rejoicing (1 Thess. 2:19)
3. The Crown of Righteousness (2 Tim. 4:8)
4. The Crown of Life (James 1:12)
5. The Crown of Glory (1 Pet. 5:1–4)

I have heard and read many arguments against the doctrine of rewards. Most of those arguments sound very pious and spiritual. "We should not serve Jesus because we are trying to earn a reward; we should serve Him simply because we love Him." That sounds right, but it does not explain why "rewards" are mentioned so many times in the Bible. I think the following statement by Jim Elliff puts this whole discussion into perspective:

> People who piously care so little about eternal rewards are often killing themselves trying to accumulate a great "reward" now. They profess to be content with a "little shack" in heaven but want a much bigger one on earth! The Bible teaches that there is nothing wrong with ambition, just as long as we focus it on heaven rather than earth.[9]

When the crowns are awarded in heaven, they will not stay in the possession of those who received them very long. According to Revelation 4, the recipients of the crowns, in an act of worship, will lay them down before the throne of the Lord.

There is an old tale about three men crossing the desert by camel at night. As they were crossing the desert, a voice came out of the darkness.

The voice commanded them to dismount, pick up some pebbles, and put them in their pockets. The voice said, "At the coming of the sun, you will be both glad and sorry."

The travelers did as they were told, and later as the sun came up, they remembered what the voice had said, "At the coming of the sun, you will be both glad and sorry." They reached into their pockets and pulled out not pebbles but diamonds. They were both glad and sorry. Glad they took as many as they did and sorry they did not take more.

Right now, God is giving us opportunities, and He is saying to us that at the coming of His Son we will be both glad and sorry—glad we used the opportunities that we did and sorry we did not use more.

CHAPTER 16

REWARDS

How does Hollywood get anything done? Every single week, it seems, the folks there put on another awards show to congratulate themselves and hand out statues to each other. It doesn't really seem fair. There are no award shows, so far as I know, for firefighters, medical professionals, police officers, or homemakers. But the entertainment industry throws one party for itself after another, so we're awash in the Academy Awards (Oscars), the Emmys, the Producers Guild Awards, the Screen Actors Guild Awards, the Grammys, the Academy of Country Music Awards, the Tony Awards, the Peabody Awards, the Daytime Emmy Awards, the BET Awards, the MTV Video Music Awards, the Golden Globes, the E! People's Choice Awards, the Billboard Music Awards, the Critics' Choice Awards, and a host of others.

These awards aren't worth as much as you think. Suppose you win an Oscar, for example. While it may boost your career, the actual value of the statue isn't going to fund your retirement. Since 1951, every Oscar recipient has signed an agreement giving the Academy the first right of refusal should the actor decide to sell the statue. If you or your heirs want to sell your award, you'll get a call from lawyers representing the Academy, informing you that by law they have first dibs on it—and the price they pay is a whopping one dollar.

The truth is, all the honors, awards, and trophies of this world have little lasting value. While we're grateful when others recognize something we have done, our chief concern shouldn't be the approval of others but the approval of God. While it's perfectly all right to honor someone for their contributions or service—the Bible tells us to give honor to whom honor is due (Rom. 13:7)—what really counts are the eternal rewards to be given out in heaven.

Some people get a little nervous about the subject of heavenly rewards because they view it as an unworthy source of motivation. Why would you need a reward to serve the Lord? Why should we need any external or eternal incentive? Let's serve the Lord because we love Him, not in order to receive a reward.

That argument sounds both logical and spiritual, yet the Bible constantly reminds us of the rewards God has for His people, and Scripture urges us to be faithful so we'll receive the prizes God offers us.

As you look at this sample of verses, perhaps you'll be surprised how often the Bible speaks of eternal rewards.

- "The LORD repay your work, and a full reward be given you by the LORD God of Israel, under whose wings you have come for refuge" (Ruth 2:12).
- "But you, be strong and do not let your hands be weak, for your work shall be rewarded!" (2 Chron. 15:7; see also Ps. 58:11; Jer. 31:16).
- "Blessed are you when they revile and persecute you, and say all kinds of evil against you falsely for My sake. Rejoice and be exceedingly glad, for great is your reward in heaven, for so they persecuted the prophets who were before you" (Matt. 5:11–12).
- "For the Son of Man will come in the glory of His Father with His

angels, and then He will reward each according to his works" (Matt. 16:27).

- "And behold, I am coming quickly, and My reward is with Me, to give to every one according to his work" (Rev. 22:12).

The Bible speaks of a reward ceremony that will take place in heaven immediately after the Rapture of the church. This event is called the judgment seat of Christ. This is where the Lord will judge us for our conduct and work as believers. At this event we will receive our rewards for the work we have done while living as Christians on the earth.

Three major passages of Scripture tell us about this event:

- "Why do you judge your brother? Or why do you show contempt for your brother? For we shall all stand before the judgment seat of Christ" (Rom. 14:10).
- "We make it our aim, whether present or absent, to be well pleasing to Him. For we must all appear before the judgment seat of Christ, that each one may receive the things done in the body, according to what he has done, whether good or bad" (2 Cor. 5:9–10).
- "Let each one take heed how he builds. . . . For no other foundation can anyone lay than that which is laid, which is Jesus Christ. Now if anyone builds on this foundation with gold, silver, precious stones, wood, hay, straw, each one's work will become clear; for the Day will declare it, because it will be revealed by fire; and the fire will test each one's work, of what sort it is. If anyone's work which he has built on it endures, he will receive a reward. If anyone's work is burned, he will suffer loss; but he himself will be saved, yet so as through fire" (1 Cor. 3:10–15).

On that day, we will approach the judgment seat of Christ, one by one, to be judged by the Lord Jesus—not for our salvation, but for what we have done as believers between the moment of our salvation and the moment when we ultimately stand before our Lord.

"Our eternal destination," according to Bruce Wilkinson, is "the consequence of what we believe on earth. Our eternal compensation is the consequence of how we behave on earth."[1]

THE DESCRIPTION OF HEAVEN'S REWARDS

What will these rewards be like? What can we expect? Does the Bible give us any clues? Yes, it does. At least five of these rewards are listed for us. The New Testament uses the word *crowns* to describe them.

THE VICTOR'S CROWN

First, there is the Victor's Crown, portrayed for us in 1 Corinthians 9:25–27:

Everyone who competes for the prize is temperate in all things. Now they do it to obtain a perishable crown, but we for an imperishable crown. Therefore I run thus: not with uncertainty. Thus I fight: not as one who beats the air. But I discipline my body and bring it into subjection, lest, when I have preached to others, I myself should become disqualified.

Paul wrote this paragraph to the Christians in the Greek city of Corinth, who were very familiar with two great athletic festivals that occurred near them—the Olympic Games and the Isthmian Games. The Isthmian Games were held at Corinth, and many of Paul's readers would have attended these exciting contests. Contestants in the games had to endure very rigorous training for ten months. The last month was spent at Corinth with supervised daily workouts in the gymnasium and athletic fields. The race was always a major attraction at the games, and that is the analogy Paul uses to illustrate the faithful Christian life.

No one would train so hard for so long without intending to win. Yet only one of the athletes would come in first and win the prize. Paul used that analogy to point out that athletes who expect to win must train diligently.

The thought, of course, has to do with developing personal discipline. Walking with God demands personal sacrifice and self-control. We need to maintain self-control even in things that are not necessarily evil, but which can dilute our full devotion to God. In an age of luxury like ours, these words have real significance for serious servants of Jesus Christ. If we want to win an award, we have to say no to some things so we can say yes to other things that are more pleasing to God.

Remember, Paul was comparing us to athletes who live under strict training so they can be effective in their pursuits. When runners are in training, they exercise when they would rather be resting. They eat a balanced meal when they would rather have rich desserts. They get up early when they'd rather stay in bed. They control their desires rather than being controlled by their desires.

In his book *No Excuses: The Power of Self-Discipline*, Brian Tracy wrote about the time he ran into M. R. Kopmeyer, a noted writer of motivation and success literature. Tracy seized the opportunity to ask Kopmeyer, "Of all the 1,000 success principles that you have discovered, which do you think is the most important?"

Kopmeyer smiled and replied without hesitation, "The most important success principle of all was stated by Elbert Hubbard, one of the most prolific writers in American history, at the beginning of the twentieth century. He said, 'Self-discipline is the ability to do what you should do, when you should do it, whether you feel like it or not.'"

Kopmeyer went on to say that without self-discipline the other 999 principles don't work, but with self-discipline they all do.[2]

It's important to remember that self-control depends on Spirit-control. Our own determination needs buttressing by grace, so we have to depend on God to strengthen us in our resolutions to live disciplined lives. Titus 2:11–13 says, "The grace of God has appeared that offers salvation to all people. It teaches us to say 'No' to ungodliness, worldly passions, and to live self-controlled, upright and godly lives in this present age, while we wait for the blessed hope—the appearing of the glory of our great God and Savior, Jesus Christ" (NIV).

The Lord will help us, but we have to do our part too. It's surely worth it, for "everyone who competes for the prize is temperate in all things. Now they do it to obtain a perishable crown, but we for an imperishable crown" (1 Cor. 9:25)

THE CROWN OF REJOICING

The next crown is the Crown of Rejoicing, mentioned in 1 Thessalonians 2:19: "For what is our hope, or joy, or crown of rejoicing? Is it not even you in the presence of our Lord Jesus Christ at His coming?"

This is the crown given for playing a part in leading others to Christ. The background for this passage is Acts 17, which tells the story of Paul and his companions arriving in the city of Thessalonica. Paul went into the synagogue "and for three Sabbaths reasoned with them from the Scriptures, explaining and demonstrating that the Christ had to suffer and rise again from the dead, and saying, 'This Jesus whom I preach to you is the Christ'" (vv. 2–3).

Some of his hearers were persuaded to follow Christ, including some Greek men and a number of prominent women. The gospel spread to their hearts, and through them to others, and a church was born in that city. Writing to them later, in 1 Thessalonians 2, Paul said they would be his "crown of rejoicing" when Christ returned (v. 19).

This is sometimes called the Soul Winner's Crown, but I suspect it isn't just reserved for those who actually lead another person to Christ. I think it will be shared by all those who play a role in bringing others to Christ. It's a team effort. Whenever I have the opportunity of leading others to receive Jesus as Savior, I almost always find that someone else has already planted the seed of the gospel in their hearts. Paul wrote, "I planted, Apollos watered, but God gave the increase" (1 Cor. 3:6).

When was the last time you shared the gospel in some form or fashion with another person? Whenever you do so, the Lord Himself is fitting you for the Crown of Rejoicing.

THE CROWN OF RIGHTEOUSNESS

The Crown of Righteousness is next, and it's described in 2 Timothy 4:8: "Finally, there is laid up for me the crown of righteousness, which the Lord, the righteous Judge, will give to me on that Day, and not to me only but also to all who have loved His appearing."

The book of 2 Timothy represents the last known writing of the apostle Paul, and we have reason to believe he was beheaded shortly after writing these words. But rather than dreading death, he was looking forward to the second coming. He was ready to meet Christ and content with his record of service for the Master. Paul's use of the athletic metaphor here is especially descriptive of the life of the believer because it describes struggle, endurance, discipline, and final victory. The Crown of Righteousness is reserved for those who have a longing for the Lord Jesus and who watch for Jesus to come back.

Psychologists tell us that anticipation, which is the opposite of surprise, is an emotion with marvelous healing powers. Can you imagine a world without anticipation? How would we feel with nothing to look forward to? Welcome to non-Christianity. Without Christ, there's no ultimate anticipation. There may be momentary prospects and incremental excitement, but lasting expectancy is missing. Everything is different for Jesus followers! Our best days are ahead of us, and we can anticipate all the glories of eternity. That should motivate our daily faithfulness as we await His return.

Denis Lyle, who was a pastor in Lurgan, Northern Ireland, tells of a tourist who visited a beautiful mansion on a lovely lakeshore in Switzerland. The house was surrounded by well-kept gardens connected by tidy pathways. Not a weed anywhere.

"How long have you been caretaker here?" the tourist asked the gardener.

"I've been here twenty years."

"And during that time how often has the owner of the property been in residence?"

The gardener smiled and said, "He has been here only four times."

"And to think," exclaimed the visitor, "all these years you've kept this house and garden in such superb condition. You tend them as if you expected him to come tomorrow."

"Oh no," replied the gardener, "I look after them as if I expected him to come today."[3]

Jesus is coming back, coming any minute, coming soon, maybe today. The Bible says that time is short (1 Cor. 7:29), and we must work, for the night is coming. The more vividly aware we are of His impending return, the more we'll be motivated in our work for Him in these last days.

THE CROWN OF LIFE

The fourth crown is called the Crown of Life, and two different verses describe it for us.

- "Blessed is the man who endures temptation; for when he has been approved, he will receive the crown of life which the Lord has promised to those who love Him" (James 1:12).
- "Do not fear any of those things which you are about to suffer. Indeed, the devil is about to throw some of you into prison, that you may be tested, and you will have tribulation ten days. Be faithful until death, and I will give you the crown of life" (Rev. 2:10).

The Crown of Life is given in recognition of enduring and triumphing over temptations and trials, even to the point of martyrdom. Motivated by our love for Christ, we persevere and never quit until He takes us home. The New Testament Christians lived in days of intense persecution, and almost every New Testament book was written to believers who lived in danger of martyrdom. The apostles counseled them to persevere so they could inherit the Crown of Life.

When we think of persecution, we often think of the Roman Empire and the brutal assaults on Christians by emperors like Nero who were determined to eradicate the church. But the most intense period of persecution in the history of the church is occurring around the world today. In 2017, the organization Open Doors, which monitors global persecution, released a report highlighting the top fifty nations where Christians face the most severe persecution. The bottom line: 100 percent of Christians in 21 countries around the world experience persecution for their faith in Christ, and more than 215 million Christians face "high levels" of persecution. "Nearly one in every 12 Christians today lives in an area or culture in which Christianity is illegal, forbidden or punished."[4]

Another report, this one published by the group International Christian Concern, highlighted three countries where religious discrimination and persecution have reached a certain threshold of concern. These countries are Mexico, Russia, and the United States of America. "While conditions in the U.S. are in no way comparable to other countries," said the report, "a certain segment of the culture and the courts seem to be intent on driving faith out of the public square."[5]

Don't be shocked by that. While we're grieved to think of America as an increasingly oppressive environment for Christians, the Bible says, "All who desire to live godly in Christ Jesus will suffer persecution" (2 Tim. 3:12). Satan will batter us all with temptations of all kinds, and we'll face trials and persecution. But that gives us a wonderful opportunity to lay claim to the Crown of Life.

THE CROWN OF GLORY

The final reward in the lineup is the Crown of Glory. Peter wrote,

> The elders who are among you I exhort, I who am a fellow elder and a
> witness of the sufferings of Christ, and also a partaker of the glory that

will be revealed: Shepherd the flock of God which is among you, serving as overseers, not by compulsion but willingly, not for dishonest gain but eagerly; nor as being lords over those entrusted to you, but being examples to the flock; and when the Chief Shepherd appears, you will receive the crown of glory that does not fade away. (1 Pet. 5:1–4)

This crown seems especially designed for Christian leaders and for those who are faithful shepherds of the people of God. Now, I don't believe you have to be an official pastor on staff at a church to receive this crown. You might be the shepherd of a small group. Your flock might be your family and your children. It might be your Sunday school class or small group. The Lord often gives us responsibility for the spiritual well-being and nurturing of others, and what an opportunity to serve Him!

Many earthly monarchs have found their crowns heavy and their reign troubled. Panic and problems have overwhelmed them. But the crowns awarded by Jesus will be nothing but delight.

Charles Haddon Spurgeon said, "Rewards, not of debt, but of grace, shall be given to the most obscure and unknown of you, who for his sake have sought to teach little children or to reclaim the adult who had fallen into sin. Take courage—your work of faith and labour of love are not in vain in the Lord, and will do wonders yet to the praise of his grace."[6]

THE GREATEST REWARD OF ALL

These may not be all the crowns awarded at the judgment seat of Christ. Perhaps thousands of other categories will be revealed on that day. But one overriding thought has lodged in my mind as I've thought about these things. As wonderful as our rewards are, they truly don't represent our core motivation. If we serve the Lord only to get a reward, it indicates we don't truly understand Christianity.

Somebody put it this way: "In theory, it might be possible to pursue eternal rewards with fleshly motives. However, I've never met anyone I've sensed was guilty of doing so. I've never heard someone say, 'I'm a missionary in the deep, dark jungle because when I get to Heaven I want a mansion that is bigger than the Joneses.' I've never heard anything like that, have you? For myself, I can't remember ever thinking, 'If I witness to that guy, God will owe me big time.'"[7]

Think of it this way. If you're really an athlete, you don't run for the trophy. You run for the joy of the race and for the discipline and for the victory that comes in your heart. The trophy is just something to keep around and remind you of the blessing of being in the race itself.

None of these crowns really represent our greatest reward. Remember what the Lord told Abraham in Genesis 15:1: "Do not be afraid, Abram. I am your shield, your exceedingly great reward." The Lord had planned many blessings for Abraham, which He outlined in Genesis 12 and 15. God promised to bless him, to make of him a great nation, to give him a great land, to give him many descendants, to bless those who blessed him and curse those who cursed him, and to make his name great. He promised that all the earth would be blessed through his lineage. But nothing compared to the blessing of personally knowing the God of all eternity. The Lord Himself exceeded all other gifts.

The Lord Himself is our exceedingly great reward. And that brings up the best thing I know to say about our rewards. What are we going to do with these crowns? Let's say you get to heaven, stand before the judgment seat of Christ, and receive three different crowns for your faithful service on earth. What are you going to do with them? The answer is in Revelation 4:10–11, which describes the great heavenly worship service that will occur when the raptured and resurrected saints arrive in heaven.

> The twenty-four elders fall down before Him who sits on the throne and worship Him who lives forever and ever, and cast their crowns before the throne, saying: "You are worthy, O Lord, to receive glory and honor and power; for You created all things, and by Your will they exist and were created."

Look at that! I believe the twenty-four elders very likely represent the redeemed of all the ages who are caught up to heaven at the Rapture and resurrection. If that is true, it tells us that after we receive our rewards humbly with gratitude, we're going to see Jesus. We're going to take the only thing we have in heaven, which is the crown He gave us, and we'll fall down at His feet and give it back to Him and say, "Thank You, Lord, for helping me to be here. Thank You, Lord, for paying for my sin. Thank You, Lord, for being my Redeemer. Thank You for using me a little bit on earth. Thank You for letting me be Your servant. I haven't got much to give You, Lord, but here is my crown."

I don't want to be standing in the background watching everybody I knew on earth bringing their crowns and giving them to the Lord Jesus but, because I was a lazy Christian, have nothing to offer. All this occurs before He wipes away all tears from our eyes because there will surely be some tears at that moment.

There is an old story I've told over the years, but because it seems such a fitting end to this chapter, I want to tell it one more time. There was an old missionary couple, Mr. and Mrs. Henry C. Morrison, who served in Africa for forty years and were returning to America to retire. This was in the days when most transcontinental travel was done by ship. As they steamed into New York Harbor, they had mixed feelings. Though glad to be home, they were concerned because they had no pension, their health was broken, and they were tired.

They discovered while aboard ship that President Theodore Roosevelt and his entourage were also on board, returning from a big-game hunting expedition in Africa. They watched the fanfare that accompanied the president as he returned from abroad. "TR" (Roosevelt) was met by a great delegation and with much excitement. Reverend Morrison couldn't help feeling some resentment. There was no one to meet him. No one came to celebrate their return after forty years of faithful service.

"Honey, you shouldn't feel that way," said Mrs. Morrison.

"I can't help it," he said. "It doesn't seem right."

The missionaries slipped off the ship unnoticed, found a cheap room on New York's East Side, and tried to figure out their future. That night, the missionary's heart broke, and he said to his wife, "I can't take this. God is not treating us fairly."

His wife replied, "Why don't you just go in the bedroom and tell that to the Lord."

A short time later, Reverend Morrison came out from the bedroom, and his face was completely different. His wife asked, "Honey, what happened?"

He said, "Well, the Lord settled it with me. I told Him how bitter I was that the president should receive this tremendous homecoming when no one met us as we returned home. And when I finished, it seemed as though the Lord put His hand on my shoulder and simply said, 'But you're not home yet.'"[8]

We're not home yet. It's rewarding to serve Christ, and we receive many rewards, even in this life. But the best awards are being reserved for the award ceremony in the heavens, and the best reward of all is our Lord Himself. What a joy to one day cast all our crowns at His feet.

CHAPTER 17

WORSHIP

On September 22, 1967, at Wheaton College in suburban Chicago, Dr. V. Raymond Edman, a revered Christian educator and devotional writer, returned to campus after an extended illness to preach in the auditorium named after him—Edman Chapel. His subject was "The Presence of the King." He began by telling of an invitation he once received to visit Haile Selassie I, the king of Ethiopia. He described in detail the preparations and the protocol that preceded his visit, and he spoke of the sense of majesty he felt upon speaking with the king. He spoke of walking down the aisle, pausing, bowing, and waiting to see if he would be allowed to proceed. It was a regal, glorious, intimidating but wonderful experience, one that Edman treasured.

Then Edman shifted gears and told the students:

> But I speak primarily of another King. This chapel is the house of the King. Chapel is designed to be a meeting on your part with the King of kings and the Lord of lords Himself. To that end, chapel is designed for the purpose of worship. . . . Chapel is to be a time of worship, not a lecture, not an entertainment, but a time of meeting the King. Coming in, sit down and wait

in silence before the Lord. In so doing, you will prepare your own hearts to hear the Lord, to meet with the King. Your heart will learn to cultivate what the Scripture says, "Be still and know that I am God." Over these years I have learned the immense value of that deep, inner silence as David, the king, sat in God's presence to hear from him.[1]

A moment later, Edman collapsed in the pulpit and went instantly into the presence of the very King of whom he was speaking. I'm sure you can feel my heart when I earnestly tell you that, being a preacher and pastor myself, I would count it an honor to be called home while preaching— particularly while preaching on the subject of heaven.

Something like that happened to the apostle John, but in this case he didn't die in the process. In Revelation 1:10–11 he wrote, "I was in the Spirit on the Lord's Day, and I heard behind me a loud voice, as of a trumpet, saying, 'I am the Alpha and the Omega, the First and the Last.'" He turned to see who was speaking, and he said, "I saw seven golden lampstands, and in the midst of the seven lampstands One like the Son of Man, clothed with a garment down to the feet and girded about the chest with a golden band. His head and hair were white like wool, as white as snow, and His eyes like a flame of fire" (vv. 12–14).

This is the opening vision in Revelation, in which John saw the glorified Christ among the golden lampstands, enthroned in splendor and full of glory. In the next two chapters, John related the messages he received to the seven churches of Asia Minor. These are recorded for us in Revelation 2 and 3.

Then we come to Revelation 4 and 5, which provide a glimpse into heaven at the great worship service that will occur around the throne of God as the time comes for the unleashing of the final events in world history leading to the return of Christ. Many commentators believe these are the two greatest chapters on the subject of worship in the Bible, for they rather literally take us up to heaven and let us see celestial worship as it unfolds before the throne of God.

I have studied these two chapters with great interest. There has never been a time in my life when I've drifted away from the practice of public worship, and I suppose I know the rituals and routines as well as anyone. In most of our worship services today, we have three integral parts: (1) we praise God; (2) we pray to God; and (3) we preach His Word. Yet as I read Revelation 4 and 5 only one of those three elements will survive to be part of worship in heaven.

I do not think we will have prayer in heaven, at least not as we practice it on earth. There will be no need to pray as we do now. We will live in the very presence of almighty God, and we will commune with and have an ongoing relationship with Him, much more intimately than we do now.

Nor will there be a need for preaching. The Bible says, "For now we see in a mirror, dimly, but then face to face. Now I know in part, but then I shall know just as I also am known" (1 Cor. 13:12). Perhaps we will still enjoy poring over God's Word, for Psalm 119:89 says, "Forever, O LORD, your word is settled in heaven." But we will not have to exhort anyone to trust it or to obey it, for we'll be living in a state of perfect spirituality; and we will certainly not have to make evangelistic appeals, for everyone will be saved and forever safe.

That leaves only one great element dominating heavenly worship— praise! Praising our God is the only one of the three elements of our common worship practices that will survive into eternity.

In his book *Called to Worship*, Dr. Vernon M. Whaley described the scene set forth in Revelation 4 and 5:

Notice that no one in these passages seems to be under compulsion to worship God. No one is standing there, cracking the whip and demanding veneration. The whole of heaven is rejoicing voluntarily and from the heart. Why? Because they know that Jesus Christ is no longer that baby in a manger, represented by so many cracked and peeling images in Nativity sets the world over. Neither is He the bleeding and broken "criminal," humbled and half-naked on a cross, the victim of those who thought they were bigger than Him. And He's not the cold and mangled corpse that once lay in a borrowed tomb either. Those whose praises fill the heavens know that Jesus Christ is exalted. He is all in all, and heaven's inhabitants never tire of worshipping Him. Neither will we. You and I will never run out of things to thank Him for, and praising Him will never become boring.[2]

And that brings us back to Revelation 4 and 5, the Bible's premier chapters on praise and worship. I want to dive into these chapters and describe the context, the center, the chorus, the crescendo, and the contrasting elements of heavenly worship.

THE CONTEXT OF WORSHIP IN HEAVEN

Revelation 4:1 says, "After these things I looked, and behold, a door standing open in heaven. And the first voice which I heard was like a trumpet speaking with me, saying, 'Come up here, and I will show you things which must take place after this.'"

What a dramatic phrase: A door was standing open in heaven. From his spot on the island of Patmos, John was somehow able to gaze through an open door into heaven and see something no one has ever seen before. He saw a heavenly worship service in full swing. When the church is raptured, triggering the final events in world history, a great celebration will break out in heaven. The angels, the cherubim, the seraphim, the principalities and powers and angelic forces in the heavenly realms, and the redeemed saints of all the ages will burst into spectacular praise, which is described for us here in Revelation 4 and 5.

John was the last surviving member of the original band of apostles, and he wrote these words while facing a difficult exile on the island of Patmos. Perhaps John felt weary. Maybe he worried and wondered whether his life's work was over. But it was then and there, during his exile, that he suddenly heard a voice and turned to see who had spoken to him: "After these things I looked, and behold, a door standing open in heaven. And the first voice which I heard was like a trumpet speaking with me, saying, 'Come up here, and I will show you things which must take place after this'" (v. 1).

For John, this was an extraordinary moment as he was able to view the worship occurring in heaven as all the angelic hosts prepared for the final events leading to our Lord's glorious return.

THE CENTER OF WORSHIP IN HEAVEN

From the context of worship we move to the very center of worship, and the scene is glorious. Revelation 4:2–3 says, "Immediately I was in the Spirit; and behold, a throne set in heaven, and One sat on the throne. And He who sat there was like a jasper and a sardius stone in appearance; and there was a rainbow around the throne, in appearance like an emerald."

The key word in this verse is the word *throne*, a term that appears forty-two times in Revelation, including a number of times here in chapters 4 and 5.

- "Immediately I was in the Spirit; and behold, a throne set in heaven, and One sat on the throne" (4:2).
- "There was a rainbow around the throne" (4:3).
- "And from the throne proceeded lightnings, thunderings, and voices" (4:5).
- "Before the throne there was a sea of glass" (4:6).
- "Around the throne, were four living creatures" (4:6).
- "The twenty-four elders fall down before Him who sits on the throne" (4:10).
- "I heard the voice of many angels around the throne" (5:11).
- "Blessing and honor and glory and power be to Him who sits on the throne, and to the Lamb, forever and ever!" (5:13).

These references to God's heavenly throne speak to His sovereignty, authority, reign, and absolute power. When we study the throne of God in the book of Revelation, we're reminded that while events on this earth seem chaotic and often meaningless, there is One in the universe seated upon His throne, sovereign and in control.

This is how John felt in Revelation 4 as he gazed in wonder at the heavenly throne and tried to describe what he saw. His dismal exile turned into heavenly excitement, and he began recording the scene: "Immediately I was in the Spirit; and behold, a throne set in heaven, and One sat on the throne. And He who sat there was like a jasper and a sardius stone in appearance; and there was a rainbow around the throne, in appearance like an emerald. . . . And from the throne proceeded lightnings, thunderings, and voices. Seven lamps of fire were burning before the throne, which are the seven Spirits of God" (vv. 2–3, 5).

As the apostle John gazed at the majesty and beauty of the throne of his eternal Creator, all he could comprehend was its diamond-like brilliance, its gemstone-like beauty, and its stormy grandeur.

God is still seated on His throne, and His throne is still a throne of glory and of grace. It's the heart and hub of all our worship both now and forevermore.

THE CHORUS OF WORSHIP IN HEAVEN

That brings us to the chorus of praise we hear around the throne. The apostle John actually eavesdropped on a worship celebration in heaven, one that will herald the beginning of the events leading to the return of Christ. Here is what he saw and heard:

> Around the throne were twenty-four thrones, and on the thrones I saw twenty-four elders sitting, clothed in white robes; and they had crowns of gold on their heads. . . . Whenever the living creatures give glory and honor

and thanks to Him who sits on the throne, who lives forever and ever, the twenty-four elders fall down before Him who sits on the throne and worship Him who lives forever and ever, and cast their crowns before the throne, saying: "You are worthy, O Lord, to receive glory and honor and power; for You created all things, and by Your will they exist and were created." (4:4, 9–11).

I believe the twenty-four elders represent the church of the living God. They represent the redeemed of all the ages, and they—we—are there, in heaven, before the throne, singing God's praises while beholding the most jaw-dropping setting of grandeur in the entire universe.

The vision continues in Revelation 5:8–10, and here we see not only God the Father but God the Son, who is the object of great interest and praise: "Now when He had taken the scroll, the four living creatures and the twenty-four elders fell down before the Lamb, each having a harp, and golden bowls full of incense, which are the prayers of the saints. And they sang a new song, saying: 'You are worthy to take the scroll, and to open its seals; for You were slain, and have redeemed us to God by Your blood out of every tribe and tongue and people and nation, and have made us kings and priests to our God; and we shall reign on the earth.'"

Oh, I wish I could hear that audibly right now, to hear the voices, to ascertain the melody, to grasp the power of the decibels as all of heaven rings the praises of the Lamb! One day we'll be there, but until then we can tune our hearts to heaven's frequency and use this as our model of praise and worship.

Outside of the words of the Bible, the most famous definition of worship I've read comes from the pen of William Temple, who served as Archbishop of Canterbury during the difficult days of World War II. He wrote, "To worship is to quicken the conscience by the holiness of God, to feed the mind with the truth of God, to purge the imagination by the beauty of God, to open the heart to the love of God, to devote the will to the purpose of God."[3]

This describes the worship in heaven, and it should be the goal of every worshipper on earth.

THE CRESCENDO OF WORSHIP IN HEAVEN

As you read through Revelation 4 and 5, visualizing yourself there amid the sacred throne, you can feel the acceleration of praise as the heavenly worship service progresses. One of the interesting observations I've made in studying the subject of worship in the book of Revelation involves what I'm calling the crescendo of worship in heaven. *Crescendo* is a musical term that refers to a gradual, steady increase in volume and force. The music grows louder and stronger until it reaches a climactic finish. In the worship songs of Revelation, there is an obvious crescendo, and we can see this in the doxologies we encounter:

- Revelation 1:6 has a two-fold doxology: "To Him be *glory* and *dominion* forever and ever. Amen" (emphasis added).
- Revelation 4:11 contains a three-fold doxology: "You are worthy, O Lord, to receive *glory* and *honor* and *power*; for You created all things, and by Your will they exist and were created" (emphasis added).
- Revelation 5:13 proclaims a four-fold doxology: "*Blessing* and *honor* and *glory* and *power* be to Him who sits on the throne, and to the Lamb, forever and ever!" (emphasis added).
- Revelation 7:12 gives us a seven-fold doxology: "Amen! *Blessing* and *glory* and *wisdom*, *thanksgiving* and *honor* and *power* and *might*, be to our God forever and ever. Amen" (emphasis added).

You can feel the movement of worship through the book of Revelation building until there is a massive crescendo of worship to the Lord.

THE CONTRAST OF WORSHIP IN HEAVEN

My final observations from Revelation 4 and 5 have to do with the contrasting patterns of worship in heaven. The great Christian apologist C. S. Lewis wrote an allegory called *The Great Divorce*, in which he described a man who rode a bus to Paradise and found it more fully and powerfully real than anything he could have imagined. Everything was alive, bursting with color, and expressed in complete reality. But hell, he discovered, was nothing more than a fleck of dust in comparison. It was concerned only with tiny things. In the same way, Lewis suggested, our lives in this world become smaller and smaller in light of the grandness of eternity.

As John looked at heaven through the mysterious open door in Revelation 4:1, everything he saw was grand in scale and gigantic in proportion. The problems around him on earth took on a different hue. For him and for us, getting a glimpse of heaven is like standing on the edge of the Grand Canyon or at the top of the Rocky Mountains and being speechless at the sight. It's being filled with wonder. We suddenly see that God is much bigger than we had thought and His plans for us are grander than we had expected.

John was allowed to experience two realities in one moment. On one hand, he was isolated on Patmos, separated from friends, and worried about the persecution of the church by the Roman emperor, Domitian. Yet in a moment of time he was ushered out of that reality, through the open door into heaven, where he saw the Lord seated on the throne with all the assembled host bowing down and ringing out praises that made the very air vibrate with energy. God gave this experience to John to encourage his heart. Worship took him from the loneliness of his discouragement, right into the control room of the universe to see God's purpose and plan for everything that would happen in the future.

How do we do this? How do we make John's experience more of our own? Here are four takeaway principles.

WORSHIP IS NOT ABOUT US—IT'S ABOUT HIM

First, worship is not about us; it's about Him. Do you really believe that? Perhaps we say, "Yes, I do believe that." But what, then, happens when the worship leader announces a hymn that's new to you or a song you don't like? What happens when some element of Sunday's worship service isn't exactly to your preference? I want to tell you humbly and sincerely that if we focus more on the Object of our worship, we'll be less agitated by the style of worship.

One of the reasons we get bent out of shape with our so-called "worship wars" is because we forget that worship is not about us; it's about Him. Worship is to be offered up to the Lord from our hearts, knowing that the Object of our worship is sitting on the throne seen through the doorway into heaven.

WORSHIP IS NOT ABOUT HERE— IT'S ABOUT THERE

Second, worship is not about here; it's about there. One of the main purposes of worship is to get our minds off the things of this earth and onto the things in heaven. Only as we're able to do that can we function with integrity. If you walk through your life focused on the here and now, forgetting about the eternal realities of God, you'll be discouraged every single day. But if you see heaven, your life down here will begin to make sense because you'll have the correct perspective.

In another place in his writings, the apostle John wrote, "Do not love the world or the things in the world. If anyone loves the world, the love of the Father is not in him. For all that is in the world—the lust of the flesh, the lust of the eyes, and the pride of life—is not of the Father but is of the world. And the world is passing away, and the lust of it; but he who does the will of God abides forever" (1 John 2:15–17).

WORSHIP IS NOT ABOUT NOW— IT'S ABOUT THEN

Third, worship is not about now; it's about then. The Bible says:

Therefore we do not lose heart. Even though our outward man is perishing, yet the inward man is being renewed day by day. For our light affliction, which is but for a moment, is working for us a far more exceeding and eternal weight of glory, while we do not look at the things which are seen, but at the things which are not seen. For the things which are seen are temporary, but the things which are not seen are eternal. (2 Cor. 4:16–18)

In this passage, Paul challenged the Corinthian believers to leverage everything that was going on in their lives against the promise of the future. Notice how he contrasted things.

- The outward man is perishing; the inward man is being renewed daily.
- The light affliction is today's problems; the eternal glory is tomorrow's promise.
- The things that are seen are temporary; the things that are not seen are eternal.

Worship is the corridor through which we make the exchange of heaven. It is the avenue that leads us from the emptiness of this world to the fullness of the next world. It is the street that leads from decay and discouragement to renewal and glory. When we fail to worship, therefore, we confine ourselves to the despair of this life.

That's why we shouldn't take worship casually, either in our churches or in our personal lives. That's why we shouldn't come into a church service tardy and disrespectful and distracted. We were created to worship our Creator, and it's our highest human pursuit. As Dr. A. W. Tozer said, "I am of the opinion that we should not be concerned about working for God until we have learned the meaning and the delight of worshipping Him."[4]

WORSHIP IS NOT ABOUT ONE—IT'S ABOUT MANY

Finally, worship is not about one; it's about many. In an age when people are dropping out of church and shunning weekend worship services, we're in danger of becoming individualistic worshipers. People sometimes tell me, "I don't have to come to church to worship. I can walk along the beach, or hike in the mountains," or—some have told me this—"I worship on the golf course."

The worship John saw in heaven was united, corporate worship. In fact, in the entire book of Revelation, the only time there is any independent worship is when John periodically fell down and worshiped God in light of the incredible visions he received. All the other worship in Revelation involves vast groups whose hearts are bound together in praise, such as:

- "Then I looked, and I heard the voice of many angels around the throne, the living creatures, and the elders; and the number of them was ten thousand times ten thousand, and thousands of thousands, saying with a loud voice: 'Worthy is the Lamb who was slain to receive power and riches and wisdom, and strength and honor and glory and blessing!'" (5:11–12).
- "And I heard a voice from heaven, like the voice of many waters, and like the voice of loud thunder. And I heard the sound of harpists playing their harps. They sang as it were a new song before the throne, before the four living creatures, and the elders; and no one could learn that song except the hundred and forty-four thousand who were redeemed from the earth" (14:2–3).
- "And I heard, as it were, the voice of a great multitude, as the sound of many waters and as the sound of mighty thunderings, saying, 'Alleluia! For the Lord God Omnipotent reigns!'" (19:6)

Get the picture? If choirs and orchestras can elevate us to such heights of enjoyment here on this earth, what will it be like when we hear the celestial choirs, accompanied by heaven-trained orchestras, lifting praise to almighty God around the throne?

Vernon M. Whaley wrote:

One day, worshipper, you and I will be a part of that great multitude, that *choir from all the nations*. No one really knows what kind of choir it will be—contemporary, classical, traditional, or gospel—but it won't matter. And even if you couldn't carry a tune on earth, or didn't have a lick of musical talent, it won't matter. You and I and all who love Christ will be *qualified* to join the eternal chorus, and together our voices will sound across the universe, in one unified statement: *"We love Jesus; He is worthy to be praised!"*[5]

So if that's where we are headed, we need to start rehearsing immediately, don't we? There's no guarantee how long we'll have to get ready. It's altogether possible that by the end of this day or by the end of this week, you or I will actually be part of the heavenly chorus. We need to sing praise to the Lord today, so if the Lord takes us while we're preaching a sermon—or listening to one—about heaven, we'll simply resume doing in heaven what we enjoy doing on earth—worshiping God.

PART 4

TRIBULATION SIGNS

In this section, we arrive at the climax of the story—the time known as the Tribulation. It's here that we'll discover some of the most inspiring, as well as infamous, characters in all of Scripture.

The Tribulation is a future seven-year period during which unspeakable horrors will be unleashed upon this world by Satan, the Antichrist, and the False Prophet. But in the midst of the calamity, as martyrs die for the name of Christ, heroes such as the Two Witnesses and the 144,000 will shine like stars in a world of darkness. Everything will culminate in the Battle of Armageddon—earth's final great battle—when the rebellious nations of the earth are defeated.

In the following chapters, we will walk together to gain a deeper understanding of nine important Tribulation signs described in God's Word.

CHAPTER 18

FOUR RIDERS

In October of 2018, police officer Peter Casuccio received a call about two boys walking around a neighborhood and displaying a gun. Arriving on the scene, Officer Casuccio found two young boys who matched the description he'd been given. One of the boys had what appeared to be a gun stuck inside the waistband of his pants.

Drawing his weapon, the officer commanded both boys to stop. They did stop, but the boy carrying the gun panicked and began to remove it from his pants. Officer Casuccio later learned this boy was only eleven years old. His friend was thirteen.

Thankfully, the policeman did not fire. Instead, he watched the boy drop the gun to the ground. Moving in for a closer look, he recognized the weapon as a realistic-looking BB gun. A toy.

That was not the end of the encounter, however. Bodycam footage shows Officer Casuccio spending several minutes talking with the boys about the dangers of their decisions on that day. "You can't do that, dude, in today's world," he told the boy carrying the gun. "Listen, that thing looks real."

Both boys apologized, but Officer Casuccio was not finished. "Do I honestly look like the type of dude that wants to shoot anybody?" he asked.

Both boys replied, "No, sir."

"But do I look like the type of dude that *would* shoot somebody?"

Both boys replied, "Yes, sir."

Then Officer Casuccio addressed the young man who had been carrying the gun. "I could've killed you," he said. His voice was stern. Even angry. "I want you to think about that tonight when you go to bed. You could be gone. Everything you want to do in this life could've been over."[1]

It's possible that people may read that story and feel Officer Casuccio went too far in speaking that way. *There's no need to rub it in*, such people might think. *He didn't have to be angry*. But I'm thankful for that police officer's anger. I'm thankful he took the time to tell the truth, even though the truth was harsh—because it showed how much he cared.

In a similar way, there are many people who don't understand the judgment of God. Nor the righteous anger of God. Such people rightly believe that God is love, but they can't comprehend how a loving God could punish people for their sin—how a loving God could be filled with both wrath and compassion at the same time.

As God's representatives in this world, it's important for us to know the truth. One theologian puts it this way:

> Take away the notion of judgment and you rob Christianity of any hope of satisfying our longing for justice, a longing built into us from our just and wise God. The judgmentless gospel fails to deal with the problem of evil and the detrimental way that we humans treat each other. . . .
>
> What the judgmentless gospel leaves us with is a one-dimensional God—a sappy, sanitized deity that we can easily manage. He nods and winks at our behavior, much like a kind elderly man who is not seriously invested in our lives. But the evil of our world is much too serious for us to view God as a pandering papa.[2]

PROPHECIES OF JUDGMENT

There are many prophecies in the Bible that reveal a future judgment against this world and the people in it. As described above, those prophecies often feel harsh and cruel. *Why did God describe such horrible atrocities in the book of Revelation?* some wonder. *Why should we read these terrible descriptions of the Tribulation?*

The truth is that, although many biblical prophecies predict disasters, their underlying purpose is merciful and benevolent. God gives us prophecies, even the dark ones, for our own benefit. These prophecies serve as warnings, alerting us to traumatic events coming in the future that we can either prepare for or avoid by following God's directives and depending on His providence. Noah escaped the doom of the prophesied Flood by building the ark (Gen. 6:13–22). Pharaoh in Egypt avoided the disaster that the prophesied seven-year famine could have brought on his nation by appointing Joseph to accumulate massive stores of food during the preceding years of plenty (Gen. 41). The citizens of the pagan city of Nineveh avoided its prophesied destruction by heeding Jonah's warning and repenting of their evil (Jonah 3).

The prophecies remaining to be fulfilled in the future are given to us for the same purpose. By revealing the disasters yet to come, God gives us warnings that we can heed, enabling us to avoid these approaching horrors. By turning to Him, we can be assured that His hand will remove us from the earth before these disasters arrive.

One of the most persistent prophecies of catastrophe yet to come concerns the Tribulation, which is introduced to us in Revelation 6. Indeed, the reality of the Tribulation and God's wrath and judgment against those who have rebelled against Him are the primary themes of Revelation 6–19. As we read those chapters, we encounter Jesus Christ poised to take back control of the earth. As the worthy Lamb, He comes to the throne and takes the scroll, which is the title deed to the earth.

As each of the seals of the scroll is broken, the scroll is unrolled to reveal multiple phases of God's wrath to be poured upon this wicked earth. By the time the seventh seal is broken, all the accumulated horrors of the entire Tribulation period have been unleashed. In the seventh seal we see the release of the seven trumpet judgments, and in the seventh trumpet judgment we see the unfolding of the seven bowl judgments. Each seal, each trumpet, and each bowl inflicts one terrible disaster after another with unrelenting regularity and intensity.

There in the sixth chapter of Revelation, the first four seals are broken to reveal the events that will initiate the seven years of trouble upon the earth—the seven years which we know as the Tribulation. As the four seals are opened, one of the four living creatures summons a rider on a horse to go forth upon the earth. Horses represent God's activity on earth and the forces He uses to accomplish His divine purposes.

It is very probable that the imagery of the horses in the first four seals is connected to the vision of Zechariah. This Old Testament prophet saw chariots drawn by red horses, black horses, white horses, and dappled horses. An angel explained to him that these were the "four spirits of heaven, who go out from their station before the Lord of all the earth" (Zech. 6:5).

RIDER ON A WHITE HORSE

"I looked, and behold, a white horse. He who sat on it had a bow; and a crown was given to him, and he went out conquering and to conquer" (Rev. 6:2).

When Rome's generals returned from war victorious, they would parade down the main thoroughfare on horses—conquerors making a grand entrance while receiving the accolades of the admiring citizens. Here also in Revelation we have a picture of a war hero who mounts a white horse. The rider is none other than the Antichrist, the coming world dictator, who rides into the world at the beginning of the Tribulation period promising to bring peace in the midst of global turmoil.

The world after the Rapture will be looking for a man on a white horse who will convince everyone that he is a man of peace. The image in Revelation 6:2 supports this peace-bringing interpretation. The crown the rider wears is one of victory, but his bow has no arrows. It is the picture of a bloodless victory gained through peaceful negotiations. In the midst of nations threatening each other with nuclear war and terrorists becoming ever more sophisticated with their weapons, the final dictator, promising peace and prosperity, will be welcomed as the savior and hope of the world. His eloquence and promises will mesmerize the masses. Armies and governments will be united under his leadership. The people of the earth will sigh in relief.

In fact, the Antichrist will actually bring peace to the Middle East. With Israel surrounded by enemies, the person who can finally resolve these endless and previously unsolvable conflicts plaguing Israel and its Islamic neighbors will be lauded as the greatest diplomat of all time. Daniel predicted this man's arrival when he said there is a "prince who is to come," who will make a covenant with Israel to protect her from her enemies (Dan. 9:26–27). He will have the support of all the nations of the earth.

But unlike the stereotypical riders of white horses we see in old western movies, this man will not be a hero. He will be a wolf in sheep's clothing with no intention of keeping his promises, bringing peace, or continuing his protection of Israel. He will, in fact, be by far the worst tyrant ever to appear on the face of the earth.

RIDER ON A RED HORSE

"Another horse, fiery red, went out. And it was granted to the one who sat on it to take peace from the earth, and that people should kill one another; and there was given to him a great sword" (Rev. 6:4).

When Jesus removes the second seal, the angel summons the second horse. This blood-red beast is ridden by a being who carries a *machaira*, the assassin's sword.

The rider on the red horse represents not only nation rising against nation and kingdom against kingdom, but also man fighting against man. He will usher in a time of murders, assassinations, bloodshed, and revolution that will far exceed even the worst we see today or have seen throughout history.

The First World War ended in 1918. The total military and civilian deaths attributed to that war are estimated at thirty-seven million. The Second World War ended in 1945. While statistics vary, estimates consistently report that between fifty and eighty million deaths resulted from that war. Since then, wars have followed one after another at a seemingly accelerated pace. Wars have claimed the lives of at least fifty million people during the past sixty-five years. In terms of war deaths alone, the last one hundred years have been bloodier than all the preceding five hundred.

The new technology employed in the manufacture of today's weapons makes them ever more destructive. It is tragic that the ability of people to settle their differences peacefully has not made the same progress as weaponry. Imagine the levels of conflict civilization will endure and volume of blood that will be spilled during the Tribulation when the Rapture will have removed all godly influence from the world!

When the second seal is opened, this is the message:

> You will hear of wars and rumors of wars. See that you are not troubled; for all these things must come to pass, but the end is not yet. For nation will rise against nation, and kingdom against kingdom. And there will be famines, pestilences, and earthquakes in various places. All these are the beginning of sorrows. . . .
>
> For then there will be great tribulation, such as has not been since the beginning of the world until this time, no, nor ever shall be. And unless those days were shortened, no flesh would be saved; but for the elect's sake those days will be shortened. (Matt. 24:6–8, 21–22)

We may wonder how those days can be shortened and even how it will be possible to survive such horror. As we explore the subsequent signs addressed in this book, we will discover the answers to these questions—questions that often go unasked for fear that the truth will be misunderstood, perceived as overly depressing, or seen as the cries of an alarmist.

Despite these possible criticisms and misunderstandings, the truth needs to be told and the alarm needs to be sounded. We must alert people to this dark shadow that looms on the horizon. Only when we are warned can we prepare.

RIDER ON A BLACK HORSE

My guess is that most of you who are reading this book have never been hungry—I mean *really* hungry. I'm not talking about the feeling you get when it's time to eat your regular meal or even the noise your stomach makes when you miss a meal. What I mean by hungry is that gnawing, clawing, painful sensation every minute of your day, a sensation which is consistently felt by many living in the poverty-stricken areas of the world. If you are like me, you might take food for granted. In America we throw enough food in our garbage cans every day to feed a family of six for a day in many countries. Our dogs and cats have a diet higher in protein than most people in the rest of the world.

In our "me-first," pleasure-seeking culture, many choose to turn a blind eye to the acute global shortage of food. Here is the grim reality: About 124 million people in fifty-one countries face a crisis every day when it comes to having enough to eat. Urgent humanitarian action is needed to save lives and reduce hunger and malnutrition. This crisis is largely due to conflict or instability in the countries affected. But as global population increases and the inevitable food shortages result, the world may lose its ability to feed itself.[3]

And this leads us to the breaking of the third seal:

When He opened the third seal, I heard the third living creature say, "Come and see." So I looked, and behold, a black horse, and he who sat on it had a pair of scales in his hand. And I heard a voice in the midst of the four living creatures saying, "A quart of wheat for a denarius, and three quarts of barley for a denarius; and do not harm the oil and the wine." (Rev. 6:5–6)

In John's time, a quart of wheat was the amount of food one person needed to survive each day. In the early days of the Tribulation period, this amount of food will sell for the equivalent of one day's wages. Or, to put it more succinctly, the price of groceries will rise so high that a person will have to work all day to buy enough food to feed one person just one meal. Widespread starvation will be inevitable.

Even today, the shadow of worldwide famine looms over the earth. The UN Department of Economic and Social Affairs says the world population is expected to reach 8.6 billion in 2030, 9.8 billion in 2050, and 11.2 billion in 2100. With the global population growing by 83 million people every year, the upward trend in population size is expected to continue.[4] If a worldwide famine does not occur before the Rapture, the "rider on the black horse" assures us that there will be one of disastrous proportions during the Tribulation.

RIDER ON A PALE HORSE

As the world experiences the devastation of the first three horsemen, John reveals the fourth rider:

When He opened the fourth seal, I heard the voice of the fourth living creature saying, "Come and see." So I looked, and behold, a pale horse. And the name of him who sat on it was Death, and Hades followed with him. And power was given to them over a fourth of the earth, to kill with sword, with hunger, with death, and by the beasts of the earth. (Rev. 6:7–8)

John now sees two persons riding out toward the earth: Death is mounted on a pale horse, and Hades is following closely behind. They have enormous power by which they will kill a fourth of the population of the earth. The Greek word used here to describe the color of Death's horse means "ashen" or "pale." It further describes the yellowish green of decomposition—the pallor of the face of a corpse in the state of advanced decay.

In his book *Insights on Revelation*, Charles Swindoll describes the carnage of the rider on the pale horse this way:

> In this terrifying scene John saw the grim reaper and the grave digger moving together across the face of the earth. "Death" slays the body while "Hades" swallows up the soul. These two figures symbolize the massive number of deaths that will follow in the wake of the first three horsemen. One-quarter of the world's population will be lost in their rampage![5]

God's judgments during the Tribulation are described as the "sword, and the famine, and the noisome beast, and the pestilence" (Ezek. 14:21 KJV). History has demonstrated a close association between these four terrible forces, but pestilence should probably be our biggest concern today.

It is tempting to believe that modern science has eliminated the fear of plague, but today we may be on the verge of the worst plagues the world has ever known. Notice I have written *plagues*, plural. It is quite possible that several deadly scourges could kill more people than have died in all the pestilences yet known to man. I am referring to plagues of bacteria that are fast becoming resistant to almost every drug and antibiotic. Even now they are called the "nightmare bacteria," and they presently stalk hospitals all over the world.

The Centers for Disease Control and Prevention recently detected more than 220 cases of illnesses caused by a rare breed of bacteria that are, as one report describes, "virtually untreatable and capable of spreading genes that make them impervious to most antibiotics. . . . Although the CDC has warned of the danger of antibiotic-resistant bacteria for years, the new report helps illustrate the scope of the problem." Research is running at top speed to curb antibiotic resistance, but some bacteria have already outpaced new treatments. These new germs contain special genes that allow them to pass their resistance to other germs, spreading disease to "apparently healthy people in the hospital—such as patients, doctors or nurses—who in turn can act as silent carriers of illness, infecting others even if they don't become sick."[6]

In addition to these "super germs," drug resistance in general has been growing, mainly because of the widespread use of antimicrobials and antibiotics in humans and animals. When antibiotics and antimicrobials kill off weak strains, stronger strains of resistant bacteria survive and keep growing. Calls for new antibiotic therapies have been issued, but new drug development is becoming rarer. Estimates are that 700,000 to several million deaths result each year from these bacteria. And each year in the United States, at least two million people become infected with bacteria that are resistant to antibiotics, causing at least 23,000 people to die as a result.[7]

Satan and the Antichrist would like nothing better than to have a worldwide plague under way at the beginning of the Tribulation to further their argument for a one-world government led by a seemingly benevolent, peace-loving dictator.

THE MOST IMPORTANT QUESTION

There are many more questions that can be asked and answered about the Tribulation—and certainly a large number of questions that cannot currently be answered, yet will be answered when the time comes.

However, the most important question on this subject applies not to the Tribulation itself, but to you. And to me. That question is simply, "How will we respond to the reality of the Tribulation?" Because, make no mistake, the Tribulation is real. It is coming. We can depend on that fact because we can depend on the truth of God's prophetic Word. So, what will we do about it?

Here are three responses I encourage you to consider, not only now but also as you read through the chapters that follow.

THE RESPONSE OF PRAISE

As a Christian, I have mixed emotions whenever I think through these trials to come, and I cannot read about these four horsemen without sensing that duality in my own heart. Having been forgiven of my sin through the salvation offered by Jesus Christ and believing what Scripture teaches about the Rapture, I'm grateful that I will never see those evil riders nor experience the terrible tragedy they will bring upon this world—I'll be worshiping the Lamb around God's throne. Even so, I feel a deep sense of grief and mourning for those who will suffer during those days.

THE RESPONSE OF PASSION

In Matthew 24:32–35, Jesus concludes His lesson on the future Tribulation by telling a story about a fig tree:

> Now learn this parable from the fig tree: When its branch has already become tender and puts forth leaves, you know that summer is near. . . . Assuredly, I say to you, this generation will by no means pass away till all these things take place. Heaven and earth will pass away, but My words will by no means pass away.

This parable points out that when leaves come out on a tree, we know summer is near. In the same way, future events cast their shadows before them.

Even though Jesus was talking here about His return, the lesson applies to all of prophecy. We will know Christ's return is not far off. Nevertheless, Jesus warned that we will only know the approximate time of His return— that is, we will know it is close. He said in verse 36: "But of that day and hour no one knows, not even the angels of heaven, but My Father only." We can only see the signs that show us the time is near.

I believe that the beginning of the end is quickly approaching, but we have no idea how soon it will arrive. The best course of action is stated in the apostle Paul's admonition in Romans 13:11: "And do this, knowing the time, that now it is high time to awake out of sleep; for now our salvation is nearer than when we first believed." If we live as if Christ will come tomorrow, we will always strive to be prepared for it.

THE RESPONSE OF PERSONAL EVALUATION

The writer of Hebrews said it this way: "How shall we escape if we neglect so great a salvation, which at the first began to be spoken by the Lord, and was confirmed to us by those who heard Him" (Heb. 2:3).

One of the reasons God gives us these prophecies, dire and foreboding as they are, is to warn us of what is coming so we can prepare in advance to avoid the terrible times that loom in the world's future. Pastor Steven Cole tells the story of one man who heeded the warning before it was too late.

Joe, by his own admission, was not a religious man. He drank too much, gambled, swore like a sailor, and lied and cheated to get what he wanted. God had no place in his thoughts or his life. When Joe finally retired, he relished the prospect of spending his days on the lake fishing. But a persistent pain in his stomach drove him to the doctor. His greatest fear was that he would be forced to stop drinking, but the doctor's report was even worse: It was cancer, and it had spread beyond control. The doctor gave Joe less than six months to live.

While Joe was in the hospital, a pastor dropped by and talked with him about eternity. Joe had heard religious talk of this sort many times before, but he had always blown it off and continued in his decadent ways. But now, for the first time in his life, Joe listened. A long-suppressed truth awoke in his heart, convicting him of squandering his entire life in utterly selfish pursuits. He trembled, knowing he would soon face God's judgment. But the pastor explained how Christ had paid the penalty for Joe's sin, and on that basis, He offered forgiveness and eternal life if Joe would only receive it. Joe gladly accepted the gift and died in peace shortly afterward.[8]

Joe's case is what we commonly call "deathbed repentance." It is neither the most noble nor the safest way to come to Christ. But God, in His infinite love and desire to have us with Him throughout eternity, accepts even those who come in at the last minute. Jesus promised salvation even to the thief who was dying on the cross next to Him (Luke 23:39–43). In His parable of the workers in the vineyard, the master paid the workers who had come in at the last hour of the day the same wage as those who came in at the first hour (Matt. 20:1–16). Our God gives us better than we deserve. He is a merciful God who is "longsuffering toward us, not willing that any should perish but that all should come to repentance" (2 Pet. 3:9). But He never forces us to come to Him; the choice is always ours.

The important thing to note is that Joe came to Christ because he heeded the warnings. He saw the signs that his end was near and took appropriate action. Deathbed repentance though it was, he did the wise thing: he acted on what he knew and took the right step in the face of it. It was late, but not too late.

Through prophecy, God has made the darkness of the world's approaching doom clear to us. The time is coming and now looms on the horizon when it will be too late. When the Tribulation arrives and God's people are taken into heaven, the door will close on those who have heard and rejected the gospel.

I urge you today to take the step Joe took—take it while the Tribulation is still just an approaching shadow and not the dooming finality of God's wrath. God's grace is available to rescue you from that wrath, so there is no need to despair. But there is a sense of urgency to His offer. Act now, and you need have no concern about being caught in the Tribulation.

CHAPTER 19

ANTICHRIST

In the late 1930s and early 1940s, when Adolf Hitler was moving through Europe and swallowing up whole nations, many believed that he was the coming Antichrist.

> Hitler offered himself as a messiah with a divine mission to save Germany. On one occasion he displayed the whip he often carried to demonstrate that "in driving out the Jews I remind myself of Jesus in the temple." He declared, "Just like Christ, I have a duty to my own people." He even boasted that just as Christ's birth had changed the calendar, so his victory over the Jews would be the beginning of a new age. "What Christ began," he said, "I will complete." . . .
>
> At one of the Nuremberg rallies, a giant photo of Hitler carried was captioned with the words, "In the beginning was the Word."[1]

It is not surprising that Bible students thought Hitler was the end-times, Satan-inspired world leader the Bible speaks of as "the Antichrist."

"Little children, it is the last hour; and as you have heard that the Antichrist is coming, even now many antichrists have come, by which we know that it is the last hour" (1 John 2:18).

There are over one hundred passages of Scripture that describe the Antichrist, and yet the word *antichrist* itself is mentioned in only four verses in the New Testament—each time by the apostle John (1 John 2:18, 22; 4:3; 2 John v. 7). As the word suggests, the Antichrist is a person who is against Christ. The prefix *anti* can also mean "instead of," and both meanings will apply to this coming world leader. He will overtly oppose Christ and at the same time pass himself off as Christ.

The Antichrist will aggressively live up to his terrible name. He will be Satan's superman, who persecutes, tortures, and kills the people of God, making Hitler, Stalin, and Mao seem weak and tame by comparison.

More than twenty-five different titles are given to the Antichrist, all of which help paint a picture of the most despicable man who will ever walk the earth. Some people think he is Satan incarnate. We know for certain that Satan gives him his power, his throne, and his authority.

Here are some of the Antichrist's aliases:

- a "fierce" king (Dan. 8:23)
- "a master of intrigue" (Dan. 8:23 NIV)
- "the prince who is to come" (Dan. 9:26)
- "a despicable man" (Dan. 11:21 NLT)
- a "worthless shepherd" (Zech. 11:16–17 NLT)
- "the one who brings destruction" (2 Thess. 2:3 NLT)
- "the lawless one" (2 Thess. 2:8)
- the "beast" (Rev. 13:1)

As a study of these references shows, the Antichrist is introduced and described in great detail in the Bible, yet his identity is not revealed. That lack of specific identification, however, has not stopped speculation on who he might be. When you google "Who is Antichrist?" you get about 15 million hits. Some of the websites post incredibly long and detailed articles—a sign of the extreme fascination generated by this sensational subject.

THE PERSONALITY OF THE COMING WORLD RULER

No, the Bible does not tell us who the Antichrist will be. In fact, Paul tells us in the second chapter of Thessalonians that this coming world ruler will not be revealed until after the Rapture of the church. "So if you ever reach the point where you think you know who he is, that must mean you have been left behind."[2]

Although the Bible does not tell us *who* he will be, it does tell us *what* he will be. Here is how he is described in the Bible.

HE WILL BE A CHARISMATIC LEADER

The prophet Daniel described the Antichrist in these graphic terms: "After this I saw in the night visions, and behold, a fourth beast. . . . And there . . . were eyes like the eyes of a man, and a mouth speaking pompous words. . . . He shall speak pompous words against the Most High" (Dan. 7:7–8, 25).

In these passages Daniel gives us one of the characteristics of the coming world ruler—his charismatic personality enhanced by his speaking ability, which he will use to sway the masses with spellbinding words of power and promise. We little realize the power of good speaking ability. An actor who is not classically handsome can land great parts and charm audiences simply by the power of his resonant and articulate voice. Often Americans are swayed by political candidates who have little to offer, but they offer it in the beautiful package of their smooth intonation and syntax. The coming world leader will be renowned for this kind of eloquence, which will capture the attention and admiration of the world.

Daniel goes on to tell us that this golden-tongued orator not only will speak in high-blown terms but also will utter pompous words against God. The apostle John described him in a similar fashion in the book of Revelation: "He was given a mouth speaking great things and blasphemies" (13:5).

Considering these and other prophecies, it's not hard to understand why Hitler has often been pegged as the prototype of the Antichrist. Hitler was a man of charisma, great oratory, and pomp. In his now classic book, *Kingdoms in Conflict*, Charles Colson described the well-orchestrated events that played out in countless crowded halls as Hitler manipulated the German people:

> Solemn symphonic music began the set-up. The music then stopped, a hush prevailed, and a patriotic anthem began and "from the back, walking slowly down the wide central aisle," strutted Hitler. Finally, the Fuhrer himself rises to speak. Beginning in a low, velvet voice, which makes the audience unconsciously lean forward to hear, he speaks his love for Germany . . . and gradually his pitch increases until he reaches a screaming crescendo. But his audience does not think his rasping shouts excessive. They are screaming with him.[3]

Daniel continued his description of the Antichrist by telling us he is a man "whose appearance was greater than his fellows" (Dan. 7:20). In terms of his outward appearance, this man will be a strikingly attractive person. The combination of magnetic personality, speaking ability, and extreme good looks will make him virtually irresistible to the masses. When he comes on the scene, people will flock to him like flies to honey, and they will fall over themselves to do anything he asks.

HE WILL BE A CUNNING LEADER

In the famous dream recorded in the seventh chapter of his book, Daniel was given a picture of this world leader. Here is what he reported: "I was considering the horns, and there was another horn, a little one, coming up among them, before whom three of the first horns were plucked out by the roots" (7:8).

If we read carefully and understand the prophetic symbol of the horns, we learn from this verse that the coming world leader subdues three other kings by plucking them out by their roots. This man will squeeze out the old to make room for the new. He will take over three kingdoms, one by one, not by making war but by clever political manipulation. He begins as the little horn, but then he succeeds in uprooting three of the first horns and thus appropriates their power for himself. Daniel reiterated this event in the eleventh chapter of his prophecy, telling us that this future world leader "shall come in peaceably, and seize the kingdom by intrigue" (11:21). The Antichrist will be a political genius, a masterful diplomat, and a clever leader. Arthur W. Pink wrote of him:

> Satan has had full opportunity afforded him to study fallen human nature . . . The Devil knows full well how to dazzle men by the attraction of power . . . He knows how to gratify the craving for knowledge . . . he can delight the ear with melodious music and the eye with entrancing beauty. . . . He knows how to exalt men to dizzy heights of worldly greatness and fame, and how to control that greatness when attained, so that it may be employed against God and his people.[4]

HE WILL BE A CRUEL LEADER

Once again we turn to the writings of Daniel to understand the personality of this coming tyrant.

> Thus he said: "The fourth beast shall be a fourth kingdom on earth, which shall be different from all other kingdoms, and shall devour the whole earth, trample it and break it in pieces. . . . He shall speak pompous words against the Most High, shall persecute the saints of the Most High, and shall intend to change times and law. Then the saints shall be given into his hand for a time and times and half a time." (Dan. 7:23, 25)

Here Daniel tells us that the Antichrist is going to devour the whole world; he will tread the world down. He will break it in pieces. These words hint at something utterly horrific. Many who become followers of Christ during the Tribulation will be martyred for their faith.

The word *persecute* in Daniel 7:25 literally means to "wear out." The same word is used to describe the wearing out of garments. The use of the word here indicates a slow, painful wearing down of the people of God—a torturous, cruel persecution reminiscent of the horrors Nero inflicted on Christians in ancient Rome, but even worse. It would be easier for the saints during the Tribulation if they were simply killed outright, but instead they will be "worn out"—mercilessly tortured by this unthinkably cruel man.

Again, we find a prototype of what is to come in the regime of Hitler. Charles Colson gives us a chilling description of what went on in Nazi concentration camps:

> The first Nazi concentration camp opened in 1933. In one camp, hundreds of Jewish prisoners survived in disease-infested barracks on little food and gruesome, backbreaking work. Each day the prisoners were marched to the compound's giant factory, where tons of human waste and garbage were distilled into alcohol to be used as a fuel additive. Even worse than the nauseating smell was the realization that they were fueling the Nazi war machine.[5]

Colson goes on to say that as the result of the humiliation and drudgery of their lives, "dozens of the prisoners went mad and ran from their work, only to be shot by the guards or electrocuted by the fence."[6]

Hitler and the Nazis did not annihilate the Jews all at once; they deliberately and systematically wore down their souls. And that gives us a picture of what will happen in the Tribulation when the Antichrist is in power. He will be a cruel, blood-shedding leader, taking out his wrath on the saints who come to Christ under his regime.

THE PROFILE OF THE COMING WORLD RULER

In the twelfth chapter of Revelation we read of the dragon, or Satan, being thrown out of heaven in a great war. Then in the thirteenth chapter we discover that the dragon comes to earth to begin his program by embodying his agent, the Antichrist. When we link this chapter with verses from Daniel, we get a good profile of this leader by looking at how he comes to power from several different viewpoints. Each of these viewpoints—the political, the national, the spiritual, and the providential—give us a good picture of what he will be like. So let's briefly explore what the Bible tells us about how the Antichrist comes to power.

HE WILL BE POLITICALLY INCONSPICUOUS

Daniel 7 tells us that the Antichrist will not make a big splash when he arrives on the political scene. He will not enter with a fanfare, announcing, "I am here! I will now take over!" Instead, he will squeeze his way in, little by little, beginning as one among many minor political leaders. In prophetic imagery, he is the little horn who grows to be the big horn. He will attract little attention as he methodically begins to grasp more and more power.

John the apostle emphasized this fact when he wrote that this ominous personality will arise from among the mass of ordinary people. "Then I stood on the sand of the sea. And I saw a beast rising up out of the sea, having seven heads and ten horns, and on his horns ten crowns, and on his heads a blasphemous name" (Rev. 13:1). The sea in biblical imagery stands for the general mass of humanity or, more specifically, the Gentile nations. We find confirmation of that meaning for the sea in Revelation 17: "Then he said to me, 'The waters which you saw, where the harlot sits, are peoples, multitudes, nations, and tongues'" (v. 15).

What we learn in these passages is that at first the Antichrist will not be obvious. He will not burst onto the scene in all his power and glory, but rather he will rise out of the sea of common humanity or emerge inauspiciously from among ordinary people.

HE WILL EMERGE FROM A GENTILE NATION

From what nation will the coming world ruler emerge? Often we hear that he must come from the Jewish nation. Since he will make a covenant with the nation of Israel, many people reason that perhaps he will be the Jew that Israel anticipates as her messiah. But the Bible gives us no evidence for determining that the Antichrist is a Jew. In fact, we have strong evidence for believing the opposite. Dr. Thomas Ice weighed in on the ethnicity of the Antichrist:

> A widely held belief throughout the history of the church has been the notion that Antichrist will be of Jewish origin. This view is still somewhat popular in our own day. However, upon closer examination we find no real Scriptural basis for such a view. In fact, the Bible teaches just the opposite that the Antichrist will be of Gentile descent.[7]

HE WILL BE SPIRITUALLY BLASPHEMOUS

Daniel said of this world leader, "He shall speak *pompous* words against the Most High, shall persecute the saints of the Most High, and shall intend to change times and law" (Dan. 7:25, emphasis added). In his second letter to the Thessalonians, Paul described him as one "who opposes and exalts himself above all that is called God or that is worshiped, so that he sits as God in the temple of God, showing himself that he is God" (2 Thess. 2:4).

As Paul wrote in Romans 1, and as the history of ancient Israel warns us over and over, it is a terrible thing to worship a *creature* instead of the *Creator*. Yet as Daniel warned, this man will defy God and demand to be worshiped instead of Him. And his demand will be met. As John wrote, "All who dwell on the earth will worship him, whose names have not been written in the Book of Life of the Lamb slain from the foundation of the world" (Rev. 13:8).

As if declaring himself to be God gives him power over nature and human nature, this ruler will also attempt to change the moral and natural laws of the universe. That may sound farfetched, but it's been tried before.

In the early days of the French Revolution, the new leaders tried to get control of the masses by changing everything that grew out of Christianity or Christian tradition. They set up a new calendar by which years were numbered not from the birth of Christ but from the date of the revolution. They issued decrees to change all Christian churches to "temples of reason" and to melt down church bells for the metal. They actually tried to replace the seven-day week established by God with a ten-day week.[8] Such extreme actions showing hostility to everything related to God will characterize the coming world leader. No doubt he would even change the length of a year if he could somehow gain control of the earth's rotation!

While the Antichrist is pictured as "the beast rising up out of the *sea*," John wrote that the beast "that ascends out of the bottomless *pit*," the one who will again be remanded to the bottomless pit until the end of the Millennium, is none other than Satan himself (9:11; 11:7; 20:1–3, emphasis added). The Antichrist, with his seven heads, ten horns with their ten crowns, and his blasphemous mouth—whom all the world "marveled at and followed"—was given his power by Satan (13:1–4).

HE WILL BE LIMITED PROVIDENTIALLY

As both Daniel and John show us, the Antichrist is a terrifying person. He is the epitome of evil, the ultimate negation of everything good, the avowed enemy and despiser of God. Every follower of Christ ought to bow before God at this moment and give thanks that he or she will not be on this earth during the reign of the Antichrist. At the same time, we must not forget that this satanic creature is not equal to God. He does not have absolute power or anything close to it. God has him on a chain. In fact, in Revelation 13, we are reminded repeatedly that the Antichrist can only do what he is allowed to do.

Twice in this chapter, we find the little phrase, *and he was given.* "And he was given a mouth speaking great things and blasphemies, and he was given authority to continue for forty-two months" (v. 5). We also find in this chapter, "It was granted to him to make war with the saints and to overcome them. And authority was given him over every tribe, tongue, and nation" (v. 7). As in the story of Job, Satan (and his puppet, the Antichrist) will be able to do only that which God allows. The Antichrist will be able to create terrible havoc and chaos, but ultimately God is still God, and no enemy of His will go beyond the boundaries He sets.

HE WILL HAVE AN INTIMIDATING PRESENCE

The four major kingdoms depicted in Daniel's other prophetic vision were likened to certain animals: Babylon was like a lion, Medo-Persia was like a bear, Greece was like a leopard, and Rome was like the ten-horned beast (Dan. 7). In the descriptions of the Beast in Revelation, we have all of these characteristics combined into one horrific creature (Rev. 13:2). This likeness of the Antichrist to ferocious beasts is meant to show us the intimidating presence of this satanic creature. He combines in his person all of the threatening characteristics of the kingdoms that have gone before him.

Dr. W. A. Criswell wrote:

Think of the golden majesty of Babylon. Of the mighty ponderous massiveness of Cyrus the Persian. Think of the beauty and the elegance and the intellect of the ancient Greek world. Think of the Roman with his laws and his order and his idea of justice. All of these glories will be summed up in the majesty of this one eventual Antichrist who will be like Nebuchadnezzar, like Cyrus, like Tiglath Pileser, like Shalmanezer, like Julius Caesar, like Caesar Augustus, like Alexander the Great, like Napoleon Bonaparte, like Frederick the Great and Charlemagne, all bound up into one.[9]

It's no wonder people will follow this man and even fall down and worship him. We see in our own political campaigns how quickly people gravitate to charisma and power. Give us a fine-looking candidate with a golden voice, a powerful presence, and the ability to enthrall people with vague rhetoric about an undefined better future, and we follow like sheep as the media bleats the candidate's praises. Completely overlooked is the substance of the man's program. The presence and charisma of the Antichrist will be similar, making his rise to power inevitable.

THE PROGRAM OF THE COMING WORLD RULER

One of the first acts of this world leader will be to make peace with Israel. And he will keep this covenant during the first three and a half years of his rule. At that point, however, he will change his tactics. He will drop all pretensions of peace and adopt a program of crushing power. He will break his covenant with Israel and subject the Jews to great persecution (Dan. 9:27; Isa. 28:18).

Then will come the leader's most sensational moment. The Antichrist will actually be killed, but to the astonishment of all the world, he will be raised back to life by the power of Satan in a grotesque counterfeit of the resurrection of Jesus Christ (Rev. 13:3–4).

After his death and satanic resurrection, the Antichrist will assassinate the leaders of three countries, and all other nations will immediately relinquish their power to him. It is then that he will set himself up to be worshiped by all the people of the world. Through his associate, the False Prophet, the mark of the Beast will be placed upon all those who will follow him. Anyone who does not bear this mark will be unable to buy or sell in the world's economy.

In a final act of rebellion against God, this vile person will set himself up in Jerusalem and desecrate the rebuilt temple in what is called the "abomination of desolation." He will then attempt to annihilate every Jew on earth, thus sounding the first ominous note in the prelude to the Battle of Armageddon.

This despot of all despots will be ultimately destroyed when Jesus Christ comes to battle against the Antichrist and his armies. In that climactic war the Antichrist will be killed, and his forces will be destroyed. The victorious Christ will assume His throne as rightful King and Ruler of the universe.

More important than speculating about the identity of the Antichrist is remembering that his power broker, Satan, is not the equal opposite of almighty God. Only God knows the day, the hour, the millisecond that will usher in Satan's reign on earth as Christ raptures the church. Like us, Satan can only look for the signs and wait. Throughout the millennia of his waiting, it is likely that he has been reading scouting reports and evaluating some choice candidates, and maybe even issuing a few letters of intent so he will be ready when his hour does come.

Is the Antichrist lurking somewhere out there in the masses of humanity right now? Is his darkened mind already plotting the evils that he will inflict in the last days? I believe it is entirely possible, if not highly probable.

Gary Frazier gives us a possible scenario:

> Somewhere at this moment there may be a young man growing to maturity. He is in all likelihood a brooding, thoughtful young man. Inside his heart, however, there is a hellish rage. It boils like a cauldron of molten lead. He hates God. He despises Jesus Christ. He detests the Church. In his mind there is taking shape the form of a dream of conquest. He will disingenuously present himself as a friend of Christ and the Church. Yet . . . he will, once empowered, pour out hell itself onto this world. Can the world produce such a prodigy? Hitler was once a little boy. Stalin was a lad. Nero was a child. The tenderness of childhood will be shaped by the Devil into the terror of the *Antichrist*.[10]

I realize that the picture of the future I've presented in this chapter is not a pretty one. Yet Christians need to know what is going on in the world concerning this dreaded person.

Of much greater importance than to be looking for the Antichrist, is to be "looking for the blessed hope and glorious appearing of our great God and Savior Jesus Christ" (Titus 2:13).

Jesus told us what to do during this time of waiting. We are to keep our hearts from being unnecessarily troubled. If we believe in Him, He will one day take us to that home He has been preparing for us, and we will be with Him! There is only one way to have that assurance. Jesus said, "I am the way, the truth, and the life. No one comes to the Father except through Me" (John 14:6).

Giving your life to Christ is the only absolute and certain guarantee that when He comes, you will be saved from personally experiencing the evil of the Antichrist by that daring air rescue called the Rapture. You will be taken out of the world into His glorious presence, never to experience the horrors Daniel and John described in their prophecies.

Keep looking up!

CHAPTER 20

FALSE PROPHET

In the spring of 1993, Americans watched their TVs in shock as the standoff between the FBI and the Branch Davidians cult ended in the fiery conflagration of the cult's Waco compound. The Branch Davidians were led by David Koresh, who claimed prophetic powers that enabled him to crack the code of the seven seals in the book of Revelation. Koresh convinced his followers that he had been called to raise an "Army of God" and began stockpiling weapons in preparation for the Apocalypse. Allegations of sexual and physical abuse of women and children led to several investigations of the cult and, finally, to the deadly standoff that ended in the burning of the compound and the deaths of more than seventy cult members, including their children.[1]

The world has suffered no shortage of false prophets. Throughout history, many self-proclaimed prophets attracted masses of followers and led them either to disappointment or disaster when their predictions failed. In the early 1840s, many sold their homes and possessions in response to William Miller's prediction that Christ would return by 1844. In 1978, the world was shocked when cult leader Jim Jones led or coerced more than nine hundred of his followers to commit suicide.

The apostle John tells us clearly that the world has not seen the last of false prophets. One is yet to come whose massive deceptions will make those of men like Koresh, Miller, and Jones seem minor and localized. In this chapter we will learn what the Bible tells us of this False Prophet's emergence, his profile, his purpose, his power, his program, and finally, his punishment.

THE PROFILE OF THE FALSE PROPHET

John introduced the False Prophet with these words:

> Then I saw another beast coming up out of the earth, and he had two horns like a lamb and spoke like a dragon. (Rev. 13:11)

The images of the beast in this passage are metaphoric; as we soon learn, John is merely using them to describe the extremely evil nature of the man who will become known as the False Prophet (16:13; 19:20; 20:10). It is significant that John's imagery combines two animals with opposite natures—the meekness and gentleness of a lamb merged with the predatory, devouring malevolence of a dragon.

There is nothing random about this description. The False Prophet will come on the scene as a reasonable, humble, self-effacing person whose magnetic personality will easily attract a large following. He will be the epitome of the type of deceiver Jesus warned us against: "Beware of false prophets, who come to you in sheep's clothing, but inwardly they are ravenous wolves" (Matt. 7:15).

Bible expositor John Phillips explains how the False Prophet will manipulate and deceive masses of people:

> The dynamic appeal of the False Prophet will lie in his skill in combining political expediency with religious passion, self-interest with benevolent philanthropy, lofty sentiment with blatant sophistry, moral platitude with unbridled self-indulgence. His arguments will be subtle, convincing,

and appealing. His oratory will be hypnotic, for he will be able to move the masses to tears or whip them into a frenzy. . . . His deadly appeal will lie in the fact that what he says will sound so right, so sensible, so exactly what unregenerate men have always wanted to hear.[2]

This combination of widespread appeal and diabolical deception leaves no doubt as to the strong relationship that will exist between the False Prophet, the Antichrist, and Satan himself. By recruiting these two malevolent accomplices, Satan will be attempting to form a trinity of his own. In this unholy trinity, Satan himself counterfeits God the Father; the Antichrist counterfeits God the Son, and the False Prophet counterfeits God the Holy Spirit.

THE PURPOSE OF THE FALSE PROPHET

Just as the profile of the False Prophet counterfeits that of the Holy Spirit, so does his purpose, as the apostle John makes clear:

> He exercises all the authority of the first beast in his presence, and causes the earth and those who dwell in it to worship the first beast, whose deadly wound was healed. (Rev. 13:12)

Understanding how Satan's unholy trinity imitates the holy Trinity of God helps us discover the False Prophet's purpose. Matthew tells us that Christ received authority from the Father (Matt. 11:27). In a similar way, the Antichrist will receive authority from the dragon, who is Satan (Rev. 13:4). The primary purpose and objective of God's Holy Spirit is to glorify the Son (John 16:14). The False Prophet will imitate this purpose by leading people to worship the Antichrist (Rev. 13:12).

The False Prophet will come on the scene as a religious leader. At the outset, he will encourage worship in all non-Christian religions, knowing that increased participation in multiple religions will dilute the influence of Christianity. But behind this façade of benign religious tolerance will crouch a demonic purpose, which is to compel all the world's diverse religions to worship the Antichrist.

Because religion has become largely irrelevant in our highly secular society, it may seem odd that a religious leader would figure so prominently in the political turmoil of the Tribulation period. But history shows that this fits a consistent pattern. Politics and religion have always worked in tandem as the primary forces that control humanity. Politics compels compliance by authority, while religion draws compliance by attraction. When these two combine forces, their power becomes virtually absolute.

W. A. Criswell offers powerful examples of this phenomenon:

> I do not suppose that in the history of mankind, it has ever been possible to rule without religious approbation and devotion. . . . In the days of Pharaoh, when Moses and Aaron stood before the sovereign of Egypt, he called in Jannis and Jambres, the magicians, the religionists of his day, to oppose Jehovah. When Balak, the king of Moab, sought to destroy Israel, he hired the services of Baalim to curse Israel. . . . Ahab and Jezebel were able to do what they did in Israel, in the debauchery of the kingdom, because they were abetted and assisted by the prophets of Baal.[3]

Religion has always been a powerful force in influencing humanity. Therefore, Satan will use religion as one of his most effective tools to bring the world under the control of the Antichrist. The False Prophet will be Satan's agent in turning the world's worship toward the Antichrist.

THE POWER OF THE FALSE PROPHET

John tells us the False Prophet will exercise enormous power, but that power will be derivative:

He performs great signs . . . in the sight of men. And he deceives those who dwell on the earth by those signs which he was granted to do in the sight of the beast. (Rev. 13:13–14)

Here we see demonic power flowing downward through a vertical chain of command: the False Prophet receives his power from the Antichrist (the Beast), and the Antichrist receives his power from Satan (the dragon). Scripture amply documents this flow of power. John states five times in Revelation 13:2–8 that the Antichrist will derive his power from Satan. Then in verses 12–15 he states three times that the False Prophet will derive his power from the Antichrist: "He exercises all the authority of the first beast in his presence. . . . He deceives those who dwell on the earth by those signs which he was granted to do in the sight of the beast . . . He was granted power to give breath to the image of the beast."

These passages leave no ambiguity as to the source of the False Prophet's power. It is satanic, both in its source and its nature. Some believe that only God gives power to work miracles, and they, therefore, assume the False Prophet's signs and wonders to be mere tricks. But Jesus himself counters that assumption: "False christs and false prophets will rise and show great signs and wonders to deceive, if possible, even the elect" (Matt. 24:24).

Let's look briefly at three of the False Prophet's miracles, which show how his demonic power will be employed.

HE WILL CALL DOWN FIRE UPON THE EARTH

John writes, "[The false prophet] performs great signs, so that he even makes fire come down from heaven on the earth in the sight of men" (Rev. 13:13). This is yet another instance of demonic mimicry of the power of God, who has often used fire in executing His judgments. He destroyed Sodom and Gomorrah with a downpour of fire and brimstone (Gen. 19:24). He used fire to consume the priests Nadab and Abihu for flouting tabernacle rituals (Lev. 10:1–2). At the end of the Millennium, God will send fire from heaven to annihilate Satan's army (Rev. 20:7–9).

Scripture indicates, however, that there may be even more purpose to the False Prophet's use of fire than mere mimicry. He will proclaim himself to be the fulfillment of Malachi's prophecy: "Behold, I will send you Elijah the prophet before the coming of the great and dreadful day of the LORD" (Mal. 4:5).

The False Prophet's use of fire will evoke a strong connection between himself and the Old Testament prophet Elijah, who ministered to Israel in the days of the divided kingdom. In a spectacular confrontation with the priests of Baal, Elijah called for God to send down fire to ignite the sacrificial bull he had prepared on an altar atop Mount Carmel. The fire descended and consumed not only the sacrifice but also the altar itself and the water in the trench surrounding it (1 Kings 18:20–39). This was the Elijah prophesied by Malachi to be the forerunner announcing the imminent coming of Christ. The False Prophet will mimic Elijah's miracle of fire and claim to be the fulfillment of Malachi's prophecy. He will pose as the promised Elijah and act as the harbinger of the Antichrist.

Many will see the power of the False Prophet as a sign of his authenticity. But biblical scholar Craig Keener warns against accepting miracles alone as validation of an authentic prophet of God: "Signs by themselves can be positive or negative; what enables us to discern true prophets from false ones is . . . to evaluate them by their moral character. The point is that we know them by their message and their fruit, not by their gifts (Deut. 13:1–5; Matt. 7:15–23)."[4]

HE WILL COMMISSION AN IMAGE TO BE BUILT

The False Prophet's occult power will gain him an enormous following. When his influence and deception become pervasive, he will commission an enormous sculpture honoring the Antichrist to be set in the reconstructed Jewish temple. John describes the statue as "an image to the beast who was wounded by the sword and lived" (Rev. 13:14). This image is a prominent feature in the book of Revelation, mentioned ten times in seven chapters (13:14–15; 14:9, 11; 15:2; 16:2; 19:20; 20:4). The worship of the Antichrist will center on this idol until the end of the Tribulation period, marking the final stage of apostasy, which is idolatry—the hallmark of all false religions.

Nineteenth-century theologian J. A. Seiss noted the factors that will lead the world to worship the image of the Beast:

> [It is not] difficult to trace what sort of arguments will be brought to bear for the making of this image. In the ages of great worldly glory and dominion statues were raised to the honor of the great of every class, but who of all the great ones of the earth is so great as the Antichrist! Statues have ever been common for the commemoration of great events; but what greater event and marvel has ever occurred than that in the history of this man, in that he was wounded to death, and yet is restored to life and activity, with far sublimer qualities than he possessed in his first life? . . . And who will there be among the proud sons of earth to stand against such arguments?[5]

Jesus apparently referred to this image of the Antichrist in this passage of His Olivet discourse: "When you see the 'abomination of desolation,' spoken of by Daniel the prophet, standing in the holy place . . . then let those who are in Judea flee to the mountains. . . . For then there will be great tribulation, such as has not been since the beginning of the world until this time, no, nor ever shall be" (Matt. 24:15–16, 21).

The apostle Paul also referred to the image of the Beast and the apostasy that will accompany it: "Let no one deceive you by any means; for that Day will not come unless the falling away comes first, and the man of sin is revealed, the son of perdition, who opposes and exalts himself above all that is called God or that is worshiped, so that he sits as God in the temple of God, showing himself that he is God" (2 Thess. 2:3–4). When this desecration of the temple occurs, the False Prophet will have achieved his goal of making the worship of the Antichrist a worldwide phenomenon.

HE WILL CONJURE THE IMAGE
TO BREATHE AND SPEAK

When the image of the Antichrist is erected in the Jewish temple, the False Prophet will then "give breath to the image . . . that the image of the beast should . . . speak" (Rev. 13:15). Ventriloquism or sophisticated electronic voice reproduction will not be sufficient to account for this wonder. Henry Morris explains:

> This image is more than a mere robot with a computer voice. That would be no great marvel today, with all the accomplishments of automation and kinemetronics (or audio-animatronics). Millions of people have observed an image of Abraham Lincoln move and "speak" at Disneyland, but they were hardly moved to bow down in worship of his image.
>
> The image of the man of sin will speak intelligibly and his words will not be preprogrammed. He will issue commands, among them the command to slay all who do not worship him. Those who observe this remarkable phenomenon, whether in person at Jerusalem or on another side of the world by television, will be convinced the image is really speaking of its own volition.[6]

Dr. Morris asserts that the image speaks and breathes through the power of a real but demonic miracle: "The False Prophet is enabled (by his own master, Satan) to impart a spirit to the image, but that spirit is one of Satan's unclean spirits. . . . This is a striking case of demon possession, with the demon possessing the body of the image rather than that of a man or woman."[7]

No sleight of hand, no electronics, no scientific application will be involved in the speech of the image. It is accomplished solely through naked demonic power. It serves as a chilling example of the dark power that will dominate the world throughout the Tribulation period—a power exercised by the False Prophet that will confer credibility to the Antichrist and enable Satan to complete his insidious program of deception in the final days.

THE PROGRAM OF THE FALSE PROPHET

While this beast from the earth is first a religious leader, he will also direct the Antichrist's sweeping economic program. As John writes:

> He causes all, both small and great, rich and poor, free and slave, to receive a mark on their right hand or on their foreheads, and that no one may buy or sell except one who has the mark or the name of the beast, or the number of his name. (Rev. 13:16–17)

After securing worldwide worship of the Antichrist, the False Prophet will capitalize on this success with a hostile takeover of the world's economic system. No one will be allowed to participate in any financial transaction without a license, which will take the form of a mark placed either on one's hand or forehead. There will be no exemptions. Those who refuse the mark will be barred from all buying or selling.

This mark is yet another satanic imitation of God's activity. God will mark 144,000 Jewish evangelists with a seal on their foreheads to signify their sanctification for God's special purpose (7:3). The False Prophet will replicate this act by forcing the followers of the Antichrist to bear a demonic mark, thus sealing them as Satan's own people.

The counterfeit mark of Satan will differ greatly from the authentic seal of God. God's seal will protect His witnesses from harm, whereas Satan's mark will inflict untold misery on his followers. God's seal will be given only to a select few—the 144,000 Jewish witnesses. But everyone will be forced to bear the mark of the Antichrist or suffer extremely severe consequences. Mark Hitchcock explains the disastrous impact on those who refuse the mark: "No one will be able to shop at the mall, eat at a restaurant, fill up at gas stations, pay utility bills, buy groceries, get prescriptions filled, pay to get the lawn mowed, or pay the mortgage without the mark of the Beast. It's the Tribulation trademark."[8]

The United States saw a brief, benign example of similar economic control during World War II. Many products were scarce due to the massive manufacturing resources funneled into the war effort. Government-issued cards or food stamps were required to purchase rationed goods such as sugar, tires, and other rare staples. That brief practice foreshadows in a mild way the conditions that will dominate the Tribulation period. Store customers will be required to present their hands or foreheads to be scanned before purchases are approved.

THE PUNISHMENT OF THE FALSE PROPHET

Despite the immense demonic power and control wielded by the False Prophet, he will finally come to the horrible end prophesied by John:

> The beast was captured, and with him the false prophet who worked signs in his presence, by which he deceived those who received the mark of the beast and those who worshiped his image. These two were cast alive into the lake of fire burning with brimstone. (Rev. 19:20)

Being cast alive into the lake of fire seems a fitting end to this demonic mass deceiver. Though his power and influence will reach throughout the world, inflicting death and misery on countless millions, his days will be cut short. He will be caught in the relentless wheels of God's justice and spend eternity with his cohorts, Satan and the Antichrist, in the everlasting lake of fire.

What will happen to the millions he deceived? They too will be severely punished. Those who received the mark from the False Prophet will "drink of the wine of the wrath of God" and "shall be tormented with fire and brimstone in the presence of the holy angels and in the presence of the Lamb . . . forever and ever" (14:10–11).

Some may question the fairness of this judgment against those who accept the mark of the Beast. They will merely be doing what is necessary for survival. But when we look at their choice from an eternal perspective, we can see that it will bring about the opposite of survival. It may briefly extend their earthly lives, but at the end of the Antichrist's regime, they will be plunged into eternal death. Conversely, those who refuse the mark will face the prospect of immediate death, but they will awaken from that death into eternal life.

As John tells us:

> I saw thrones, and they sat on them, and judgment was committed to them. Then I saw the souls of those who had been beheaded for their witness to Jesus and for the word of God, who had not worshiped the beast or his image, and had not received his mark on their foreheads or on their hands. And they lived and reigned with Christ for a thousand years. (20:4)

In this fallen world, Christians are not called to a life where all choices lead to comfort or safety. We are called to a life of commitment to the One who loves us enough to die for us. The Bible often tells us this commitment will mean trouble and pain. We must draw encouragement from the words of Jesus when He said, "Do not fear those who kill the body but cannot kill the soul. But rather fear Him who is able to destroy both soul and body in hell" (Matt. 10:28).

CHAPTER 21

MARTYRS

It was not a large gathering. Only a few dozen worshippers assembled in the courtyard of the Virgin Mary Church in the village of al-Our, 150 miles south of Cairo, Egypt. A preacher stood and spoke in somber tones to the equally somber group: "The life we live is but numbered days that will quickly pass, the Bible says."[1]

He was not beginning a sermon on time management or stewardship. He was addressing the reason the congregation had grown smaller. Just a few days earlier, in February 2015, the organization known as the Islamic State of Iraq and Syria (ISIS) had decapitated thirteen of their members on a beach in Libya.

These Coptic Christian men were among twenty that ISIS murdered on that day. All twenty hailed from Egyptian farming communities and had traveled to Libya in search of work. But they had been kidnapped in late December and early January and held in the Libyan coastal town of Sirte.

A month later, the condemned men were led single file onto a beach, where they were lined up on their knees with one black-clad ISIS soldier, each with knife in hand, standing behind each man. The Christians were dressed in orange coveralls in malicious mockery of the orange suits worn by radical Muslims incarcerated at the American Guantanamo Bay prison in Cuba. The prisoners were given the opportunity to recant their faith, but each refused. In the video of the executions released by ISIS, the Christian men can be seen, on their knees, mouthing prayers and praise to their Lord.

The story of these men is only one example of the uncountable hosts of believers who have been martyred for their faith over the centuries. It has been said that the entire history of redemption is written in the blood of martyrs. We see this early in the Bible when Pharaoh determined to slaughter all newborn Hebrew males. This was a precursor of worse to come. Before the Israelites entered their promised land, Moses prophesied that they would be severely persecuted throughout history.

> The LORD will scatter you among all peoples, from one end of the earth to the other, and there you shall serve other gods, which neither you nor your fathers have known—wood and stone. And among those nations you shall find no rest . . . but there the LORD will give you a trembling heart, failing eyes, and anguish of soul. Your life shall hang in doubt before you; you shall fear day and night. . . . In the morning you shall say, "Oh, that it were evening!" And at evening you shall say, "Oh, that it were morning!" because of the fear which terrifies your heart, and because of the sight which your eyes see. (Deut. 28:64–67)

This grim prophecy has been more than amply fulfilled. No people have suffered martyrdom and persecution like the Jews. In the sixth century BC, the Babylonians destroyed Jerusalem and deported its citizens. A few generations later, Haman, a high official in the court of Xerxes, conspired to annihilate all the Jews in the Persian Empire. Some three hundred years afterward, the Seleucid king Antiochus Epiphanes massacred forty thousand Jews and sold another forty thousand into slavery for their refusal to worship Zeus.

Jews dispersed among the nations have suffered persecution and deprivation throughout the subsequent centuries. The most intense occurred under Hitler in twentieth-century Europe. Synagogues were destroyed, Jewish shop windows shattered, and concentration camps at Auschwitz and Dachau tortured and executed more than six million Jews, possibly reducing their number in Europe to less than those who followed Moses out of Egypt.[2]

Adolf Eichmann, a principle player in the Nazi persecution, expressed the kind of hatred Jews have endured throughout history: "I shall leap laughing into my grave, for the thought that I have five million human lives on my conscience is to me a source of inordinate satisfaction."[3]

Christians seem to have inherited the hatred directed at the Jews, for Christian history is saturated with persecution from the outset. Herod tried to prevent the rise of Jesus by killing all the infant males born in Bethlehem. The Christian church had barely taken root when the Jewish leaders stoned to death the deacon Stephen for accusing them of murdering Israel's Messiah (Acts 7). Herod Agrippa executed the apostle James (Acts 12:1–2). In fact, all the apostles of Jesus suffered martyrdom except for John, who was exiled.

The Roman emperor Domitian executed countless Christians who refused to renounce their faith. The second-century Christian bishop Polycarp was burned at the stake for refusing to bow to Caesar. Roman Christians were fed to lions. Christians in medieval Spain suffered the Inquisition. Many Protestants of the Reformation era were massacred or exiled. Several hundred Chinese Christians were slain in the Boxer Rebellion. Twentieth-century Christians in Communist Russia endured Siberia and slave labor camps. Even in the "enlightened" twenty-first century we are seeing an alarming increase of Christian persecution and martyrdom throughout the world.

John tells us that there is much more Christian martyrdom yet to come—the result of unprecedented persecution to be inflicted by the Antichrist during the Tribulation period. Let's look deeper into the lives of these heroic Christians and the circumstances that lead to their martyrdom.

THE CONTEXT OF THEIR MARTYRDOM

Who, exactly, are these martyrs? John gives us the answer:

> When [the Lamb] opened the fifth seal, I saw under the altar the souls of
> those who had been slain for the word of God and for the testimony which
> they held. And they cried with a loud voice, saying, "How long, O Lord,
> holy and true, until You judge and avenge our blood on those who dwell
> on the earth?" (Rev. 6:9–10)

These martyrs are believers who will be killed after the church is raptured and the dead in Christ have been resurrected. The fact that they will
be slaughtered for their faith and taken into heaven while their murderers
still thrive on the earth gives strong evidence that they will be martyred
during the Tribulation period.

These souls under the altar will apparently be converted Jews. Let's look
at how this conversion will come about. After the rapture of the church,
God will redirect His focus, placing it again on Israel. The seven years of
Tribulation will see a great turning of Jews toward Christ. Paul affirms that
the salvation of Israel is a key element in God's ultimate plan: "Blindness in
part has happened to Israel until the fullness of the Gentiles has come in.
And so all Israel will be saved, as it is written: 'The Deliverer will come out
of Zion, and He will turn away ungodliness from Jacob'" (Rom. 11:25–26).
It appears that God's plan to save the nation of Israel will come to fru-
ition during the Tribulation period. This turning to God will infuriate the
Antichrist, provoking him to martyr so many Jews that their spilled blood
will flow like a river.

This massive conversion of Jews raises a question. If the Rapture
removes all believers from the earth at the beginning of the Tribulation
period, who will be available to teach Christ to these Jews? One answer is
that God will send to the earth two witnesses who will proclaim Christ
and confirm their message with spectacular miracles. God will then "seal"

144,000 of these Israelis to evangelize their people during the Tribulation (Rev. 7:4).

Dr. Henry Morris suggests another means—a silent witness—by which the Jews may be evangelized.

> Millions upon millions of copies of the Bible and Bible portions have been published in all major languages, and distributed throughout the world. . . . Removal of believers from the world at the rapture will not remove the Scriptures, and multitudes will no doubt be constrained to read the Bible. . . . Thus, multitudes will turn to their Creator and Savior in those days, and will be willing to give their testimony for the Word of God and even . . . their lives as they seek to persuade the world that the calamities it is suffering are judgments from the Lord.[4]

Martyrdom will be an everyday occurrence in the Tribulation period. Even in the face of certain death, believers will proclaim that they love God more than their own lives. As John writes, "they did not love their lives to the death" (12:11).

We find an inspiring example of the attitude of martyrs in a famous incident involving three young godly Jewish men during Judah's Babylonian captivity. When told they must either bow to the king's golden image or be cast into a furnace of fire, their response was unequivocal: "If that is the case, our God whom we serve is able to deliver us from the burning fiery furnace, and He will deliver us from your hand, O king. But if not, let it be known to you, O king, that we do not serve your gods, nor will we worship the gold image which you have set up" (Dan. 3:17–18).

According to the prophet Zechariah, in the Tribulation period two-thirds of all the Jews on earth will be slaughtered. Yet God has promised to preserve His people, saying "I will bring the one-third through the fire, will refine them as silver is refined, and test them as gold is tested" (Zech. 13:8–9). Jesus addressed the terrible suffering of the Tribulation period in his Olivet discourse: "Then they will deliver you up to tribulation and kill you, and you will be hated by all nations for My name's sake. And then many will be offended, will betray one another, and will hate one another" (Matt. 24:9–10).

Revelation presents the Tribulation period as a time when every faithful Christian must look martyrdom in the face. As Bible scholar Richard Bauckham explains it, "It is not a literal prediction that every faithful Christian will in fact be put to death. But it does require that every faithful Christian must be prepared to die."[5]

THE CAUSE OF THEIR MARTYRDOM

John leaves no ambiguity about the reason the martyrs in Revelation 6 had been slain:

> I saw under the altar the souls of those who had been slain for the word of God and for the testimony which they held. (Rev. 6:9)

These martyrs will suffer death for the same reason John was exiled. In fact, John's description of the cause of his exile is almost exactly like his description of the cause of their martyrdom. He had been exiled "for the word of God and for the testimony of Jesus Christ" (1:9).

These souls will be martyred for "the testimony which they held," which surely refers to their proclamation of coming judgment as the Tribulation period descends into its darkest horrors. They will urge repentance and give warnings of a day of reckoning soon to come for those who do not repent. But their message will be rejected, and they will be executed. At the Rapture of the church, the Holy Spirit will withdraw from the earth, removing all restraints on evil. Unprecedented malevolence will be unleashed as the demonic rulers express their rebellion against God by venting their anger on His people.

The faithful will be ruthlessly killed for bearing God's message, joining an exalted list of courageous prophets who suffered for speaking boldly against the evils of their times:

- The evil queen Jezebel threatened Elijah's life because he condemned the prophets of Baal (1 Kings 18–19).
- Isaiah told Judah's kings that Jerusalem and the temple would be razed and the people marched into captivity (2 Kings 20). Tradition says he was ordered sawn in two by King Manasseh (Heb. 11:37).
- Jeremiah was chained in stocks for delivering to Judah's kings essentially the same message as Isaiah (Jer. 20:2–3).
- John the Baptist was beheaded for denouncing the immorality of Herod Antipas (Matt. 14:1–12).
- Jesus consistently denounced the Jewish religious leaders and prophesied judgment. He was crucified.

W. A. Criswell tells us that despite the possibility of severe consequences, it is always the prophet's nature and duty to proclaim judgment.

Whenever there is a true prophet of God, he will preach judgment. These modern so-called ministers of God speak all things nice. . . . There is not any hell and there is not any Devil and there is not any judgment of God. . . . In our enlightened and sophisticated day . . . we stand up and we speak of the love of Jesus, and we speak of peace, and we speak of all things pretty and beautiful. But remember . . . the same Book that tells us about the good, tells us about the bad. The same Revelation that speaks to us about heaven, speaks about hell. The Bible that presents the Lord Jesus as the Savior, is the same Bible that presents to us the Devil as our enemy and adversary of damnation and destruction. The two go together. If there is not anything to be saved from, we do not need a savior.[6]

THE CONSEQUENCE OF
THEIR MARTYRDOM

As we have noted above, these faithful martyrs will suffer and give their lives for their dedication to the Lord. How will they benefit from their sacrifice? John gives us a clue:

> When He opened the fifth seal, I saw under the altar the souls of those who had been slain for the word of God and for the testimony which they held. (Rev. 6:9)

Remember that in this part of John's account, he is describing his visions of scenes in heaven. In this vision, he sees an altar, and the souls martyred for their faithful testimony are situated "under the altar." To appreciate the full impact of what this means, we must turn back to the Old Testament. The altar was a prominent feature of the Israelite tabernacle (and later, the temple) where the people offered animal sacrifices to God. "Under the altar" is where the priests poured out the blood of the sacrificed animals (Ex. 29:12).

The Greek word John uses to indicate the martyrdom of these souls is rendered as "slain" in the English translation we are using. But it can just as accurately be translated as "slaughtered," which is the term applied to Old Testament sacrifices killed as offerings to God. In the eyes of the world, these martyrs will be annihilated—their lives ended. But in reality, they will be slaughtered as a sacrifice offered to God, who will bring them into His holy presence. This is the glorious meaning of their being "under the altar."

THE CRY OF THEIR MARTYRDOM

The Tribulation martyrs under the heavenly altar will remember the severity of their persecution on earth and will call to the Lord for justice:

> They cried with a loud voice, saying, "How long, O Lord, holy and true, until
> You judge and avenge our blood on those who dwell on the earth?" (Rev. 6:10)

This cry for vengeance places these martyrs squarely within the Tribulation period rather than in the prior church age. Notice how different their plea is from that of Stephen, the first martyr of the church. Stephen prayed for mercy: "Lord, do not charge them with this sin" (Acts 7:60). But those who suffer Tribulation atrocities will be justified in calling for vengeance because the age of grace will have ended and the day of God's judgment will have arrived.

Pastor and educator Louis T. Talbot explains, "A man prays according to the attitude God is taking toward the world in the dispensation in which he lives. This present age is the age of grace. God is showing . . . mercy to the worst of men, and we are told to pray for them that despitefully use us. But in the Tribulation period God will be meting out judgment upon the earth."[7] The martyrs' cry for vengeance will be in perfect accord with God's will.

THE COMFORT OF THEIR MARTYRDOM

The Lord heard the cry of the martyrs under the altar, and John records His response:

> A white robe was given to each of them; and it was said to them that they should
> rest a little while longer, until both the number of their fellow servants and
> their brethren, who would be killed as they were, was completed. (Rev. 6:11)

Although the time has not yet come for God to act on the martyrs' request for justice, He will provide them with five comforts as they wait.

1. REFUGE
God gives these faithful servants a refuge by placing them under the altar, a position of safety and redemption. We have the wrong picture if we think

of them as hiding and peeping out as from underneath a bed. Donald Grey Barnhouse explains that "under the altar" will be a position of honor. "To be 'under the altar' is to be covered in the sight of God by that merit which Jesus Christ provided in dying on the cross. It is a figure that speaks of justification ... These martyred witnesses are covered by the work of the Lord Jesus Christ."[8]

2. ROBES

God graciously awards to each martyr a white robe. We are familiar with clothing being awarded for singular achievement. Varsity high school athletes are awarded a letter jacket, Masters Golf Tournament winners a green sport coat, and judo masters a belt. When the prodigal son returned in Luke 15:22, his father called for the best robe to be put on him. Earlier John told us that white garments will be the standing reward issued to overcomers (Rev. 3:5). The white robe will be awarded to these martyrs for facing and overcoming the extreme evil of the Tribulation.

The issuing of these robes raises a perplexing question. John tells us that Tribulation martyrs will not receive their resurrection bodies until the Tribulation ends (20:4–6). How can they wear clothing if they do not yet have their resurrected bodies? Dr. John F. Walvoord offers a possible answer. He posits that they will have a body of some kind, but:

> It is not the kind of body that Christians now have, that is, the body of the earth; nor is it the resurrection body of flesh and bones of which Christ spoke after His own resurrection. It is a temporary body suited for their presence in heaven but replaced in turn by their everlasting resurrection body given at the time of Christ's return.[9]

3. REST

When the martyrs call for judgment against their slayers, they are told to "rest a little while longer, until both the number of their fellow servants and their brethren, who would be killed as they were, was completed" (6:11). The fifth seal, under which these events occur, will initiate the first of two periods of the Tribulation in which believers will suffer martyrdom. God must delay His answer to their cry for justice until the believers under the second Tribulation period have been martyred.

As the first set of martyrs wait, they are invited to take advantage of the delay and enjoy rest from their labors. As John wrote, "I heard a voice from heaven saying to me, 'Write: "Blessed are the dead who die in the Lord from now on." 'Yes,' says the Spirit, 'that they may rest from their labors, and their works follow them'" (14:13).

4. RETRIBUTION

The time for judgment will finally arrive, and God will fulfill his promise to the Tribulation martyrs.

> Another angel came out from the altar, who had power over fire, and he cried with a loud cry to him who had the sharp sickle, saying, "Thrust in your sharp sickle and gather the clusters of the vine of the earth, for her grapes are fully ripe." So the angel thrust his sickle into the earth and gathered the vine of the earth, and threw it into the great winepress of the wrath of God. And the winepress was trampled outside the city, and blood came out of the winepress, up to the horses' bridles, for one thousand six hundred furlongs. (14:18–20)

Here in one of the Bible's most graphic depictions of God's wrath, the martyrs' cry for justice is answered when the blood of their crushed oppressors will flow in a stream five feet deep and two hundred miles long.

5. REWARD

The honor God bestows on these martyrs will be eternal. Even prior to their heavenly reward, they will receive honor during Christ's reign on earth during the Millennium:

> Then I saw the souls of those who had been beheaded for their witness to Jesus and for the word of God, who had not worshiped the beast or

his image, and had not received his mark on their foreheads or on their hands. And they lived and reigned with Christ for a thousand years. (20:4)

When these martyrs are resurrected after the Tribulation period, they will rule with Christ in His millennial kingdom. Finally, these heroic believers will enjoy the peace and justice so long denied them.

THE COURAGE OF MARTYRDOM

We tend to think of Christian martyrdom as a thing of the past—a phenomenon of ancient history like the many stories described in *Foxe's Book of Martyrs*. But martyrdom is widespread around the world today. The Center for the Study of Global Christianity estimates that over half of all historical Christian martyrdoms have occurred in the twentieth century. They estimate that 100,000 Christians were killed each year between 2000 and 2010.[10] The following facts shed additional light on these appalling figures.

- Between 7,000 and 8,000 Christians are martyred worldwide each year. And this is a conservative estimate.[11]
- The US State Department reports that Christians in more than sixty countries are persecuted by their government or their neighbors.[12]
- In North Korea Christianity is illegal, and about 50,000 Christians are now held in labor camps.[13]
- In 2013, almost 300 churches were destroyed and 612 Christians killed in Nigeria.[14]
- The government of Iran monitors Christian church services and arrests new converts.[15]
- Eight states in India have passed anti-conversion laws, which are used to disrupt church services, force Christians from their homes, destroy church buildings, and even kill pastors.[16]
- Increased persecution in Iraq since the fall of Saddam Hussein has

forced almost two-thirds of the one million Iraqi Christians to flee the country.[17]

Whether we look at history, current events, or the future revealed in Revelation 6, we find that persecution and martyrdom have always accompanied Christianity—and always will. Satan, who in Eden usurped the lordship of this fallen world, is determined to annihilate anyone exuding the aroma of goodness and godliness.

In the opening story of this chapter, I told you that ISIS had beheaded twenty Christians on that Libyan beach. But the actual number beheaded was twenty-one. I withheld the name of the last one so I could end this chapter with his inspiring story. When ISIS published the video of the mass beheading, there was one face among the Egyptians whom no one could identify. It was later learned that he was an African from Chad, Mathew Ayairga, who had migrated to Libya to find work. He was not a Christian at all. For reasons that are not clear, he had been swept up with the twenty Egyptian Coptic Christians and marched to the beach to die.

Ayairga knelt in his orange suit in the line as the executioners asked each of the Christians to reject Christ and then beheaded them when they refused. Finally, the butchers reached Ayairga. Although he was not a Christian, they demanded that he reject the Christian's God. "Do you reject Christ?" they asked.

Having observed the faith and courage of the Egyptian Christians throughout the ordeal, Ayairga was deeply moved by the unbending power of their belief. At that moment he knew he wanted what they had more than life itself. He calmly confessed to his captors, "Their God is my God."[18]

Moments later, like the repentant thief on the cross who confessed his faith in Christ (Luke 23:39–43), I believe Ayairga entered paradise along with his fellow martyrs. In attempting to shrink the size of the church triumphant, ISIS actually caused it to grow by one. Heaven will one day reveal how many others, like Ayairga, will have entered paradise after witnessing the faith and martyrdom of those Egyptian Christians.

I hope the courage of the martyrs we have studied in this chapter will inspire you to stand strong in your commitment to Christ regardless of the severity of the cost. Even if it means giving up your own life, what is that compared to the glory of the reward?

CHAPTER 22

144,000

Sometimes the most unexpected people accomplish the most outstanding feats. Dean Hess was such a person. As the newly ordained pastor of a church in Cleveland, Ohio, Hess expected to spend his life in Christian ministry. But when the Japanese attacked Pearl Harbor in 1941, he left his pastorate to join the Aviation Cadet Program, explaining to his stunned congregation, "If we believe our cause is just and necessary, how in all conscience can I ask others to protect it—and me—while I keep clean of the gory mess of war?" Hess flew sixty-three combat missions in France.

After the war, Hess returned to civilian life. But he was recalled to active duty at the outbreak of the Korean War to command a training program for Korean fighter pilots, in addition to flying more combat missions.

During that time, Hess felt a keen burden for the large number of Korean children who had been orphaned by the war. He joined forces with Chaplain Russell L. Blaisdell to provide food and shelter for hundreds of children, first on a military airbase and then in a makeshift orphanage in Seoul.

Shortly after the orphanage was established, however, the Communist army marched on Seoul, forcing thousands to evacuate the city. Hess and

Blaisdell devised a plan to transfer the children to a permanent orphanage on Jeju Island. Military command blocked these arrangements at first, but Hess and Blaisdell persisted until sixteen C-54 transports were approved for the mission.[1] All told, those airlifts and subsequent arrangements for food and supplies for the orphanage saved the lives of more than a thousand Korean orphans.[2]

The heroic acts of Col. Dean Hess required extraordinary courage and determination. In that same spirit, the apostle John tells of a group of heroes who will save millions of people in the coming Tribulation period.

This period could well be called the era of the Antichrist. During this terrible time, his power will become virtually absolute. He will control the world's economy and religion, exalting himself with an enormous statue erected in the new Jewish temple in Jerusalem. He will ruthlessly annihilate all who refuse to bow to him.

Yet, while the unprecedented cruelty of the Antichrist increases, God will not forget His promise to take care of His people. As Paul wrote, "God has not cast away His people whom He foreknew" (Rom. 11:2). In the depths of the Tribulation horrors, the world will witness the greatest spiritual awakening ever to occur on planet earth. Our loving and creative God continually surprises us with the methods He devises to care for His people in their darkest hours. During this time, His care will rise through the agency of 144,000 specially-chosen Jewish evangelists.

John writes of these evangelists in Revelation 7:1–8 and 14:1–5. We will explore who these 144,000 evangelists are and what they will do as we examine both Bible passages.

THEY WILL BE SELECTED FROM ISRAEL'S TWELVE TRIBES

In John's vision of heaven, he sees four angels ready to unleash the winds of God's judgment upon the earth. But another angel approaches, calling for a delay of the destruction until after these "servants of God" are sealed. Then John writes:

> I heard the number of those who were sealed. One hundred and forty-four thousand of all the tribes of the children of Israel were sealed. (7:4)

John is unequivocally specific in telling us that these 144,000 witnesses are Jewish. Yet some expositors insist they will emerge from out of the Christian church. This is impossible. When the 144,000 begin their witness, the redeemed church will already be in heaven, swept up universally by the Rapture, which occurs between Revelation 3 and 4. It amazes me that this error can survive in the face of Revelation 7:4–8, which lists with no ambiguity each of the twelve tribes of Israel from which these evangelists will emerge. As J. A. Seiss wrote, no error "so beclouds the Scriptures, and so unsettles the faith of men, as this constant attempt to read *Church* for *Israel*, and Christian peoples for Jewish tribes."[3]

Twelve thousand witnesses will be called out of each of the twelve tribes of Israel, bringing their total to 144,000 (vv. 4–8). The number twelve here is significant, for it is repeatedly connected with the nation of Israel. The breastplate of the Jewish high priest was set with twelve precious stones; the tabernacle table of showbread bore twelve holy loaves; the city of God will have twelve gates. In each of these cases, the number twelve symbolizes Israel's twelve tribes. The consistent use of the number twelve in connection with Israel climaxes in the sealing of 144,000 individuals—twelve times twelve—chosen from the nation of Israel for a special ministry during the darkest period in earth's history.

THEY WILL BE SEALED ON THEIR FOREHEADS

The angel who introduces the 144,000 witnesses tells us that they will receive their seal from God:

I saw another angel ascending from the east, having the seal of the living God. And he cried with a loud voice to the four angels to whom it was granted to harm the earth and the sea, saying, "Do not harm the earth, the sea, or the trees till we have sealed the servants of our God on their foreheads." (7:2–3)

What is this seal? We are told only that it will be "the seal of the living God." Later, John tells us the seal means "having His Father's name written on their foreheads" (14:1). Clearly, the seal identifies the 144,000 as God's own and serves as a shield, protecting them as He pours out His devastating judgments upon the earth.

The Old Testament offers several examples of God sealing off His people to protect them from an outpouring of judgmental wrath. For example:

- God sealed Noah and his family in the ark to protect them from the destruction of the worldwide Flood (Gen. 6–8).
- God led Lot's family out of Sodom, sealing them from the fiery judgment soon to descend on that city (Gen. 19).
- The firstborn of Jewish families in Egypt were protected from death by the seal of lamb's blood applied to their doorposts (Ex. 12).
- Rahab and her family were sealed from the destruction of Jericho by means of a scarlet cord (Josh. 2:18–21).
- In Elijah's day, God sealed seven thousand Israelites who refused to worship Baal (1 Kings 19).

The sealing of the 144,000 witnesses tells us that God will continue to protect those to whom He assigns special ministries during the Tribulation.

THEY WILL BE SERVANTS OF GOD

The angel in heaven indicates that the seal placed on the 144,000 witnesses will set them apart for a special purpose of God:

Do not harm the earth, the sea, or the trees till we have sealed the servants of our God on their foreheads. (Rev. 7:3)

By describing these witnesses as "servants of our God," the angel is saying they will not worship the Antichrist or take the mark of the Beast. Despite the resulting pressure and opposition, they will devote themselves entirely to God, doing His will and evangelizing relentlessly during the Tribulation period. This points to the seal being something other than a mere external mark of identification. It will be more like a badge of office, indicating the task with which they are charged.

In a similar way, Jesus spoke of God's seal being set on Him (John 6:27). This occurred when the Holy Spirit descended on Him at His baptism, which empowered Him to fulfill His mission on earth.

The Old Testament prophet Joel foresaw the result of the ministry of the 144,000 witnesses and described how they will be agents of the Holy Spirit's power in the Tribulation period:

It shall come to pass afterward
That I will pour out My Spirit on all flesh;
Your sons and your daughters shall prophesy,
Your old men shall dream dreams,
Your young men shall see visions.
And also on My menservants and on My maidservants
I will pour out My Spirit in those days.

And I will show wonders in the heavens and in the earth:
Blood and fire and pillars of smoke.
The sun shall be turned into darkness,
And the moon into blood,
Before the coming of the great and awesome day of the Lord.
And it shall come to pass
That whoever calls on the name of the Lord

Shall be saved.

For in Mount Zion and in Jerusalem there shall be deliverance,

As the LORD has said,

Among the remnant whom the LORD calls. (Joel 2:28–32)

God's seal is not limited to the past or to the future. We who are Christians in the present are also given a seal. Paul affirms this fact in three passages:

- "He who establishes us with you in Christ and has anointed us is God, who also has sealed us and given us the Spirit in our hearts as a guarantee" (2 Cor. 1:21–22).
- "In Him you also trusted, after you heard the word of truth, the gospel of your salvation; in whom also, having believed, you were sealed with the Holy Spirit of promise" (Eph. 1:13).
- "Do not grieve the Holy Spirit of God, by whom you were sealed for the day of redemption" (Eph. 4:30).

In all eras—past, present, and future—God seals those whom He calls to fulfill His purposes and to display the power of His Holy Spirit in this fallen world.

THEY WILL BE SEPARATED UNTO GOD

After John describes the 144,000 standing with the Lamb on Mount Zion after their redemption from the earth, he adds an unexpected detail:

These are the ones who were not defiled with women, for they are virgins. (Rev. 14:4)

Commentators hardly know what to make of this passage. Many spiritualize it, claiming it means the 144,000 will not commit spiritual adultery by consorting with false gods (2 Cor. 11:2; James 4:4). That may be correct, but I think it more likely that it means these witnesses will be celibates. The unprecedented terrors and pressures of the Tribulation period will make it extremely difficult for a dedicated preacher, always on the run from the Antichrist's authorities, to maintain a marriage. Paul endorses singleness as the best option for such troubled times:

> Brethren, the time is short, so that from now on even those who have wives should be as though they had none. . . . I want you to be without care. He who is unmarried cares for the things of the Lord—how he may please the Lord. But he who is married cares about the things of the world—how he may please his wife. . . . And this I say for your own profit, not that I may put a leash on you, but . . . that you may serve the Lord without distraction. (1 Cor. 7:29, 32–33, 35)

If there is ever a time when serving God requires total concentration without distraction, that time will be the Tribulation.

THEY WILL BE STRONG IN THEIR FAITH

John describes the 144,000 witnesses as utterly dedicated to Christ and displaying tremendous strength of character:

> These are the ones who follow the Lamb wherever He goes. . . . And in their mouth was found no deceit, for they are without fault before the throne of God. (Rev. 14:4–5)

The witnesses' sterling example of unimpeachable character coupled with their persistent declaration of the gospel will draw millions of Jews to Christ as the world suffers increasing natural and human-caused disasters. Living a pure life establishes a solid platform for spiritual power, and that power will ignite a turning to God like the world has never seen.

THEY WILL BE SPARED FROM COMING JUDGMENT

Chapter 6 of Revelation ends with an announcement that the day will arrive when God's wrath will be unleashed on the earth. Following this announcement comes the rhetorical question, "Who is able to stand?" Chapter 7 begins with a response:

> After these things I saw four angels standing at the four corners of the earth, holding the four winds of the earth, that the wind should not blow on the earth, on the sea, or on any tree. Then I saw another angel ascending from the east, having the seal of the living God. And he cried with a loud voice to the four angels to whom it was granted to harm the earth and the sea, saying, "Do not harm the earth, the sea, or the trees till we have sealed the servants of our God on their foreheads." (vv. 1–3)

John's report of four angels standing at the four corners of the earth is not an assertion that the earth is square. He is telling us the angels are positioned at the earth's strategic compass points, ready to unleash four destructive winds that will inflict God's judgments over the entire earth—north, south, east, and west.

Then John sees a fifth angel emerge from the east, telling the four angels to delay the destruction they are about to release until the 144,000 witnesses have been sealed (vv. 2–3). Thus, the question raised in the last verse of Revelation 6 is answered: Who can stand when the great day of God's wrath comes? These faithful Jewish witnesses can stand because God's seal of divine protection will preserve them from the soon-to-be-released winds of judgment.

THEY WILL BE SECURE DURING THE TRIBULATION

John gives an after-the-fact assurance that the 144,000 witnesses will be sealed and protected through the terrible Tribulation period:

> I looked, and behold, a Lamb standing on Mount Zion, and with Him one hundred and forty-four thousand, having His Father's name written on their foreheads. (14:1)

Here the apostle sees the 144,000 evangelists in heaven, standing triumphantly with the Lamb on Mount Zion. Their ordeal is over, and they have reaped the reward for their faithfulness. Just as God protected Shadrach, Meshach, and Abed-Nego in Babylon from Nebuchadnezzar's fiery furnace, this heavenly scene shows that the 144,000 will be protected through the Tribulation and delivered safely into the portals of heaven.

As Mark Hitchcock writes, "John sees the 144,000 at the end of the Tribulation standing triumphantly on Mount Zion—the city of Jerusalem. Notice he doesn't see 143,999. All 144,000 have been divinely preserved by the Lord. Not one has been overlooked."[4]

THEY WILL BE SUCCESSFUL IN THEIR MINISTRY

Here on earth, ministers tend to evaluate their success by the growth of their congregations. But there is a better way, which John shows us in picturing the result of the 144,000 witnesses' ministry.

> After these things I looked, and behold, a great multitude which no one could number, of all nations, tribes, peoples, and tongues, standing before

the throne and before the Lamb, clothed with white robes, with palm branches in their hands. (7:9)

I wish the optimistic predictions of a great religious revival sweeping the earth prior to the Rapture were true. But Scripture indicates the opposite—that before the end, Christianity will experience a great "falling away" (2 Thess. 2:3). Yes, an unprecedented revival is coming, but it will occur after the Rapture, when the 144,000 Jewish witnesses evangelize the world during the Tribulation period. The calamitous events of this period will shake millions out of their complacency, shattering their resistance to the message of the 144,000 as they blanket the world with the gospel.

How many souls will be saved by the message of these evangelists? "A great multitude which no one could number, of all nations, tribes, peoples, and tongues" (Rev. 7:9). The astonishing success of their final campaign will fulfill this prophecy of Jesus: "This gospel of the kingdom will be preached in all the world as a witness to all the nations, and then the end will come" (Matt. 24:14).

THEY WILL BE SET APART FOR THE KINGDOM

When John in his heavenly vision sees the multitude arrayed in white robes, an elder comes to him and explains who they are:

These are the ones who come out of the great tribulation, and washed their robes and made them white in the blood of the Lamb. (Rev. 7:14)

As we noted earlier, the 144,000 will be sealed and protected throughout the Tribulation period. These evangelists, who will survive the Tribulation and be alive when the Millennium begins, will reign with Christ throughout that thousand-year period.

In the Millennium, each tribe of Israel will have its own specified geographical area (Ezek. 48). Each of these faithful evangelists will live within the area assigned to his own tribe. They are the remnant of Israel prophesied by the prophet Zephaniah to be set apart for salvation when the Lord will "restore to the peoples a pure language, that they all may call on the name of the LORD, to serve Him with one accord" (Zeph. 3:9). The prophet goes on to say of them, "The remnant of Israel shall do no unrighteousness and speak no lies, nor shall a deceitful tongue be found in their mouth; for they shall feed their flocks and lie down, and no one shall make them afraid" (v. 13).

THEY WILL SING A NEW SONG IN HEAVEN

When the devastation of the Tribulation ends and the 144,000 stand with the Lamb on Mount Zion, John tells us what they will do next:

> And I heard a voice from heaven, like the voice of many waters, and like the voice of loud thunder. And I heard the sound of harpists playing their harps. They sang as it were a new song before the throne, before the four living creatures, and the elders; and no one could learn that song except the hundred and forty-four thousand who were redeemed from the earth. (Rev. 14:2–3)

These evangelists will have survived the worst seven years in the history of the world. You might expect them to be hauled off to a hospital and treated for PTSD, as many brave soldiers are treated after suffering the horrors of war. But no; these 144,000 survivors will stand up and *sing*!

Others in the Bible have responded with song after God gave them a victory or saved them from disaster. When the Lord led Israel safely through the Red Sea and drowned their Egyptian pursuers, Moses led the people in a joyful song: "I will sing to the LORD, for He has triumphed gloriously! The horse and its rider He has thrown into the sea!" (Ex. 15:1). When Barak defeated the Canaanites, he and the judge Deborah sang a song of praise and victory (Judges 5). David penned songs of victory in 2 Samuel 22 and Psalm 18.

It is this kind of song John hears as he gazes at the triumphant Lamb standing on Mount Zion. It's a new song, arising from an enormous, exultant choir accompanied by harps. It's a song that only these 144,000 saints can learn and sing because it grows out of the unique ordeals they have experienced, as well as out of their exultation over the massive numbers their ministry has turned to God. This is not the enormous choir that John heard singing earlier, which numbered "ten thousand times ten thousand, and thousands of thousands" (Rev. 5:11). The choir he hears now is composed of a mere 144,000 voices!

I remember the first day I attended chapel at Dallas Theological Seminary. Under the direction of the chaplain, 500 men stood and blended their voices in praise to God. I could not hold back the tears. If a choir of 500 choked me up, I suppose a choir of 144,000 men singing praises to God might reduce me to an emotional basket case!

There's no way to experience what a choir of this size will sound like, but we might get a small taste from the music of American Grammy Award-winning composer Eric Whitacre. Whitacre is the creator of a Virtual Choir composed of recorded voices from around the world singing his compositions. He selects the best recordings, merges them into a single track, and posts the results on YouTube. His first Virtual Choir 1.0 consisted of 185 voices from 12 countries. At this writing, his most current recording is Virtual Choir 4.0, which blends 5,905 voices from 101 countries. As beautiful as Whitacre's "choir as big as the Internet"[5] may be, it will not hold a candle to 144,000 voices from the twelve tribes of Israel singing their joyful hearts out to the Lord who saved them.

It is significant that harps will accompany this choir. The Old Testament speaks of harps almost fifty times, and each time they are linked with joy. Harps were never played to express sorrow or distress. The Jewish captives in Babylon wept when they remembered Zion and hung up their harps rather than play them (Ps. 137:1–2). Conversely, harps accompanying a new song is considered an appropriate way to praise God when He delivers His people from trouble. David wrote, "I will sing a new song to You, O God; on a harp of ten strings I will sing praises to You, the One who gives salvation to kings, who delivers David His servant from the deadly sword" (144:9–10).

Almost everyone recognizes the power of music not only to express emotions but also to encourage them. Professor Jeremy Begbie gives us a striking example of music's extraordinary power in this story of his experience one Sunday in a poor South African church:

> I was told, immediately before the service, that a house just around the corner from the church had just been burned to the ground because the man who lived there was a suspected thief. A week before that, a tornado had cut through the township, ripping apart fifty homes; five people were killed. And then I was told that the very night before, a gang hounded down a fourteen-year-old, a member of the church's Sunday school, and stabbed him to death.
>
> The pastor began his opening prayer: "Lord, you are the Creator and the Sovereign, but why did the wind come like a snake and tear our roofs off? Why did a mob cut short the life of one of our own children, when he had everything to live for? Over and over again, Lord, we are in the midst of death."
>
> As he spoke, the congregation responded with a dreadful sighing and groaning. And then, once he finished his prayer, very slowly, the whole congregation began to sing, at first very quietly, then louder. They sang and they sang, song after song of praise—praise to a God who in Jesus had plunged into the very worst to give us a promise of an ending beyond all imagination. The singing gave that congregation a foretaste of the end.[6]

That "foretaste of the end," which we experience in song, gives evidence that what we call the end is not the end at all. When the curtain falls on this world, it will open to the beginning of all things new.

The Tribulation period will wreak devastation like the earth has never seen. But those who turn to God will experience this new beginning, which will be more glorious than the mind can imagine. God's raising up, sealing, and rewarding His dear 144,000 Jewish evangelists gives evidence that regardless of the depths the world may sink into, God remains sovereign. His plan for ultimate victory will not be thwarted. Because we who trust Him understand that, in our darkest hours we can sing praises to Him with great joy.

CHAPTER 23

TWO WITNESSES

On June 23, 2018, twelve boys ranging in age from eleven to sixteen—all members of a Thailand soccer team—took an after-practice excursion with their coach into the Tham Luang cave in northern Thailand. They had traversed two of the cavern's six miles when monsoon rains flooded the caves, trapping the team on an underground ledge.

When families reported the boys missing, a search party found their bicycles and packs near the cave entrance. Authorities immediately instigated operations to search the caves. Thai Navy SEALs entered the caverns, feeling their way through murky water, an experience they described as "swimming through coffee."

When additional rains and rushing water prevented further penetration, pumps were brought in to lower the water level. Then divers set up air pumps at intervals along the passages, creating breathing stations that enabled them to move deeper into the caves.

After nine days, divers finally located the boys and delivered survival supplies while they devised a complex rescue system. Over the next week, they strung underwater guidewires from the team's location to the entrance. Then they equipped the boys with scuba gear and brought them out one by one, each escorted between two experienced divers. The first round trip took eleven hours and delivered four boys. Although subsequent trips went faster, the entire operation took three additional days. But all the boys were brought out safely as the watching world applauded the heroic efforts of the divers and their support teams.[1]

Given the complexity of the caves, the underwater distance to be traversed, the darkness, and the impending danger of further monsoon deluges, it would have been easy for the authorities to write off the rescue attempt as too dangerous—even impossible.

Using similar logic, God could just as easily write off the people who will be caught in the deadly danger and darkness of the Tribulation period. The Rapture will draw all authentic Christians out of the world and leave only unbelievers to endure the horrors of the Tribulation. But God will not write off these billions groping in darkness. He will send rescuers—voices to proclaim the gospel—offering a secure lifeline out of the depths of their impending doom.

This lifeline will take the form of the two witnesses introduced in Revelation 11. Some scholars believe these witnesses will arrive at the center point of the Tribulation period. I believe they will arrive at the beginning, immediately following the Rapture. For God, in His infinite love, will never leave men and women without a means of turning to Him.[2]

In Revelation 11 John reveals much about these two witnesses, including their personalities, their prophecies, their power, their persecution, and their preservation.

THE PERSONALITY OF THE WITNESSES

John introduces the two witnesses with these words spoken by an angel of God: "I will give power to my two witnesses, and they will prophesy one thousand two hundred and sixty days, clothed in sackcloth" (11:3).

Many interpreters have spiritualized the identity of these witnesses, claiming they are symbolic representations of the law and the gospel or the Old and New Testaments. But the interpretation most consistent with Scripture is that they will be actual persons who will speak with human voices and perform miracles by the power of God.

Let's explore how John affirms their humanity with two significant metaphors: "These are the two olive trees and the two lampstands standing before the God of the earth" (v. 4). John's readers would have recognized these metaphors as echoes from a vision of the prophet Zechariah, who describes a golden candlestick bearing seven lamps flanked by two olive trees, which produce golden oil for the lamps. Zechariah identifies the olive trees as actual people—"the two anointed ones, who stand beside the Lord of the whole earth" (Zech. 4:14).

These two "anointed ones" in Zechariah's prophecy were prominent men of faith in his time: the high priest Joshua and Jerusalem's governor Zerubbabel, who restored the Jewish temple. In Zechariah's day, Joshua and Zerubbabel were two witnesses to the fact that God does His work through the power of His Spirit (vv. 6–10). The zeal of these two men provided fuel for God's work, like an olive tree. Their zeal also gave light for God's work, like a lampstand. Given this background, it's easy to see why John identified the two witnesses in Revelation as olive trees and lampstands. Like the godly Zerubbabel and Joshua, they will be men fueled by the power of God's Holy Spirit to shine lights into the darkness of the Tribulation period.[3]

While the purpose of these two witnesses is clear, their exact identity remains a source of controversy. Most scholars identify one of the witnesses as Elijah the Old Testament prophet. Here are the factors supporting this view:

- Malachi prophesied that Elijah would return to prepare the way for Christ's second coming: "Behold, I [the Lord] will send you Elijah the prophet before the coming of the great and dreadful day of the LORD. And he will turn the hearts of the fathers to the children, and the hearts of the children to their fathers" (Mal. 4:5–6). Some believe

John the Baptist fulfilled this prophecy. Luke 1:17 tells us that John came in the "spirit and power of Elijah," but this simply means that John did his work by the power of the Spirit, just as Elijah did. He was not literally Elijah reincarnated. John himself affirmed this fact. When Jewish leaders asked him, "Are you Elijah?" he answered unequivocally, "I am not" (John 1:21). Clearly, Malachi's prophecy points to someone other than John the Baptist—someone yet to come.

- God miraculously took up Elijah into heaven (2 Kings 2:11). The two witnesses will experience the same miracle (Rev. 11:12).
- The two witnesses will prevent rain from falling. Elijah did the same (1 Kings 17:1; Rev. 11:6).
- Elijah called down fire from heaven. The witnesses will also employ fire in their ministry (2 Kings 1:10; Rev. 11:5).
- The drought Elijah imposed lasted three years and six months (1 Kings 17:1; Luke 4:25; James 5:17–18). This is exactly the duration of the two witnesses' ministry (Rev. 11:3).

As to the identity of the second witness, some scholars propose Enoch. I believe the more likely candidate is Moses. Here is why:

- Both Moses and Elijah appeared at Christ's transfiguration (Matt. 17:3).
- By God's power, Moses turned water into blood (Ex. 7:19–20). The two witnesses will perform the same miracle (Rev. 11:6).
- Moses' body was miraculously preserved for restoration (Deut. 34:5–7). When the witnesses die, their bodies will also be restored (Rev. 11:11).
- Satan fought the archangel Michael for possession of Moses' body (Jude v. 9). He may have intended to prevent God's program of restoration in the last days.
- Moses represents the law and Elijah the prophets. Since the witnesses will minister within the nation of Israel, this connection with Jewish Scriptures will underscore their message.

Prophecy scholars Timothy Demy and John Whitcomb present strong reasons for identifying Moses and Elijah as the two witnesses:

> No two men in Israel's entire history would receive greater respect and appreciation than Moses and Elijah. Moses was God's great deliverer and lawgiver for Israel (Deut. 34:10–12). First-century Jews actually thought that Moses had given them the manna in the wilderness (John 6:32). And God raised up Elijah to confront Israel in a time of great national apostasy. God vindicated him by sending fire from heaven and "a chariot of fire and horses of fire" to escort him out of this world. So highly did the Jews of Jesus' day think of Elijah that when they saw Jesus' miracles, some people concluded that Elijah had returned (Matt. 16:14).[4]

THE PROPHECIES OF THE WITNESSES

In the same passage we explored above, John gives us two details indicating the duration and character of the witnesses' prophecies: "I will give power to my two witnesses, and they will prophesy one thousand two hundred and sixty days, clothed in sackcloth" (Rev. 11:3).

The duration of their ministry is stated in exact terms. It will last 1,260 days, which is equivalent to forty-two months or three-and-a-half years.

The nature of their prophecy is indicated in their attire. They will wear sackcloth, a course mohair fabric Jews wore to express mourning, distress, or repentance. Jacob donned sackcloth when told his son Joseph was dead (Gen. 37:34). David wore sackcloth when told that Joab had slain Abner (2 Sam. 3:31).

These witnesses will prophesy to both Jews and Gentiles, which may be God's purpose in sending two of them. To both groups, however, the content of their prophecy will be the same: judgment. They will preach impending judgment daily and relentlessly throughout their entire three-and-a-half-year ministry.

Another reason for sending two witnesses is to comply with the legal standards of Jewish law. At least two witnesses were required to establish the truth of a testimony: "Whoever is deserving of death shall be put to death on the testimony of two or three witnesses; he shall not be put to death on the testimony of one witness" (Deut. 17:6). One witness may be mistaken or corrupted. But the corroboration of two witnesses confirms the truth.

The Bible often records God using two witnesses to confirm a truth. Two angels testified to the women at the tomb that Christ had risen. Two angels testified to the disciples that He had ascended. God has often paired people to perform His missions: Moses and Aaron, Joshua and Caleb, Zerubbabel and Joshua, Peter and John, Paul and Silas, Timothy and Titus. Jesus sent out the apostles in pairs (Mark 6:7), as well as the seventy (Luke 10:1). These two witnesses will confirm God's message of judgment and His call to repentance with their perfectly meshing testimony.

THE POWER OF THE WITNESSES

The first thing we are told about the two witnesses is the source of their power: "I will give power to my two witnesses, and they will prophesy one thousand two hundred and sixty days, clothed in sackcloth" (Rev. 11:3).

They will be filled with the Spirit of God, who will empower them with both speech and actions to convict their audiences of coming judgment and the urgency of repentance.

THE POWER OF THEIR PREACHING

The message of the two witnesses will provoke intense hatred, and we can see why. They will not pull any punches. As William R. Newell wrote, "They will testify unsparingly of human wickedness to men's very faces. You have probably never heard a preacher that told you to your face just how bad you were. . . . These witnesses will tell to the teeth of a horrid godlessness which is ready to worship the Devil, just what they are before God!"[5]

The witnesses will warn that the disasters of the Tribulation period are judgments the people have brought down upon themselves by rejecting Christ as Lord. They will accuse the people of turning Jerusalem, God's holy city, into a pit of depravity. They will refute the claims of the Antichrist and expose him for the Satan-controlled being he is. They will denounce the lie that man is innately good and improvable. They will warn of more terrible judgments to come if the people do not turn from their gross depravity.

We see it in our own day. Unbelievers do not merely reject the truth; they go all-out to silence it. Why? Because planted in every heart is the innate knowledge of right and wrong. This knowledge is stifled and buried when people give themselves over to sinful behavior. To hear truth proclaimed arouses their dormant consciences and inflicts a sense of guilt, which the sinner cannot tolerate (Rom. 1:18–21). This explains why the message of the two witnesses will so outrage the people that they will demand their deaths. They will think killing the messengers will eradicate the message.

THE POWER OF THEIR PLAGUES

Disasters often shake people out of their complacency and spur them to seek more stability than the world offers. That will be the primary purpose of the three plagues the witnesses will inflict during their ministry.

- **The plague of death:** As opposition intensifies, many attempts will be made on the witnesses' lives. But since their ministry is vital in the Tribulation period, God will give them power to defend themselves. In his confrontation on Mount Carmel, Elijah called down fire from heaven (1 Kings 18:37–38). The two witnesses will also employ fire, but in a unique way: "If anyone wants to harm them, fire proceeds from their mouth and devours their enemies" (Rev. 11:5).
- **The plague of drought:** The two witnesses possess "power to shut heaven, so that no rain falls in the days of their prophecy" (Rev. 11:6).

The "days of their prophecy" will span three-and-a-half years—the first half of the Tribulation period—which matches the duration of the drought Elijah imposed on Israel when "he prayed earnestly that it would not rain; and it did not rain on the land for three years and six months" (James 5:17). These two miraculously imposed droughts will be the longest the earth has ever experienced.

- **The plague of disease:** The two witnesses will "have power over waters to turn them to blood" (Rev. 11:6). This power reflects that which was given to Moses, who turned the Nile River red with blood (Ex. 7:20). This plague correlates to those announced by the second trumpet in Revelation 8: "The second angel sounded: And something like a great mountain burning with fire was thrown into the sea, and a third of the sea became blood. And a third of the living creatures in the sea died, and a third of the ships were destroyed" (vv. 8–9). The contaminated water will cause epidemics of disease.

None of these miracles will be performed out of anger or vindictiveness. Their primary purpose will be to shake people out of their delusion that all is well, convict them of their sinfulness, and awaken their need to repent. One effect of both the preaching and the miracles of the witnesses may be that the turmoil they arouse will delay the completion of the Antichrist's quest for world dominion. Only when they are annihilated will his path to power be clear of obstruction.

THE PERSECUTION OF THE WITNESSES

Although God will protect the two witnesses until they have completed their ministry, he will finally allow the Antichrist to destroy them. "When they finish their testimony, the beast that ascends out of the bottomless pit will make war against them, overcome them, and kill them" (Rev. 11:7).

The death of the witnesses will expose the extreme depravity of the

Antichrist and the unregenerate people of the Tribulation period. But as we shall soon see, their deaths are merely a prelude to a spectacular demonstration of God's reality and power.

THE DEATH OF THE WITNESSES

As the passage above says, the witnesses will be killed by "the beast that ascends out of the bottomless pit." Here we are first introduced to the Beast (the Antichrist), who will be mentioned thirty-five more times in the book of Revelation. Though not previously referred to, his career at this point will have been highly active and successful. He will have manipulated events, taken over governments, and signed a peace treaty with Israel, setting the stage for world domination.

Halfway through the Tribulation period, the Beast will order the two witnesses assassinated. This act will greatly expand his popularity and consolidate his power.

THE DISPLAY OF THEIR BODIES

After the witnesses are killed, "Their dead bodies will lie in the street of the great city which spiritually is called Sodom and Egypt, where also our Lord was crucified" (Rev. 11:8). Throughout history most cultures have buried corpses quickly—often on the day of death—or at least preserved them until burial could be accomplished (Deut. 21:22–23). But not so with these two witnesses. The Antichrist will defile their bodies by leaving them unburied to demonstrate his contempt for them and their message.

The "great city" where these bodies will be displayed is Jerusalem. At this time, the holy city will be a sewer of corruption like ancient Sodom and Egypt—places associated in the Jewish mind with the most depraved sexual perversions and the cruelest tyranny.

Throughout the Tribulation period, Jerusalem will be a city of contrasts. After God delivers it from the armies of Gog, it will descend into extreme wickedness and debauchery, even as their temple is rebuilt on its original site and the Jews' ancient sacrifices are restored. On the surface

Jerusalem will seem to have reached its peak of glory and holiness. But from within it will emanate the stench of decay and death. Henry Morris calls Jerusalem "the holy city and the city of peace" as well as "the city where God's prophets die" and the place where the Beast's soldiers "will apprehend and slay [the witnesses] and leave their bodies unburied in the street for all their enemies to see."[6]

The unburied bodies of the two witnesses will be seen worldwide: "Those from the peoples, tribes, tongues, and nations will see their dead bodies three-and-a-half days, and not allow their dead bodies to be put into graves" (Rev. 11:9). Decades ago, critics dismissed this passage as impossible. How could this grisly spectacle be seen around the world? Today, however, with satellite TV, social media, and the Internet, the question no longer even arises.

THE DELIGHT OF THEIR ENEMIES

The masses will celebrate the deaths of the two witnesses with a holiday rivaling Christmas: "Those who dwell on the earth will rejoice over them, make merry, and send gifts to one another, because these two prophets tormented those who dwell on the earth" (v. 10).

Here we have the only report of joy of any kind occurring throughout the Tribulation period. What does this tell us about the state of the human heart in the end times? William Newell answers: "Now comes the real revelation of the heart of man: glee, horrid, insane, inhuman, hellish, ghoulish glee! There is actual delight at the death of God's witnesses—utter unbounded delight! . . . A regular Christmastime-of-Hell ensues."[7]

THE PRESERVATION OF THE WITNESSES

The story of the two witnesses will not end with their deaths or the ignominious display of their corpses: "After the three-and-a-half days the breath of life from God entered them, and they stood on their feet, and great fear fell on those who saw them" (v. 11).

Three-and-a-half days will pass while the world celebrates their deaths, and then two astounding events will turn their celebration into abject terror.

THEIR RESURRECTION

As the world celebrates, the "breath of life from God" will infuse the two corpses—the same breath that resurrected the body of Jesus. The wild celebrations will cease suddenly, and the watching world will gape in shock as the two corpses stir and rise to their feet, whole and healthy. The horror these resurrections generate will be indescribable. The Beast will find no way to counterfeit this miracle.

THEIR RAPTURE

After their resurrection, "a loud voice from heaven" will call to the witnesses, saying, "Come up here." A cloud will envelop them, and they will rise into heaven as their enemies gape in astonishment (v. 12).

The two witnesses will experience a rapture much like that of the church, but with one significant difference. The church will be taken "in a moment, in the twinkling of an eye, at the last trumpet" (1 Cor. 15:52). The event will be so sudden that no eye will see it happen. The rapture of the two witnesses, however, will not occur in a flash but will be visible to their enemies (Rev. 11:12). It is yet another display of God's power to jar them out of unbelief and into repentance. John Phillips vividly describes the event:

> Picture the scene—the sun-drenched streets of Jerusalem, the holiday crowds flown in from the ends of the earth for a firsthand look at the corpses of these detested men, the troops in the Beast's uniform, the temple police. There they are, devilish men from every kingdom under heaven, come to dance and feast at the triumph of the Beast. And then it happens! As the crowds strain at the police cordon to peer curiously at the two dead bodies, there comes a sudden change. Their color changes from cadaverous hue to the blooming, rosy glow of youth. Those stiff, stark

limbs—they bend, they move! Oh, what a sight! They rise! The crowds fall back, break, and form again.[8]

Henry Morris adds:

The sight will be enough to strike terror into the hearts of the most arrogantly rebellious of their enemies. A moment before, such men were rejoicing in supreme confidence that Christ was finally defeated and Satan's man was on the victor's throne. But now Christ had triumphed again. The ascent of the prophets into heaven was a dire prediction that even greater judgments were about to descend from heaven. The three-and-a-half-day festivities were about to be followed by another three-and-a-half years of judgments more severe than ever.[9]

As great as the fear of these watching enemies will be, an even greater terror will quickly descend upon them.

THEIR REVENGE

When the heavens close over the two risen witnesses, a sudden earthquake will reduce a tenth of the city to rubble, killing seven thousand people in Jerusalem alone (Rev. 11:13). In the original text, the word translated "people" actually means "men of name." This indicates that the seven thousand fatalities will likely be famous people or political leaders—those most responsible for the persecution of the two witnesses.

The survivors, quaking and groveling in terror, will have no choice but to acknowledge the resurrection and ascension of the two witnesses and the subsequent earthquake as acts of divine power. John tells us that they "were afraid and gave glory to the God of heaven." It's unlikely that they truly turn to God in faith and repentance. A surge of terror can trigger a momentary emotional response without producing a permanent change of heart.

We saw this temporary revival of the religious impulse in the wake of the 9/11 attacks on the World Trade Center towers. For weeks afterward, we witnessed a seeming turn toward God. Prayers ascended. Church atten-dance soared. A renewed sense of community prevailed. But it was not long before attitudes reverted to their pre-9/11 norm. Fear dissipated, everyday routine resumed, and God slipped out of people's minds.

Yet even amid the horrors of the Tribulation period, some will heed the two witnesses' message of redemption and respond to the loving call of God. As always, He will offer a way out of the darkness and into His light. His love and mercy never ceases.

CHAPTER 24

DRAGON

William Golding's classic novel *Lord of the Flies* tells the chilling tale of a group of pre-adolescent British boys marooned by an air crash on an uncharted Pacific island. They choose a leader who tries to establish order to ensure survival. But jealousy and dissention soon undermine his authority, and order disintegrates into chaos as rebellion and sheer malice divide the boys into hostile camps. The chaos quickly descends into savagery as the boys yield to superstition and paranoia, smear themselves with pig's blood, and perform barbaric rituals. The rituals climax when a decaying boar's head, swarming with flies, is impaled on a pole and worshiped as the Lord of the Flies. All semblance of order evaporates as some boys are killed in ritualistic frenzies and a rebelling faction maliciously ignites a forest fire that will destroy the island.

It's the story of our world—past, present, and future. We've all sensed the reality of it. It seems there is more evil operating in the world than mere human sin can account for. Ever since humanity rejected God's authority, there has been an ever-present, lurking, persistent, dark force poised to invade the human heart given the slightest opening—a force that is pushing the world toward a cataclysmic end of ruin and destruction.

Lord of the Flies is a literal translation of "Beelzebub" or "Baal-Zebub" from 2 Kings 1:2–3, 6, 16. The name is applied to "the ruler of the demons" in the New Testament (Matt. 12:24). Lord of the Flies actually means "the lord of death, to which flies are attracted." Beelzebub is often synonymous with Satan, the antagonist in the drama of human history from its beginning to its prophesied end. Satan, the lord of death, is our perennial adversary, the archenemy of God and His creation. It was his rebellion that corrupted creation and brought death and evil into the world. He has been mankind's bitter enemy, tempter, and inflictor of grief ever since.

In Revelation 12 we learn much about this archfiend's role in the end times drama—his objective, his character, his vendetta, his rebellion, and his doom. These elements are revealed in five phrases of such cosmic significance that all but one are preceded by the adjective *great*—a great sign, a great dragon, a great war, a great wrath, and finally, the wings of a great eagle. Let's explore these revealing elements one by one.

THE GREAT SIGN

> A great sign appeared in heaven: a woman clothed with
> the sun, with the moon under her feet, and on her head a
> garland of twelve stars. Then being with child, she cried
> out in labor and in pain to give birth. (Rev. 12:1–2)

This woman, bathed in light, crowned with stars, and laboring in the throes of childbirth, has endured many interpretations, but only one is fully consistent with the Bible. She is certainly the nation of Israel, the target of Satan's deadly malice.

The Old Testament often characterizes Israel as a woman enduring the travail of childbirth. Isaiah writes, "As a woman with child is in pain and cries out in her pangs, when she draws near the time of her delivery, so have we been in Your sight, O LORD. We have been with child, we have been in pain; we have, as it were, brought forth wind; we have not accomplished any deliverance in the earth" (Isa. 26:17–18, see also 66:7–8; Micah 4:10; 5:3). This unhappy image of a pregnant woman failing to deliver her child pictures Israel's failure to deliver God's light of hope to the nations. Yet even after centuries of failure, the Jews had the honor of delivering Christ to the world. As John says, "She bore a male Child who was to rule all nations with a rod of iron. And her Child was caught up to God and His throne" (Rev. 12:5).

This power-packed verse highlights three of the most momentous events defining the role of Christ in human history:

1. Christ's Incarnation: "She bore a male Child."
2. Christ's Ascension: "Her child was caught up to God and His throne."
3. Christ's Second Coming: He will "rule all nations with a rod of iron."

The prediction that Christ will "rule all nations with a rod of iron" is reaffirmed in the final chapters of Revelation where John describes Christ as He descends to fight mankind's final battle: "Out of His mouth goes a sharp sword, that with it He should strike the nations. And He Himself will rule them with a rod of iron" (19:15).

Here in this first great sign we see Satan's objective. He is determined to destroy the woman's Child to prevent both God's redemptive purpose and his own destruction.

THE GREAT DRAGON

Another sign appeared in heaven: behold, a great, fiery red dragon
having seven heads and ten horns, and seven diadems on his
heads. His tail drew a third of the stars of heaven and threw them

> to the earth. And the dragon stood before the woman who was
> ready to give birth, to devour her Child as soon as it was born. . . .
> So the great dragon was cast out, that serpent of old, called the
> Devil and Satan, who deceives the whole world; he was cast to
> the earth, and his angels were cast out with him. (12:3–4, 9)

Here we see Satan thwarted in his attempt to destroy the Christ child. He and his army of angels are driven from heaven and plunge headlong to the earth. From that moment on, his trajectory is always downward. Like a crashing plane caught in a tailspin, he falls from heaven to earth; from earth to the bottomless pit; and from the pit to the lake of fire.

Revelation 12 gives us more concentrated information about the dragon, Satan, than any other chapter in the Bible. Here we learn of his personality, his power, his partners, and his purpose.

SATAN'S PERSONALITY

Revelation 12:9 pictures Satan as a great dragon, an old serpent, the Devil, and the world's deceiver. These repugnant descriptions refer not to his physical appearance but to his character. Art and cinema often portray Satan as physically hideous. But in reality, his appearance is bright and glorious, as you would expect of an archangel—even a fallen one. According to Paul, Satan "transforms himself into an angel of light" (2 Cor. 11:14). Isaiah calls him Lucifer, which means "the morning star" (Isa. 14:12).

Satan is the instigator of sin, which reflects his nature—appealing on the surface but deadly when followed. Peel away his superficial attractiveness and you confront the shocking truth: he is vile, vicious, ferocious, depraved, and diabolical. Red is his traditional color—the color of blood, which stains his murderous hands. Satan's serpentine nature was on full display in Eden, where through cunning deception he plotted the annihilation of humanity and succeeded in bringing about our fall. This is why Jesus called him "a murderer from the beginning" (John 8:44).

The word *Satan* means "adversary"—a name he notoriously lives up to, being the archenemy of God and mankind. Peter calls him "a roaring lion, seeking whom he may devour" (1 Pet. 5:8). Satan's name occurs fifty-four times in the Bible, fourteen times in the Old Testament and forty in the New Testament.

The New Testament also refers to Satan as the Devil. The term for *Devil* in Greek is *diabolos*, which means "slanderer." It's the term John uses when describing Satan as "the accuser of our brethren" (Rev. 12:10). He acts as a corrupt prosecuting attorney, falsely accusing and defaming Christian believers, viciously intent on destroying our reputation in the courtroom of heaven.

Satan is the being who "deceives the whole world" (v. 9). Having failed to keep Christ from the world, he is now determined to keep the world from Christ. Utterly devoid of scruples or conscience, he lies, misrepresents, and hides truth to plant the seeds of doubt about the reality and goodness of God. As Paul explains it, Satan has blinded people's minds "lest the light of the gospel of the glory of Christ, who is the image of God, should shine on them" (2 Cor. 4:4).

SATAN'S POWER

John describes Satan as "a great, fiery red dragon having seven heads and ten horns, and seven diadems on his heads" (Rev. 12:3). In the Bible, the number seven generally symbolizes completeness or totality. We recognize the head as the seat of intelligence. Horns are often biblical symbols of strength (see Deut. 33:17; 1 Kings 22:11; Ps. 69:31). Therefore, the dragon's seven heads and ten horns symbolize extreme intelligence and enormous power.

The diadems crowning the dragon's heads symbolize a fact that surprises many people. Satan is the ruler of the world. Jesus Himself tells us that the Devil has a kingdom (Matt. 12:25–26). Paul describes him as the ruler of this age (Eph. 6:12), "the god of this age" (2 Cor. 4:4), and "the prince of the power of the air" (Eph. 2:2). On three occasions, John calls him "the prince of this world" (John 12:31; 14:30; 16:11 KJV). He adds that "the whole world lies under the sway of the wicked one" (1 John 5:19).

In his role as "the prince of the world," Satan's subjects are men and women who reject Christ. As "the prince of the power of the air," his subjects are the evil spirits in the invisible realm. In both realms, he rules over all who rebel against God.

How did the lord of death become the lord of the world? It certainly was not by God's appointment. Satan usurped the title from its legitimate owners—Adam and Eve. God charged them to "fill the earth and subdue it; have dominion over . . . every living thing that moves on the earth" (Gen. 1:28). When the human couple rebelled against God, they lost the power to hold their kingdom, and Satan seized the throne for himself.

SATAN'S PARTNERS

One reason for Satan's inordinate power is the fact that he commands a vast army, which he assembled by drawing to himself "a third of the stars of heaven" (Rev. 12:4). These "stars" are actually angels, called stars here as they are in Job 38:7, where we're told they sang in exultation as God created the earth. One-third of these angels joined Satan in a mass rebellion against God.

None of these fallen angels retain their original, pre-rebellion goodness. Some have been imprisoned already (2 Pet. 2:4; Jude v. 6). Those that remain free function as Satan's accomplices, subverting mankind, manipulating world events, and stirring up chaos to bring about the ultimate destruction of humanity. As Paul put it, "We do not wrestle against flesh and blood, but against principalities, against powers, against the rulers of the darkness of this age, against spiritual hosts of wickedness in the heavenly places" (Eph. 6:12).

Satan and these yet unbound angels have immense freedom to rove about at will. He infiltrated Eden to seduce our primeval parents. He confronted Christ in the Judean wilderness. He is even allowed limited access to stand before God and accuse believers (Job 1:6–12; Rev. 12:10). Satan's angels imitate their master, working out their diabolical plots among us to undermine goodness and accomplish humanity's downfall.

SATAN'S PURPOSE

From the beginning, Satan's obsession has been the eradication of God's people. In Eden he seduced the first couple into disobeying God, no doubt thinking God would destroy them for their disobedience. But to his dismay, God promised redemption to the couple and told Satan he would eventually be crushed by a descendant of the woman (Gen. 3:15). Naturally, the Devil began plotting to prevent the fulfillment of that prophecy. He learned from God's promise to Abraham that his nemesis would arise out of Israel, so he strove to abort the formation of that nation. He ignited in Esau's heart a murderous rage against Jacob, who would beget Israel's twelve tribes. But Esau failed to kill Jacob, so Satan induced Pharaoh to slaughter the male babies of the Israelites in Egypt—a plot which Moses survived. Had Satan eradicated either Jacob or Moses, there would be no nation of Israel.

During the reign of Judah's kings, Satan's scheme came within a hair's breadth of succeeding. Knowing that the Messiah would emerge from the royal descendants of David, he set about to cut off that line. After the death of King Jehoshaphat, Satan incited a series of assassinations that eradicated all but one family of David's line—King Ahaziah and his children. When Ahaziah was also murdered, his mother, Athaliah, ordered all his royal heirs slaughtered (her own grandchildren!) and took the throne herself.

Finally, Satan had succeeded. The royal line of David was ended and would never produce the Messiah. Or so it seemed. But a sister to the murdered king managed to whisk away and hide his youngest son, Joash, until he could safely be revealed and crowned as the rightful king (2 Chron. 22:10–12). Again Satan was thwarted and the line of the Promised One preserved.

Next, Satan provoked a high Persian official, Haman, to plot the mass extermination of all the Jews. The brave Queen Esther exposed Haman's conspiracy, shattering Satan's scheme yet again (Est. 4:14).

Despite the dragon's machinations, Christ was born. Frustrated but undaunted, Satan goaded the already-evil Herod to slaughter all the baby boys in Bethlehem, thinking this insidious mass infanticide would take out the infant Christ (Matt. 2:16). But through a dream, God directed Joseph to get the child out of Bethlehem before the killings began. The child was born—and lived.

As Jesus neared the end of His forty-day wilderness fast, Satan laid before Him three successive temptations designed to destroy His redemptive mission. But using no weapon other than Scripture, Jesus repelled Satan's attacks and sent him scurrying away in defeat (Luke 4:1–13).

The Devil made two more attempts on Jesus' life. He incited Nazareth's leaders to throw Him off a cliff (Luke 4:29) and the Pharisees to stone Him (John 8:59). Jesus miraculously escaped both attempts.

Finally, however, Satan succeeded. On Friday before the Jewish Passover celebration, the hatred he infused into the hearts of the Jewish leaders finally paid off. He watched in gleeful triumph as they beat Jesus unmercifully and nailed his battered body to a cross to die. When that body was sealed within a tomb, Satan's victory was complete. Or so he thought. He did not realize that Jesus' death was but a prelude to His resurrection—the event that would ensure Satan's ultimate doom.[1]

THE GREAT WAR

War broke out in heaven: Michael and his angels fought with the
dragon; and the dragon and his angels fought, but they did not prevail,
nor was a place found for them in heaven any longer. (Rev. 12:7–8)

The war described here is not merely a single battle; it is more like World War II, a conflict fought by many antagonists on many fronts. Michael battles Satan; God's angels battle Satan's angels; God-led humans battle Satan-led humans. These battles are ongoing, building toward a final, cataclysmic conflict that will forever destroy Satan and his diabolic influence.

We can better understand the nature of this war when we realize that evil does not exist in the abstract. Though all evil originates in Satan's heart, he has no power to create anything that is inherently evil. All evil is simply damage done to good. Evil consists solely of destroying, warping, marring, co-opting, or misusing the good that God created. Satan, in his hatred of God, has made it his whole purpose to inflict all the evil he can upon God's creation.

To secure his usurped position as lord of the earth, Satan has organized his fallen angels into a hierarchy, placing the most powerful ones over nations and provinces. We see this order demonstrated in Daniel 10. Daniel had been fasting and praying for three weeks without an answer when suddenly an angel of God appeared. The angel explained that God had heard Daniel's prayer from its beginning and had immediately dispatched the angel to answer him. But as this angel sped toward Daniel, he was attacked by a satanic angel, the prince of Persia, who was determined to prevent the delivery of God's message. The two angels battled to a standoff until the archangel Michael joined the combat and held the prince of Persia at bay, freeing the heavenly angel to complete his mission.

We know that this "prince of Persia" is an angelic being for two reasons: First, no mere human could withstand the might of one of God's angels. Second, Cyrus the Great was at that time the human ruler of Persia, and he was a benefactor to the Jews, not an enemy.

Satan's capacity to wage war raises a theological question: If he has already been judged by the cross, why is he free to continue the war? It's true that Satan has been judged, as these two passages tell us: "When [the Holy Spirit] has come, He will convict the world of sin, and of righteousness, and of judgment . . . because the ruler of this world is judged" (John 16:8, 11). "Inasmuch then as the children have partaken of flesh and blood, [Christ] Himself likewise shared in the same, that through death He might destroy him who had the power of death, that is, the devil" (Heb. 2:14).

Yes, Satan has been judged, but the sentence has not yet been enforced. We see examples of delay between sentence and execution in our nation's courts. In most capital cases, execution is carried out years after sentencing. Satan has been defeated and judged, but God has chosen to delay execution until the time is right.

The still-free Satan continues to inflict heinous evil on us, but we believers need not despair. We can engage the battle and enforce Christ's victory over Satan through prayer. Daniel is our example. His three-week prayer was instrumental in defeating the satanic prince of Persia. Victories on earth and in heaven are dependent on each other, just as in World War II the ground troops invading Normandy were dependent on air power to soften their invasion sites. As we combat evil on earth, our angelic fellow warriors battle evil in the invisible spiritual dimension. Churches and godly homes are battle stations from which prayers emanate in a vast communication network that connects both fronts. As prayer warriors, we often turn the tide of human events. Someone has said, "It's not the mayors that make the world go 'round; it's the prayers."

The defeated Satan fights on in sheer vindictiveness, but he cannot conquer those of us who have joined the army of the Lord and claim Christ's victory as our own. We may endure persecution or even death, inflicted by the dragon's dying throes. But we are assured of ultimate victory, and this is our source of courage. We are fully equipped and protected in every encounter with Satan or his angels. "The weapons of our warfare are not carnal but mighty in God for pulling down strongholds, casting down arguments and every high thing that exalts itself against the knowledge of God, bringing every thought into captivity to the obedience of Christ" (2 Cor. 10:4–5).

THE GREAT WRATH

Rejoice, O heavens, and you who dwell in them! Woe to the inhabitants
of the earth and the sea! For the devil has come down to you, having
great wrath, because he knows that he has a short time. (Rev. 12:12)

In this passage, the reason for the contrast between the joyful people and the woeful ones is clear: One group, now safely in heaven, is protected forever from Satan. The other group is about to face the Devil's final rampage of evil. Satan is aware of reality; he knows that with the resurrection of Christ, the game is up. He is forever defeated. Yet in the interim between his defeat and his final sentence, his wrath will explode, wreaking death and destruction like never before.

AN AGGRAVATED ASSAULT

The Greek word for *wrath* in the passage above means "strong passion or emotion." Donald Grey Barnhouse likens the Devil's wrath to that of a caged animal: "The animal that was dangerous enough when he roamed through the whole forest is now limited to a stockade, where, mad with the restrictions which he sees around him, and raging because he feels the end near, he throws the insane strength of the death struggle into all of his movements."[2]

AN ANTI-SEMITIC ASSAULT

Before the end, Satan will mount an all-out assault on God's people, the Jews, launching a tsunami of anti-Semitism over the world like nothing yet seen in human history. "When the dragon saw that he had been cast to the earth, he persecuted the woman who gave birth to the male Child. . . . So the serpent spewed water out of his mouth like a flood after the woman, that he might cause her to be carried away by the flood" (12:13, 15). Satan hates Israel because it is the nation that birthed Christ. He is bent on destroying the Jews to prevent fulfillment of Israel's role in prophecy when Christ returns to establish His kingdom.

Satan knows his days are numbered, but like a spiteful child who breaks a playmate's toy because he can't have it, he will go all-out to crush Israel. He spews water from his mouth to sweep Israel off the face of the earth (v. 15). This may indicate a literal flood that will inundate Israel, or it may be a symbolic picture of the Devil's overall campaign to obliterate the Jews. Either way, his intent is clear: before the end, he will launch an unprecedented offensive against Israel.

AN ANGRY ASSAULT

John tells us that "the dragon was enraged with the woman, and he went to make war with the rest of her offspring, who keep the commandments of God and have the testimony of Jesus Christ" (v. 17). This passage refers specifically to Jewish believers in Christ. These believers are undoubtedly the 144,000 Jewish witnesses introduced in Revelation 7. Satan's fury will descend on these converted Jews simply because they will have joined forces with his ultimate enemy.

THE GREAT WINGS

The woman was given two wings of a great eagle, that she might
fly into the wilderness to her place, where she is nourished
for a time and times and half a time, from the presence of
the serpent. . . . But the earth helped the woman, and the
earth opened its mouth and swallowed up the flood which
the dragon had spewed out of his mouth. (vv. 14, 16)

Jews would immediately recognize the "two wings of a great eagle" as symbolic of the grace of God, who spoke of delivering them from bondage in Egypt, saying, "I bore you on eagles' wings and brought you to Myself" (Ex. 19:4). This reference assures Israel that during Satan's aggressive assault, God will again deliver them as he did from Egypt. He will move them to a secure, protected place. Some think this place will be the ancient, rock-carved city-fortress Petra, hidden deep within the cliffs south of the Dead Sea. Revelation 12:14 says these Jews will be "nourished," indicating a recurrence of His supernatural provision which sustained Elijah at the brook Cherith and Israel during the Exodus. By whatever means, God assures Israel that a godly remnant of their number will be saved.

Carolyn Arends tells of an incident that vividly illustrates why the world suffers continuing damage from Satan despite the fact that he has been defeated. She recounts the story as reported by a missionary couple stationed in a steamy jungle:

> One day, they told us, an enormous snake—much longer than a man—slithered its way right through their front door and into the kitchen of their simple home. Terrified, they ran outside and searched frantically for a local who might know what to do. A machete-wielding neighbor came to the rescue, calmly marching into their house and decapitating the snake with one clean chop.
>
> The neighbor reemerged triumphant and assured the missionaries that the reptile had been defeated. But there was a catch, he warned: It was going to take a while for the snake to realize it was dead.
>
> A snake's neurology and blood flow are such that it can take considerable time for it to stop moving even after decapitation. For the next several hours, the missionaries were forced to wait outside while the snake thrashed about, smashing furniture and flailing against walls and windows, wreaking havoc until its body finally understood that it no longer had a head. . . .
>
> At some point in their waiting, [the missionaries] told us, they had a mutual epiphany. . . .
>
> "Do you see it?" asked the husband. "Satan is a lot like that big old snake. He's already been defeated. He just doesn't know it yet. In the meantime, he's going to do some damage. But never forget that he's a goner."

Arends reminds us that a day is coming when Satan's thrashing will cease: "The story haunts me because I have come to believe it is an accurate picture of the universe. We are in the thrashing time, a season characterized by our pervasive capacity to do violence to each other and ourselves. The temptation is to despair. We have to remember, though, that it won't last forever. Jesus has already crushed the serpent's head."[3]

CHAPTER 25

MARK OF THE BEAST

Jakob Frenkiel grew up as one of seven sons in a Jewish family outside Warsaw, Poland. Jakob was ten years old when Germany declared war against Poland in 1939—old enough to remember the German soldiers invading his town and burning down the wooden synagogue close to his home. Like so many Jews during that time, Jakob and the other males of his family were eventually shipped to a concentration camp.

For Jakob and his brothers, it was Auschwitz:

At age 12, I was put in a group of men to be sent to labor camps. More than a year later, we were shipped to Auschwitz. The day after we arrived, my brother Chaim and I were lined up with kids and old people. I asked a prisoner what was going to happen to us. He pointed to the chimneys. "Tomorrow the smoke will be from you." He said if we could get a number tattooed on our arms, we'd be put to work instead of being killed. We sneaked to the latrine, then escaped through a back door and lined up with the men getting tattoos.[1]

The Jewish Virtual Library offers an explanation for the use of tattoos:

While it cannot be determined with absolute certainty, it seems that tattooing was implemented mainly for ease of identification whether in the case of death or escape; the practice continued until the last days of Auschwitz.[2]

As citizens of the modern world and participants in a "civilized" culture, we like to think the Holocaust represents the last time a mark will be used for identification as a way of perpetuating evil in our world on such a large scale. But it won't be. Satan plans to use another mark during the Tribulation, the mark of the Beast, and its use will be worldwide.

I'm often asked a wide range of questions about this mark of the Beast and how it might affect the lives of those enduring the Tribulation. Let's explore some of those questions together.

THE PERSONALITIES BEHIND THE MARK

Many Christians are surprised to learn that the mark of the Beast will not be implemented personally by the Antichrist—the Beast that arises from the sea (Rev. 13:1). Later in the same chapter, John tells us that this mark will be initiated by a second beast, the "beast coming up out of the earth" (v. 11) who is later identified as the False Prophet (16:13).

While the False Prophet will be the implementor of the mark, he will be acting on authority that comes from higher up. As John tells us, "He exercises all the authority of the first beast" (13:12). And where does the first beast, the Antichrist, get his power? "The dragon [Satan] gave him his power, his throne, and great authority" (v. 2). Satan himself will instigate all the terrible evil of the Tribulation period with the Antichrist and the False Prophet acting as his diabolical agents.

The False Prophet, working on behalf of the Antichrist, will use the mark to subjugate the world during the Tribulation period. John tells us that "he causes all, both small and great, rich and poor, free and slave, to receive a mark on their right hand or on their foreheads, and that no one may buy or sell except one who has the mark or the name of the beast, or the number of his name" (vv. 16–17).

As the word *prophet* indicates, the False Prophet will be a religious leader, the kind Jesus warned of when He said, "Beware of false prophets, who come to you in sheep's clothing, but inwardly they are ravenous wolves" (Matt. 7:15). Many false prophets have come and gone, but none have had the devastating impact on the world's population that the False Prophet of Revelation will inflict. He will use religion to deceive the world, and once deceived, he will use the mark of the Beast to enslave all people economically, forcing them to endure the unrelenting tyranny of Satan and the Antichrist.

THE PURPOSE OF THE MARK

Revelation 13:17 tells us what the mark will do on a day-to-day basis: "No one may buy or sell except one who has the mark or the name of the beast, or the number of his name." Only those who have the mark or the Antichrist's name or his number, identifying them as his followers, will be able to sell goods and services to support themselves and secure what they need. Anyone refusing to wear the mark will struggle to survive.

It's notable that the word *mark* is translated from the Greek *charagma*. The *charagma* was a symbol used somewhat like notary seals are used today. The symbol consisted of a portrait of the emperor and the year of his reign. It was required to complete commercial transactions and was stamped in wax on official documents to authenticate their validity. The mark of the Beast will function in a similar way, identifying those who bear it as worshipers of the Beast and permitting them to conduct financial transactions.

This fusion of government and religion will put the squeeze on rebels, leaving them nowhere to turn. Those who refuse the mark will be shut out of society altogether. No one will buy their products or services. Barred from employment and from shopping in stores or online, they will face bankruptcy and starvation.

Given our modern financial system, it's hard to imagine a scenario in which Christians are shut out like this. But the Bible is clear that Satan's intent is not only to keep them from means of survival, but also to force them to a decision: Will they continue to stand for Christ, refusing the mark despite the hardship promised? Or will they succumb to the loyalty demands of Satan and take on the mark to relieve that hardship?

In many countries now, Christians face persecution and even death when they stand for Christ, just as those without the mark will during the Tribulation. During that time, these questions will be put before the entire world's population, without exception. They will come in the form of the offered mark, supposedly to promote a good life, but with the intent to make clear who will live for Christ and who will yield to Satan.

THE PERPLEXITY ABOUT THE MARK

It's not unusual for people who have never read the Bible or heard a sermon to know something about the mark of the Beast and its associated number, 666. The mark and number have been featured in novels and feature films, invoking mystery and terror, but usually with little to no solid biblical context. In fact, some TV and film scripts make jokes about the mark, as if Satan's work can ever be a laughing matter.

This exposure is enough to make people wary of the number 666. For example, in the same way many high-rise building owners refuse to designate a floor number thirteen, many people try to eliminate the 666 sequence from their phone numbers, home addresses, license plate numbers, and almost any other personal number you can think of. Maybe you have done that as well; the number itself can be unsettling.

No one knows what form the mark of the Beast will take. John gives us a mysterious clue that has tantalized theologians for centuries: "Here is wisdom. Let him who has understanding calculate the number of the beast, for it is the number of a man: His number is 666" (v. 18).

Theories about the meaning of the number 666 run rampant, ranging from the ridiculous to the absurd. No coincidence or fact from the Bible or from history is safe from becoming fodder for speculation. For example, Goliath stood six cubits high; the head of his spear weighed six hundred shekels; and he wore six items of armor (1 Sam. 17:4–7). Will the Antichrist be another Goliath? The statue of Nebuchadnezzar stood sixty cubits high, six cubits wide, and six musical instruments summoned the Babylonians to worship it (Dan. 3:1, 15 NIV). Will the Antichrist be a revived Babylonian emperor? Numbers in names and calendars have been manipulated to designate the Pope, Hitler, and many US presidents as the Antichrist. But these interpretations are nothing more than contrivances.

Bottom line: no one yet knows the real meaning of 666.

The most likely answer is probably the least sensational. John tells us that 666 is the number of a man. Could he be saying simply that this number refers to humanity in general? The Bible often connects the number six with mankind. Humans were created on the sixth day. We are enjoined to work six days a week. Hebrew slavery was limited to six years.

By contrast, the number associated with God is seven. He created many things in sets of sevens—seven colors in the spectrum; seven notes in the diatonic musical scale; and seven days in a week. God also ordained many events in series of sevens: seven feasts of Jehovah (Lev. 23); seven priests bearing seven trumpets led the Israelite army around Jericho for seven days—then seven times on the seventh day—causing the city walls to fall (Josh. 6). The number seven is found more than thirty times in the book of Revelation, which includes seven of each of the following items:

- churches
- spirits
- stars
- lamps

- lampstands
- seals
- horns
- eyes
- angels
- plagues
- bowls
- mountains
- kings
- beatitudes
- judgments
- letters
- songs
- "I am" statements of Christ

Seven is often called a perfect number, while six is an incomplete number. When you try to indicate the fraction two-thirds decimally, your calculator strings out an endless succession of sixes, never quite completing a precise rendition of two-thirds. This may indicate the significance of 666. It is the number of humanity, and no matter how many sixes you add, it never reaches the perfection of seven—God's number. Man without God is always incomplete, and we long for the completeness we can find only in relationship with Him.

It would be more fruitful to abandon our quest for the meaning of 666 and focus instead on the desire which that incomplete number should arouse in us—the desire to rise above our fallen nature and find completeness in God.

Humans seem to have a built-in desire for completeness. We see this desire at work in a story about a trick the mischievous children of the composer Johann Sebastian Bach sometimes played on their father. According to legend, shortly after he went upstairs to bed, the children would sneak to the parlor harpsichord and play all the notes of the scale except the last one.

Bach, freshly snuggled into his bed, could not stand hearing the incomplete scale lingering in his mind. He had to rise, don his robe, descend the stairs, and plunk that final, scale-completing key.

Our very nature longs for completion, not only of the musical scale, but also of ourselves. We should use the number 666 to remind us that since the fall of mankind, something has been missing from our lives. That "something" is found in a Someone—Christ Himself, the perfect number who can give us the completeness we lack.

THE PRECURSORS TO THE MARK

The apostle John didn't know how the False Prophet could cause a mark to have such power to divide and conquer; he just knew he would. But I think we in the twenty-first century have some idea of what can make it possible for the False Prophet to effectively weaponize the mark of the Beast: technology.

Living in the first century, John would likely have understood the mark to be like a tattoo or a brand on the skin. The possibility of using the microchip or other technologies we have today would have been an unfathomable mystery to him. But these technologies are advancing almost at mach speed, and there is little doubt that the technology for implementing the mark of the Beast is either already here or a new one will arise to be fully developed and realized in the time of Tribulation.

I'll say it again: I believe we are already in the last days, and we know the Rapture could come at any time. We also know that the mark of the Beast will be fully employed in the middle of the seven-year Tribulation period. Therefore, the extreme hardship caused by the mark could be only a mere three-and-a-half years away from the time you are reading this book, making it a very real danger for much of the world's present population.

As I write this, we have no idea exactly how technology might be employed to implement the coming mark of the Beast. But present technology already indicates a couple of ways by which it could happen.

The first is through microchips and sensors. The practice of implanting microchips in humans is growing because people are attracted to the benefits of ease and safety they provide. Microchips can be implanted invisibly under the skin. They can be read via short-range frequency identification (RFID) signals to enable the wearer to buy goods in stores without using a plastic card or cell phone. Microchips can also be used to identify everyone who walks through a security checkpoint.

But there is a downside. As *Fox News* reported, there are "concerns about the wrong people accessing personal information and tracking you via the chips."[3] Think about that: "the wrong people." What people could be more wrong than the Beast and his conspirators? Yet despite the serious and obvious downsides, more and more people are willingly acquiring[4] and submitting to[5] microchip implants to take advantage of their perceived convenience and benefits.

In January 2018, Amazon opened a convenience store in Seattle testing new technology that could become common nationwide. It's based on a grab-and-go concept with no cashiers, no shopping carts, and no checkout lines. Using a combination of cell phone technology and in-store scanners, shoppers' accounts are automatically debited electronically as they carry goods out of the store.[6]

Now picture this: during the Tribulation, store scanners reading data from shoppers' implanted microchips as they attempt to buy food or other necessities. If they don't have the mark of approval, if they've refused to worship the Antichrist and acquiesce to the system put into place by the False Prophet, they'll go without.

Another possible precursor to the mark of the Beast is Bitcoin. Bitcoin is completely virtual money not issued or controlled by a centralized government. Physical coins and currency are completely eliminated, and all money is electronic, tracked either by implanted chips or on the Internet. Some believe Bitcoin could pave the way for the future mark of the Beast.

How or if these particular technologies will be used to implement the mark would be mere speculation at this point in time. The False Prophet might use either one of these technologies, a combination of both, or some technology yet to be invented. Those who read this book years after its publication date may well experience technologies far more sophisticated than anything imaginable today. We won't know for certain how the mark of the Beast will be incorporated until it's too late.

WHAT WILL HAPPEN IN THE END?

The form and nature of the mark will remain a mystery until it is actually implemented. But there is no mystery about the future of those who accept the mark. As long as the Beast maintains control, all will be well with those who accept it. But their time of prosperity will be short, followed swiftly by the inevitable judgment of God:

> If anyone worships the beast and his image, and receives his mark on his forehead or on his hand, he himself shall also drink of the wine of the wrath of God, which is poured out full strength into the cup of His indignation. He shall be tormented with fire and brimstone in the presence of the holy angels and in the presence of the Lamb. And the smoke of their torment ascends forever and ever; and they have no rest day or night, who worship the beast and his image, and whoever receives the mark of his name. (Rev. 14:9–11)

Followers of Christ who refuse the mark will experience a complete inversion of the fate of those who receive it. While the Beast maintains control, they will experience deadly persecution. But after that, John tells us:

> And I saw thrones, and they sat on them, and judgment was committed to them. Then I saw the souls of those who had been beheaded for their witness to Jesus and for the word of God, who had not worshiped the

beast or his image, and had not received his mark on their foreheads or on their hands. And they lived and reigned with Christ for a thousand years. (20:4)

Christians who reject the mark will be acting on the admonition of Christ, who said, "And do not fear those who kill the body but cannot kill the soul. But rather fear Him who is able to destroy both soul and body in hell" (Matt. 10:28).

You may believe you are safely exempted from this warning because Christ will take the church into heaven before the horrors of the Tribulation begin. You will never have to make the decision to refuse the mark and face the suffering that will follow. That is quite true, but it does not exempt you from the possibility of facing persecution. Christians have suffered for their faith throughout history, and many around the world are suffering severely even as you read these words. We live in a fallen world, which means "the whole creation groans and labors with birth pangs together until now" (Rom. 8:22). These "birth pangs" will get increasingly worse as we move toward the time when all comes crashing down in the Tribulation period.

Even today, we must choose. Will we be marked as God's own in our hearts and in our actions? Or will we be marked as Satan's own? Will we stand for Christ, His Son, no matter the personal cost? Will we endure any hardship or persecution for His sake?

I will end this chapter by posing to you one final question, which you may find difficult to answer. If you were forced to choose between standing with God by rejecting the mark or taking it to ensure the immediate safety and security of your family, which would you do? We see the right answer superbly demonstrated in a story of three young Jewish men as related in the book of Daniel:

Nebuchadnezzar the king made an image of gold, whose height was sixty cubits and its width six cubits. He set it up in the plain of Dura, in the province of Babylon. . . . Then a herald cried aloud: "To you it is commanded, O peoples, nations, and languages, that at the time you hear the sound of the horn, flute, harp, lyre, and psaltery, in symphony with all kinds of music, you shall fall down and worship the gold image that King Nebuchadnezzar has set up; and whoever does not fall down and worship shall be cast immediately into the midst of a burning fiery furnace." (Dan. 3:1, 4–6)

After the image was unveiled, the people of Babylon were ordered to assemble before it. The musical call to worship was sounded, and immediately the entire population fell to their knees. That is, all but three young men who stood tall and unbending among the carpet of worshippers surrounding them. These three men were Jews taken from Jerusalem whom we know by their Babylonian names: Shadrach, Meshach, and Abed-nego. Their refusal to worship the image infuriated King Nebuchadnezzar. Yet he offered them a second chance, warning if they refused to bow a second time, they would be cast alive into a superheated furnace of fire.

Read the response of these three courageous men and see if you don't love them as I did when I first read their story. They became my models for courage, and even now I pray that if I am ever tested as they were, I will find within my heart the same kind of courage they so eloquently expressed to the king in these fine words:

O Nebuchadnezzar, we have no need to answer you in this matter. If that is the case, our God whom we serve is able to deliver us from the burning fiery furnace, and He will deliver us from your hand, O king. But if not, let it be known to you, O king, that we do not serve your gods, nor will we worship the gold image which you have set up. (vv. 16–18)

These three brave men were precursors to those in the coming Tribulation period who will refuse the mark of the Beast. Like Shadrach, Meshach, and Abed-nego, they will refuse the safe and easy path and choose to stand for God rather than bow to evil.

We often tend to make right choices much too complex. When the outcome seems doubtful or ominous, we want to hold off the decision while we weigh all the factors, examine all the nuances, and consider all the outcomes. But in essence, almost all moral decisions are starkly simple: either we stand for God or we fall for Satan. Whether the result will be inconvenient or painful or even fatal should never be a factor. The only decision to be made is whether you are on God's side, which means you will follow Him regardless of the cost.

The decision may mean repression or loss of freedom. It may even mean death. But if we stand tall and true to God while all others are taking the mark and bowing to the image, we can rely on His promise that we will ultimately reign with Him (2 Tim. 2:12; Rev. 20:6).

CHAPTER 26

ARMAGEDDON

General Douglas MacArthur stood tall on the deck of the USS *Missouri* in Tokyo harbor. It was September 2, 1945, and this man who had engineered America's hard-fought victory in the Pacific had just witnessed the signatures of Japan's leaders ending the bloody global struggle known as World War II. On that day, this authentic American hero uttered a profound warning, which he later repeated in his famous farewell address before the United States Congress: "We have had our last chance," he said. "If we will not devise some greater and more equitable system, Armageddon will be at our door."[1]

Shortly after he was inaugurated as the fortieth president of the United States, Ronald Reagan was astounded by the complexities of the Middle East. Israel, on its thin strip of land, was surrounded by well-armed Arab enemies who were splintered like broken glass into countless factions and divisions impossible to reconcile. On Friday, May 15, 1981, scribbling in his diary, Reagan noted the intractable problems involving Lebanon, Syria, Saudi Arabia, the Soviet Union, and Israel. "Sometimes I wonder," he wrote, "if we are destined to witness Armageddon."[2]

Armageddon. The very word chills the soul. There are probably very few adults who are not familiar with that word and what it implies. Why have our national leaders, in the twentieth and twenty-first centuries, begun to use that doomsday word in their speaking and writing? I believe it is because they can see how modern weaponry and international tensions are showing how quickly global equilibrium could get out of control, leading to a cataclysmic war such as the world has never seen before.

This war, called Armageddon, makes all the wars fought to date look like minor skirmishes. This war will draw the final curtain on modern civilization.

THE PREPARATION FOR THE BATTLE OF ARMAGEDDON

In the twelfth chapter of Revelation, the apostle John revealed how this conflagration will come about. "So the great dragon was cast out, that serpent of old, called the Devil and Satan, who deceives the whole world; he was cast to the earth, and his angels were cast out with him . . . Now when the dragon saw that he had been cast to the earth, he persecuted the woman who gave birth to the male Child" (vv. 9, 13).

These verses tell us that during the Tribulation, when Satan is cast out of heaven to the earth, he will begin immediately to persecute the woman who brought forth the male child. The "woman" is a metaphor for Israel, through whom the child Jesus was born. Satan's first attempt at persecution will be the Battle of Gog and Magog. This battle, which precedes the Battle of Armageddon, will be a massive, Russian-led coalition of nations coming against Israel like swarms of hornets against a defenseless child. As Revelation tells us, Satan will be the motivating force behind this invasion. But before he can accomplish his intended annihilation of Israel, she will be rescued by almighty God.

The thwarting of the battle of Gog and Magog will be a setback to Satan, but he will not give up; he is relentless in his persecution of the Jews. His purpose, beginning in the middle of the Tribulation period, is to destroy the Jewish people before Christ can set up His kingdom, thus wrecking God's prophesied rule over the earth. According to Revelation 16, Satan will employ two fearful personalities in these plans: "I saw three unclean spirits like frogs coming out of the mouth of the dragon, out of the mouth of the *beast*, and out of the mouth of the *false prophet*" (v. 13, emphasis added).

Here John tells us that Satan will empower the Beast, who is the head of the reestablished Roman Empire, and the False Prophet, the head of the new world religious system. Thus Satan (the dragon), the Beast (the Antichrist), and the False Prophet become the unholy trinity committed to the destruction of Israel. When the church of Jesus Christ is taken safely into heaven and the Tribulation period begins, the unrestrained satanic persecution of Israel will propel the entire world toward the Battle of Armageddon.

THE PLACE OF THE BATTLE
OF ARMAGEDDON

"They gathered them together to the place called in Hebrew, Armageddon" (v. 16).

Given the enormous attention this word receives, it may surprise you that *Armageddon* is mentioned only once in the Bible—right here in the sixteenth chapter of Revelation. The word originates from the Hebrew *har megiddo* meaning "the mount of Megiddo." *Har* means "mount," and *megiddo* means "slaughter"; so the meaning of Armageddon is "Mount of Slaughter."

The mountain of Megiddo is an actual geographical feature located in northern Israel. It includes an extended plain that reaches from the Mediterranean Sea to the northern part of the land of Israel. Megiddo is about eighteen miles southeast of Haifa, fifty-five miles north of Jerusalem, and a little more than ten miles from Nazareth, the town where Jesus grew up.

Why Megiddo? Why will this be the location of the world's final conflict? One of the world's greatest military figures gives us the answer. In 1799, Napoleon stood at Megiddo before the battle that ended his quest to conquer the East and rebuild the Roman Empire. Considering the enormous plain of Armageddon, he declared: "All the armies of the world could maneuver their forces on this vast plain . . . There is no place in the whole world more suited for war than this . . . [It is] the most natural battleground on the whole earth."[3]

This war will be so horrific that the Bible says blood will flow in staggering torrents. "The winepress was trampled outside the city, and blood came out of the winepress, up to the horses' bridles, for one thousand six hundred furlongs" (14:20). If you translate these ancient measurements into the terminology of today, sixteen hundred furlongs is almost exactly two hundred miles—about the distance from the northern to the southern tip of the land of Israel.

We would actually be more accurate to refer to this conflict as the "*Campaign* of Armageddon." The word translated as "battle" in Revelation 16:14 is the Greek word *polemos*, which signifies a war or campaign. Armageddon will involve many battles fought throughout the entire land of Israel over a three-and-one-half-year period of time.

THE PURPOSE OF THE BATTLE OF ARMAGEDDON

Our sensibilities revolt when we read of the carnage the Bible describes in the Battle of Armageddon. And the horrible scene raises all kinds of questions that many people find difficult to answer. We wonder what is going on, not only in the world but also in the mind of God. Just what are His purposes?

TO FINISH HIS JUDGMENT UPON ISRAEL

The Tribulation period is a time of divine indignation against the people of Israel, the people who rejected their Messiah and—time and time again after given the chance to return—failed to heed the corrective and punitive judgment of God. It is no accident that this future period of time is often referred to as "the time of Jacob's trouble" (Jer. 30:7).

TO FINALIZE HIS JUDGMENT UPON THE NATIONS THAT HAVE PERSECUTED ISRAEL

Those nations that have persecuted the Jewish people are finally gathered together in the Battle of Armageddon, in the Valley of Jehoshaphat, giving God the perfect opportunity to deal with them finally and decisively.

> I will also gather all nations,
> And bring them down to the Valley of Jehoshaphat;
> And I will enter into judgment with them there
> On account of My people, My heritage Israel,
> Whom they have scattered among the nations;
> They have also divided up My land. (Joel 3:2)

TO FORMALLY JUDGE ALL THE NATIONS THAT HAVE REJECTED HIM

"Now out of His mouth goes a sharp sword, that with it He should strike the nations. And He Himself will rule them with a rod of iron. He Himself treads the winepress of the fierceness and wrath of Almighty God" (Rev. 19:15).

This verse gives us another of God's purposes in bringing about Armageddon. Notice particularly that last phrase: "He Himself treads the winepress of the fierceness and wrath of Almighty God." To our time-bound senses, God's activity often seems so slow and ponderous that people pursuing ungodly goals tend to dismiss His judgment as a factor to be taken seriously. Thus the nations do not believe that a time is coming when God's judgment will inevitably descend. But be assured, He is storing up judgment against a day to come. The Bible is clear: one of these days God will have had enough, and His judgment will pour down like consuming fire against the world's wicked nations. "And men were scorched with great heat, and they blasphemed the name of God who has power over these plagues; and they did not repent and give Him glory" (16:9).

This verse tells us just how incredibly wicked the nations will have become when God's judgment descends. Even when these men are writhing and screaming with the excruciating pain God inflicts upon them, they will continue to curse Him to His face. They will be so far gone, so given over to evil, that in their prideful defiance they will refuse to repent, even in the grip of fatal judgment.

THE PARTICIPANTS IN THE BATTLE OF ARMAGEDDON

As we have noted, all the nations of the world will be involved in the Battle of Armageddon, and they will be led by the Antichrist. But the Bible gives us many more details about the motives and actions of the participants in this battle. These are worth exploring, as they provide insights into the nature of the war and why it will be fought.

THE DEAL BETWEEN ISRAEL AND ANTICHRIST

Referring specifically to the Antichrist, Daniel tells us that "he shall confirm a covenant with many for one week" (Dan. 9:27). In prophetic language, this means a week of years, so the covenant will be made for seven years. The Antichrist will sign such a covenant with Israel, guaranteeing peace and security for seven years. Israel will view this man not as the evil Antichrist but as a beneficent and charismatic leader.

THE WORSHIP OF THE ANTICHRIST

On the heels of the covenant with Israel, this self-appointed world ruler will begin to strengthen his power by performing amazing signs and wonders, including even a supposed resurrection from the dead (Rev. 13:3). Then with his grip on the world greatly enhanced, he will boldly take the next step in his arrogant defiance of God: "Then the king shall do according to his own will: he shall exalt and magnify himself above every god, shall speak blasphemies against the God of gods" (Dan. 11:36).

Daniel goes on to give us a further description of the Antichrist's insidious methods:

> He shall regard neither the God of his fathers nor the desire of women, nor regard any god; for he shall exalt himself above them all. But in their place he shall honor a god of fortresses; and a god which his fathers did not know he shall honor with gold and silver, with precious stones and pleasant things. Thus he shall act against the strongest fortresses with a foreign god, which he shall acknowledge, and advance its glory; and he shall cause them to rule over many, and divide the land for gain. (Dan. 11:37–39)

The Antichrist will be the epitome of the man with a compulsion to extend his dominion over everything and everyone. To achieve this end, the Antichrist will bow to no god but the "god of fortresses." That is, he will build enormous military might and engage in extensive warfare to extend his power throughout the world.

Daniel describes how the swollen megalomania of the Antichrist will drive him to take his next step in Daniel 11:36, quoted earlier. John expanded on Daniel's description of the Antichrist's blasphemous acts by telling us that every living person will be required to worship this man. "He was granted power to give breath to the image of the beast, that the image of the beast should both speak and cause as many as would not worship the image of the beast to be killed" (Rev. 13:15). Step by step, the Antichrist will promote himself from a European leader, to a world leader, to a tyrannical global dictator, and finally to a god.

THE DECISION TO FIGHT AGAINST
THE ANTICHRIST

The Antichrist's grip on global power will not last long. The world will become increasingly discontented with the leadership of this global dictator, who will have gone back on every promise he made. Major segments of the world will begin to assemble their own military forces and rebel against him.

The king of the south and his armies will be the first to come after the Antichrist, followed by the armies of the north. "At the time of the end the king of the South shall attack him; and the king of the North shall come against him like a whirlwind, with chariots, horsemen, and with many ships" (Dan. 11:40). John Walvoord pinpoints the source of this army and describes the magnitude of the initial thrust against the Antichrist:

> Daniel's prophecy described a great army from Africa, including not only Egypt but other countries of that continent. This army, probably numbering in the millions, will attack the Middle East from the south. At the same time Russia and other armies to the north will mobilize another powerful military force to descend on the Holy Land and challenge the world dictator. Although Russia will have had a severe setback about four years earlier in the prophetic sequence of events, she apparently will have been able to recoup her losses enough to put another army in the field.[4]

The Antichrist will put down some of these first attempts at rebellion against him. But before he can celebrate and move on toward his goal of destroying Israel and Jerusalem, something will happen.

THE DISTURBING NEWS FROM THE EAST

"But news from the east and the north shall trouble him; therefore he shall go out with great fury" (v. 44). The Bible leaves no doubt as to the source of the news that so disturbs and enrages the Antichrist: "Then the sixth angel poured out his bowl on the great river Euphrates, and its water was dried up, so that the way of the kings from the east might be prepared" (Rev. 16:12).

The Euphrates is one of the greatest rivers in the world. It flows from the mountains of western Turkey through Syria, and continues on right through the heart of Iraq, not far from Baghdad. It eventually unites with the Tigris to become the Shatt al Arab, and finally empties into the Persian Gulf. The entirety of the Euphrates flows through Muslim territory. In Genesis 15 and Deuteronomy 11, the Lord specified that the Euphrates would be the easternmost border of the promised land. It serves both as a border and a barrier between Israel and her enemies.

What is the significance of the drying up of the Euphrates River, and why will that event have such a disturbing effect on the Antichrist? For an explanation, let's turn once more to John Walvoord:

> The drying-up of the Euphrates is a prelude to the final act of the drama, not the act itself. We must conclude then, that the most probable interpretation of the drying-up of the Euphrates is that by an act of God its flow will be interrupted even as were the waters of the Red Sea and of Jordan. This time the way will open not for Israel but for those who are referred to as the Kings of the East. . . . The evidence points, then, to a literal interpretation of Revelation 16:12 in relation to the Euphrates.[5]

It's no wonder the world dictator is disturbed and frustrated. He has just put down rebellions by defeating armies from the south and the north, and just when it appears that he is about to gain control of everything, he gets word that the Euphrates River has dried up and massive armies of the east are crossing it to come against him. He had thought himself safe, as no army could cross this barrier and come into the Israeli arena where he fought. But now that barrier is down, and an army of unprecedented numbers is marching toward him.

Just how large is that army? Listen to what John tells us: "Now the number of the army of the horsemen was two hundred million; I heard the number of them" (Rev. 9:16). Suddenly the Antichrist must divert the major portion of his attention to defending himself against an amassed force the size of which the world has never seen.

When this unprecedented army crosses the bed of the Euphrates against the Antichrist, the greatest war of all history, involving hundreds of millions of people, will be set in motion. The major battleground for that war will be the land of Israel.

As if this news were not frightening enough, John tells us that all these events are inspired and directed by the demons of hell: "For they are spirits of demons, performing signs, which go out to the kings of the earth and of the whole world, to gather them to the battle of that great day of God Almighty" (16:14).

> No doubt demonism in every shape and form will manifest itself more and more as the end draws near, until at last it all ends in Armageddon....
> But besides these hosts of human armies, there will also be present at Armageddon an innumerable host of supernatural beings. . . . So Armageddon will truly be a battle of heaven and earth and hell.[6]

So just at the moment when the Antichrist is about to attack and destroy Israel and Jerusalem, a diversion occurs in the form of another massive army entering the field of conflict. Thus the stage is set for the last, stunning movement in the Battle of Armageddon.

THE DESCENDING LORD FROM THE HEAVENS

If you are a follower of Christ, what happens next may instill an urge to stand up and shout like a football fan watching the star quarterback come onto the field.

> Now I saw heaven opened, and behold, a white horse. And He who sat on him was called Faithful and True, and in righteousness He judges and makes war. His eyes were like a flame of fire, and on His head were many

crowns. He had a name written that no one knew except Himself. He was clothed with a robe dipped in blood, and His name is called The Word of God. And the armies in heaven, clothed in fine linen, white and clean, followed Him on white horses. Now out of His mouth goes a sharp sword, that with it He should strike the nations. And He Himself will rule them with a rod of iron. He Himself treads the winepress of the fierceness and wrath of Almighty God. And He has on His robe and on His thigh a name written: KING OF KINGS AND LORD OF LORDS. (19:11–16)

The great Lord Jesus, the captain of the Lord's hosts, the King over all kings will descend to defend and protect His chosen people and put a once-and-for-all end to the evil of the Antichrist.

DESCENDING WITH HIS SAINTS

But the Lord Jesus, captain of the Lord's hosts, will not descend alone, as the following scriptures make abundantly clear:

- "Thus the LORD my God will come; and all the saints with You" (Zech. 14:5).
- "The coming of our Lord Jesus Christ with all His saints . . ." (1 Thess. 3:13).
- "Behold, the Lord comes with ten thousands of His saints" (Jude v. 14).

All those who have died in the Lord, along with those who were raptured before the years of the Tribulation, will join with the Lord and participate in the battle to reclaim the world for the rule of Christ.

DESCENDING WITH HIS ANGELS

The saints are not the only ones who will comprise the army of the Lord. Both Matthew and Paul tell us that the angels will also descend with Christ. "When the Son of Man comes in His glory, and all the holy angels with Him, then He will sit on the throne of His glory" (Matt. 25:31); "and to give you who are troubled rest with us when the Lord Jesus is revealed from heaven with His mighty angels" (2 Thess. 1:7).

How many angels are available for conscription into this army? Hebrews 12:22 sums it up by talking about innumerable angels in "joyful assembly" (NIV). Angels as far as the eye can see and the mind can imagine.[7]

This admixture of saints and angels calls to mind scenes from great fantasies such as *The Chronicles of Narnia* and *The Lord of the Rings*, where humans fight alongside otherworldly creatures to defeat the forces of evil. It's a thrilling picture to think of human saints side by side with God's angels doing battle.

The inception of the Battle of Armageddon has something of a historical precedent in miniature. Author Randall Price recounts the event:

The Yom Kippur War began at 2 P.M. on October 6, 1973. It was a surprise attack on Israel from the Arab nations of Egypt and Syria, which were intent on the destruction of the Jewish State. Overwhelming evidence of large-scale Arab military preparations on the morning of October 6 had compelled Chief of Staff David Elazar to ask the United States to help restrain the Arabs. U.S. Secretary of State Henry Kissinger urged Prime Minister Golda Meir to not issue a preemptive strike, but to trust international guarantees for Israel's security. To which Mrs. Meir, in her characteristic up-front manner, retorted, "By the time they come to save Israel, there won't be an Israel!"

When international intervention finally came in calling for cease-fire negotiations, Israel's casualties had mounted to 2,552 dead and over 3,000 wounded. And it would have been much worse if Israel hadn't realized that if nobody was going to fight for them, they were going to have to fight for themselves. For that reason, Israel has come to rely upon their own defenses for their security. That attack is just a foretaste of what Israel can expect in the future, when the worst attack in its history will come and will be centered on Jerusalem. In that day there will be no allies, not even reluctant ones. . . . But Scripture has prophesied otherwise. At the right time, Jerusalem's Savior will return.[8]

As Price tells us, Israel in this last war will be forced to rely on herself and not depend on assistance from allies. That is the similarity between the inception of the Battle of Armageddon and the Yom Kippur War, its miniature historical precedent. But what about the outcome? Will the end of the final war be anything like the end of Israel's Yom Kippur War? We will answer that question by telling the full story of the event in the next chapter.

Terrible and terrifying as the events we've discussed in this chapter may be, there is still good news. We may be disturbed by the signs we see of coming catastrophic events. We may feel uneasy due to the continual reports of wars and wanton terrorism. We may quail at reports of nature turning against us. But here is the bottom line: we who trust the Lord as our Savior need have no fear. He loves and protects His own, and whatever comes, if we seek Him and His will for our lives, we will be among those whom He saves from the wrath to come.

PART 5

END SIGNS

We've come to the last act in the cosmic drama featuring the signs of the Apocalypse.

Our story continues with the second coming of Christ, which is a central theme in the Bible's narrative and one of the best-attested signs in all of Scripture. Following the return of Christ, the glorious Millennium will be established—an era of unprecedented peace on earth.

After one thousand years, all the spiritually dead will stand before God at the Great White Throne Judgment where they will face the consequences for rejecting Jesus Christ as Savior and Lord. Then, the entire universe will be transformed by God's grace as a new heaven and new earth emerges, and a glorious city—with dazzling foundations whose architect and builder is God—descends from the sky and becomes the capital city of God's everlasting kingdom.

The final act ends. The curtain closes. Eternity begins. Let's conclude our study with five end signs God has given us to fill our hearts with anticipation and hope as the end of the world approaches.

CHAPTER 27

RETURN OF THE KING

In a room decorated for an Albanian funeral, our missionary to Albania, Ian Loring, delivered a powerful Good Friday sermon on the sacrificial death of Jesus Christ. Afterward, he invited everyone to come back on Sunday to observe the "third day ritual." In Albanian culture, friends return three days after a funeral to sit with the family, drink bitter coffee, and remember the one who has died. More than three hundred people filled the room that Easter Sunday. Ian preached about the "not quite empty tomb," observing that Christ's empty grave clothes still bore His shape, but the napkin, which had been wrapped around His head, was placed away from the other grave clothes, folded. To Ian's congregation, that minor detail held great meaning and promise. In Albania, when a person finishes a meal and prepares to leave the table, he crumples up his napkin to indicate that he is finished. But if he leaves his napkin folded, it is a sign that he plans to come back.

The application was obvious to the Albanians: Jesus is coming back!

The second coming of Christ is a central theme of much of the Bible, and it is one of the best-attested promises in all of Scripture. Christians can rest in the sure conviction that just as Jesus came to earth the first time, so He will return at the conclusion of the Great Tribulation.

THE ANTICIPATION OF CHRIST

Although Christians are most familiar with the first coming of Christ, it is the second coming that gets the most ink in the Bible. References to the second coming outnumber references to the first by a factor of eight to one. Scholars count 1,845 biblical references to the second coming, including 318 in the New Testament. Christ's return is emphasized in no less than seventeen Old Testament books and seven out of every ten chapters in the New Testament. The Lord Himself referred to His return twenty-one times. The second coming is second only to faith as the most dominant subject in the New Testament.

THE PROPHETS FORETOLD THE SECOND COMING OF CHRIST

While many of the Old Testament prophets wrote concerning the second coming of Christ, it is Zechariah who has given us the clearest and most concise prediction of it:

> Then the LORD will go forth
> And fight against those nations,
> As He fights in the day of battle.
> And in that day His feet will stand on the Mount of Olives,
> Which faces Jerusalem on the east.
> And the Mount of Olives shall be split in two,
> From east to west,
> Making a very large valley;
> Half of the mountain shall move toward the north
> And half of it toward the south. (Zech. 14:3–4)

Notice how Zechariah deals in specifics, even pinpointing the geographic location to which Christ will return: "In that day His feet will stand on the Mount of Olives" (14:4). Like Armageddon, the Mount of Olives is an explicitly identifiable place that retains its ancient name even today. Recently I visited a Jewish cemetery that has been on this site since biblical times. The prophet's specificity gives us confidence that his prophecy is true and accurate.

JESUS HIMSELF ANNOUNCED HIS SECOND COMING

Jesus, speaking from the Mount of Olives, affirmed His second coming to His disciples in dramatic and cataclysmic terms:

> "For as the lightning comes from the east and flashes to the west, so also will the coming of the Son of Man be. . . . Immediately after the tribulation of those days the sun will be darkened, and the moon will not give its light; the stars will fall from heaven, and the powers of the heavens will be shaken. Then the sign of the Son of Man will appear in heaven, and then all the tribes of the earth will mourn, and they will see the Son of Man coming on the clouds of heaven with power and great glory." (Matt. 24:27, 29-30)

THE ANGELS ANNOUNCED THAT JESUS WOULD RETURN

Immediately following Christ's ascension into heaven, two angels appeared to the stunned disciples and spoke words of comfort to them. "Men of Galilee," they said, "why do you stand gazing up into heaven? This same Jesus, who was taken up from you into heaven, will so come in like manner as you saw Him go into heaven" (Acts 1:11). The next verse tells us, "They returned to Jerusalem from the mount called Olivet" (v. 12). Did you catch that? Jesus ascended to heaven from the Mount of Olives. According to the angels, Christ will return to that very same spot—the Mount of Olives. The words of the angels conveyed both consolation for the disciples' present loss of Jesus and confirmation of His future return.

JOHN THE APOSTLE FORETOLD
JESUS' SECOND COMING

The prophecies of Christ's return are like bookends to John's Revelation. In the first chapter he wrote: "Behold, He is coming with clouds, and every eye will see Him, even they who pierced Him. And all the tribes of the earth will mourn because of Him" (Rev. 1:7). And in the last pages of the last chapter—indeed, almost the last words of the New Testament—our Lord emphatically affirms His second coming: "He who testifies to these things says, 'Surely I am coming quickly.' Amen. Even so, come, Lord Jesus!" (22:20).

Obviously we have excellent reason to anticipate the return of Christ. The Bible affirms it throughout as a certainty, describing it in specific terms and with ample corroboration.

THE ADVENT OF CHRIST

Twice in the book of Revelation we are told that the door to heaven will be opened. It is first opened to receive the church into heaven at the time of the Rapture: "After these things I looked, and behold, a door standing open in heaven. And the first voice which I heard was like a trumpet speaking with me, saying, 'Come up here, and I will show you things which must take place after this'" (4:1). The door swings open a second time for Christ and His church to proceed from heaven on their militant march back to earth (19:11, 14). The first opening is for the Rapture of the saints; the second is for the return of Christ!

When Jesus arrives on earth the second time, His landing will dramatically herald the purpose of His coming. The moment His feet touch the Mount of Olives, the mountain will split apart, creating a broad passageway from Jerusalem to Jericho. As you can imagine, this will be an unprecedented geological cataclysm.

Let's look briefly at the Bible's description of the glory and majesty Christ will display at His second coming.

HIS DESIGNATION

In Revelation 19, the descending Lord is given three meaningful titles.

> Now I saw heaven opened, and behold, a white horse. And He who sat on him was called Faithful and True, and in righteousness He judges and makes war. . . . He had a name written that no one knew except Himself . . . and His name is called THE WORD OF GOD. . . . And He has on His robe and on His thigh a name written: KING OF KINGS AND LORD OF LORDS. (vv. 11–13, 16)

I like the way one scholar summarizes these verses: "In these three names we have set forth first, our Lord's dignity as the Eternal Son; second, His incarnation—the Word became Flesh; and last, His second advent to reign as King of Kings and Lord of Lords."[1]

HIS DESCRIPTION

The eyes of the returning Christ are described as burning like a flame of fire, signifying His ability as a judge to see deeply into the hearts of men and ferret out all injustice (1:14; 2:18; 19:12). His eyes will pierce through the motives of nations and individuals and judge them for what they really are—not for how they hope their masks of hypocrisy will make them appear!

The head of the returning Christ is crowned with many crowns (19:12), testifying to His status as the absolute sovereign King of kings and Lord of lords—the undisputed monarch of the entire earth.

The robe of the returning Christ is dipped in blood, reminding us that He is the sacrificial Lamb of God. Earlier in Revelation, John described Him as "the Lamb slain from the foundation of the world" (13:8). In fact, Jesus will be represented to us as the Lamb of God throughout eternity.

THE ARMIES OF CHRIST

When Jesus returns to this earth to put down the world's ultimate rebellion, the armies of heaven will accompany him. John described these armies as "clothed in fine linen, white and clean, [following] Him on white horses" (19:14).

In the short epistle that immediately precedes the book of Revelation, Jude described this epic event in verses 14 and 15:

> Now Enoch, the seventh from Adam, prophesied about these men also, saying, "Behold, the Lord comes with ten thousands of His saints, to execute judgment on all, to convict all who are ungodly among them of all their ungodly deeds which they have committed in an ungodly way, and of all the harsh things which ungodly sinners have spoken against Him."

In one short verse, Jude used the word *ungodly* four times. This repetition is not accidental. Jude was emphasizing the fact that when Christ comes the second time, His long-suffering patience will have run its course. He will come to impose judgment upon those who have defied Him, and that judgment will be massive. At this point the people on the earth will have rejected the ministry of the 144,000 preachers and the two witnesses that God sent to them for their salvation, just as the prophet Jonah was sent to the Ninevites. In His loving mercy, God endeavored to turn them away from their fatal rebellion. But unlike the Ninevites, the people in the last days will have hardened their hearts beyond repentance.

THE AUTHORITY OF CHRIST

When the Lord returns to earth at the end of the Tribulation, the men and nations who have defied Him will no more be able to stand against Him than a spiderweb could stand against an eagle. His victory will be assured, and His authority undisputed. Here is how John described the finality of His judgment and the firmness of His rule: "And He Himself will rule them with a rod of iron. He Himself treads the winepress of the fierceness and wrath of Almighty God. And He has on His robe and on His thigh a name written: KING OF KINGS AND LORD OF LORDS" (Rev. 19:15–16).

This grand title, King of kings and Lord of lords, identifies our Lord at His second coming. It speaks of His unassailable authority. At this name every king on earth will bow, and every lord will kneel.

When Christ returns the second time, He will finally fulfill the prophecy of Isaiah that we often quote and hear choirs sing to Handel's lofty music at Christmastime: "For unto us a Child is born, unto us a Son is given; and the government will be upon His shoulder. And His name will be called Wonderful, Counselor, Mighty God, Everlasting Father, Prince of Peace" (Isa. 9:6). At His first coming, Jesus fulfilled the first part of Isaiah's prophecy, the heartwarming Christmas part. At His second coming, He will fulfill the second part—the part that reveals His iron-hard power and authority over all the nations. The government of the world will at last be upon His shoulder!

THE AVENGING OF CHRIST

The book of Revelation is divided into three sections. At the beginning of the book we are introduced to the world ruined by humanity. As we move to the latter half of the Tribulation period, we witness the world ruled by Satan. But now as we come to Christ's return at the end of the Tribulation period, we see the world reclaimed by Christ.

Reclaiming the earth, however, is not merely a simple matter of Christ stepping in and planting His flag. Before the earth can be reclaimed, it must be cleansed. You wouldn't move back into a house infested with rats without first exterminating and cleaning it up. That is what Christ must do before He reclaims the earth. All rebellion must be rooted out. He must avenge the damage done to His perfect creation by wiping the rebels from the face of the earth. The last verses of Revelation 19 give us an account of this purging and cleansing, and each step in the process is a dramatic story within itself. Let's briefly examine these avenging acts that will cleanse and reclaim the earth.

THE FOWLS OF HEAVEN

In the classic Alfred Hitchcock film *The Birds*, a coastal California town is terrorized by the escalating attacks of vicious birds. Throughout the film the terror increases to the point that birds merely sitting in rows on highline wires look ominous and foreboding. Instead of closing the film with his typical "The End," Hitchcock simply fades the screen to black, leaving the viewer with a lingering sense of terror as he drives from the theater and sees birds sitting on the high wires in his neighborhood. As horrifying as that story is, it pales in comparison to the grisly bird scene that John unveils.

> Then I saw an angel standing in the sun; and he cried with a loud voice, saying to all the birds that fly in the midst of heaven, "Come and gather together for the supper of the great God, that you may eat the flesh of kings, the flesh of captains, the flesh of mighty men, the flesh of horses and of those who sit on them, and the flesh of all people, free and slave, both small and great." . . . And all the birds were filled with their flesh. (19:17–18, 21)

Words are hardly adequate to describe the horror of this appalling scene. The fowl of the earth's air all gather at Armageddon to feast upon the massive piles of human flesh that will litter the battlefield for miles upon miles. The word translated *fowl* or *birds* is found only three times in the Bible: twice here in Revelation 19 (verses 17 and 21), and once more in Revelation 18:2. It is the Greek word *orneon*, which designates a scavenger bird that is best translated into English as *vulture*.

In John's vision the angel is calling the vultures of the earth to Armageddon to "the supper of the great God," where they will feast on the fallen carcasses of the enemies of the Lord. The text says that these corpses include both great and small, kings and generals, bond and free.

THE FOES OF HEAVEN

"And I saw the beast, the kings of the earth, and their armies, gathered together to make war against Him who sat on the horse and against His army" (19:19). Could there be anything more futile than creatures fighting against their Creator? Than little men stuck on one tiny planet, floating in the immeasurable cosmos, striking back at the Creator of the universe? Yet futility is not beyond hearts turned away from God. John warned that the Beast and the False Prophet will persuade the armies of the earth to go to war against Christ and the armies of heaven. It's like persuading mice to declare war against lions. This final war will be the culmination of all of the rebellion that men have leveled against almighty God from the beginning of time! And there's not one iota of doubt about the outcome.

THE FATALITY OF THE BEAST
AND FALSE PROPHET

The Bible tells us that God simply snatches up the Beast (the Antichrist) and the False Prophet and flings them into the fiery lake. "Then the beast was captured, and with him the false prophet who worked signs in his presence, by which he deceived those who received the mark of the beast and those who worshiped his image. These two were cast alive into the lake of fire burning with brimstone" (19:20).

These two evil creatures have the unwanted honor of actually getting to hell before Satan, whose confinement occurs much later: "The devil, who deceived them, was cast into the lake of fire and brimstone where the beast and the false prophet are. And they will be tormented day and night forever and ever" (20:10). Satan does not join the Beast and the False Prophet there until the end of the Millennium, one thousand years later.

Note that two men, are taken alive . . . These two men are "cast alive into [the lake burning with fire and brimstone]" where a thousand years later, they are still said to be "suffering the vengeance of eternal fire" (Jude 7). . . . The lake of fire is neither annihilation nor purgatorial because it neither annihilates nor purifies these two fallen foes of God and man after a thousand years under judgment.[2]

THE FINALITY OF CHRIST'S VICTORY OVER REBELLION

"And the rest were killed with the sword which proceeded from the mouth of Him who sat on the horse" (Rev. 19:21). Here is how John F. Walvoord describes the victory:

When Christ returns at the end of the Tribulation period, the armies that have been fighting with each other for power will have invaded the city of Jerusalem and will have been engaged in house-to-house fighting. When the glory of the second coming of Christ appears in the heavens, however, these soldiers will forget their contest for power on earth and will turn to fight the army from heaven (16:16; 19:19). Yet their best efforts will be futile because Christ will smite them with the sword in His mouth (19:15, 21), and they will all be killed, along with their horses.[3]

THE APPLICATION OF CHRIST'S SECOND COMING

In spite of the high value I place on understanding future events, I find that studying prophecy has an even higher and more practical value. It provides a compelling motivation for living the Christian life. The immediacy of prophetic events shows the need to live each moment in Christlike readiness. As revered Southern Baptist evangelist Vance Havner has put it, "The Devil has chloroformed the atmosphere of this age." Therefore, in view of the sure promises of Christ's return, as believers, we are to do more than merely be ready; we are to be expectant. In our day of "anarchy, apostasy, and apathy," Havner suggests that expectant living means: "We need to take down our 'Do Not Disturb' signs . . . snap out of our stupor and come out of our coma and awake from our apathy."[4] Havner reminds us that God's Word calls to us to awake out of our sleep and to walk in righteousness in the light Christ gives us (Rom. 13:11; 1 Cor. 15:34; Eph. 5:14).

Prophecy can provide the wake-up call that Dr. Havner calls for. When we have heard and understood the truth of Christ's promised return, we cannot just keep living our lives in the same old way. Future events have present implications that we cannot ignore. When we know that Christ is coming again to this earth, we cannot go on being the same people.

One of the finest stories I've heard about men longing for their leader's return is that of explorer/adventurer Sir Ernest Shackleton. On Saturday, August 8, 1914, one week after Germany declared war on Russia, twenty-nine men set sail in a three-masted wooden ship from Plymouth, England, to Antarctica on a quest to become the first adventurers to cross the Antarctic continent on foot. Sir Ernest Shackleton had recruited the men through an advertisement: "Men wanted for hazardous journey. Small wages. Bitter cold. Long months of complete darkness. Constant danger. Safe return doubtful. Honour and recognition in case of success."

Not only was Shackleton an honest man, for the men did experience all that his handbill promised, but he was also an able leader and a certified hero. His men came to refer to him as "the Boss," although he never thought of himself that way. He worked as hard as any crew member and built solid team unity aboard the ship, aptly named *Endurance*. In January 1915, the ship became entrapped in an ice pack and ultimately sank, leaving the men to set up camp on an ice floe—a flat, free-floating slice of sea ice. Shackleton kept the men busy by day and entertained by night. They played ice soccer, had nightly songfests, and held regular sled-dog competitions. It was in the ice floe camp that Shackleton proved his greatness as a leader. He willingly sacrificed his right to a warmer, fur-lined sleeping bag so that one of his men might have it, and he personally served hot milk to his men in their tents every morning.

In April 1916, their thinning ice floe threatened to break apart, forcing the men to seek refuge on nearby Elephant Island. Knowing that a rescue from such a desolate island was unlikely, Shackleton and five others left to cross eight hundred miles of open Antarctic sea in a twenty-foot lifeboat with more of a hope than a promise of a return with rescuers. Finally, on August 30, after an arduous 105-day trip and three earlier attempts, Shackleton returned to rescue his stranded crew, becoming their hero.

But perhaps the real hero in this story is Frank Wild. Second in command, Wild was left in charge of the camp in Shackleton's absence. He maintained the routine the Boss had established. He assigned daily duties, served meals, held sing-alongs, planned athletic competitions, and generally kept up morale. Because "the camp was in constant danger of being buried by the snow . . . [and becoming] completely invisible from the sea, so that a rescue party might look for it in vain," Wild kept the men busy shoveling away drifts.

The firing of a gun was to be the prearranged signal that the rescue ship was near the island, but as Wild reported, "Many times when the glaciers were 'calving,' and chunks fell off with a report like a gun, we thought that it was the real thing, and after a time we got to distrust these signals." But he never lost hope in the return of the Boss. Confidently, Wild kept the last tin of kerosene and a supply of dry combustibles ready to ignite instantly for use as a locator signal when the "day of wonders" would arrive.

Barely four days' worth of rations remained in the camp when Shackleton finally arrived on a Chilean icebreaker. He personally made several trips through the icy waters in a small lifeboat in order to ferry his crew to safety. Miraculously, the leaden fog lifted long enough for all the men to make it to the icebreaker in one hour.

Shackleton later learned from the men how they were prepared to break camp so quickly and reported: "From a fortnight after I had left, Wild would roll up his sleeping bag each day with the remark, 'Get your things ready, boys, the Boss may come today.' And sure enough, one day the mist opened and revealed the ship for which they had been waiting and longing and hoping for over four months." Wild's "cheerful anticipation proved infectious," and all were prepared when the evacuation day came.[5]

Shackleton's stranded crew desperately hoped that their leader would come back to them, and they longed for his return. But as diligent and dedicated as Shackleton was, they could not be certain he would return. He was, after all, a mere man battling elements he could not control, so they knew he might not make it back. Unlike that desperate crew, we have a certain promise that the Lord will return. Ours is not a mere longing or a desperate hope, as theirs was, for our Lord is the Creator and Master of all, and His promise is as sure as His very existence.

The prophets, the angels, and the apostle John all echo the words of promise from Jesus Himself that He will return. God's Word further amplifies the promise by giving us clues in prophecy to help us identify the signs that His return is close at hand. As we anticipate His return, we are not to foolishly set dates and leave our jobs and homes to wait for Him on some mountain. We are to remain busy doing the work set before us, living in love and serving in ministry, even when the days grow dark and the nights long. Be encouraged! Be anticipating! We are secure; we belong to Christ. And as the old gospel song says, "Soon and very soon, we are going to see the King!"

CHAPTER 28

MILLENNIUM

Isaac Watts began writing poems when he was seven, and, after his college years, he began writing hymns. Isaac lived in a time when hymns were frowned upon, for many British believers only sang the psalms in church. But Isaac wrote hymns anyway, and he is remembered today as the father of English hymnody. He also served as a pastor in London and wrote textbooks on logic used by the major universities of his day. He was small in size, eccentric in habit, and great of heart. Even now, more than two hundred years later, many of his hymns are widely sung, including his great Christmas carol, "Joy to the World."

But Watts would be chagrinned to know "Joy to the World" is sung today as a Christmas carol, because he wasn't thinking of the birth of Christ when he wrote it, but of our Lord's return and the golden age that would follow the second coming.

This hymn first appeared in a 1719 hymnbook, in which Watts took many of the biblical psalms and paraphrased them through the eyes of the New Testament. "Joy to the World" is based on his interpretation of Psalm 98, and the words don't refer to the birth of Christ at all. Let's put it to a test. Review the words below and see if you can determine what they are really about:

Joy to the world, the Lord is come!
Let earth receive her King;
Let every heart prepare Him room,
And heaven and nature sing,
And heaven and nature sing,
And heaven, and heaven, and nature sing.

Joy to the earth, the Savior reigns!
Let men their songs employ;
While fields and floods, rocks, hills and plains
Repeat the sounding joy,
Repeat the sounding joy,
Repeat, repeat, the sounding joy.

No more let sin and sorrow grow,
Nor thorns infest the ground;
He comes to make His blessing flow
Far as the curse is found,
Far as the curse is found,
Far as, far as, the curse is found.

He rules the world with truth and grace,
And makes the nations prove
The glories of His righteousness,
And wonders of His love,
And wonders of His love,
And wonders, wonders, of His love.

Did those things happen when Jesus came the first time to be wrapped in swaddling clothes and placed in a manger? Did earth receive her King? Was nature transformed—fields and floods, rocks, hills, and plains? Did thorns stop infesting the ground? Was the curse lifted? Did sin and sorrow cease, and does Christ currently rule the world with grace and truth? Do the nations of the world acknowledge His righteousness and the wonders of His love?

Those statements do reflect biblical promises, but they're not about the first coming of Christ. They reference His Second Coming and the glorious Millennium that will occur when He returns. Now, I don't intend to stop singing "Joy to the World" at Christmas, but as I sing the words I'll be looking forward to His return and to the era of peace He will establish on earth. I'm eager for the day when earth will receive her King; when every heart will prepare Him room; when thorns stop infesting the ground; and when Christ will rule the world with truth and grace. That is what will happen during the thousand-year reign of Christ, which comes after His Second Coming. Only then will the words to "Joy to the World" be truly fulfilled.

We often refer to this period of time by a certain title—the Millennium. The word *millennium* doesn't actually occur in most of our English Bibles, yet this topic is one of the Bible's premier subjects; and it is astonishing to notice how many chapters and verses describe this golden age of Christ, which will last for a thousand years on this planet.

WHAT IS THE MILLENNIUM?

Let's begin by taking the mystery out of the term *millennium*. It comes to us from a combination of the Latin words *mille*, which means "a thousand," and *annum*, which means "years." The word *millennium*, then, simply means "a thousand years."

The Millennium is a literal period of a thousand years, which is scheduled for the future and will begin when Jesus comes again at the end of history to set up His earthly kingdom.

FOUR PURPOSES OF THE MILLENNIUM

Of course, all this raises very good questions. Why did God plan it like this? Why have a Millennium at all? Why not begin the eternal state at the moment of Christ's return without having to wait another thousand years? I don't know all the answers to that, although I'm fully confident that God, in His infinite wisdom, knows exactly what He is doing and why. But from our study of Scripture, we can ascertain several critical and obvious purposes for the Millennium. Let me give you four of them.

TO REWARD THE PEOPLE OF GOD

The first purpose of the Millennium is to reward the people of God. Scores of biblical promises reassure God's people they will receive rewards for faithful service. For instance, Isaiah 40:10 says, "Behold, the Lord God shall come with a strong hand, and His arm shall rule for Him; behold, His reward is with Him, and His work before Him."

Jesus said, "The Son of Man will come in the glory of His Father with His angels, and then He will reward each according to his works" (Matt. 16:27). A little later He added, "Then the King will say to those on His right hand, 'Come, you blessed of My Father, inherit the kingdom prepared for you from the foundation of the world'" (25:34). And Revelation 22:12 says, "I am coming quickly, and My reward is with Me, to give to every one according to his work."

The Bible teaches that when we serve the Lord here on earth as Christians we will be rewarded when we get to the kingdom with the opportunity to serve in a new and special way.

In the parable of the talents, Jesus taught that our role as servants and rulers will be based upon our faithfulness. Remember the words we want to hear from the Lord when we get to heaven? "Well done, good and faithful servant; you have been faithful over a few things, I will make you ruler over many things. Enter into the joy of your lord" (Matt. 25:23). Our opportunity to "rule over many things." These words will be part of our millennial experience. In the Millennium we will be ruling the earth with Jesus. He will be our King and we will serve Him, not as a punishment but as a reward.

Randy Alcorn said:

> Service is a reward, not a punishment. This idea is foreign to people who dislike their work and only put up with it until retirement. We think that faithful work should be rewarded by a vacation for the rest of our lives. But God offers us something very different: more work, more responsibilities, increased opportunities, along with greater abilities, resources, wisdom, and empowerment. We will have sharp minds, strong bodies, clear purpose, and unabated joy.[1]

Imagine the wonder of helping Jesus rule and reign on earth for a thousand golden years!

TO RESPOND TO THE PROPHETS' PREDICTIONS

During the thousand-year reign of Christ, the prophecies and promises of the Old Testament prophets will be fulfilled, and that is another major purpose of the Millennium. It's difficult to make sense of large parts of the Old Testament if we expunge the Millennium from God's program for the ages. J. Dwight Pentecost wrote, "A larger body of prophetic Scripture is devoted to the subject of the millennium, developing its character and conditions, than any other one subject."[2] Many of the promises God made to Israel have yet to be literally fulfilled, but they will be—during the Millennium. I've selected some verses to serve as a sample of this, and I hope you'll not skip over them. Read each one and visualize the predictions God has given us for this thousand-year period.

> Yes, all kings shall fall down before Him; all nations shall serve Him. (Ps. 72:11)

Of the increase of His government and peace there will be no end, upon the throne of David and over His kingdom, to order it and establish it with judgment and justice from that time forward, even forever. The zeal of the LORD of hosts will perform this. (Isa. 9:7)

Also your people shall all be righteous; they shall inherit the land forever, the branch of My planting, the work of My hands, that I may be glorified. (Isa. 60:21)

He will be great, and will be called the Son of the Highest; and the Lord God will give Him the throne of His father David. And He will reign over the house of Jacob forever, and of His kingdom there will be no end. (Luke 1:32–33).

Without the coming kingdom age, none of those could be fulfilled. Biblical prophecy is full of predictions of a coming day when King Jesus will rule over the earth with His saints as co-regents with Him. The first time, He came to redeem us, but the world rejected Him. When He comes the second time, He will come to rule this world in righteousness; and during this period the great predictions of His earthly kingdom will be fulfilled. Kings will fall down before Him. Nations will serve Him. He will sit on the throne of David and establish His kingdom with justice and judgment. His people will be righteous, and Israel will inherit its land. War will be suspended, and the Lord's dominion will stretch from sea to sea.

The greatest prediction of all may have to do with the factual promise that a descendant of David will sit on Israel's throne, in keeping with the covenant God made with David in 2 Samuel 7:16, "Your house and your kingdom shall be established forever before you. Your throne shall be established forever." This is the promise Gabriel quoted to Mary about her miracle Child in Luke 1:32–33: "He will be great, and will be called the Son of the Highest; and the Lord God will give Him the throne of His father David. And He will reign over the house of Jacob forever, and of His kingdom there will be no end."

Jesus has not yet reigned as an acknowledged King over the house of Jacob, but that will change when He returns.

TO RECEIVE THE ANSWER TO
THE DISCIPLES' PRAYER

The Millennium is also the time when the Lord's Prayer—or, as I like to call it, the Disciples' Prayer—will be completely fulfilled. Jesus taught us to pray in Matthew 6:10, "Your kingdom come. Your will be done on earth as it is in heaven." Every day, millions of Christians utter that prayer, in hundreds of languages, in thousands of diverse settings and situations. Someone, somewhere, dispatches that plea heavenward every hour of every single day, and we have done so for the last two thousand years. God can answer our prayers in intermediate ways now; but the ultimate fulfillment awaits the Millennium. That's when the kingdom will come in its fullness, and His will will be done on earth as it is done in heaven.

TO REEMPHASIZE MAN'S DEPRAVITY AND
THE NECESSITY OF CHRIST'S DEATH

We also need the Millennium to create the conditions necessary for the end of history, the final judgment, and the dawn of the eternal state. The Millennium is necessary to reemphasize human depravity and to demonstrate the utter necessity of Christ's death.

What do I mean by that? An incredible statement in Revelation 20:7–9 tells us how the thousand-year reign of Christ will end. It's one of the most unexpected and shocking realities in Scripture. John wrote:

> Now when the thousand years have expired, Satan will be released from his prison and will go out to deceive the nations which are in the four corners of the earth, Gog and Magog, to gather them together to battle, whose number is as the sand of the sea. They went up on the breadth of the earth and surrounded the camp of the saints and the beloved city. And fire came down from God out of heaven and devoured them.

According to the earlier verses in the chapter, when Jesus comes again Satan will be bound and cast into the bottomless pit for a thousand years. But at the end of the Millennium, the Devil will be temporarily released to stage one final worldly rebellion. This tells us things will not be perfect during the Millennium. Death, though rare, will occur. Sin, though diminished, will still be possible. And the human heart will still be capable of rebellion. When Satan, newly released and furious, goes out into the world, he will deceive the nations again—demonstrating with absolute finality the utter inability of human beings to chart their own way and to save themselves. This will be the final proof of the hopeless depravity of the human heart apart from grace. The generations have a way of spiraling downward into corruption because our biggest problem isn't our environment. After all, Adam and Eve were in a perfect garden at the heart of a sinless world, yet they sinned. The population of the earth will enjoy a thousand years of teaching and testimony and peace, yet it will still end in rebellion. Our primary problem isn't our environment, but the sinful nature we inherited from our first parents.

The Millennium will prove God's righteousness when those at the Great White Throne Judgment say, "Lord, God, I just didn't have the right environment." The Lord will reply, "I gave you a thousand years of peace and righteousness, yet you still rebelled. Depart from Me; I never knew you."

FIVE PROFILES OF THE MILLENNIUM

Let's shift gears and end this chapter on a positive note. I want to give you five wonderful facts about the Millennium. What will it be like? How will we enjoy it? Imagine what it would be like on this earth if all sin were removed; if all rebellion were removed; if all unrighteousness were removed. These are the sorts of blessings the Millennium will bring, and the resulting conditions will be characterized by peace, prosperity, purity, prolonged life, and personal joy.

IT WILL BE A TIME OF PEACE

First, the Millennium will be a time of great peace. If you visit the gardens of the United Nations in New York City, you may see the sculpture by Soviet artist Yevgeny Vuchetich depicting a figure of a man holding a hammer aloft in one hand and beating a sword into a plow. The sculpture depicts Isaiah 2:4 and suggests that one of the missions of the United Nations is converting implements of war into implements of peace and productivity. But the United Nations has utterly failed in the attempt. That mission cannot happen by human effort, for the passage in Isaiah talks about the millennial reign of Christ. He alone can bring peace to the planet. The Bible repeatedly speaks of the reign of peace that will characterize this vast expanse of history called the Millennium.

- "In His days the righteous shall flourish, and abundance of peace" (Ps. 72:7).
- "For out of Zion the law shall go forth, and the word of the LORD from Jerusalem. He shall judge between many peoples, and rebuke strong nations afar off; they shall beat their swords into plowshares, and their spears into pruning hooks; nation shall not lift up sword against nation, neither shall they learn war anymore" (Mic. 4:2–3).
- "The wolf also shall dwell with the lamb, the leopard shall lie down with the young goat, the calf and the young lion and the fatling together; and a little child shall lead them. The cow and the bear shall graze; their young ones shall lie down together; and the lion shall eat straw like the ox. The nursing child shall play by the cobra's hole, and the weaned child shall put his hand in the viper's den. They shall not hurt nor destroy in all My holy mountain, for the earth shall be full of the knowledge of the LORD as the waters cover the sea" (Isa. 11:6–9).

War will be utterly unknown during the earthly reign of Christ. Not a single armament plant will be operating. Not a soldier or sailor will be in uniform. No military camps will exist; not one cent will be spent on a military budget. Even wild animals will become dear friends, as it were. Can you imagine such an age in which all the kingdoms of this world—and even the animal kingdoms—will be in perfect peace; when all the resources of the earth will be available for enjoyment; and when all industries will engage in the manufacture of articles of peaceful luxury? Is that really possible? Not here, not now—but when Jesus comes.

IT WILL BE A TIME OF PROSPERITY

The Millennium will also be a time of prosperity. The whole world will be economically healthy, and the land of Israel will flourish beyond anything imaginable. Once again, listen to the Word of God:

- "I will cause showers to come down in their season; there shall be showers of blessing. Then the trees of the field shall yield their fruit, and the earth shall yield her increase. They shall be safe in their land; and they shall know that I am the LORD" (Ezek. 34:26–27).
- "I will call for the grain and multiply it, and bring no famine upon you. And I will multiply the fruit of your trees and the increase of your fields, so that you need never again bear the reproach of famine among the nations" (Ezek. 36:29–30).
- "'Behold, the days are coming,' says the LORD, 'when the plowman shall overtake the reaper, and the treader of grapes him who sows seed; the mountains shall drip with sweet wine, and all the hills shall flow with it'" (Amos 9:13).

IT WILL BE A TIME OF PURITY

The Millennium will also be a wonderful time of holiness and purity. Sin will be kept in check and disobedience will be dealt with. Let me show you some verses about that.

- "They shall not hurt nor destroy in all My holy mountain, for the earth shall be full of the knowledge of the LORD as the waters cover the sea" (Isa. 11:9).
- "It shall come to pass that from one New Moon to another, and from

one Sabbath to another, all flesh shall come to worship before Me"
(Isa. 66:23).

- "'It shall be in that day,' says the LORD of hosts, 'that I will cut off the
names of the idols from the land, and they shall no longer be remembered. I will also cause the prophets and the unclean spirit to depart
from the land'" (Zech. 13:2).

IT WILL BE A TIME OF PROLONGED LIFE

Another feature of the millennial reign of Christ will involve human
lifespan. This is an interesting study in the Bible. Before the Flood of Noah's
day, people lived to incredible ages. According to Genesis 5:27, Methuselah
lived to be 969 years old. Some scientists believe the climate of earth was
so different, the genetic pool was so young, and the grace of God was so
fresh that people lived for many centuries. Many people believe the Flood
changed the nature of the earth. Before the Flood, perhaps a vapor canopy
protected us from the ultraviolet rays of the sun and enhanced longevity.
The climate of the world was the healthiest in history. But some experts
believe the vapor canopy collapsed during the Flood and from that point
onward, human lifespan was a fraction of what it was prior to the Flood.
Now, according to Psalm 90:10, our lifespan is about seventy or eighty
years, give or take some. Despite the best efforts of our medical experts,
there's little chance any of us will be a Methuselah.

But in the Millennium that will change, and human longevity will
return to pre-Flood levels. It's as though history will come full circle. Isaiah
65:20 says, "Never again will there be in it an infant who lives but a few days,
or an old man who does not live out his years; the one who dies at a hundred
will be thought a mere child; the one who fails to reach a hundred will be
considered accursed" (NIV).

IT WILL BE A TIME OF PERSONAL JOY

Finally, the Millennium will be a time of personal joy, an exhilarat-
ing era of happiness and contentment. It will be the answer to many of the

anguished prayers of the Jews and many of the hopes we harbor in our hearts today. Once again, let me offer Scripture to show you the preponderance of these truths in the Old Testament.

- "You have multiplied the nation and increased its joy; they rejoice before You according to the joy of harvest, as men rejoice when they divide the spoil" (Isa. 9:3).
- "Therefore with joy you will draw water from the wells of salvation" (Isa. 12:3).
- "The whole earth is at rest and quiet; they break forth into singing" (Isa. 14:7).
- "He will swallow up death forever, and the Lord GOD will wipe away tears from all faces; the rebuke of His people He will take away from all the earth; for the LORD has spoken. And it will be said in that day: 'Behold, this is our God; we have waited for Him, and He will save us. This is the LORD; we have waited for Him; we will be glad and rejoice in His salvation'" (Isa. 25:8–9).

These are only a few representative verses we run across as we read the Bible—especially the Old Testament—and notice the endless references to the golden age of Jewish history, a promised period of peace, prosperity, purity, prolonged life, and personal joy. During this thousand years, King Jesus will reign and rule on the throne of His ancestor, David, in the city of Jerusalem. And out of Jerusalem will flow this wonderful reign of peace over all the world as we know it today. Can you imagine? Isn't it interesting to see what God has planned?

But here is the main thing. All this is simply the prelude to heaven. This is the overture of eternity. Whenever you go to an elaborate musical, the orchestra begins with an overture that has little strains and snippets of all the different songs in the program. Listening to the music gives you inklings of what is to come. The Millennium is an overture of heaven. It gives a limited, advanced snapshot of what heaven will be like. The millennial earth will simply be a precursor of the new earth—not as perfect, wonderful, or spectacular as the eternal earth, but a preview of some of its coming features.

Jesus came the first time to become our Savior, and He's coming the second time to be our King. The coming of Christ to set up His kingdom will be so much different than when He came before. Consider the contrast between His first and second comings.

> He entered the world the first time in swaddling clothes;
> He will reign the second time in majestic purple.
>
> He came the first time as a weary traveler;
> He will return the second time as the untiring God.
>
> Once when He came, He had nowhere to lay His head;
> When He comes back, He will be revealed as the heir of all things.
>
> Once He was rejected by tiny Israel;
> When He returns, He will be accepted by every single nation.
>
> Once He was a lowly Savior, acquainted with grief;
> Then He will be the mighty God, anointed with the oil of gladness.
>
> Once He was smitten with a reed;
> Then He will rule the nations with a rod of iron.
>
> Once wicked soldiers bowed the knee in mockery;
> Then every knee will bow and every tongue confess that He is Lord.
>
> Once He received a crown of thorns;
> Then He will receive a crown of gold.

Once He delivered up His Spirit in death;
Then He will be alive forevermore.

Once He was laid in a tomb;
Then He will sit on a throne.

When He comes again, there will be no doubt and no delay. He will be "KING OF KINGS AND LORD OF LORDS" (Rev. 19:16). We need to prepare our hearts now by installing Him as King of our lives. The Bible says one day "that at the name of Jesus every knee should bow, of those in heaven, and of those on earth, and of those under the earth, and that every tongue should confess that Jesus Christ is Lord, to the glory of God the Father" (Phil. 2:10–11).

On that day we truly will sing with fresh meaning and everlasting exuberance:

Joy to the world, the Lord is come!
Let earth receive her King;
Let every heart prepare Him room,
And heaven and nature sing,
And heaven and nature sing,
And heaven, and heaven, and nature sing.

CHAPTER 29

GREAT WHITE THRONE
JUDGMENT

In 2017, four young adult women went for a swim in New Zealand's Waikato River. The girls dived in at their favorite spot, oblivious to any danger. But danger lurked. An upstream power station regularly opens its dam to release excess water. During these runoffs, the river rises precipitously and becomes a raging torrent. Warning signs are posted along the banks, and a siren always sounds five minutes before the dam opens, giving swimmers ample time to get out of the river.

But the girls ignored the signs. Though they heard the siren, either they didn't grasp its meaning, or they failed to realize the extent of the danger. As the water rose, the four students scrambled to a rock midstream, which was quickly submerged under the rising torrent. A man edged out on a nearby rock and urged the girls to come to him before it was too late. Three of the girls finally plunged toward him, and he pulled them out of the rushing water. But for the fourth, it was too late. Before she could reach safety, the flood swept her downriver to her death.[1]

Too late. It's one of the saddest phrases in the English language. It speaks of tragic finality, of irrevocable decisions, of forever missed opportunities. In this chapter we will address the ultimate tragedy that will befall those who do not turn to God before it is too late.

The apostle John described this scene from his vision of mankind's final judgment: "Anyone not found written in the Book of Life was cast into the lake of fire" (Rev. 20:15). This must be the most chilling passage in the Bible, but today it is broadly ignored or dismissed as fantasy. Most Christians understand that everyone on earth faces final judgment, for the Bible says, "It is appointed for men to die once, but after this the judgment" (Heb. 9:27). Many believe this means God will assess our lives, weigh our good deeds against the bad, and then decide whether we should be rewarded or condemned.

The biblical picture of judgment is nothing like that. Our eternal fate will be sealed at death, not by God weighing evidence after the fact. In the end times there will actually be two altogether separate judgments occurring at different times and being tried in different courts. The first is called the judgment seat of Christ; the second is the Great White Throne Judgment.

All authentic Christians will be judged in the first court, which will immediately follow the Rapture. "We must all appear before the judgment seat of Christ, that each one may receive the things done in the body, according to what he has done, whether good or bad" (2 Cor. 5:10). The object of this court is not to determine guilt or to condemn, because every person who passes through it will be a Christian. They are reprieved because grace covers their sins. In this court, believers' works will be evaluated to determine how lavishly they should be rewarded.

All unbelievers and pseudo-Christians will be judged in the second court, the Great White Throne Judgment. They will not be graded on the curve system or evaluated by cultural opinions of right and wrong. They will be judged by the unbending standard of God's truth, and this judgment will be forever unalterable.

These two contrasting judgments will follow the two resurrections yet to occur in the future. Jesus mentioned both: "Do not marvel at this; for the hour is coming in which all who are in the graves will hear His voice and come forth—those who have done good, to the resurrection of life, and those who have done evil, to the resurrection of condemnation" (John 5:28–29).

Seventh-Day Adventists, Jehovah's Witnesses, and a growing number of evangelical Christians are teaching a doctrine called conditional immortality, which jettisons the concept of hell. They assert that the wicked will be destroyed. This belief contradicts biblical teaching, which says that everyone who has ever lived will be resurrected and judged, and those who are condemned will suffer torment forever (Luke 16:19–31).

The first resurrection, which Jesus calls the "resurrection of life" (John 5:29), will occur in two stages. The first will be simultaneous with the Rapture, when the saved of the present age are raised to meet Christ along with those who are raptured. The second stage will occur seven years later when the saints martyred during the Tribulation period are resurrected to enter the Millennium. The Old Testament saints will also be raised in this second stage (Dan. 12:1–2; Isa. 26:19). This means when Christ returns to reign in the Millennium, the first resurrection will be completed. Every believer who has ever lived will have been raised from the dead.

In Revelation 20, John describes the second resurrection, which Christ calls the "resurrection of condemnation" (John 5:29) because all the dead unbelievers will be raised to face eternal punishment.

> The rest of the dead did not live again until the thousand years were finished. . . . And I saw the dead, small and great, standing before God, and books were opened. And another book was opened, which is the Book of Life. And the dead were judged according to their works, by the things which were written in the books. The sea gave up the dead

who were in it, and Death and Hades delivered up the dead who were in them. And they were judged, each one according to his works. Then Death and Hades were cast into the lake of fire. This is the second death. And anyone not found written in the Book of Life was cast into the lake of fire. (Rev. 20:5, 12–15)

In this second resurrection, all the unsaved dead from creation to the Millennium will be raised to face final condemnation. It will occur one thousand years after the completion of the first resurrection at the end of the Tribulation period. With this resurrection, everyone who ever lived will have been raised—some to eternal glory, others to eternal condemnation.

THE PLACE OF THE GREAT WHITE THRONE

I saw a great white throne and Him who sat on it, from
whose face the earth and the heaven fled away. And
there was found no place for them. (Rev. 20:11)

We are not told when the Great White Throne Judgment will occur, but we do know where it will not occur. It cannot occur on earth because when Christ appears, the earth and heaven will have "fled away" (v. 11). It cannot occur in heaven because sinners are barred from the presence of God. John Walvoord suggests that it could occur in what we might call another dimension: "It will not happen in our present universe, either on earth or in the atmospheric, stellar, or divine heavens. No planet in our solar system will qualify. It could take place somewhere beyond our universe that has not been affected by angelic sin. Whether the assigned place actually exists today, it is hard to say."[2]

THE PERSON ON THE GREAT WHITE THRONE

I saw a great white throne and Him who sat on it. . . . And I
saw the dead . . . standing before God. (Rev. 20:11–12)

Jesus made it clear that He will be the Judge sitting upon the Great White Throne: "The Father judges no one, but has committed all judgment to the Son . . . and has given Him authority to execute judgment also, because He is the Son of Man" (John 5:22, 27). Paul affirms Christ's judiciary role: "God will judge the secrets of men *by Jesus Christ*" (Rom. 2:16, emphasis added). Peter says God ordained Christ "to be Judge of the living and the dead" (Acts 10:42).

Christ will be the Judge at both of the final judgments of mankind. At the first, He will judge the faithful; at the second, He will judge the unredeemed. No one is better qualified than Christ. He offered salvation to mankind, so it is fitting that He should judge those who both accept and reject His generous and costly offer.

THE PEOPLE BEFORE THE GREAT WHITE THRONE

I saw the dead, small and great, standing before
God. . . . The sea gave up the dead who were
in it, and Death and Hades delivered up the
dead who were in them. (Rev. 20:12–13)

In John's vision, he saw all the bodies and souls of unbelievers in all ages called up from Death and Hades to stand before the Great White Throne. This vast throng will include both the "small and great," which encompasses all classes and ranks of people—even religious people. Erwin Lutzer wrote:

This multitude is diverse in its religions. We see Buddhists, Muslims, Hindus, Protestants, and Catholics. We see those who believed in one God and those who believed in many gods. We see those who refused to believe in any God at all. We see those who believed in meditation as a means of salvation and those who believed that doing good deeds was the path to eternal life. We see the moral and the immoral, the priest as well as the minister, the nun as well as the missionary.[3]

Religious people who stand before the Great White Throne will be shocked to hear their judgment. But Jesus gave them fair warning: "Many will say to Me in that day, 'Lord, Lord, have we not prophesied in Your name, cast out demons in Your name, and done many wonders in Your name?' And then I will declare to them, 'I never knew you; depart from Me, you who practice lawlessness!'" (Matt. 7:22–23). These words shatter the popular opinion that believing in your own personal "truth" makes it true for you. The Bible makes it clear: There is one truth and one truth only—Jesus Christ (John 14:6). Your only choice is Christ or eternal death.

Wealth, class, fame, or accomplishment lose all meaning before the Great White Throne.

Both the small and the great of this life (as men view other men) will be there: the banker and the beggar, the prince and the pauper, the statesman, the scientist, the lawyer, the doctor, the professor, the author, the mechanic, the housewife, the bricklayer, the farmer, and the criminal. In this life men have station, but before Christ, there will be no respect of persons. Although they will stand there in mass, they will be judged individually.[4]

Whether rich, poor, famous, obscure, beautiful, plain, powerful, weak, intelligent, dull, religious, or agnostic, all who stand before the Great White Throne will share one common attribute: they will be utterly without hope because they died outside of Christ. In the words of Donald Grey Barnhouse, "Only one group will be seen at this judgment, the dead . . . the spiritually dead."[5]

THE PURPOSE OF THE GREAT WHITE THRONE

I saw the dead, small and great, standing before
God, and books were opened. And another book
was opened, which is the Book of Life. And the dead
were judged according to their works, by the things
which were written in the books. (Rev. 20:12)

When all the unregenerate dead stand before God, the books will be opened. This simply means their past deeds will be exposed. One of the books is identified—the Book of Life. The others are not mentioned here, but various Scriptures indicate their identity and purpose in this final judgment.

THE BOOK OF LAW

Jesus and Paul contended with Jews who taught that salvation was earned by obeying the law. That error lives on today in the minds of many Christians. Paul reveals the illogic of this position: If law is the standard, then obedience to law must be perfect in order to attain salvation. And perfect obedience is impossible for fallen humans. "By the deeds of the law no flesh will be justified in His sight . . . for all have sinned and fall short of the glory of God" (Rom. 3:20, 23). The only path to salvation, Paul asserts, is to claim the grace of Christ by submission to Him, for there is "no condemnation to those who are in Christ Jesus" (8:1). Those who claim justification by law sign their own death warrant, for the law itself will condemn those who fail to obey it perfectly.

THE BOOK OF WORKS

John saw the unregenerate dead "judged, each one according to his works" (Rev. 20:13). Paul writes of those "whose end will be according to their works" (2 Cor. 11:15). Jesus promised, "The Son of Man will come in the glory of His Father with His angels, and then He will reward each according to his works" (Matt. 16:27). God will possess a detailed record of every act ever committed by every person on earth. Every sordid sin will be revealed, which will dash the hopes of those who rely on their good works to get them into heaven.

The saved, who will be judged at the judgment seat of Christ, will also have committed sins. But their sins will be treated quite differently; they will not even come up before the court. All record of their sins will be erased the moment they place their trust in Christ, and they will appear before the court with their slate wiped clean. Scripture emphatically affirms this truth:

- "He who overcomes shall be clothed in white garments, and I will not blot out his name from the Book of Life; but I will confess his name before My Father and before His angels" (Rev. 3:5).
- "Most assuredly, I say to you, he who hears My word and believes in Him who sent Me has everlasting life, and shall not come into judgment, but has passed from death into life" (John 5:24).
- "There is therefore now no condemnation to those who are in Christ Jesus" (Rom. 8:1).

THE BOOK OF SECRETS

Lincoln is famously credited with saying, "You can fool all the people some of the time, and some of the people all the time, but you cannot fool all the people all the time." We can fool God none of the time. "Nothing is secret that will not be revealed, nor anything hidden that will not be known and come to light" (Luke 8:17). Paul adds, "God will judge the secrets of men by Jesus Christ" (Rom. 2:16). Solomon wrote, "God will bring every work into judgment, including every secret thing, whether good or evil" (Eccl. 12:14).

It's as if there's a video camera focused on the heart of every person, running continually throughout life and recording every ungodly thought or misdeed hatched in secret. At the Great White Throne Judgment that video will be played before the Judge, and every dark secret will be exposed as condemning testimony against the unsaved.

THE BOOK OF WORDS

According to acoustic physicists, no sound is ever lost. Though sound waves diminish with distance, they reverberate perpetually, available for recovery in the future. Similarly, every word spoken will be available as evidence against the unsaved at the Great White Throne Judgment. Christ said, "For every idle word men may speak, they will give account of it in the day of judgment. For by your words you will be justified, and by your words you will be condemned" (Matt. 12:36–37). When a defendant's book of words is opened, no excuse will stand against the record of one's own revealed utterances.

THE BOOK OF CONSCIENCE

Paul wrote that people's consciences will bear witness to their thoughts, "accusing or else defending them, on the day when . . . God will judge the secrets of men through Christ Jesus" (Rom. 2:15–16 NASB). Conscience is our built-in, God-given guide to right and wrong. But the conscience is not infallible because it can be manipulated, ignored, retrained, or stifled. Those who tamper with their conscience, like those who tamper with evidence in a criminal investigation, will face condemnation for their deliberate repression of right and wrong.

THE BOOK OF LIFE

Scripture contains several references to the Book of Life (Ex. 32:32–33; Ps. 69:28; Dan. 12:1; Phil. 4:3; Rev. 3:5; 13:8; 17:8; 21:27; 22:19). First-century cities kept bound registers listing the names of everyone born within their walls. Citizens convicted of heinous crimes could be blotted from the register and exiled from the city. While the Book of Life may not be a literal book, the mind of God contains a list that functions in the same way: every person born is recorded in God's register, but any name can be removed with just cause.

Henry M. Morris elaborates:

One can speculate that beside each person's name as entered in the book at time of conception will be recorded the time of his "age of accountability," the date of his conversion to Christ as His Savior, and evidence demonstrating the genuineness of that conversion. However, if there are no entries for the last two items by the time that person dies, the entire entry will be blotted out (Rev. 3:5), and an awful blank will be left in the book at the place where his name would have been. Exhibiting this blank spot in the book will be the final and conclusive evidence that the person being judged must be consigned to the lake of fire.[6]

THE PUNISHMENT FOLLOWING
THE GREAT WHITE THRONE

Then Death and Hades were cast into the lake of fire. This is
the second death. And anyone not found written in the Book
of Life was cast into the lake of fire. (Rev. 20:14–15)

In this passage, we see the final phase of judgment against all unregenerate humans who ever lived. John calls it "the second death." To explain the two deaths, we must realize that death always involves a separation. The first death occurs when a person's physical body ceases to function. When heartbeats and breathing cease, we pronounce the person dead, which means the soul has separated from the body. The body is buried, while the soul is taken to an interim holding place called Hades to await judgment. At the last resurrection, the bodies of the unsaved will rise from the grave and their souls will emerge from Hades to be judged. After judgment, they will be cast into the lake of fire—hurled into hell—where they will be eternally separated from God. This is the second death.

This ultimate separation from God is irrevocable. Dr. Isaac Massey Haldeman wrote:

> From this second death there is no resurrection. . . . [The condemned] will be sent out into the wide universe, into the "outer darkness." They will be as "wandering stars, to whom is reserved the blackness of darkness forever." They shall wander through this unlit darkness of eternity as derelicts of humanity, tossed upon an endless and shoreless sea; souls that have missed the purpose for which created—union and fellowship with God.[7]

In an age which asserts that everyone has a right to live by his own choices without consequence, the doctrine of hell is highly unpopular and often rejected, even among many Christians. But Scripture consistently affirms the existence of hell. For every word Jesus spoke about heaven, He spoke three about hell. For example: "[The King] will also say to those on the left hand, 'Depart from Me, you cursed, into the everlasting fire prepared for the devil and his angels.' . . . And these will go away into everlasting punishment" (Matt. 25:41, 46). Paul affirms Jesus' words, writing that those who reject God "shall be punished with everlasting destruction from the presence of the Lord" (2 Thess. 1:9).

The Bible pictures hell in horrific terms. It is a place

- of torment and flames (Luke 16:20–28).
- of "wailing and gnashing of teeth" (Matt. 13:42).
- where the "worm does not die and the fire is not quenched" (Mark 9:48).
- of "fire and brimstone" (Rev. 14:10–11; 21:8).

The Bible presents this molten lake of fire and brimstone as the final destination of all who rebel against God throughout time. It will swallow the Beast and the False Prophet (19:20). At the end of the Millennium, it will become the eternal home of Satan (20:10). He will be joined there by all whose names are not found in the Book of Life (v. 15).

As horrible as hell is, it will be worse for some than for others. There will be degrees of punishment, with the worst reserved for the most heinous sins. In explaining His parable of the faithful and evil servants, Jesus said, "That servant who knew his master's will, and did not prepare himself or do according to his will, shall be beaten with many stripes. But he who did not know, yet committed things deserving of stripes, shall be beaten with few" (Luke 12:47–48). In three Jewish cities, Chorazin, Bethsaida, and Capernaum, Christ performed spectacular miracles designed to produce repentance. But these cities rejected Christ, which will bring down on their heads punishment more severe than on the notoriously wicked cities of Tyre, Sidon, and Sodom (Matt. 11:20–24).

It grieves me to see this rejection of Christ occurring in Western nations today. Despite the abundance of Christian churches and the widespread availability of the gospel, belief in God and obedience to Him are plummeting. I sorrow at the punishment awaiting those who turn their backs on God where knowledge of Him is so prevalent.

The church I lead is saturated with Bible teaching. We offer classes, fellowships, and small-group Bible studies for all age levels. We offer women's and men's ministries; recreational and international ministries; radio, television, Internet, and print ministries. Opportunities like these create responsibilities. Those who spurn such opportunities to hear and respond to Jesus Christ place themselves in perilous jeopardy.

Who will end up in the lake of fire? John gives us a list: "The cowardly, unbelieving, abominable, murderers, sexually immoral, sorcerers, idolaters, and all liars shall have their part in the lake which burns with fire and brimstone" (Rev. 21:8). This list includes all the evildoers you would expect to be condemned to hell, but there is one entry that may surprise you: the "unbelieving." To be unbelieving is to reject God, which aligns one with those who commit the worst sins imaginable.

You, the reader of this chapter, are in a happy position. If you have not put your trust in Jesus Christ as your Savior and come into an obedient relationship with Him, the opportunity lies open before you. It's not too late. You can still escape the rising torrent before it takes you under. But a time is coming when death will close your eyes. At that point, your eternal future will be sealed. I urge you to turn to Christ today—at this moment! Christ Himself said, "He who believes in Him is not condemned; but he who does not believe is condemned already, because he has not believed in the name of the only begotten Son of God. . . . Most assuredly, I say to you, he who hears My word and believes in Him who sent Me has everlasting life, and shall not come into judgment, but has passed from death into life" (John 3:18; 5:24).

Come to Christ now, before it is too late. Your eternal future depends on it.

CHAPTER 30

NEW HEAVEN AND NEW EARTH

Utopia.

That strange word was coined more than five hundred years ago by Thomas More, a Roman Catholic philosopher, as the title of his fictional book describing a perfect society that existed on a remote island somewhere in the uncharted Atlantic. More invented the word *utopia* by combining the Greek term *ou*, meaning "no," with *topos*, meaning "place" (as in topological). In other words, Utopia is no place, a nonexistent society that lives only in our dreams.

Thomas More didn't picture Utopia as a perfect place, and scholars haven't been able to determine why he actually wrote the book or what it meant. Still, it's one of the most famous books in Western literature merely because of the word Thomas More coined for its title—*Utopia*. After the publication of his book, that word entered the English lexicon to depict the concept of an idyllic place where things are somehow more perfect than we see them in our current world.

People long for a more perfect world. We hear it in the dreams of the poets. We read it in literature. We see it in the paintings of the famous artists whose works fill the walls of the great museums of the world.

It's as if we instinctively understand that our paradise in the garden of Eden was the normal state of affairs for humanity, but we lost it after Adam and Eve sinned against God. Now we yearn for its restoration. We want it back. We intuitively know things should be different than they are. We were made for a more perfect world.

Jesus taught us to pray, "Your kingdom come. Your will be done on earth as it is in heaven" (Matt. 6:10). While this prayer won't be fully answered during this current epoch of history, it represents the hope that is in every heart. Whether we know it or not, we're homesick for the garden of Eden. In every beating heart, there is a desire for what our first parents enjoyed—a perfect heaven on earth. We want everything restored that was lost. We can't help ourselves. It's programmed into the software of our humanity. This often unspoken yearning corresponds with God's plans for the future, for everywhere we turn in the Bible we uncover prophecies and predictions about God's true utopia—the new heaven and the new earth, wherein righteousness dwells.

THE PROMISE OF THE NEW HEAVEN AND NEW EARTH

If you read the Bible carefully, you will find promises salted throughout Scripture on this glorious subject. Listen to these incredible words in Isaiah 65:

> For behold, I create new heavens and a new earth;
> And the former shall not be remembered or come to mind.
> But be glad and rejoice forever in what I create;
> For behold, I create Jerusalem as a rejoicing,
> And her people a joy.

I will rejoice in Jerusalem,
And joy in My people;
The voice of weeping shall no longer be heard in her,
Nor the voice of crying. (vv. 17–19)

In the next chapter, Isaiah added:

"For as the new heavens and the new earth
Which I will make shall remain before Me," says the LORD,
"So shall your descendants and your name remain.
And it shall come to pass
That from one New Moon to another,
And from one Sabbath to another,
All flesh shall come to worship before Me,"
        says the LORD. (66:22–23)

When we turn to the closing books of the New Testament, we run into the same emphasis, expanded, highlighted, and amplified for our benefit. Simon Peter excitedly shares these truths with us in 2 Peter 3 and describes the dramatic events leading up to the new heaven and the new earth:

The heavens and the earth which are now preserved by the same word, are reserved for fire until the day of judgment and perdition of ungodly men. . . . But the day of the Lord will come as a thief in the night, in which the heavens will pass away with a great noise, and the elements will melt with fervent heat; both the earth and the works that are in it will be burned up. Therefore, since all these things will be dissolved, what manner of persons ought you to be in holy conduct and godliness, looking for and hastening the coming of the day of God, because of which the heavens will be dissolved, being on fire, and the elements will melt with fervent heat? Nevertheless we, according to His promise, look for new heavens and a new earth in which righteousness dwells. (vv. 7, 10–13)

Visualize this passage. Think in terms of an apocalyptic movie in which the world and, indeed, the whole universe explodes and collapses into flames, and somehow out of the cataclysm a new heaven and a new earth appear.

More information comes our way in Hebrews 1:10–12: "You, LORD, in the beginning laid the foundation of the earth, and the heavens are the work of Your hands. They will perish, but You remain; and they will all grow old like a garment; like a cloak You will fold them up, and they will be changed. But You are the same, and Your years will not fail."

Here, the writer of Hebrews, quoting from Psalm 102:25–27, avows that one day God will take this world and fold it up and change everything, just as you would take off your coat, fold it up, and store it away.

All this prepares us for the Bible's greatest passage on this—Revelation 21–22. Look at the way John begins this final section of Scripture: "Now I saw a new heaven and a new earth, for the first heaven and the first earth had passed away. Also there was no more sea. Then I, John, saw the holy city, New Jerusalem, coming down out of heaven from God, prepared as a bride adorned for her husband" (21:1–2).

We can't fully conceive of what this will be like, and we struggle to imagine what it will look like. But use your God-given imagination and take these God-given words into your heart. Picture them. See the current ages drawing to a close, the universe collapsing like an old house in flames, a new earth emerging from the carnage, and a new city glistening and descending and ready to lead us into eternity with Jesus on the throne. Talk about utopia! That word is hopelessly insufficient to describe the place God is preparing for us. It is our heavenly home—the place where Christ rules forever.

THE PURIFICATION OF THE NEW HEAVEN AND NEW EARTH

As we drill into the information contained in these passages, we tap into some astounding facts and start asking some logical questions, such as:

When will the new heaven and new earth arrive on the scene? Well, notice the order of events in Revelation.

The bulk of the middle chapters in the book, Revelation 6–18, describe the unfolding events of the coming period of the Tribulation, with their seven seals, seven trumpets, and seven bowls of wrath, leading up to the final climactic battle in world history—the Battle of Armageddon. In the next chapter, Revelation 19, the angelic host bursts into praise as Christ returns to earth to defeat the forces of the Antichrist and rescue His people.

The first part of Revelation 20 describes the millennial kingdom that Christ will establish when He comes again. The last part of chapter 20 describes the Great White Throne Judgment. This is when all Christ-rejecters will be condemned.

Then we turn the page, as it were, and begin reading in Revelation 21:1 about the creation of the new heaven and the new earth. Chronologically, then, we're reading about an event that will occur after the Rapture of the church, after the Tribulation and the Battle of Armageddon, after the second coming of Christ, after the millennial kingdom, and after the Great White Throne Judgment.

After the final events in human history have concluded, the curtain will fall on time and will arise on eternity.

Let's go back to Peter's words in 2 Peter 3:10–12 and see how he describes this moment:

> The day of the Lord will come as a thief in the night, in which the heavens will pass away with a great noise, and the elements will melt with fervent heat; both the earth and the works that are in it will be burned up. Therefore, since all these things will be dissolved, what manner of persons ought you to be in holy conduct and godliness, looking for and hastening the coming of the day of God, because of which the heavens will be dissolved, being on fire, and the elements will melt with fervent heat?

I believe that is when the new heaven and new earth will appear; but that leads to another question: How will they come into being? What does the Bible mean when it says heaven and earth will pass away? Earlier in my ministry, I believed the current earth and universe would be totally annihilated and completely destroyed. I've heard others teach about how the Lord will thoroughly wipe out every vestige of the old universe and start over from scratch.

Over the years, I've grown in my understanding of this event; and after years of studying this subject, it seems clear to me that the Lord will create the new heaven and earth by renovating, overhauling, refurbishing, and reconstituting the old heaven and the earth. Rather than being totally annihilated, the present heaven and earth will be cleansed, glorified, and equipped for our eternal use.

Several phrases and insights suggest this is the case.

"BURNED UP"

Take, for example, the words *burned up*. Notice again what Peter said: "Both the earth and the works that are in it will be burned up . . . the heavens will be dissolved, being on fire" (2 Pet. 3:10, 12).

The phrase *burned up* literally means "laid bare" or "exposed." The actual Greek word chosen by Peter in this text conveys the idea of being uncovered or laid open for exposure. It isn't a matter of utter destruction but of stripping everything away and getting back down to the original elements. The great universal conflagration that Peter describes will be a purification of the cosmos, a burning away of everything associated with sin, death, the curse, and the temporal. Peter didn't use a word that meant annihilation but one having to do with renovation.

The basic materials of earth's structure will not be annihilated but will undergo tremendous processes of disintegration. All the ingrained evidences of decay wrought into the earth's crust, especially the fossils and the cemeteries and all the other monuments belonging to the long march of death, will be completely destroyed. As the material elements of the former cosmos will melt in the intense heat, God will once more exercise His creative power to re-create the universe, to make the new heaven and the new earth. As God created Adam out of the dirt of the ground, so He will re-create the heaven and the earth from the elements remaining after the universe is destroyed by fire.

In one of his inimitable sermons, Dr. W. A. Criswell put it this way:

God someday shall purge this earth and this universe of all of its sin and unrighteousness and darkness and death. It will be dissolved in a fervent heat. The elements shall return to their primordial form, and that whole creation of God shall be burned with fire (2 Peter 3:10, 12). It shall be cleansed. It shall be purged. Everything that is wrong and everything that is transgressing and sinful shall be taken out of it. Then shall come to pass this ultimate and final revelation described for us in the twenty-first chapter (Revelation 21). Out of this purged mass of God's creative work, He will reshape, He will remake, He will re-create all of the heavens and this earth. There will be no destruction of what God has made. It is a renewal. It is a renaissance. It is a regeneration. It is a re-creation (Revelation 21:1–5).[1]

"NEW"

We get another indication of this in Revelation 21:5, when the Lord declares, "Behold, I make all things new." The word *new* is significant. The apostle John originally wrote the book of Revelation in the prevailing Greek language of his day, and there are two Greek words for "new." One of those words (*neos*) contained the idea of creating something from nothing—new in terms of time. The other word (*kainos*) suggested newness in terms of quality.

It is this second word that John uses of the new creation at the end of the age—not utter destruction but utter transformation.

"PASS AWAY"

Yet another indication of this is the Greek term for "pass away" in Revelation 21:1: "Now I saw a new heaven and a new earth, for the first heaven and the first earth had passed away." This Greek word does not mean to cease to exist but to change form, to pass from one state into another. "It is the same heaven and earth, but gloriously rejuvenated, with no weeds, thorns, or thistles, and so on."[2]

We use similar terminology. When I speak of a loved one who passes away, I don't mean to say they are now nonexistent. They haven't ceased to exist because "God is not the God of the dead, but of the living" (Matt. 22:32). They have simply moved from one state to another.

LIKE THE FLOOD

There's another strong hint about the nature of the transition from the old creation to the new creation. Peter compared it to the Flood of Noah's day. Remember what he wrote in 2 Peter 3:5–7?

> By the word of God the heavens were of old, and the earth standing out of water and in the water, by which the world that then existed perished, being flooded with water. But the heavens and the earth which are now preserved by the same word, are reserved for fire until the day of judgment and perdition of ungodly men.

Now, think about this parallel. Was the world of Noah's day destroyed? Well, it was cleansed. It was purified by the waters of the Flood. The judgment of God fell over the earth, and the very topography of the globe changed dramatically as the waters fell, rose, and dissipated. But the essential elements making up the earth were not annihilated. God did not obliterate the earth's core and erase all of creation from existence, returning everything to emptiness. He renovated it.

The renovation at the end of the age will be far more extensive and miraculous. The universe will pass through the smelt furnace of God's judgment and emerge in a pristine state, glorified, transformed, imperishable, and fitted for eternity. Peter helps us comprehend the meaning of the final purging of heaven and earth by describing the earlier purification that took place in the days of Noah. The Flood was certainly destructive and cataclysmic, but it did not obliterate the world. God preserved Noah and his family so they could re-inhabit the world that was made ready for them by the cleansing and purification of the Flood.

In the same manner, God will not cause the present earth to cease to exist by the fire that will come at the end of the age. The fire will have a much greater purifying effect upon the world than water did, but it will not destroy the world.

LIKE THE RESURRECTION OF THE BODY

Notice how this process parallels the resurrection of the human body. When Jesus died and rose again, His old body wasn't obliterated and recreated from scratch. The body that rose again was the same that had died on the cross; but in that wondrous flash of resurrection power, it was glorified, transformed, and fitted for eternity. The same is true with our own bodies. Our bodies may decay to dust, but God knows where every molecule has landed; and somehow in His omnipotent energy, the physical bodies we have now will be resurrected and instantly glorified and equipped for eternal life. Yes, we will have new bodies—not new in terms of time but in terms of quality or in their essence.

TO DENY SATAN

Let me suggest a final reason for viewing the new heaven and new earth in terms of renovation. I don't believe God intends to give Satan the satisfaction of having irreparably ruined the divine creation. When God created heaven and the earth in the book of Genesis, He was very pleased with His handiwork. Genesis 1:31 says, "Then God saw everything that He had made, and indeed it was very good." There is no evidence the Lord ever changed His mind about that. His purpose for redeeming the world was not to abandon His creation but to restore it.

Anthony Hoekema wrote:

> If God would have to annihilate the present cosmos, Satan would have won a great victory. For then Satan would have succeeded in so devastatingly corrupting the present cosmos and the present earth that God could do nothing with it but to blot it totally out of existence. But Satan did not win such a victory. On the contrary, Satan has been decisively defeated. God

will reveal the full dimensions of that defeat when he shall renew this very earth on which Satan deceived mankind and finally banish from it all the results of Satan's evil machinations.[3]

To summarize, then, after the Rapture of the church, the seven years of Tribulation, the Battle of Armageddon, the return of Christ, the Millennium, and the Great White Throne Judgment, God will draw the curtains on human history, and the entire universe will undergo a purifying conflagration. All evidence of disease will be burned up. All evidence of disobedience will melt away. All the remnants and results of sin, sorrow, and suffering will be destroyed. Out of the smoldering ruins, God will recreate all physical reality, and He will bring forth a fresh universe—a new heaven and a new earth.

THE PRINCIPLES OF THE NEW HEAVEN AND NEW EARTH

Having discussed the promise and the purification of the new heaven and the new earth, let's return to Revelation 21 to uncover some startling principles about our new universe. I want to tell you what this is all going to be like. When this new creation is finished and God has purified it, it's still the same earth and still the same heaven, but it will have been purged. It will be made fresh. All the stains of sin will be gone. All the evidences of death. All the signs of disease. What, then, will the world be like? Among the glorious things we're told in the book of Revelation, three have struck me with particular force—the removal of the sea, the reversal of the curse, and the restoration of all things.

THE REMOVAL OF THE SEA
The first thing we have to grapple with is the question of the oceans of the world. Revelation 21:1 says, "Now I saw a new heaven and a new earth,

for the first heaven and the first earth had passed away. Also there was no more sea." If you're like me, that's a little disconcerting, at least when I first heard about it. I live in Southern California near the ocean, and I love watching the sun fall like a blazing orb into the Pacific in the evenings at sunset. Many of us who love the oceans cock a troubled eyebrow when we read the last phrase of verse 1.

But the Bible doesn't tell us there won't be beautiful bodies of water. When you think about it, the surface of our planet is primarily water—about 71 percent. The oceans hold over 96 percent of all the earth's water, and these vast wastelands of salt water are essentially uninhabitable by humans. The new earth will be more beautiful than anything we can imagine and more gorgeous than anywhere we've ever been. There will clearly be bodies of water, as I'll explain in a moment. But evidently, there will not be huge wastelands of salty seas.

The composition of the planet will be so different—and the nature of our glorified bodies will be so superior—that the very ecology of the new creation will be altered.

Certainly the fresh waters flowing throughout the coming world will be more beautiful than anything we can imagine, with trees growing alongside them providing fruit and beauty and a quality of life beyond anything that we have ever known. So don't worry about the phrase, "Also there was no more sea." Give God a little bit of credit here, for if He made the seas so beautiful and pleasant in the first place, He will certainly design the new world with even greater levels of marvel and magnificence.

THE REVERSAL OF THE CURSE

We uncover another glorious feature of the new world with these words in Revelation 22:3: "And there shall be no more curse, but the throne of God and of the Lamb shall be in it, and His servants shall serve Him."

What curse is that? When most of us think of the word *curse* we think of an obscenity or profanity, the kind we hear at work or school or all too often on television. But when John used the word *curse* he was pointing back to the words God spoke in the garden of Eden in Genesis 3, after Adam and Eve had rebelled and brought sin and shame upon the world.

In Genesis 3:17–19, the Lord said to Adam:

"Because you have heeded the voice of your wife, and have eaten from the tree of which I commanded you, saying, 'You shall not eat of it': Cursed is the ground for your sake; in toil you shall eat of it all the days of your life. Both thorns and thistles it shall bring forth for you, and you shall eat the herb of the field. In the sweat of your face you shall eat bread till you return to the ground, for out of it you were taken; for dust you are, and to dust you shall return."

The curse is why everything goes wrong in our world and why life is such a fight all the time. Humanity always has to run uphill, and nature often works against us.

In a million ways, we see the earth deteriorating around us. Look at an empty field. It doesn't sprout into flowerbeds or ornamental gardens; it descends into a patch of weeds. Look at our human bodies. At a certain point, they begin to deteriorate, age, break down, and fail. Look across our planet at the ravages of droughts, earthquakes, hurricanes, tornadoes, fires, and floods—not to mention the evils perpetuated by humanity's sinful nature. All this is summed up in that one word: *curse*.

Now think of the power of these words from Revelation 22:3: "And there shall be no more curse."

When we get to the new heaven and the new earth, the curse will be reversed. It will be lifted; it will be dispelled forever. Oh, think of it! The weariness that accompanies our work will be a forgotten memory. Nature will work as it should, the weather will always be in our favor, and the ground will grow flowers as naturally as it produces thorns and thistles today. We ourselves will not fall into the ground in death because we will never die.

God sent His Son into the world, not only to save our souls but also to redeem creation from the results of sin. The work of Christ goes beyond the incredible goal of saving an innumerable throng of blood-bought people. The total work of Christ is nothing less than redeeming this entire creation from the effects of sin. That purpose will not be accomplished until God has ushered in the new earth, until Paradise lost becomes Paradise regained. But it will be accomplished!

THE RESTORATION OF ALL THINGS

That brings us to the final feature I want to mention about the new heaven and the new earth—the restoration of all things. Revelation 21:4–5 says, "The former things have passed away. Then He who sat on the throne said, 'Behold, I make all things new.'"

Randy Alcorn explained it like this:

Heaven is God's home. Earth is our home. Jesus Christ, as the God-man, forever links God and mankind, and thereby forever links Heaven and Earth. As Ephesians 1:10 demonstrates, this idea of Earth and Heaven becoming one is explicitly biblical. Christ will make Earth into Heaven and Heaven into Earth. Just as the wall that separates God and mankind is torn down in Jesus, so too the wall that separates Heaven and Earth will be forever demolished. There will be one universe, with all things in Heaven and on Earth together under one head, Jesus Christ.

Alcorn continued, "God's plan is that there will be no more gulf between the spiritual and physical worlds. There will be no divided loyalties or divided realms. There will be one cosmos, one universe united under one Lord— forever. This is the unstoppable plan of God. This is where history is headed."[4]

This is why Revelation 21:3 is so exuberant: "I heard a loud voice from heaven saying, 'Behold, the tabernacle of God is with men, and He will dwell with them, and they shall be His people. God Himself will be with them and be their God.'"

When you think about it, this new paradigm doesn't simply give us a sense of adventure about the future; it also gives us a new appreciation for the world in which we currently live. That's why Christians are—or should be—in a proper sense, the world's best ecologists. We realize that God loves the world He has made, and from the beginning, back in Genesis 2:15, we're told that we are responsible for this planet, to "tend and keep it."

In his narrative about heaven, David Haney wrote about going to his favorite restaurant in Dallas, Texas, that features creative Southwestern cuisine. The most famous item on the menu is a specially prepared rib eye steak, but the restaurant is also known for its extensive menu of exotic appetizers. One day David sat down at his table, studied the menu, and ordered a marvelous shrimp fajita appetizer that was unlike anything he had ever tasted in his life. "I discovered taste buds that I did not even know I had," he said. "I could not believe that anyone could make something so odd-sounding taste so good."

When the waiter returned to inquire about the entrée, David told him he didn't want to eat anything else all night. The shrimp fajita had done him in, and he didn't even plan to brush his teeth that evening because he wanted to savor the memory of the marvelous taste. But the waiter told him, "If you thought that was good, just wait for the rib eye."[5]

Afterward David thought about that simple conversation, and he pondered the whole idea of "foretaste." In a sense, the beauties of our world—the hills, the plains, the mountains, the oceans, the spangling vault of heaven—are like appetizers that whet our appetites for the main course, for God's new creation.

I don't know anything more about these realities than what the Bible tells us; Scripture is our only source of truth about the life hereafter. But based upon these biblical truths, I believe the same God who magnificently created this present world is preparing for that moment when He will make all things new. The scene in Revelation 21 and 22 is not some fictional utopia. It is absolute reality, revealed for us in God's book, designed for us by God's heart, and provided for us by God's own Son.

CHAPTER 31

HOLY CITY

In June 2016, the magazine *Business Insider* assigned a team of technology reporters to determine the greatest cities in world history, the greatest city on earth today, and the nature of the megacities of the future. In 2100 BC the leading city in the world was Ur, with an estimated 100,000 inhabitants. Several centuries later, the top honor passed to Yinxu, with 120,000 souls.

During the days of the kings of Israel, the world's greatest city was Nineveh, which Jonah famously evangelized in the days of the prophets. When Christ was born, Rome had eclipsed all other cities in history to reach the one million mark.

Skipping through time, London became the largest city on earth in 1825, with nearly 1.5 million people; but after World War I New York City sprinted to the top with a whopping 7.8 million. Tokyo took over in 1968 with 20.5 million people, and today it still holds the distinction of being the most heavily populated city in human history with more than 38 million inhabitants.[1]

The purpose of this chapter, however, is to tell you about a city that far surpasses all the cities of the past, present, and future. The Bible delights in telling us about this place, which we sometimes call the celestial city,

Mount Zion, or New Jerusalem. The final two chapters of the Bible use the word *city* eleven times to describe our eternal home, and I don't believe it's a figure of speech. It is an actual physical place—a real city. Since our resurrected bodies will be physical bodies, real and tangible, they will need a real place and an actual home—a physical city.

It's in the book of Revelation that we have our fullest glimpse of this city, starting with this promise from the lips of the glorified Christ in Revelation 3:12: "He who overcomes, I will make him a pillar in the temple of My God, and he shall go out no more. I will write on him the name of My God and the name of the city of My God, the New Jerusalem, which comes down out of heaven from My God. And I will write on him My new name."

The apostle John tells us of the creation of the new heaven and the new earth, and then, we're told, the great city of New Jerusalem will descend from the sky and become the capital city of God's eternal kingdom.

It's important to realize that the city of New Jerusalem is not really heaven, per se. It is the capital city of heaven. Here, in one of the Bible's most climactic passages, this great city is described as it descends, fully designed and built, to the earth:

Now I saw a new heaven and a new earth, for the first heaven and the first earth had passed away. Also there was no more sea. Then I, John, saw the holy city, New Jerusalem, coming down out of heaven from God, prepared as a bride adorned for her husband. And I heard a loud voice from heaven saying, "Behold, the tabernacle of God is with men, and He will dwell with them, and they shall be His people. God Himself will be with them and be their God. And God will wipe away every tear from their eyes; there shall be no more death, nor sorrow, nor crying. There shall be no more pain, for the former things have passed away." Then He who sat on the throne said, "Behold, I make all things new." And He said to me, "Write, for these words are true and faithful." (21:1–5)

This description implies that the holy city was designed, built, and ready—made for the new earth. John did not see the New Jerusalem created; he says he saw the city already built and coming down out of the highest heaven. In other words, the New Jerusalem is an actual, physical city presently located within the third heaven. Jesus referred to New Jerusalem in Revelation 3:12 as the "city of My God." Here in Revelation 21, John saw this city descending to the new earth. Some Bible scholars believe this city will hover over the earth during the Millennium, then descend to the earth during the eternal state to serve as the everlasting capital of God's renovated and glorious universe.

This city of New Jerusalem is the place Jesus is preparing for us, and the Bible draws to a close with a breathtaking description of its dimensions, its description, and a warning about the one thing that could deny us access through its gates—the failure to trust Christ as our Savior.

THE DIMENSIONS OF THE CITY

These final pages of the Bible begin by telling us about the size of this city. The boundaries of the New Jerusalem exceed anything ever envisioned by human engineers or politicians. Sometimes people ask me, "How in the world can heaven be large enough to hold all the redeemed of all the ages?"

Well, first of all, I assume the entirety of the new heaven and new earth will be inhabitable. But if we limit our thinking simply to the city of New Jerusalem, our minds are still boggled by its immensity. Revelation 21:15–16 says, "He who talked with me had a gold reed to measure the city, its gates, and its wall. The city is laid out as a square; its length is as great as its breadth. And he measured the city with the reed: twelve thousand furlongs. Its length, breadth, and height are equal."

In today's terms, that means New Jerusalem will be about 1,500 miles wide, 1,500 miles long, and 1,500 miles high. That's more than 2 million square miles on the first "floor" alone! And given that this city is cubical and rises far beyond the stratosphere (the stratosphere starts about eleven miles above the surface of the earth; New Jerusalem ascends to 1,500 miles), we can assume that in some way it will have more than one level. There will be vertical elements to it.

F. W. Boreham was a brilliant pastor and essayist who carefully considered the size and capacity of the great city. In one of his writings he tells of discussing this with a man named Tammas, who was an Australian engineer and a member of his church. Boreham shared the dimensions of the Celestial City with Tammas, asking him, "Did you ever think about the size of the city God has prepared?" Tammas replied:

Man, it's amazing; it's astounding; it beats everything I ever heard of! John says that each of the walls of the city measures twelve thousand furlongs. Now, if you work that out . . . it will give you an area of 2,250,000 square miles! . . . The only "city foursquare" that I ever saw was Adelaide in South Australia. The ship that brought me out from the Old Country called in there for a couple of days, and I thought it a fine city. But, as you know very well, the city of Adelaide covers only one square mile. Each of the four sides is a mile long. London covers an area of one hundred and forty square miles. But this city—the City Foursquare! It is 2,250,000 times as big as Adelaide! It is 15,000 times as big as London! It is twenty times as big as all New Zealand! It is ten times as big as Germany and ten times as big as France! It is forty times as big as all England! It is ever so much bigger than India! Why, it's an enormous continent in itself. I had no idea of it until I went into the figures with my blue pencil here.

But Tammas wasn't done.

Wait a minute—I've been going into the matter of population, and it's even more wonderful still. Look at this! Working it out on the basis of the number of people to the square mile in the city of London, the population of the City Foursquare comes out at a hundred thousand millions—seventy times the present population of the globe.[2]

Another writer has compared the footprint of New Jerusalem to the size of the United States, saying:

> If you compare the New Jerusalem to the United States, you would measure from the Atlantic Ocean coastal line and westward, it would mean a city from the furthest Maine to the furthest Florida, and from the shore of the Atlantic to Colorado. And from the United States' Pacific coast eastward, it would cover the United States as far as the Mississippi River, with the line extending north through Chicago and continuing on the west coast of Lake Michigan, up to the Canadian border.[3]

To me, one of the most amazing things about the dimensions of this city involves its height. According to Revelation 21:16, it is just as high as it is long and wide, which means it will ascend 1,500 miles into the air. Now, just for discussion's sake, let's say the city was divided into floors with very high ceilings, say, twenty feet high per floor. There are 5,280 feet in a mile, so if the city of New Jerusalem reaches 1,500 miles into the air, that's 7,920,000 feet. Let's suppose every floor was a mile high. That gives us a city of 1,500 floors, every floor the size of a continent. And that's just the capital city! Don't forget what's all around it—the new heaven and the new earth.

Some people are overwhelmed as they begin to wonder how we'll ever get around in a city like that. We're used to the congestion and traffic jams of earth. But remember what we said about our new bodies. We may have the ability, like Christ, to travel instantly and by the impulses of thought. Transportation will be no problem. I don't want to become too speculative, but I want you to share my excitement about the sheer, overwhelming, mind-boggling size of the city. It will exceed anything we've ever imagined.

There's one other interesting aspect to the dimensions. The city is obviously described as a cube—1,500 miles long, high, and wide. The Holy of Holies inside the tabernacle and, later, inside the temple, was also in the shape of a cube. Many people believe the city of New Jerusalem is like an immense Holy of Holies, which serves as the dwelling place of God in the temple of His new universe. In fact, Revelation 21:3 says of this city, "Behold, the tabernacle of God is with men, and He will dwell with them, and they shall be His people. God Himself will be with them and be their God."

THE DESCRIPTION OF THE CITY

The dimensions of this vast city serve as only the beginning point of our observations. As we continue reading through Revelation 21 and 22, we're awestruck by the multifaceted descriptions of the city. I encourage you to read these final two chapters of Scripture for yourself and make them an object of ongoing study. To help you, I want to point out the sevenfold depiction these chapters give us of New Jerusalem.

On that basis, then, let's look at these seven wonderful features of New Jerusalem.

THE HOLY CITY

First, this will be a holy city. Notice the emphasis on this in Revelation 21:

- "Then I, John, saw the holy city, New Jerusalem" (v. 2).
- "And he carried me away in the Spirit to a great and high mountain, and showed me the great city, the holy Jerusalem, descending out of heaven from God" (v. 10).

The chief characteristic of this city is its holiness. *The Wycliffe Bible Commentary* says, "A holy city will be one in which no lie will be uttered in one hundred million years, no evil word will ever be spoken, no shady business deal will ever even be discussed, no unclean picture will ever be seen, no corruption of life will ever be manifest. It will be holy because everyone in it will be holy."[4]

Without sin, there will be no death. There will be no jails, courtrooms, prisons, hospitals, or funeral homes in heaven. This is a holy place for holy people, for those who have been made holy by God's infinite grace through the blood of Jesus Christ.

THE GATES OF PEARL

The Bible also tells us about a vast, high, broad wall surrounding New Jerusalem, punctuated by twelve gates, each of which is made of pearl. Revelation 21:17–21 says:

> Then he measured its wall: one hundred and forty-four cubits, according to the measure of a man, that is, of an angel. The construction of its wall was of jasper; and the city was pure gold, like clear glass. . . . The twelve gates were twelve pearls: each individual gate was of one pearl. And the street of the city was pure gold, like transparent glass.

Perhaps you're wondering what kind of oyster is required to produce such a gigantic pearl! But do you think God is limited to creating pearls only by oysters? God can make a pearl just by speaking a word if He wishes. If He can speak a word and create a star, He can certainly do so with pearls. That said, I'm not sure how God will do it; but each of the twelve gates will be as beautiful and stunning as a giant pearl, and each will have the name of one of the tribes of Israel.

Think of it. The wall is made of jasper, which, in biblical times, was a crystal stone like a diamond; and the gigantic gates are made of solid pearl. Imagine seeing this from afar. It will sparkle and shine as it rotates down to the earth, and all the hues of the glory of the city will be overwhelming. It will take your breath away.

One of my mentors, Dr. W. A. Criswell, had an interesting view of these gates of pearl. He once preached:

There is a sermon in the fact that the gates are pearl. [Because] heaven is entered through suffering and travail, through redemption and blood, through the agony of the cross. A pearl is a jewel made by a little animal that is wounded. Without the wound, the pearl is never formed.[5]

When we walk through the gates of pearl, we'll be reminded the only reason we're there is because of the suffering and the pain of the Lord Jesus, who bore His wounds for us that we might be redeemed.

THE FOUNDATIONS OF PRECIOUS STONES

The third descriptive element of this city is its foundation. This seems to be a very important feature because we have an earlier reference to it in Hebrews 11:10, where the city is described as one with "foundations, whose builder and maker is God."

Revelation 21:19–20 describes it this way:

The foundations of the wall of the city were adorned with all kinds of precious stones: the first foundation was jasper, the second sapphire, the third chalcedony, the fourth emerald, the fifth sardonyx, the sixth sardius, the seventh chrysolite, the eighth beryl, the ninth topaz, the tenth chrysoprase, the eleventh jacinth, and the twelfth amethyst.

The names of those stones have been rendered from the original Greek words John used, and they may not represent the exact stones as those bearing the same names today. But they certainly describe a set of stones with all the colors and hues of the rainbow.

Can you imagine approaching heaven's capital and seeing it from afar? We'll witness this magnificent city, soaring 1,500 miles into the atmosphere, built upon gemstone foundations, with each gate brilliantly crafted from a single pearl. We'll walk into this holy city with jaws dropped and eyes widened in absolute wonder, for even the most beautiful places on earth don't hold a candle to what God has prepared for us.

THE STREETS OF GOLD

But that's not all! Revelation 21 also says the city is constructed of gold, and even its central boulevard will be made of solid gold paving stones: "The twelve gates were twelve pearls: each individual gate was of one pearl. And the street of the city was pure gold, like transparent glass" (v. 21).

Interestingly, the gold of New Jerusalem is described as being like "transparent glass." The earthly gold that currently fills our vaults isn't transparent, of course; but the gold of heaven will be so pure that we will seem to look into it and through its clear depths as we walk upon it. Some scholars interpret this as being like a finely polished mirror and therefore not so much transparent as translucent. But remember: we'll be walking around in our glorified bodies, and we can assume our eyesight will be enhanced so we can see things as we've never seen them before.

THE LAMB THAT IS THE LIGHT

The next thing we encounter in Revelation 21 and 22 has to do with the light and energy sources for the city of New Jerusalem. Where will its power plant be located? Where will its electrical generators be? How can such an immense city be illumined? Four different verses are devoted to this subject:

- "Her light was like a most precious stone, like a jasper stone, clear as crystal" (Rev. 21:11).
- "The city had no need of the sun or of the moon to shine in it, for the glory of God illuminated it. The Lamb is its light" (Rev. 21:23).
- "And the nations of those who are saved shall walk in its light" (Rev. 21:24).
- "There shall be no night there: They need no lamp nor light of the sun, for the Lord God gives them light" (Rev. 22:5).

There will be no light posts in New Jerusalem, no lanterns, no flood-lights or flashlights or table lights. A strange presence of brilliant light will emanate throughout the city from the throne of God and of the Lamb. The brilliance of the light will beam forth from the Lord Jesus in His glorification, and it will fill the city with radiance. Were it not for our new glorified eyesight, we would be blinded. But it won't hurt our eyes at all; in fact, our new eyes will be perfectly made for such light. I can't imagine that, but I can anticipate it.

This is the New Jerusalem described in Scripture, and it's the fulfillment of a prophecy made hundreds of years before the birth of Christ, in Isaiah 60:19: "The sun shall no longer be your light by day, nor for brightness shall the moon give light to you; but the LORD will be to you an everlasting light, and your God your glory."

THE TREE OF LIFE

Having looked at its holiness, its dimensions, its gates and foundations and streets, and at its lighting source, there's another wonderful feature to discover—the presence of the tree of life. Revelation 22:2 says, "In the middle of its street, and on either side of the river, was the tree of life, which bore twelve fruits, each tree yielding its fruit every month. The leaves of the tree were for the healing of the nations."

One of the topographical features of New Jerusalem is a river flowing down from the throne of God, its waters as clear as crystal; and on both sides of the river are the trees of life—not just one tree but multiple trees. Notice that verse 2 refers to "each tree." The Greek term indicates a plurality of the trees, such as we'd find in an orchard. These trees will bear fruit every month, and it will be like eating fruit from the garden of Eden.

Notice the phrase that speaks of the leaves being used for the healing of the nations. The word for "healing" in the Greek language is *therapeia*, from which we get *therapeutic*. We'll be able to eat the leaves of the tree, and those leaves will somehow give us a greater sense of our lives and our presence in heaven. This "therapy" will not enhance our holiness, because we will be perfectly holy; but somehow it will give us a greater sense of enjoyment and fulfillment. It will be heaven's therapy for our ever-increasing well-being.

THE RIVER OF LIFE

That brings us to the final feature in our tour of New Jerusalem—the river of life. Look again at Revelation 22:1–2: "He showed me a pure river of water of life, clear as crystal, proceeding from the throne of God and of the Lamb. In the middle of its street, and on either side of the river, was the tree of life, which bore twelve fruits, each tree yielding its fruit every month. The leaves of the tree were for the healing of the nations."

I believe this is the same river mentioned in Psalm 46:4: "There is a river whose streams shall make glad the city of God, the holy place of the tabernacle of the Most High."

Almost all the great cities of the world have the ribbon of a river running through them—Cairo has the Nile; Baghdad has the Tigris; Budapest has the Danube; London has the Thames; Paris, the Seine; Rome, the Tiber. Visit New York and you can take a boat trip up and down the Hudson River; and if you're in Washington, you can walk along the Potomac. If you visit the city of Jerusalem right now, you'll be visiting one of the few great world cities without a river. But one day, the new city of Jerusalem—the heavenly Zion—will have a river of waters that are clear as crystal, flowing from the throne of God. It will be the most beautiful river ever created in time or eternity.

This is our destination, our eternal home. Heaven is a city foursquare, 1,500 miles wide, 1,500 miles long, and 1,500 miles high. It will have plenty of room to house all the people who have ever trusted God from the beginning of time.

Think of the most beautiful spot you've ever seen on earth. For me, it's a place called Santorini. My wife, Donna, and I took a little break a few years ago and visited Greece and Turkey. One of the Greek islands in the southern Aegean Sea is Santorini, a volcanic island only about thirty-five square miles in size. As we stood on the deck of the boat and looked at the blindingly white little town with its rounded roofs and quaint simplicity, elevated along the clifftops above the blue sea and jutting upward toward the blue sky, it almost appeared to be suspended in space.

"Wow," we said, "what a beautiful place!"

But it doesn't compare to what God has envisioned for those who have put their trust in Him.

THE DENIAL TO THE CITY

I don't want to end this chapter on a negative note, but all the way through Revelation 21 and 22 we see repeated warnings about the danger of being denied access to this city. We've discussed the dimensions of the city and the description of the city, but I need to remind you about this denial of entrance to the city.

Not everyone will be admitted to the heavenly city. See for yourself the emphasis on this in the following verses:

- He who overcomes shall inherit all things, and I will be his God and he shall be My son. But the cowardly, unbelieving, abominable, murderers, sexually immoral, sorcerers, idolaters, and all liars shall have their part in the lake which burns with fire and brimstone, which is the second death. (Rev. 21:7–8)
- Its gates shall not be shut at all by day (there shall be no night there). And they shall bring the glory and the honor of the nations into it. But there shall by no means enter it anything that defiles, or causes an abomination or a lie, but only those who are written in the Lamb's Book of Life. (21:25–27)
- Blessed are those who do His commandments, that they may have the right to the tree of life, and may enter through the gates into the city. But outside are dogs and sorcerers and sexually immoral and murderers and idolaters, and whoever loves and practices a lie. (22:14–15)

Now, of course, all of us are sinners. We have all practiced lying. Many Christians have episodes of sorcery or immorality or idolatry or even murder in their pasts. These verses do not mean to imply that those sins will keep us out of heaven if the blood of Christ has redeemed us. But if we have not repented of our sins and placed our faith in Christ, those sins will certainly prevent us from walking the streets of gold.

If you are living in sin without any regard for the forgiveness of God, and if you are failing to respond to His gracious invitation found in the gospel, you will have no part in the new heaven, the new earth, or the city of New Jerusalem. The only people allowed there are those whose names are written in the Lamb's Book of Life. There are no exceptions. You won't be able to argue your way into that city, or con your way in, or sneak in, or bribe your way in. If you have not accepted God's plan for your life and received His forgiveness for your sin, when the moment comes, you will be denied entrance into heaven and into the city we have described. I don't want that to happen to you!

I believe the reason God gives us health and life and energy as His people is so we can be His ambassadors, going all over the world, in and out of cities, and on the radio and television, distributing Christian literature, sharing our testimonies, contributing our resources, and giving out the gospel—all so we can take as many people to heaven with us as possible.

Let me end with this analysis of Revelation 21–22 by the great Scottish preacher of an earlier era, Horatius Bonar, who said that the city of New Jerusalem was a great city, a well-built city, a well-lit city, a well-watered city, a well-provisioned city, a well-guarded city, a well-governed city, a well-peopled city, a holy city, a glorious city.

"Blessed city!" wrote Bonar. "City of peace, and love, and song! Fit accompaniment of the new heavens; fit metropolis of the new earth, wherein dwelleth righteousness! How eagerly should we look for it! How worthy of it should we live!"[6]

Have you made your reservation for the holy city? I urge you to do that now! The last invitation in the book of Revelation says:

And the Spirit and the bride say, "Come!"
And let him who hears say, "Come!"
And let him who thirsts come.
Whoever desires, let him take the water of life freely. (22:17)

EPILOGUE

The Nazi blitz on London began in late 1940. People had to endure the terrifying screams of falling bombs, the roar of planes overhead, the staccato bursts of anti-aircraft gunfire, and the booming explosions of bombs.

One little girl was returning home from school when the sirens suddenly sounded. She dropped her books and ran headlong toward her home. A bomb exploded a block away. When she arrived home, her frantic father scooped her up and rushed the family to the nearest shelter. They huddled in the darkness as the terrifying cacophony of war raged outside.

The little girl clung to her father and said, "Daddy, can we please go somewhere where there isn't any sky?"

After coming this far on our journey together through the "Thirty-One Undeniable Prophecies of the Apocalypse," you might be wishing the same thing. But my hope is that while you are wide awake and more aware of the "signs" than you've ever been—alert, watchful, and vigilant, with one eye on the headlines and the other on the eastern skies—you would also be more hopeful, now realizing that there is high value on understanding future events which in addition to painting a sometimes terrifying picture also show us God is the author of history. He is in control, and our Lord's return is certain, and I believe, soon.

In addition to enabling us to live with hope about our world and its future, studying prophecy has an even higher and more practical value. It provides a compelling motivation for living the Christian life. The immediacy of prophetic events shows the need to live each moment in Christlike readiness. When we have heard and understood the truth of Christ's promised return, we cannot just keep living our lives in the same old way. Future events have present implications that we cannot ignore. When we know that Christ is coming again to this earth, we cannot go on being the same people. We need to make a positive impact on the world.

WHAT SHALL WE DO?

It's my sincere hope that you have increased your knowledge of the end times by reading this book. But knowledge is not enough. In fact, knowledge is only helpful to us if it leads us to action.

Therefore, based on my readings in the New Testament epistles, here are ten ways we as Christians should be different as a result of our prophetic knowledge. In each of the following Scripture passages, I have italicized the words connecting the admonition with the promise of Christ's return.

1. **Refrain from judging others:** "Therefore judge nothing before the time, *until the Lord comes*, who will both bring to light the hidden things of darkness and reveal the counsels of the hearts. Then each one's praise will come from God" (1 Cor. 4:5).
2. **Remember the Lord's Table:** "For as often as you eat this bread and drink this cup, you proclaim the Lord's death *till He comes*" (1 Cor. 11:26).
3. **Respond to life spiritually:** "If then you were raised with Christ, seek those things which are above, where Christ is, sitting at the right hand of God. Set your mind on things above, not on things on the earth. For you died, and your life is hidden with Christ in God.

When Christ who is our life appears, then you also will appear with Him in glory" (Col. 3:1–4).

4. **Relate to one another in love:** "And may the Lord make you increase and abound in love to one another and to all, just as we do to you, so that He may establish your hearts blameless in holiness before our God and Father at *the coming of our Lord Jesus Christ* with all His saints" (1Thess. 3:12–13; Jude v. 21).

5. **Restore the bereaved:** "But I do not want you to be ignorant, brethren, concerning those who have fallen asleep, lest you sorrow as others who have no hope. For if we believe that Jesus died and rose again, even so God will bring with Him those who sleep in Jesus. For this we say to you by the word of the Lord, that we who are alive and remain *until the coming of the Lord* will by no means precede those who are asleep. For the Lord Himself will descend from heaven with a shout, with the voice of an archangel, and with the trumpet of God. And the dead in Christ will rise first. Then we who are alive and remain shall be caught up together with them in the clouds to meet the Lord in the air. And thus we shall always be with the Lord. Therefore comfort one another with these words" (1 Thess. 4:13–18).

6. **Recommit ourselves to the ministry:** "I charge you therefore before God and the Lord Jesus Christ, who will judge the living and the dead *at His appearing* and His kingdom: Preach the word! Be ready in season and out of season. Convince, rebuke, exhort, with all longsuffering and teaching" (2 Tim. 4:1–2).

7. **Refuse to neglect church:** "And let us consider one another in order to stir up love and good works, not forsaking the assembling of ourselves together, as is the manner of some, but exhorting one another, and so much the more *as you see the Day approaching*" (Heb. 10:24–25).

8. **Remain steadfast:** "Therefore be patient, brethren, until the coming of the Lord. See how the farmer waits for the precious fruit of the earth, waiting patiently for it until it receives the early and

latter rain. You also be patient. Establish your hearts, for *the coming of the Lord is at hand* " (James 5:7–8).

9. **Renounce sin in our lives:** "And now, little children, abide in Him, that *when He appears*, we may have confidence and not be ashamed before Him *at His coming*. If you know that He is righteous, you know that everyone who practices righteousness is born of Him" (1 John 2:28–29).

10. **Reach the lost:** "Keep yourselves in the love of God, *looking for the mercy of our Lord Jesus Christ* unto eternal life. And on some have compassion, making a distinction; but others save with fear, pulling them out of the fire, hating even the garment defiled by the flesh" (Jude vv. 21–23).

Perhaps you have come to the final pages of this book uncertain of what eternity holds in store for you. If that's the case, I'd like to take you all the way back to the beginning of this book, where I asked you to remember the last time you drove along an interstate or highway. Now, I'd like you to imagine yourself doing just that—driving down the road toward an important destination. Imagine also that you are receiving directions from a GPS device or an app on your phone, and you've just missed your exit. You are now going in the wrong direction.

How would that GPS device respond? Would it chide you in a cold, computerized voice? Would it call you names or disparage your intelligence? Would it remind you of all the other times you missed a turn or failed to go the right way?

No. Your computerized navigator would simply say, "At the next opportunity, make a u-turn." It would gently but firmly inform you that you need to turn around and get back on track.

In a similar way, by reading this book and gaining a deeper understanding of God's Word, you may have become aware that you are heading in the wrong direction along the road of life. You have missed the exits and opportunities God has called you to take through the gentle prompting of

His Holy Spirit, and you are cruising along your own path—a path that ultimately leads to destruction.

If you find yourself in that place even now, then I humbly but urgently encourage you to heed the voice of God at this very moment. "Make a u-turn." Repent. Turn away from the road that leads to destruction and choose instead the road that leads to life. Jesus talked about that road when He said, "I am the way, the truth, and the life. No one comes to the Father except through Me" (John 14:6).

Choose to embrace God's gift of salvation. Choose to embrace Jesus as the Truth and allow Him to set you free.

When you make that choice, you will encounter one final sign at the conclusion of your life's journey. Standing before Christ on that final day, you may even see Him holding that sign as He beckons you to join Him in the place He has prepared for you. It's a sign that will simply say:

"WELCOME HOME."

NOTES

CHAPTER 1: ISRAEL

1. Romesh Ratnesar, "The Dawn of Israel," *Time*, March 31, 2003, http://content
.time.com/time/specials/packages/article/0,28804,1977881_1977887
_1978201,00.html.

2. "Declaration of Establishment of State of Israel," Israel Ministry of Foreign
Affairs, May 14, 1948, http://www.mfa.gov.il/MFA/ForeignPolicy/Peace
/Guide/Pages/Declaration%20of%20Establishment%20of%20State%20of%20
Israel.aspx.

3. "Israel Population 2018," World Population Review, accessed September 24,
2018, http://worldpopulationreview.com/countries/israel-population/.

4. "The Major Religions in Israel," World Atlas, accessed September 24, 2018,
https://www.worldatlas.com/articles/the-major-religions-in-israel.html.

5. Pew Research Center, "A Portrait of Jewish Americans: Chapter 1: Population
Estimates," Pew Forum, October 1, 2013, http://www.pewforum.org/2013/10
/01/chapter-1-population-estimates/.

6. David Jeremiah, *Before It's Too Late* (Nashville, TN: Thomas Nelson, Inc.,
1982), 126.

7. David Jeremiah, *The Jeremiah Study Bible* (Franklin, TN: Worthy
Publishing, 2013), 23.

8. J. Correspondent, "Peace Won't Be Instant, but Dream Can't Be Dropped,"
The Jewish News of Northern California, May 9, 2003, http://www.jweekly.
com/article/full/19844/peace-won-t-be-instant-but-dream-can-t-be
-dropped/.

9. J. F. Walvoord, "Will Israel Possess the Promised Land?" in *Jesus the King Is Coming*, ed. Charles Lee Feinberg (Chicago, IL: Moody, 1975), 128.

10. *2 Maccabees 9, Apocrypha* (London: Oxford University Press, 1953), 408.

11. "The Six-Day War," Committee for Accuracy in Middle East Reporting in America, accessed June 4, 2016, http://www.sixdaywar.org/content/israel.asp.

12. "Full Transcript of Netanyahu's Address to UN General Assembly," *Haaretz*, October 2, 2015, http://www.haaretz.com/israel-news/1.678524.

13. Tim LaHaye and Ed Hindson, *Target Israel: Caught in the Crosshairs of the End Times* (Eugene, OR: Harvest House, 2015), 9–10.

14. Lidar Gravé-Lazi, "Israel's Population to Reach 20 Million by 2065," *Jerusalem Post*, May 21, 2017, https://www.jpost.com/Israel-News/Report-Israels-population-to-reach-20-million-by-2065-492429.

15. Milton B. Lindberg, *The Jew and Modern Israel* (Chicago, IL: Moody Press, 1969), 7.

16. Rufus Learsi, *The Jews in America: A History* (Cleveland, OH: World Publishing Company, 1954), 230.

17. David McCullough, *Truman* (New York, NY: Simon & Schuster, 1992), 620.

CHAPTER 2: EUROPE

1. Donald Goldsmith and Marcia Bartusiak, eds., *E=Einstein* (New York, NY: Sterling, 2006), 140.

2. Dr. Walter Veith, "The Mists of Time," Amazing Discoveries, accessed September 24, 2018, https://amazingdiscoveries.tv/media/1519/7720-the-mists-of-time/.

3. Tim LaHaye and Ed Hindson, eds., *The Popular Bible Prophecy Commentary* (Eugene, OR: Harvest House Publishers, 2006), 226.

4. "The European Union," *Time*, May 26, 1930, http://www.time.com/time/magazine/article/0,9171,739314,00.html.

5. William R. Clark, *Petrodollar Warfare: Oil, Iraq and the Future of the Dollar* (New Society Publishers, 2005), 198; see also W. S. Churchill, *Collected Essays of Winston Churchill*, vol. 2 (London: Library of Imperial History, 1976), 176–86.

6. "The History of the European Union," Europa.eu, accessed October 10, 2018, https://europa.eu/european-union/about-eu/history_en.

7. "Countries," Europa.eu, accessed September 24, 2018, https://europa.eu/european-union/about-eu/countries_en.

8. "Institutions and Bodies," Europa.eu, accessed March 5, 2008, https://europa .eu/european-union/about-eu/institutions-bodies_en.

9. Quoted in David L. Larsen, *Telling the Old, Old Story: The Art of Narrative Preaching* (Grand Rapids, MI: Kregel, 1995), 214.

CHAPTER 3: RUSSIA

1. Sarah Rainsford, "Ukraine Crisis: Putin Shows Who Is Boss in Crimea," BBC.com, August 19, 2015, http://www.bbc.com/news/world-europe -33985325.

2. "Russian Spy Poisoning: What We Know So Far," BBC News, October 8, 2018, https://www.bbc.com/news/uk-43315636.

3. John F. Walvoord, *The Nations in Prophecy* (Grand Rapids, MI: Zondervan, 1978), 108.

4. Mark Hitchcock, *The Coming Islamic Invasion of Israel* (Sisters, OR: Multnomah Books, 2002), 31–32.

5. C. I. Scofield, *The Scofield Study Bible* (New York, NY: Oxford University Press, 1909), 883.

6. Mustafa Fetouri, "Libya Looks to Russia for Arms," *Al-Monitor,* April 20, 2015, http://www.al-monitor.com/pulse/originals/2015/04/libya-us-uk -france-russia-uneast-west-armament-deal-morocco.html.

7. John Phillips, *Exploring the Future: A Comprehensive Guide to Bible Prophecy* (Nashville, TN: Thomas Nelson, 1983), 327.

8. Henry M. Morris, *The Genesis Record: A Scientific and Devotional Commentary on the Book of Beginnings* (Grand Rapids: Baker Book House, 1976), 247.

9. Mark Hitchcock, *The End: A Complete Overview of Bible Prophecy and the End of Days* (Carol Stream, IL: Tyndale House, 2012), 310.

10. Steven M. Williams, "How Israel Became the Startup Nation Having the 3rd Most Companies on the Nasdaq," Seeking Alpha, February 27, 2018, https:// seekingalpha.com/article/4151094-israel-became-startup-nation-3rd-companies-nasdaq.

11. Matan Bordo, "Israeli Tech's Identity Crisis: Startup Nation or Scale Up Nation?" *Forbes,* May 14, 2018, https://www.forbes.com/sites/startup nationcentral/2018/05/14/israeli-techs-identity-crisis-startup-nation-or -scale-up-nation/#15a07a43ef48.

12. Roi Bergman, "Israel's Wealthy: 105,000 Millionaires and 18 Billionaires,"

Ynet News, November 25, 2016, https://www.ynetnews.com/articles/0,7340,L
-4884381,00.html.

13. John F. Walvoord and Roy B. Zuck, eds., *The Bible Knowledge Commentary* (Wheaton, IL: Victor, 1985), Logos Bible Software.

14. Adapted from Ray C. Stedman, *God's Final Word: Understanding Revelation* (Grand Rapids, MI: RBC Ministries, 1991), 123.

CHAPTER 4: BABYLON

1. "Titanic Facts," *Titanic Facts*, accessed October 30, 2018, http://www.titanic
-facts.com/titanic-infographic.html.

2. Charles H. Dyer, *The Rise of Babylon* (Chicago, IL: Moody Publishers, 2003), 21.

3. Henry M. Morris, *The Revelation Record* (Wheaton, IL: Tyndale House, 1983), 348–49.

4. Morris, 351.

5. John Phillips, *Exploring Revelation: An Expository Commentary* (Grand Rapids, MI: Kregel Publications, 2001), 222.

CHAPTER 5: AMERICA

1. Adapted from Newt Gingrich, *Rediscovering God in America* (Nashville, TN: Integrity, 2006), 130.

2. Peter Marshall and David Manuel, *The Light and the Glory* (Old Tappan, NJ: Revell, 1977), 17, 18.

3. "President's Proclamation," *New York Times*, November 21, 1982, https:// www.nytimes.com/1982/11/21/us/president-s-proclamation.html.

4. "George Washington's First Inauguration Address, April 30, 1789," National Archives, accessed October 16, 2018, https://www.archives.gov/legislative /features/gw-inauguration.

5. Gordon Robertson, "Into All the World," Christian Broadcasting Network, accessed November 1, 2007, http://www.cbn.com/spirituallife /churchandministry/churchhistory/Gordon_Into_World.aspx.

6. Luis Bush, "What Is Joshua Project 2000?" Mission Frontiers, accessed October 18, 2018, http://www.missionfrontiers.org/issue/article/what-is -joshua-project-2000.

7. Abba Eban, *Abba Eban: An Autobiography* (New York, NY: Random House, 1977), 134.

8. "Freedom in the World 2018," Freedom House, accessed October 16, 2018, https://freedomhouse.org/report/freedom-world/freedom-world-2018.

9. Ronald Reagan, "Inaugural Address, January 20, 1981," Ronald Reagan Presidential Library and Museum, https://www.reaganlibrary.gov/research /speeches/inaugural-address-january-20-1981.

10. Quoted in Newt Gingrich, *Winning the Future: A 21st Century Contract with America* (Washington, DC: Regnery Publishing, Inc., 2005), 200.

11. John Gilmary Shea, *The Lincoln Memorial: A Record of the Life, Assassination, and Obsequies of Abraham Lincoln* (New York, NY: Bunce and Huntington Publishers, 1865), 237.

12. Benjamin Franklin, "Speech to the Constitutional Convention, June 28, 1787," Library of Congress, accessed October 11, 2018, http://www.loc.gov /exhibits/religion/rel06.html.

13. William J. Federer, ed., *America's God and Country—Encyclopedia of Quotations*, (St. Louis, MO: Amerisearch, Inc., 2000), 696.

14. Federer, *America's God,* 697–98.

15. Tim LaHaye, "Is the United States in Bible Prophecy?" *National Liberty Journal,* 26:2 (February 1997), 16.

16. Tim LaHaye, "The Role of the U.S.A. in End Times Prophecy," Tim LaHaye's Perspective, August 1999, accessed October 16, 2018, https://www.scribd .com/document/23562573/Tim-LaHaye-The-Role-of-the-USA-in-End-Times -Prophecy.

17. John Walvoord and Mark Hitchcock, *Armageddon, Oil and Terror* (Carol Stream, IL: Tyndale House Publishers, 2007), 67.

18. "President Bush Meets with EU Leaders, Chancellor Merkel of the Federal Republic of Germany and President Barroso of the European Council and President of the European Commission," White House Press Release, April 30, 2007, accessed October 16, 2018, https://georgewbush-whitehouse .archives.gov/news/releases/2007/04/text/20070430–2.html.

19. Walvoord and Hitchcock, *Armageddon,* 68.

20. Ed Timperlake, "Explosive Missing Debate Item," *Washington Times,* March 5, 2008, http://www.washingtontimes.com/news/2008/mar/05 /explosive-missing-debate-item.

21. Timperlake, "Explosive."

22. Timperlake, "Explosive."

23. Walvoord and Hitchcock, *Armageddon,* 65.

24. Adapted from Carle C. Zimmerman, *Family and Civilization* (Wilmington, DE: ISI Books, 2008), 255.

25. Herbert C. Hoover, *Addresses upon the American Road 1950–1955* (Palo Alto, CA: Stanford University Press, 1955), 111–13, 117.

26. Mark Hitchcock, *America in the End Times*, newsletter, The Left Behind Prophecy Club.

27. Herman A. Hoyt, *Is the United States in Prophecy?* (Winona Lake, ID: BMH Books, 1977), 16.

CHAPTER 6: MATERIALISM

1. Luisa Kroll and Kerry Dolan, eds., "Meet the Members of the Three-Comma Club," *Forbes,* March 6, 2018, https://www.forbes.com/billionaires/#5d4c2828251c.

2. CNBC Prime, "A Different Side of Warren Buffett, Told by Those Whose Lives He Has Changed," CNBC, May 4, 2018, https://www.cnbc.com/2018/05/04/the-warren-buffett-story-as-told-by-those-whose-lives-he-has-changed.html.

3. Mark Hitchcock, *Cashless: Bible Prophecy, Economic Chaos, and the Future Financial Order* (Eugene, OR: Harvest House Publishers, 2009), 100.

4. Donagh O'Shea, "God and Mammon," Jacob's Well, accessed October 1, 2009, http://www.goodnews.ie/jacobswelljuly.shtml.

5. Wilfred J. Hahn, *The Endtime Money Snare: How to Live FREE* (West Columbia, SC: Olive Press, 2002), 144.

6. Simon Critchley, "Coin of Praise," *New York Times*, August 30, 2009, http://opinionator.blogs.nytimes.com/2009/08/30/in-cash-we-trust/.

7. John Piper, *Desiring God* (Sisters, OR: Multnomah, 2011), 156.

8. Eleanor Goldberg, "Legendary Shoe Shiner Who Donated All His Tips ($220,000!) Retires . . . but Not from Our Hearts," *Huffington Post*, December 19, 2013, http://www.huffingtonpost.com/2013/12/19/albert-lexie-shoe-shiner_n_4474990.html.

9. C. S. Lewis, *Mere Christianity* (New York, NY: HarperCollins, 1980), 144–45.

10. Tim Worstall, "Astonishing Numbers: America's Poor Still Live Better than Most of the Rest of Humanity," *Forbes*, June 1, 2013, https://www.forbes.com/sites/timworstall/2013/06/01/astonishing-numbers-americas-poor-still-live-better-than-most-of-the-rest-of-humanity/#53f24e2054ef.

11. Quoted in Randy Alcorn, *Money, Possessions, and Eternity* (Carol Stream, IL: Tyndale House Publishers, Inc., 2003), Kindle locations 8750–70.

12. Samantha Grossman, "Allow This Man to Remind You that People Can Be Surprisingly Generous," *Time*, April 21, 2015, http://time.com/3830073/new -york-city-subway-roses/.

CHAPTER 7: IMMORALITY

1. Joan Tupponce, "Tony Bennett," *Richmond Times-Dispatch*, December 7, 2014, https://www.richmond.com/entertainment/music/tony-bennett /article_32fca731-6e36-517f-b66e-ac027d39c188.html.
2. Erin Strecker, "Lady Gaga and Tony Bennett Release 'Cheek to Cheek' Album Cover, Track List and New Song," Billboard, August 19, 2014, https://www .billboard.com/articles/news/6221858/lady-gaga-tony-bennett-cheek-to -cheek-track-list.
3. William McBrien, *Cole Porter* (New York: Vintage Books, 2000), 394–95. See also Dan Barker, "Cole Porter out of Both Closets?," Freedom from Religion Foundation, October 2004, https://ffrf.org/faq/feeds/item/13332 -cole-porter-out-of-both-closets.
4. McBrien, 395.
5. George Eells, *The Life That Late He Led: A Biography of Cole Porter* (New York, NY: G. P. Putman's Sons, 1967), 312.
6. David Jeremiah, *I Never Thought I'd See the Day!: Culture at the Crossroads* (New York, NY: Faith Words, 2011), 126–27.
7. Charles R. Swindoll, *Growing Deep in the Christian Life: Essential Truths for Becoming Strong in the Faith* (Grand Rapids, MI: Zondervan, 1995), 204.
8. Philip Yancey, *Vanishing Grace: What Ever Happened to the Good News?* (Grand Rapids, MI: Zondervan, 2014), 154.
9. Dave Breese, *Seven Men Who Rule the World from the Grave* (Chicago, IL: Moody Publishers, 1990), 153.
10. Ibid., 170.
11. Ibid., 175.
12. Ravi Zacharias, *Deliver Us from Evil* (Nashville, TN: Word Publishing, 1996), 23.
13. Albert Mohler, "Everything That Is Solid Melts into Air—the New Secular Worldview," Albert Mohler.com, March 3, 2016, http://www.albertmohler .com/2016/03/03/everything-that-is-solid-melts-into-air-the-new-secular -worldview/#_ftn1.
14. D. M. Baillie, *God Was in Christ* (New York, NY: Scribner's Publishing, 1948), 52.

15. Jeremiah, *The Jeremiah Study Bible*, 1543.

16. Donald Grey Barnhouse, *Man's Ruin, God's Wrath: Romans Vol. I* (Grand Rapids, MI: W. B. Eerdmans Publishing Co., 1959), 271.

17. D. Martyn Lloyd-Jones, *Romans: Exposition of Chapter 1, The Gospel of God* (Grand Rapids, MI: Zondervan, 1985), 392.

18. Cornelius Plantinga, Jr., *Not the Way It's Supposed to Be: A Breviary of Sin* (Grand Rapids, MI: W. B. Eerdmans Publishing Co., 1995), 199.

19. Ibid., xiii.

20. D. Martyn Lloyd-Jones, *Romans: An Exposition of Chapters 3:20–4:25, Atonement and Justification* (Grand Rapids, MI: Zondervan, 1970), 57.

CHAPTER 8: RADICAL ISLAM

1. Georges Sada, *Saddam's Secrets: How an Iraqi General Defied and Survived Saddam Hussein* (Brentwood, TN: Integrity Publishers, 2006), 285–86.

2. Ibid., 289.

3. Daniel Cox and Robert P. Jones, PhD, "Nearly Half of Americans Worried That They or Their Family Will Be a Victim of Terrorism," PRRI, December 10, 2015, https://www.prri.org/research/survey-nearly-half-of-americans -worried-that-they-or-their-family-will-be-a-victim-of-terrorism/.

4. Sada, *Saddam's Secrets*, 289–90.

5. Walvoord and Hitchcock, *Armageddon, Oil and Terror*, 44.

6. Adapted from "New Poll Shows Worry Over Islamic Terror Threat, to Be Detailed in Special Fox News Network Report," Fox News, February 3, 2007, https://www.foxnews.com/story/new-poll-shows-worry-over-islamic-terror -threat-to-be-detailed-in-special-fnc-report.

7. Reza F. Safa, Foreword to Don Richardson, *The Secrets of the Koran* (Ventura, CA: Regal Books, 2003), 10.

8. Michael Lipka, "Muslims and Islam: Key Findings in the U.S. and Around the World," Pew Research Center, August 9, 2017, http://www.pewresearch .org/fact-tank/2017/08/09/muslims-and-islam-key-findings-in-the-u-s-and -around-the-world/.

9. Abd El Shafi, *Behind the Veil* (Caney, KS: Pioneer Book Company, 1996), 32.

10. Winfried Corduan, *Pocket Guide to World Religions* (Downers Grove, IL: InterVarsity Press, 2006), 80–85.

11. Information on the five pillars adapted from Norman L. Geisler and Abdul Saleeb, *Answering Islam*, 2nd ed. (Grand Rapids, MI: Baker Books, 2006), 301.

12. Tony Blankley, *The West's Last Chance* (Washington, DC: Regnery Publishing, Inc., 2005), 21–23, 39.

13. Sada, *Saddam's Secrets*, 287.

14. Philip Johnston, "Reid Meets the Furious Face of Islam," *London Telegraph*, September 21, 2006, http://www.telegraph.co.uk/news/uknews/1529415/Reid-meets-the-furious-face-of-Islam.html (accessed 13 March 2008).

15. "Sharia Law in UK is 'Unavoidable'," *BBC News*, February 7, 2008, http://news.bbc.co.uk/2/hi/uk_news/7232661.stm.

16. "Vatican: Muslims Now Outnumber Catholics," *USA Today,* March 30, 2008, http://www.usatoday.com/news/religion/2008–03–30-muslims-catholics_N.htm.

17. "Address by H.E. Dr. Mahmood Ahmadinejad President of the Islamic Republic of Iran Before the Sixtieth Session of the United Nations General Assembly New York," September 17, 2005, United Nations, http://www.un.org/webcast/ga/60/statements/iran050917eng.pdf.

18. "Roman Catholic Bishop Wants Everyone to Call God 'Allah,'" Fox News, August 16, 2007, https://www.foxnews.com/story/roman-catholic-bishop-wants-everyone-to-call-god-allah.

19. Stan Goodenough, "Let's Call Him Allah," *Jerusalem Newswire*, August 21, 2007.

20. Tom Gross, "Dutch Catholic Bishop Tells Christians to Call God 'Allah,'" *National Review,* August 20, 2007, https://www.nationalreview.com/media-blog/dutch-catholic-bishop-tells-christians-call-god-allah-tom-gross/.

21. "Roman Catholic Bishop," Fox News.

22. Adapted from Dr. Robert A. Morey, *Islam Unveiled* (Shermandale, PA: The Scholar's Press, 1991), 60.

23. Edward Gibbon, *The Decline and Fall of the Roman Empire* (London: Milman Co., n.d.), 1:365.

24. "A Testimony from a Saudi Believer," Answering Islam: A Christian-Muslim Dialog and Apologetic, accessed April 20, 2006, http://answering-islam.org/Testimonies/saudi.html.

CHAPTER 9: PERSECUTION

1. David French, "How the Atlanta Fire Chief's Christian Views Cost Him His Job," *National Review*, February 25, 2016, http://www.nationalreview.com/article/431859/kelvin-cochrans-christian-views-cost-atlanta-fire-chief-his-job.

2. J. Paul Nyquist, Prepare: *Living Your Faith in an Increasingly Hostile Culture* (Chicago: Moody Publishers, 2015), 14.

3. Ibid. 14.

4. "Inside the Persecution Numbers," *Christianity Today*, 58, no. 2 (March 2014): 14.

5. Fay Voshell, "Persecution of Christians in America: It's Not Just 'Over There,'" *American Thinker*, May 10, 2015, https://www.americanthinker.com /articles/2015/05/persecution_of_christians_in_america_its_not_just_over _there.html.

6. "Christian Fired for Sharing God," WND.com, March 28, 2007, https://www .wnd.com/2007/03/40820/.

7. "Christian Fired," WND.com.

8. Sarah McBride, "Mozilla CEO Resigns, Opposition to Gay Marriage Drew Fire," Reuters, April 3, 2014, http://www.reuters.com/article/us-mozilla-ceo -resignation-idUSBREA321Y320140403.

9. "ACLU vs. Civil Liberties," *National Review*, December 10, 2013, http://www .nationalreview.com/article/365947/aclu-vs-civil-liberties-editors.

10. Nyquist, *Prepare*, 13.

11. Todd Starnes, "Christian Bakers Fined $135,000 for Refusing to Make Wedding Cake for Lesbians," Fox News Opinion, July 3, 2015, http://www .foxnews.com/opinion/2015/07/03/christian-bakers-fined-135000-for -refusing-to-make-wedding-cake-for-lesbians.html.

12. Eugene H. Peterson, *Christ Plays in Ten Thousand Places: A Conversation in Spiritual Theology* (Grand Rapids, MI: Eerdmans, 2005), 288.

13. Gordon Franz, "The King and I: The Apostle John and Emperor Domitian," Part 1, Associates for Biblical Research, January 18, 2010, http://www .biblearchaeology.org/post/2010/01/18/The-King-and-I-The-Apostle-John -and-Emperor-Domitian-Part-1.aspx.

14. Gemma Betros, "The French Revolution and the Catholic Church," HistoryToday.com, December 2010, http://www.historytoday.com /gemma-betros/french-revolution-and-catholic-church.

15. Rev. Archimandrite Nektarios Serfes, "In Memory of the 50 Million Victims of the Orthodox Christian Holocaust," Serfes.org, October 1999, http://www .serfes.org/orthodox/memoryof.htm.

16. James M. Nelson, *Psychology, Religion, and Spirituality* (New York, NY: Springer Science and Business Media, 2009), 427.

17. See Open Doors, accessed November 14, 2018, http://www.opendoorsusa.org /christian-stories.

18. "Persecution at a Glance," Open Doors, accessed November 14, 2018, http:// www.opendoorsusa.org/persecutionataglance.

19. John Ortberg, "Don't Waste a Crisis," *Christianity Today*, accessed June 22, 2016, http://www.christianitytoday.com/pastors/2001/winter /dontwastecrisis.html.

20. A.W. Tozer, *Man: The Dwelling Place of God* (Seattle, WA: Amazon Digital Services, 2010), Kindle edition, location 1404.

21. D. Martyn Lloyd-Jones, *Romans: An Exposition of Chapter 8:5–17, The Sons of God* (Grand Rapids, MI: Zondervan, 1974), 433.

22. Sabina Wurmbrand, "The Authentic Pastor Richard Wurmbrand Biography," accessed June 22, 2016, http://richardwurmbrandbio.info/.

23. Quoted in John Piper, *Let the Nations Be Glad!* (Grand Rapids, MI: Baker Publishing Group, 2010), 101.

24. Adapted from "John Chrysostom," *Christianity Today*, accessed June 15, 2016, http://www.christianitytoday.com/history/people/pastorsand preachers/john-chrysostom.html; and Justin Taylor, "Chrysostom: Nothing You Can Do to Harm Me," Gospel Coalition, August 10, 2009, https://www .thegospelcoalition.org/blogs/justin-taylor/chrysostom-nothing-you-can-do -to-harm/.

CHAPTER 10: SPIRITUAL WARFARE

1. Sun Tzu, *The Art of War* (Hollywood, FL: Simon and Brown, 2010), 11.

2. John Phillips, *Exploring Ephesians and Philippians: An Expository Commentary* (Grand Rapids, MI: Kregel, 1995), 187.

3. Billy Graham Evangelistic Association, "Answers," accessed December 12, 2018, https://billygraham.org/answer/ive-heard-the-bible-says-somewhere -that-the-devil-is-a-liar-and-im-sure-its-true-but-what-is-his-biggest-lie/.

4. Randy Alcorn, *If God Is Good: Faith in the Midst of Suffering and Evil* (Colorado Springs, CO: Multnomah Books, 2009), 51.

5. Erwin Lutzer, *How You Can Be Sure You Will Spend Eternity with God* (Chicago, IL: Moody Publishers, 2015), 67–68.

6. Peter T. O'Brien, *The Letter to the Ephesians, The Pillar New Testament Commentary* (Grand Rapids, MI: Wm. B. Eerdmans Publishing Co., 1999), 480.

7. John MacArthur, *How to Meet the Enemy: Arming Yourself for Spiritual Warfare* (U.S.A.: Victor Books, 1992), 141.

8. Ray C. Stedman, *Spiritual Warfare: Winning the Daily Battle with Satan* (Portland, OR: Multnomah Press, 1985), 116.

9. Donald S. Whitney, *Spiritual Disciplines for the Christian Life* (Colorado Springs, CO: NavPress, 1991), 85.

10. Jack R. Taylor, *Prayer: Life's Limitless Reach* (Kent: Sovereign World, 2004), 127–28.

CHAPTER 11: APATHY

1. A. W. Tozer, *Man: The Dwelling Place of God* (Camp Hill, PA: Christian Publications, 1966), 151.

2. William Barclay, *The Gospel of Matthew, Volume Two* (Louisville, KY: Westminster John Knox Press, 2001), 370.

3. *On the Mountain's Brink* (Washington, DC, US Forest Service, 1980), 25.

4. Rowe Findley, *Mount St. Helens: Mountain with a Death Wish* (Washington, D.C.: National Geographic Magazine, 1981), 20.

CHAPTER 12: RAPTURE

1. "Firefighters Gain Ground as Santa Ana Winds Decrease," *KNBC Los Angeles*, October 24, 2007, http://www.knbc.com/news/14401132/detail.html.

2. Mark Hitchcock, *The Complete Book of Bible Prophecy* (Wheaton, IL: Tyndale House, 1991), 70.

3. Renald Showers, *Maranatha—Our Lord, Come!: A Definitive Study of the Rapture of the Church* (Bellmawr, NJ: Friends of Israel Ministry, 1995), 127.

4. "100 Nations' Leaders Attend Churchill Funeral," International Churchill Society, accessed December 1, 2018, https://winstonchurchill.org/the-life -of-churchill/in-memoriam/110-nations-leaders-attend-funeral-service/.

5. Dr. Arnold G. Fruchtenbaum, *The Footsteps of the Messiah: A Study of the Sequence of Prophetic Events* (San Antonio, TX: Ariel Press, 2004), 149.

6. Arthur T. Pierson, *The Gospel, Vol. 3* (Grand Rapids, MI: Baker Book House, 1978), 136.

7. Gig Conaughton, "County Buys Reverse 911 System," *San Diego Union-Tribune*, August 2005, https://www.sandiegouniontribune.com/sdut-county-buys -reverse-911-system-2005aug12-story.html; see also Scott Glover, Jack Leonard, and Matt Lait, "Two Homes, Two Couples, Two Fates," *Los Angeles*

Times, October 26, 2007, http://www.latimes.com/news/local/la-me-pool 26oct26,0,3755059.story.

CHAPTER 13: RESURRECTION

1. Sarah Knapton, "World's First Anti-Ageing Drug Could See Humans Live to 120," *Telegraph*, November 29, 2015, https://www.telegraph.co.uk/science/2016/03/12 /worlds-first-anti-ageing-drug-could-see-humans-live-to-120/.
2. Clive Cookson, "Bionic Advances to Defeat Death," *Financial Times*, January 20, 2016, https://www.ft.com/content/c6a4797c-a25b-11e5–8d70 –42b68cfae6e4.
3. Amy Carmichael, *Thou Givest . . . They Gather* (Fort Washington, PA: CLC Publications, 2013), 220-21.
4. Marie Monsen, *A Present Help: Standing on the Promises of God* (Shoals, IN: Kingsley Press, 2011), 59–60.
5. Joni Eareckson Tada, *Heaven: Your Real Home* (Grand Rapids, MI: Zondervan, 1995), 53.
6. Jack Welch with Suzy Welch, *Winning* (New York, NY: HarperBusiness, 2005), 358–59.
7. Matthew Henry, *Matthew Henry's Commentary*, BibleGateway, accessed September 25, 2018, https://www.biblegateway.com/resources/matthew -henry/1Cor.15.35–1Cor.15.50.

CHAPTER 14: HEAVEN

1. Jennifer Smith, "REVEALED: Grieving Boy Who Sent Heartbreaking Message in a Balloon to His Law Professor Father 'in Heaven' Was by His Side When He Was Shot Dead in Street Mugging," *Daily Mail*, December 8, 2016, http://www.dailymail.co.uk/news/ article-4013544/Little-boy-s -heartbreaking-note-dead-father-lands-woman-s-garden-balloon-child -hoped-reach-time-Christmas.html.
2. Sarah Knapton, "Mysterious 'Supervoid' in Space Is Largest Object Ever Discovered, Scientists Claim," *Telegraph*, April 20, 2015, www.telegraph .co.uk/news/science/space/11550868/Giant-mysterious-empty-hole-found -in-universe.html.
3. Ruthanna Metzgar, "It's Not in the Book!," Eternal Perspective Ministries, March 29, 2010, https://www.epm.org/resources/2010/Mar/29/Its-Not-in -the-Book/.

CHAPTER 15: JUDGMENT SEAT OF CHRIST

1. Erwin W. Lutzer, *Your Eternal Reward: Triumph and Tears at the Judgment Seat of Christ* (Chicago, IL: Moody Publishers, 1998), 116.
2. Warren W. Wiersbe, *Be Victorious: In Christ You Are an Overcomer* (Colorado Springs, CO: David C. Cook, 2010), 176.
3. L. Sale-Harrison, *Judgment Seat of Christ* (New York, NY: Hepzibah House, Sale-Harrison Publications, 1938), 8.
4. J. I. Packer, *Knowing God* (Downers Grove, IL: InterVarsity, 1973), 138.
5. George Sweeting, *Who Said That?: More Than 2,500 Usable Quotes and Illustrations* (Chicago, IL: Moody Publishers, 1995), 283.
6. Hitchcock, *The End*, 210–11.
7. J. Dwight Pentecost, *Prophecy for Today: God's Purpose and Plan for Our Future* (Grand Rapids, MI: Zondervan, 1961), 152.
8. Pentecost, *Prophecy for Today*, 158.
9. Jim Elliff, "The Starving of the Church," in *Reformation and Revival: A Quarterly Journal for Church Leadership 1* (1992), 115.

CHAPTER 16: REWARDS

1. Bruce Wilkinson, *A Life God Rewards: Why Everything You Do Today Matters Forever* (Colorado Springs, CO: Multnomah, 2012), 25.
2. Brian Tracy, *No Excuses: The Power of Self-Discipline* (New York, NY: Vanguard Press, 2010), 6–7.
3. Denis Lyle, *Countdown to Apocalypse* (Belfast: Ambassador, 1999), 21.
4. Samuel Smith, "100% of Christians Face Persecution in These 21 Countries," January 11, 2017, *Christian Post*, www.christianpost.com/news/100-percent -of-christians-face-persecution-in-21-countries-open-doors-world-watch -list-2017-172850/.
5. Stoyan Zaimov, "12 Worst Christian Persecution Nations; US Makes List for First Time," *Christian Post*, January 4, 2017, https://www.christianpost.com /news/12-worst-christian-persecution-nations-us-makes-list-for-first-time -172551/.
6. Charles Haddon Spurgeon, "The Fruits of Grace," June 8, 1916, The Spurgeon Archive, http://www.romans45.org/spurgeon/sermons/3515.htm.
7. Manfred Koehler, "What Will I Do With a Crown?" *Discipleship Journal*, Sept/Oct, 2002.
8. Ray Stedman, "On Living Together," September 15, 1968, transcript posted

by Peninsula Bible Church, https://cdn.pbc.org/Main_Service/1968/09/15
/0284.pdf.

CHAPTER 17: WORSHIP

1. Dr. V. Raymond Edman, "The Presence of the King," Chapel, Wheaton College,
   September 22, 1967, www2.wheaton.edu/learnres/ARCSC/exhibits/edman/.
2. Vernon M. Whaley, *Called to Worship: The Biblical Foundations of Our
   Response to God's Call* (Nashville, TN: Thomas Nelson, 2009), 323–24.
3. William Temple, *Nature, Man and God* (MacMillan and Co. Limited, 1940).
4. A. W. Tozer, *Whatever Happened to Worship?: A Call to True Worship* (Camp
   Hill, PA: Christian Publications, 1985), 12.
5. Whaley, *Called to Worship*, 327.

CHAPTER 18: FOUR RIDERS

1. Caitlin O'Kane, "'Do You Think I Want to Shoot An 11-Year-Old?': Cop
   Confronts Boys Carrying BB Gun," CBS News, accessed October 31, 2018,
   https://www.cbsnews.com/news/columbus-ohio-cop-confronts-two-black
   -boys-carrying-realistic-looking-bb-gun/.
2. Trevin Wax, "Rob Bell and the Judgmentless 'Gospel': Holy Love Wins,"
   February 27, 2011, The Gospel Coalition, http://thegospelcoalition.org/blogs
   /trevinwax/2011/02/27/rob-bell-and-the-judgmentless-gospel/.
3. World Food Programme, "2018 Global Report on Food Crises," WFP.org,
   March 21, 2018, https://www.wfp.org/content/global-report-food-crises-2018.
4. United Nations Department of Economic and Social Affairs, "World
   Population Projected to Reach 9.8 Billion in 2050, and 11.2 Billion in 2100,"
   UN.org, June 21, 2017, https://www.un.org/development/desa/en/news
   /population/world-population-prospects-2017.html.
5. Charles R. Swindoll, *Swindoll's Living Insights New Testament Commentary:
   Revelation* (Carol Stream, IL: Tyndale, 2014), 113.
6. Liz Szabo, "'Nightmare' Bacteria, Resistant to Almost Every Drug, Stalk U.S.
   Hospitals," *USA Today*, April 3, 2018, https://eu.usatoday.com/story/news
   /nation/2018/04/03/nightmare-bacteria-antibiotic-resistant-stalk-hospitals
   /482162002/.
7. Centers for Disease Control and Prevention, "Antimicrobial Resistance,"
   CDC.gov, https://www.cdc.gov/drugresistance/index.html and World Health
   Organization, "Antimicrobial Resistance," World Health Organization,

February 15, 2018, http://www.who.int/news-room/fact-sheets/detail
/antimicrobial-resistance.

8. Adapted from Steven J. Cole, "Lesson 110: A Deathbed Conversion (Luke
23:39-43)," Bible.org, June 21, 2013, https://bible.org/seriespage/lesson-110
-deathbed-conversion-luke-2339-43.

CHAPTER 19: ANTICHRIST

1. Erwin Lutzer, *Hitler's Cross* (Chicago, IL: Moody Publishers, 1995), 62–63.
2. Tim LaHaye and Ed Hinson, *Global Warning* (Eugene, OR: Harvest House,
2007), 195.
3. Charles Colson, *Kingdoms in Conflict* (Grand Rapids, MI: Zondervan, 1987),
129–30.
4. Arthur W. Pink, *The Antichrist* (Minneapolis, MN: Kloch & Kloch, 1979), 77.
5. Colson, *Kingdoms in Conflict*, 68.
6. Colson, *Kingdoms in Conflict*, 68.
7. Thomas Ice, "The Ethnicity of the Antichrist," Pre-Trib Research Center,
accessed October 22, 2018, https://www.pre-trib.org/articles/all-articles
/message/the-ethnicity-of-the-antichrist/read.
8. Major Dan, "'Goddesses of Reason' Replace Catholic Church in France!"
History and Headlines, accessed November 8, 2018, https://www.history
andheadlines.com/goddesses-reason-replace-catholic-church-france/.
9. W. A. Criswell, *Expository Sermons on Revelation*, vol. 4 (Dallas, TX:
Criswell Publishing, 1995), 109.
10. Gary Frazier, *Signs of the Coming of Christ* (Arlington, TX: Discovery
Ministries, 1998), 149.

CHAPTER 20: FALSE PROPHET

1. "David Koresh Biography," Biography.com, accessed September 4, 2018,
https://www.biography.com/people/david-koresh-9368416.
2. Phillips, *Exploring*, 171.
3. Criswell, *Expository Sermons on Revelation*, 115.
4. Craig S. Keener, *The NIV Application Commentary: Revelation* (Grand
Rapids, MI: Zondervan, 2009), 357.
5. J. A. Seiss, *The Apocalypse: A Series of Special Lectures on the Revelation of
Jesus Christ*, rev. ed. (New York, NY: Charles C. Cook, 1901), 345.
6. Morris, *The Revelation Record*, 251.

7. Ibid., 251
8. Hitchcock, *The End*, 275.

CHAPTER 21: MARTYRS

1. Jared Malsin, "Christians Mourn Their Relatives Beheaded by ISIS," *Time*, February 23, 2015, http://time.com/3718470/isis-copts-egypt/.
2. United States Holocaust Memorial Museum, "Remaining Jewish Population of Europe in 1945," *Holocaust Encyclopedia*, accessed September 19, 2018, www.ushmm.org/wlc/en/article.php?ModuleId=10005687.
3. Jacob Presser, *Ashes in the Wind: The Destruction of Dutch Jewry* (New York, NY: Dutton, 1969), 336.
4. Morris, *The Revelation Record*, 119.
5. Richard Bauckham, *Climax of Prophecy: Studies in the Book of Revelation* (Edinburgh: T. & T. Clark, 1993), 424–25.
6. W. A. Criswell, *Expository Sermons on Revelation,* vol. 3 (Grand Rapids, MI: Zondervan, 1962), 106–7.
7. Louis T. Talbot, *The Revelation of Jesus Christ* (Grand Rapids, MI: Eerdmans, 1973), 99.
8. Donald Grey Barnhouse, *Revelation: An Expository Commentary* (Grand Rapids, MI: Zondervan, 1971), 133–34.
9. John F. Walvoord, *The Revelation of Jesus Christ* (Chicago, IL: Moody Press, 1966), 134–35.
10. Todd M. Johnson and Gina A. Zurlo, "Christian Martyrdom as a Pervasive Phenomenon," Gordon Conwell University, December 2014, http://www .gordonconwell.edu/ockenga/research/documents/2Countingmartyrs methodology.pdf.
11. Julia A. Seymour, "Counting the Cost: How Many Christians Are Actually Martyred?" *World*, accessed September 24, 2018, https://world.wng.org /2013/11/counting_the_cost_how_many_christians_are_actually_martyred.
12. "Frequently Asked Questions," Open Doors USA, accessed September 24, 2018, https://www.opendoorsusa.org/about-us/frequently-asked-questions/.
13. Linda Lowry, "Trump's Historic Opportunity to Press Kim Jong Un to Free 50,000 Christians from Auschwitz-Like Prison Camps," Open Doors USA, accessed September 24, 2018, https://www.opendoorsusa.org/christian -persecution/stories/trumps-historic-opportunity-to-press-kim-jong-un -to-free-50000-christians-from-auschwitz-like-prison-camps/.

14. Raymond Ibrahim, "Thousand Churches Destroyed in Nigeria," Gatestone Institute, accessed September 24, 2018, https://www.gatestoneinstitute.org /4986/nigeria-churches-destroyed.

15. "How Christians are Suffering in Iran," Open Doors USA, accessed September 24, 2018, https://www.opendoorsusa.org/christian-persecution /world-watch-list/iran/.

16. Anugrah Kumar, "Christians Face 2 Years in Prison for Evangelism in 8th India State to Pass 'Anti-Conversion' Law," *Christian Post*, accessed September 24, 2018, https://www.christianpost.com/news/8th-state-india -anti-conversion-law-christians-face-2-years-prison-for-evangelism-223463/.

17. "Urgent Prayers Needed: Hundreds of Iraqi Christians Are Fleeing for Their Lives," Open Doors USA, June 12, 2014, https://www.opendoorsusa.org /christian-persecution/stories/urgent-prayers-needed-hundreds-iraqi -christians-fleeing-lives/.

18. "Their God Is My God," The Voice of the Martyrs Canada, April 23, 2015, https://www.vomcanada.com/ly-2015-04-23.htm.

CHAPTER 22: 144,000

1. Sam Roberts, "Dean Hess, Preacher and Fighter Pilot, Dies at 97," *New York Times*, March 7, 2015,https://www.nytimes.com/2015/03/08/us/dean-hess -preacher-and-fighter-pilot-dies-at-97.html.

2. "Fact Sheet: Col. Dean Hess," National Museum of the US Air Force, accessed September 25, 2018, https://web.archive.org/web/20091006080639 /http://www.nationalmuseum.af.mil/factsheets/factsheet.asp?id=1913.

3. J. A. Seiss, *The Apocalypse: An Exposition of the Book of Revelation* (Grand Rapids, MI: Zondervan, 1965), 161.

4. Hitchcock, *The End*, 291.

5. Eric Whitacre, "A Choir as Big as the Internet," Ted.com, accessed September 26, 2018, https://www.ted.com/talks/a_choir_as_big_as_the_internet.

6. Jeremy Begbie, "The Sense of an Ending," October 27, 2001, http://veritas.org /talks/sense-ending/?view=presenters&speaker_id=1955.

CHAPTER 23: TWO WITNESSES

1. Seán Clarke, Paul Torpey, Paul Scruton, Michael Safi, Daniel Levitt, Pablo Gutiérrez, and Chris Watson, "Thailand Cave Rescue: How Did the Boys Get Out?" *Guardian*, July 9, 2018, https://www.theguardian.com/world/ng

-interactive/2018/jul/03/thailand-cave-rescue-where-were-the-boys-found
-and-how-can-they-be-rescued.

2. John C. Whitcomb, "The Two Witnesses of Revelation 11," Pre-Trib.org, accessed September 17, 2018, https://www.pre-trib.org/articles/all-articles /message/the-two-witnesses-first-or-second-half-of-the-tribulation/read.

3. For more on this topic, see David Jeremiah, *Escape the Coming Night* (Nashville: Thomas Nelson, 2001), 122.

4. Timothy J. Demy and John C. Whitcomb, "Witnesses, Two," in *The Popular Encyclopedia of Bible Prophecy*, eds. Tim LaHaye and Ed Hindson (Eugene, OR: Harvest House, 2004), 402–403.

5. William R. Newell, *Revelation: Chapter-by-Chapter* (Chicago: Moody Press, 1935), 152.

6. Morris, *The Revelation Record*, 201.

7. Newell, *Revelation*, 155.

8. Phillips, *Exploring Revelation*, 150.

9. Morris, *Revelation Record*, 204.

CHAPTER 24: DRAGON

1. Adapted from Criswell, *Expository Sermons on Revelation, vol. 4*, 85–87.

2. Barnhouse, *Revelation*, 229.

3. Carolyn Arends, "Satan's a Goner," *Christianity Today*, March 25, 2011, www .christianitytoday.com/ct/2011/february/satansagoner.html.

CHAPTER 25: MARK OF THE BEAST

1. "Jakob Frenkiel," Holocaust Encyclopedia, accessed September 28, 2018, https://encyclopedia.ushmm.org/content/en/id-card/jakob-frenkiel.

2. George Rosenthal, "Auschwitz-Birkenau: The Evolution of Tattooing in the Auschwitz Concentration Camp Complex, accessed September 28, 2018, https://www.jewishvirtuallibrary.org/the-evolution-of-tattooing-in-the -auschwitz-concentration-camp-complex.

3. John Brandon, "Is There a Microchip Implant in Your Future?" Fox News, accessed September 26, 2018, http://www.foxnews.com/tech/2014/08/30/is -there-microchip-implant-in-your-future.html.

4. Chris Stein, "Meet the Humans with Microchips Implanted in Them," CBS News, June 22, 2016, https://www.cbsnews.com/news/meet-the-humans-with -microchips-implanted-in-them/.

5. Maggie Astor, "Microchip Implants for Employees? One Company Says Yes," *New York Times*, July 25, 2017, https://www.nytimes.com/2017/07/25/technology/microchips-wisconsin-company-employees.html.

6. Drew Harwell and Abha Bhattarai, "Inside Amazon Go: The Camera-filled Convenience Store that Watches You Back," *Washington Post*, January 22, 2018, https://www.washingtonpost.com/news/business/wp/2018/01/22/inside-amazon-go-the-camera-filled-convenience-store-that-watches-you-back/?noredirect=on&utm_term=.041dca4a888c.

CHAPTER 26: ARMAGEDDON

1. Douglas MacArthur, "Farewell Address to Congress," American Rhetoric, April 19, 1951, www.americanrhetoric.com/speeches/douglasmacarthur farewelladdress.htm.

2. Ronald Reagan and Douglas Brinkley, ed., *The Reagan Diaries* (New York, NY: HarperCollins, 2007), 19.

3. Quoted in Vernon J. McGee, *Through the Bible*, vol. 3 (Nashville: Thomas Nelson, Inc., 1982), 513.

4. Walvoord and Hitchcock, *Armageddon, Oil and Terror*, 174.

5. John F. Walvoord, "The Way of the Kings of the East," in *Light for the World's Darkness*, ed. John W. Bradbury (New York, NY: Loizeaux Brothers, 1944), 164.

6. Walter Scott and J. Wachite, *The Coming Great War: The Greatest Ever Known in Human History* (Toronto, Canada: A. Sims, Publisher, 1932), 12–13.

7. Robert J. Morgan, *My All in All* (Nashville: B&H, 2008), entry for July 16.

8. Randall Price, *Jerusalem in Prophecy* (Eugene, OR: Harvest House, 1998), 1179–80.

CHAPTER 27: RETURN OF THE KING

1. Harry A. Ironside, *Revelation* (Grand Rapids, MI: Kregel, 2004), 187–188.

2. Ironside, *Revelation*, 189–90.

3. John F. Walvoord, *End Times* (Nashville, TN: Word Publishing, 1998), 171.

4. Vance Havner, *In Times Like These* (Old Tappan, NJ: Fleming H. Revell Company, 1969), 29.

5. Based on Sir Ernest Henry Shackleton, "South! The Story of Shackleton's Last Expedition, 1914–1917, Project Gutenberg, accessed October 2, 2018, http://www.gutenberg.org/ebooks/5199.

CHAPTER 28: MILLENNIUM

1. Randy Alcorn, *Heaven* (Wheaton, IL: Tyndale, 2004), 226.
2. J. Dwight Pentecost, *Things to Come: A Study in Biblical Eschatology* (Grand Rapids, MI: Zondervan, 1958), 476.

CHAPTER 29: GREAT WHITE THRONE JUDGMENT

1. Sinead MacLaughlin, "Chilling Moment Four Women Are Stranded on a Rock in the Middle of a River as a Dam's Flood Gates Open—Before One Is Washed Away and Drowned," *Daily Mail*, February 8, 2017, https://www.dailymail.co.uk/news/article-4202416/New-Zealand-woman-21-drowns-raging-Waikato-river.html.
2. Quoted in Robert Glenn Gromacki, *Are These the Last Days?* (Old Tappan, NJ: Revell, 1970), 175.
3. Lutzer, *Your Eternal Reward*, 166.
4. Gromacki, *Are These the Last Days?*, 178.
5. Barnhouse, *Revelation*, 390.
6. Morris, *The Revelation Record*, 433.
7. Isaac Massey Haldeman, *Ten Sermons on the Second Coming of Our Lord Jesus Christ* (New York, NY: Revell, 1917), 739.

CHAPTER 30: NEW HEAVEN AND NEW EARTH

1. Dr. W. A. Criswell, "The New Creation," W. A. Criswell Sermon Library, September 16, 1984, www.wacriswell.com/sermons/1984/the-new-creation1/.
2. William Hendriksen, *More Than Conquerors* (Grand Rapids, MI: Baker, 1982), 198.
3. Anthony A. Hoekema, *The Bible and the Future* (Grand Rapids, MI: William B. Eerdmans, 1979), 281.
4. Alcorn, *Heaven*, 101.
5. Quoted in Richard Leonard and JoNancy Linn Sundberg, *A Glimpse of Heaven* (New York, NY: Howard, 2007), 45.

CHAPTER 31: HOLY CITY

1. Robert Johnson and Gus Lubin, "The 16 Greatest Cities in History," *Business Insider*, January 21, 2013, http://uk.businessinsider.com/largest-cities-throughout-history-2013-1?op=1&r=UK&IR=T.
2. F. W. Boreham, *Wisps of Wildfire* (London: Epworth Press, 1924), 202–3.

3. J. B. Smith, *A Revelation of Jesus Christ* (Scottsdale, PA: Herald Press, 1961), 289.

4. Charles F. Pfeiffer and Everett F. Harrison, eds., *The Wycliffe Bible Commentary: A Phrase by Phrase Commentary of the Bible* (Chicago: Moody Publishers, 1962), 1522.

5. W. A. Criswell, *Expository Sermons on Revelation,* vol. 5 (Grand Rapids, MI: Zondervan Publishing House, 1969), 130.

6. Reverend William Jones, *New Testament Illustrations* (Hartford, CT: J. B. Burr, 1875), 939–41.

INDEX

A

Aaron (high priest), 262, 303
Abaddon and Apollyon, 129
abortion, 113, 122
Abraham, 4–9, 11–12, 14, 15, 37, 174, 215, 317
Abrahamic covenant, 4–12, 14, 15
Abu Bakr, 101
ACLU (American Civil Liberties Union), 113
Adam and Eve, 195, 316, 371, 392, 402
Afghanistan, 34
Age of Reason, 89
Ahaziah (king), 317
Ahmadinejad, Mahmoud, 105
Albanian culture (re: funerals), 351
Alcorn, Randy, 129–30, 403
Alexander the Great, 20, 255
Ali (son-in-law of Muhammad), 101
Allah, 99, 100, 101, 102, 106–7
Allied forces, 137
America (*also*, United States; US, *in text*). See
    chapter 5, "America" (57–69); *also* 1, 4, 5, 15–16,
    25, 31, 35, 38, 85, 87, 88, 90, 97–98, 99, 100,
    103–4, 107, 110, 111–12, 114, 118, 124, 151, 155,
    168, 182, 187, 189, 213, 216, 239, 242, 267–68,
    336, 347, 409
    the Bible's silence on the future of, 63–69
    footprint of the New Jerusalem compared
        with the United States, 409
    reasons for God's favor on, 59–63
American Civil Liberties Union (ACLU), 113
Amin, Idi, 99
angels, 56, 141, 158, 161, 162, 173, 185, 207, 221,
    222, 229, 243, 268, 285–86, 287, 291, 303, 314,
    316, 318, 319, 320, 329, 332, 337, 346–47, 353,
    363, 367, 385, 388
antibiotic-resistant bacteria, 241–42
Antichrist. *See chapter 19*, "Antichrist" (246–58);
    also 1, 27, 28, 39, 46, 64, 128, 143, 231, 236–37,
    242
    is the rider on a white horse (Rev. 6:2), 236–37,
        261–69, 272, 273, 285, 288, 290, 304, 305–6,
        325–26, 328, 331, 338, 341–46, 359, 395
    the deal between Israel and the, 341
    ethnicity of the, 253–54
    other names of the, 247
    the personality of the, 248–51
    the profile of the, 251–55
    the program of the, 256–57
    the rebellion against the, 343
    the worship of the, 341–42
Antiochus IV Epiphanes, 9, 271
anti-Semitism, 5, 321
"Anything Goes" (Porter song), 85–86
apathy. *See chapter 11*, "Apathy" (139–52); *also*,
    66, 361
apostasy, 265, 302, 361
Arab-Israeli controversy, 28, 39
Arabs, 7, 10, 37, 347
Arends, Carolyn, 322–23
Armageddon. *See chapter 26*, "Armageddon"
    (336–48); *also*, 28, 139, 231, 256, 352, 358–59,
    395, 400
    the location of the Battle of, 338–39
    origin and meaning of the word, 338
    the participants in the Battle of, 341–48
    the preparation for the Battle of, 337–38

the purpose of the Battle of, 339–41
armor of God, 128, 130–37
Art of War, The (Sun Tzu), 125
Ascension, 162, 172, 175, 313, 353
Assyria, 23
Athaliah (queen), 317
Auschwitz, 272, 324–25
Augustine, Saint, 158
Austria, 25
awards (in the entertainment industry), 205
"axis of terror," 99
Ayairga, Mathew, 282

B

Babylon. *See chapter 4*, "Babylon" (44–56); *also* 1,
    9, 10, 18–20, 23, 27, 255, 292, 296, 333–34
    the destruction of
        our response to, 55–56
        the reactions to, 52–54
        reasons for, 48–51
        rejoicing over, 54–55
        the utter finality of, 51–52
    rebirth of, 46–48
bacteria (antibiotic-resistant), 241–42
Baillie, Donald, 92–93
banks, 47, 52, 53
Barnhouse, Dr. Donald Grey, 93, 279, 321, 384
Barroso, Jos, 64–65
Battle of Armageddon. *See* Armageddon
Battle of Gettysburg, 137
Battle of Gog and Magog, 38, 337, 370
Beast (/beast) (of Revelation), the, 49, 50, 53, 127,
    254, 255, 260, 263–69, 280, 305–8, 325–26,
    328, 331, 332–33, 338, 342, 359, 389. *See also*
    Antichrist; false prophet; mark of the beast;
    Satan
        the fatality of the, 359
beasts, the birds and the, 41
Beelzebub, 312
Begbie, Jeremy, 296
Belgium, 24, 25, 168
belt of truth (*or*, girdle of truth), 130–31, 136
bema seat, 195
Benelux Conference (1948), 24
Ben-Gurion, David, 3
Bennett, Tony, 85, 86
bereaved, the, 421
Berlin Wall, fall of, 25
Bible
    past presidents on the importance of the, 62, 63

the superiority of the, 107–8
Birds, The (Hitchcock film), 358
birds and beasts, 41–42. *See also* fowls of heaven
"birth pangs," 333
Bitcoin, 331
Blaisdell, Russell L. (chaplain), 284–85
Blankley, Tony, 103–4
blasphemies, 248, 253–54, 342
bodies, the nature of our resurrected, 163–64,
    169–80
Bonar, Horatius (early Scottish preacher), 417
Book of Life, 167, 190–91, 192, 253, 379, 380–81,
    384, 385, 386–87, 389, 416, 417
Boreham, F. W., 408
bowls of wrath (judgments), 236, 329, 395
Boxer Rebellion, 273
Branch Davidians, 259
breastplate of righteousness, 131–32, 136
Breese, Dave, 89–90
Briand, Aristide (French statesman), 24
Buffett, Warren, 73
Bulgaria, 25
burning
    of the earth, 396–97
    of weapons (Ezekiel), 41
Bush, George W., 64–65
Business Insider, 405

C

Caleb (Israelite), 303
Carmichael, Amy, 174
Casuccio, Peter, 233–34
Catholic Church, 105
Centers for Disease Control and Prevention
    (CDC), 241–42
character and suffering, 119
China, 38, 83, 88, 117, 125, 176, 187
chips (microchips), 331
Chorazin, Bethsaida, and Capernaum, 389
Christ
    the armies of, 355
    ascension of, 162, 172, 175, 313, 353
    the authority of, 356–57
    the avenging of, 357–58
    the dead in, 165, 166, 421, 157, 163
    description of the returning, 355
    His warnings about our attitude (in the last
        days), 144–45, 147–50
    incarnation of, 313, 355
    judgment seat of. *See* judgment seat of Christ

Lamb, the, 139, 188, 222, 224, 225, 229, 243, 253, 268, 273, 289, 290, 292, 293, 294, 332, 355, 401, 413–14, 415
resurrection of, 96, 116, 137, 163, 166, 170, 171, 172–73, 175, 179, 189, 256, 279, 318, 321, 399
return/second coming of. *See* Second Coming
three meaningful titles given to (Rev. 19), 355
the three most momentous events defining the role of, 313
Transfiguration of, 171, 301
Christianity Today, 112
Christians
number killed, abducted, detained each month, 118
persecution of
in the Bible, 115–16
in history, 116
today, 116–17
ten ways we should be different due to our prophetic knowledge, 420–22
Chronicles of Narnia, 347
Chrysostom, John, 123–24
church attendance, 123, 310, 421
Churchill, Winston, 24, 161
cities in world history, the greatest, 405
citizenship, our heavenly, 123, 143, 171, 189–90
civilizations
eight stages in the cycle of, 66
eleven observable "symptoms of final decay" in the fall of the Greek and Roman, 67
Civil War, 137
Cochran, Kelvin, 110–11
Cole, Steven (pastor), 244
Colson, Charles, 249, 251
Columbus, Christopher, 57, 58
Common Market, 24
conditional immortality, 380
conscience, 115, 123, 224, 304, 315, 386
Coolidge, Calvin, 63
Corduan, Winfried, 101
corporations, 47, 49, 52
Council on American-Islamic Relations, 107
Council of European Union, 25, 26
courage and suffering, 119–20
covenant
Abrahamic, 4–12, 14, 15
Antichrist's (with Israel), 28, 39, 237, 252–53, 256, 341
Davidic, 369
creation
the act, 91, 115, 122, 147, 184, 381

of the new heaven and the new earth, 395, 406
a sign of God's love for His, 182
new, 397–98, 400, 401, 404
the work of Christ for, 402–3
crescendo, 225
Crimea, 30–31
Criswell, W. A., 255, 262, 276, 397, 412
Critchley, Simon, 78
Croatia, 25
crowns available to the believer, five, 203
the Crown of Glory, 213–14
the Crown of Life, 212–13
the Crown of Rejoicing (aka Soul Winner's Crown), 210–11
the Crown of Righteousness, 211
the Victor's Crown, 208
curse, reversal of the, 400, 401–3
cycle of civilization, 66
Cyprus, 25
Czech Republic, 25

D

Daniel (prophet), 18–24, 26, 27, 28, 33, 39, 49, 71, 237, 248–55 *passim*, 258, 265, 319–20, 341, 342, 343
Darwin, Charles, 89
David (king), 8, 13, 162, 166, 219, 295, 296, 302, 317, 369, 375
Davidic covenant, 369
dead in Christ, the, 165, 166, 421, 157, 163
"deathbed repentance," 244–45
deaths
of Christians during the Ottoman Empire, estimated, 117
per year from antibiotic-resistant bacteria, 242
in World Wars I and II, estimated, 238
Declaration of Independence, 111
deism, 89
demons, 49, 126, 129, 138, 312, 345, 383
Demy, Timothy, 302
Denmark, 25
depravity, 49, 51, 87–89, 93, 95, 304, 305–6, 370–71
despotism, 61
Devil, origin and meaning of the word, 315. *See* Satan
Dewey, John, 90
disease, xii, 40, 89, 169, 170, 241–42, 251, 305, 400
disqualified, origin and meaning of the word, 202
division (satanic) 128–29

divorce rate, 88
Domitian (emperor), 117, 226, 272
doxologies, 225
dragon (of Revelation), the. *See chapter 24,*
"Dragon" (311–23); also, 251–52, 260, 261, 263,
325, 337, 338. *See* Satan
dreams
Daniel's, 18, 22–23, 27, 248, 249, 255
Einstein's dream, 17
Joseph's, 318
Muslims confronted by the gospel in, 108–9
Nebuchadnezzar's dream, 18–22
drought, 301, 304–5, 402
Dulles, John Foster, 60
Dyer, Charles H. (OT scholar), 45

E

Eareckson Tada, Joni, 178–79
earthquakes, 40, 118, 151, 155, 157, 238, 309, 402
Eban, Abba (Jewish statesman), 60
Ebbers, Bernard, 77
Eden, 55, 127, 195, 282, 314, 316, 317, 392, 402, 414
Edman, Dr. V. Raymond (Christian educator),
218–19
Edwards, Suzanne, 181–82
EEC (European Economic Community), 25
Egypt, 9, 35, 45, 117, 121, 235, 262, 270, 272, 282,
306, 317, 322, 343, 347
Egyptian Christians, martyrdom of twenty, 282
Eich, Brendan, 113
Eichmann, Adolf, 272
Elazar, David (chief of staff), 347
Elijah (prophet), 164, 174, 264, 276, 287, 300–302,
304–5, 322
Elliff, Jim, 203
empires
Babylonian, 20. *See* Babylon
British, 35
Byzantine, 23
Greek, 20, 21, 255
Medo-Persian, 20, 255
Ottoman, 117
Persian, 271
Roman, 10–11, 21–28, 64, 133, 213, 255, 338,
339
Soviet, 34
end-time events, sequence of the five major,
162–65
entertainment industry, 111, 205
Einstein, Albert, 17

Enlightenment, 89
Enoch (patriarch), 164, 301, 356
Esther (queen), 317
Estonia, 25
Ethiopia, 34–35, 218
EU (European Union), 24–28, 30, 64–65
Eudoxia (Aelia Eudoxia, empress consort), 124
Euphrates, 7, 343–45
euro, 25
European Commission, 25, 26
European Economic Community (EEC), 25
European Parliament, 25–26, 27
European Union (EU), 24–28, 30, 64–65
Europe. *See chapter 2,* "Europe" (17–29); also
1, 46, 64, 89, 101, 103–5, 246, 272. *See also*
European Union
evolution, 89, 145
Ezekiel (prophet), 1, 7, 13, 32–33, 35–41, 71, 99

F

fallen angels, 316, 319. *See also* demons
false prophet, the. *See chapter 20,* "False Prophet"
(259–69); also 127, 231, 256, 325–26, 330,
331–32, 338, 359–60, 389
the fatality of the beast and, 359–60
the power of the, 262–66
the profile of the, 260–61
the program of the, 267–68
the punishment of the, 268–69
the purpose of the, 261–62
three miracles performed by the, 263–66
famine, 51, 56, 74, 118, 157, 235, 238, 240, 241, 373
fatah (Muslim infiltration), 104, 107
fig tree, 243
Finland, 25
fire and brimstone, 41, 127, 263, 268, 332, 359,
360, 388–89, 416
First World War, 238
Fitzsimmons, Cotton, 193
Flood, the, 87, 141, 144–45, 169, 235, 287, 374, 398
Forbes, 73, 83
"form of godliness," 76–77, 87
four horsemen of the Apocalypse. *See chapter 18,*
"Four Riders" (233–45)
rider on a black horse, 239–40
rider on a pale horse, 240–42
rider on a red horse, 237–38
rider on a white horse, 236–37
fowls of heaven (Rev. 19), 358–59
Foxe's Book of Martyrs, 281

Fox News, 99, 331
France, 24, 25, 89, 104, 284, 408
Franklin, Benjamin, 62
Frazier, Gary, 257
freedom, 14, 58, 60–61, 63, 100, 111, 115, 118, 121, 335
Freedom House, 60
French Revolution, 117, 253
Frenkiel, Jakob, 324
Fruchtenbaum, Arnold, 163–64

G

Gaddafi, Muammar, 35
Garcia-Herreros, Alejandro, 181–82
Garcia-Herreros, Carlos, 181–82
Gates, Bill, 83
gates of pearl, 411–12, 413
Gaza Strip, 10
generosity, 79, 80–82, 84
Germany, 10, 24, 25, 35, 36, 189, 246, 249, 324, 361, 408
Gibbon, Edward, 108
giving, 81–82, 84
globalism; global market, 52
God
    America and the sovereignty of, 58–59
    America was founded on, 61–62
    nothing can separate us from, 56
    signs from. See signs
    the only source of real security, 56
    wrath of, 91, 199, 235, 236, 245, 268, 280, 287, 291, 332
godliness
    "a form of," 76–77, 87
    suffering and, 120
gold, 9, 19, 20, 36, 47, 53, 56, 83, 197, 200, 207, 223, 274, 333–34, 342, 376, 411, 413, 417
Gog, 33–34, 37, 38, 39, 42, 306, 337, 370
Golan Heights, 10
Golding, William, 311
Gomer, 35
Goodenough, Stan, 106–7
Graham, Billy, 128
Great Britain, 32, 105, 137
Great White Throne. See chapter 29, "Great White Throne Judgment" (378–90); also 194, 349, 371, 395, 400
    the people before the, 382–84
    the person on the, 382
    the place of the, 381

the punishment following the, 387–90
the purpose of the, 384–87
Greece, 20, 25, 255, 415
Greek Empire, 20, 21, 255

H

Hades, 240, 241, 381, 382, 387, 388
Hahn, Wilfred J., 78
Haile Selassie I (king), 218
Haldeman, Dr. Isaac Massey, 388
Haman (official in court of Xerxes), 271, 317
Hamas, 99
Handel's Messiah, 357
Haney, David, 404
harps, 294, 295–96
Havner, Vance, 360–61
heaven. See chapter 14, "Heaven" (181–92); also 4, 8, 19, 20, 22, 50, 54, 55, 57, 68, 82, 83, 91, 93, 123, 124, 136, 141–80 passim, 194–388 passim, 406–21 passim
    dimensions of, 407–9, 415
    the first (or, the atmospheric), 183–84
    the fowls of, 358–59
    the location of, 186–87
    the new. See chapter 30, "New Heaven and New Earth" (391–404)
    a new song in, 294–97
    number of biblical mentions of, 183
    the plurality of, 183–85
    the preciousness of, 188–91
    the second (the universe), 183, 184
    the third, 183, 184–85, 187, 407
    the way to get to, 180
    worship in, 221–26, 229–30
hell, 94, 108–9, 129, 151, 199, 226, 269, 276, 333, 345, 359, 380, 388–89
    the horrific biblical picture of, 388
helmet of salvation, 130, 133–34, 137
Henry, Matthew, 180
Herod Agrippa, 272
Herod Antipas, 116, 276
Herod the Great, 115, 116, 272, 317–18
Herodotus, 20
Herzog, Isaac Halevi, 16
Hess, Dean, 284–85
Hitchcock, Alfred, 358
Hitchcock, Mark, 34, 37–38, 74, 197, 267, 292
Hitler, Adolf, 10, 246, 247, 249, 251, 257, 272, 328
Hoekema, Anthony, 399–400
Hollywood, 90, 205

INDEX

Holocaust, 10, 325
holy city, the (New Jerusalem). *See* New Jerusalem
Hoover, Herbert, 67
horns, 23, 27, 249–50, 252, 254, 260, 313, 315, 329
horsemen of Revelation. See four horsemen of the Apocalypse
Hoyt, Herman A., 68
Hubbard, Elbert, 209
Huffington Post, 84
humanistic secularism, 90
Hungary, 25
hunger, 98, 239–40

I

Ice, Dr. Thomas, 253
idolatry, 9, 92, 265, 417
imminent, an exploration of the word, 157–58
immorality, 9, 49. *See chapter 7, "Immorality"* (85–96), esp. 93
Incarnation, 313, 355
India, 101, 281, 408
ingratitude, 92
iniquity, 49, 93–94
Inquisition, 10, 272
International Christian Concern, 213
Internet, xii, 59, 295, 307, 331, 389
intimidation (of Christians), 113–14
Iraq, 8, 97, 98, 101, 270, 281–82, 344
Iran, 34, 35, 36, 39, 66, 99, 105, 117, 281
Ireland, 25, 211
ISIS, 270–71, 282
Islam. *See chapter 8, "Radical Islam"* (97–109);
    also 34–36, 64, 66, 71
    five pillars of, 102
    the hatred of, 102–3
    the history of, 100–101
    the hope of, 103–6
    responding to the threat of, 106–8
    the two sects of, 101
    the ultimate goal of, 97–98
Islamic Republic of Iran. *See* Iran
Islamic revolution, 97
Islamification, 103–4
Israel. *See chapter 1, "Israel"* (3–16); *also* 1, 59–60, 63, 64, 66, 71, 99, 103, 107, 173, 206, 237, 253, 256, 262, 264, 272, 273, 286, 294–95, 301, 302, 305, 306, 312, 313, 317, 321–22, 336–41, 343–45, 347–48, 368, 369, 373, 376, 405, 411
    birth of the modern nation of, 13–14, 15–16
    the condition for the Antichrist's treaty with, 28

geographical boundaries of (in Scripture), 7–8
national achievements of, 7
notable example of God's vengeance against an enemy of, 9
number of millionaires and billionaires in, 38
population of, 14
return of the Jews to, 14–15
the return to the God of, 12–13
the ten named countries in the future coalition against, 34–36
two pivotal unfulfilled prophecies concerning, 13
when and where the end-time Russian invasion will occur, 37–38
why Russia and its allies will attack, 36–37
Isthmian Games, 208–9
Italy, 24, 25

J

Jacob (patriarch), 174, 302, 317, 369, 370
James (apostle), 143, 199, 272
Japan, 117, 284, 336
Japheth, 34, 35
Jehoshaphat (king), 317
Jehovah's Witnesses, 380
Jeremiah (prophet), 48, 276
Jeremiah Study Bible, 6
Jerusalem, 7, 9, 13, 33, 38, 46, 56, 81, 116, 256, 266, 271, 276, 285, 289, 292, 300, 304, 306–9, 324, 338, 343, 345, 347–48, 352, 353, 354, 360, 372, 375, 392–93, 415. *See also* New Jerusalem
Jesus Christ. *See* Christ
JESUS film, 59
Jewish Virtual Library, 324–25
Jews
    number of (in Israel, the United States), 5
    summary of the miraculous preservation of the, 10–11
Jezebel (queen), 262, 276
jihad, 66, 99, 102–5 *passim*
Joel (prophet), 288
John (apostle), 47–56 *passim*, 74–75, 116, 119, 143, 160, 163, 167, 176, 219, 221–23, 226, 227, 229, 240–412 *passim*
John the Baptist, 116, 276, 300–301
Jonah (prophet), 235, 356, 405
Jones, Jim, 259, 260
Jordan, 8, 10, 344
Joseph (husband of Mary), 318
Joseph (son of Jacob), 235, 302

Joseph of Arimathea, 170
Joshua (high priest), 300, 303
Joshua (successor of Moses), 126, 303
joy
    millennial, 374–75
    from suffering, 120
"Joy to the World" (carol), 364–66, 377
Jude (author of epistle), 356
judging others, 420
judgment
    first. *See* judgment seat of Christ
    Great White Throne. *See* Great White Throne
    prophecies of judgment, 235–36
    seat of Christ. *See* judgment seat of Christ
    second. *See* Great White Throne
judgment seat of Christ. *See chapter 15,*
    "Judgment Seat of Christ" (193–204); *also* 153,
    207–8, 214, 215, 379, 385
    the chronology of the, 199
    the criteria for the, 199–201
    three central passages on, 197–98
    two possible outcomes from the, 201

K

Kazakhstan, 34
Khadija (wife of Muhammad), 100
Khomeini, Ayatollah, 99
King, Stephen, 83–84
"King of Kings and Lord of Lords," 346, 355, 357,
    377
Kissinger, Henry, 347
Klein, Melissa and Aaron (Christian bakers), 114
Kopmeyer, M. R., 209
Koran (*also* Qu'ran *in text*), 99, 100, 101, 105, 107,
    108, 109
Koresh, David, 259, 260
Kozlowski, Dennis, 77
Kyrgyzstan, 34

L

Lady Gaga, 85
LaHaye, Tim, 63–64
lake of fire, 127, 268, 314, 359–60, 379, 381, 387,
    388, 389
    who will end up in the, 389–90
Lamb, the. *See under* Christ
Lamb's Book of Life, 167, 190–91, 192, 253, 379,
    380–81, 384, 385, 386–87, 389, 416, 417
Latvia, 25

law, the (Mosaic), 300, 301, 384
Lay, Kenneth, 77
Lebanon, 8, 336
Lewis, C. S., 82, 225–26
Lexie, Albert, 80–81
Libya, 35, 36, 270, 282
lifespan
    human, 169
    increased millennial, 374
    of the world's greatest civilizations, average,
        66
Lincoln, Abraham, 58, 62, 109, 266, 385
Lindberg, Milton B., 15
Lithuania, 25
litigating (against Christians), 114
little horn. *See* Antichrist
Lloyd-Jones, Dr. Martyn, 94, 96, 120
London, 47, 66, 104, 364, 405, 408, 415, 419
longevity, millennial, 374
Lopez, Maria, 84
Lord of the Flies (deity), 311–12
Lord of the Flies (Golding), 311
Lord of the Rings, 347
Lord's Table, a call to remember the, 420
Loring, Ian (missionary), 351
lost, the: a call to reach, 422
Lot (patriarch), 287
love
    of money, 74, 75–76
    relating to one another in, 421
    self-, 56, 77
lovers
    of money, 78–79
    of self, 77
Lucifer, 126, 187, 314. *See* Satan
Lutzer, Erwin (pastor), 131, 382–83
Luxembourg, 24, 25
Lyle, Denis (pastor), 211–12

M

MacArthur, Douglas, 336
Maccabean revolt, 9
Madoff, Bernie, 77
Magog, 33, 34, 38, 41, 337, 370
Mahdi, 101, 105
Malachi (prophet), 264, 300, 301
male Child (of Revelation), 313, 321, 337
Malta, 25
Manasseh (king), 276
Manuel, David, 57, 58

Marduk (Babylonian chief deity), 20
marginalizing (of Christians), 113
mariners, 53, 54
mark of the beast. *See chapter 25,* "Mark of the Beast" (324–35); *also* 51, 54, 256, 267–69, 288, 359
   perplexity concerning the, 327–30
   the personalities behind the, 325–26
   precursors to the, 330–32
   the purpose of the, 326–27
Marshall, George (secretary of state), 60
Marshall, Peter, 57, 58
martyrdom, 124, 212–13. *See chapter 21,* "Martyrs" (270–83)
martyrs. *See chapter 21,* "Martyrs" (270–83); *also* 51, 54, 55, 124, 231
   estimated number killed each year, 281
   of Revelation 6
      the cry of the, 277–78
      five comforts for the, 278–81
      the identity of the, 273
materialism, 71. *See chapter 6,* "Materialism" (73–84)
   the antidote to, 79
   defined, 74
Matthew (gospel writer), 261, 346
Matthews, Chris, 113
May, Theresa (British prime minister), 32
Medo-Persian Empire, 20, 255
Medo-Persians, 20, 21
Megiddo, 338–39
Meir, Golda, 347
Mere Christianity (Lewis), 82
Merkel, Angela, 64–65
merchants, 49, 53, 54. 55
Mercy Health Partners, 113
Meshech, 33, 34
Metformin, 168
Methuselah, 374
Metzgar, Ruthanna and Roy, 191–92
Mexico, 189, 213
Michael (archangel), 130, 301, 318, 319
microchips, 331
Middle Ages, 10, 89
Millennium. *See chapter 28,* "Millennium" (364–77); *also,* 7, 38, 254, 263, 280–81, 294, 349, 359, 380, 381, 389, 400, 407
   defined, 366
   five facts about the, 371–76
   four purposes of the, 367–71
Miller, William, 259, 260

mind of Christ, 134
ministry, commitment to the, 421
missionary movement, the force behind the, 59
Mohler, Albert, 90
monarchs, 53, 54, 214
money
   changing the way you think about, 79–80
   the love of, 74, 75–76
   lovers of, 78–79
Monsen, Marie (missionary), 176–77
moral decline
   the escape from our, 95–96
   the explanation for our, 89–95
   the expression of our, 87–89
moral relativism, 86, 90
More, Thomas, 391
Morris, Henry, 46, 47, 266, 274, 307, 309, 387
Morrison, Mr. and Mrs. Henry C. (missionaries), 216–17
Moscow, 34, 47
Moses, 6, 9, 107, 121, 126, 171, 174, 185, 262, 271, 272, 292, 301–2, 303, 305, 317
Mount of Olives, 161, 186, 352–53, 354
Mount Saint Helens, 151–52
Mount Zion, 289, 292, 294, 295, 405
Muhammad, 99, 100–101, 102, 105, 108
multiculturalism, 103
music, the power of, 296
Muskens, Martinus Petrus Maria (Dutch Catholic bishop), 106, 107
Muslims, 5, 98, 100, 102–5, 107, 108–9, 271, 383. *See also* Islam
   number in the United States, globally, 100
   percent of public who know about the religious beliefs and practices of, 98

N

Nadab and Abihu, 263
Napoleon, 137, 255, 339
National Review, 110–11, 113
Nazareth, proximity of Megiddo to, 338
Nazis, 103, 251
Nebuchadnezzar, 18–22, 49, 255, 292, 328, 333–34
Nero, 117, 213, 251, 257
Netanyahu, Benjamin, 10–11
Netherlands, 24, 25
Newell, William R., 303–4, 307
new heaven and new earth, 349. *See chapter 30,* "New Heaven and New Earth" (391–404)
New Jerusalem. *See chapter 31,* "Holy City"

(405–18); *also*, 171, 175, 394
  biblical description of the, 410–16
  chief characteristic of, 410
  denial of entrance into the, 416–17
  the dimensions of the, 407–9
  the light and energy sources for the, 413–14
"news from the east," 343
new world order, 27, 139
New York City, 84, 85, 372, 405
Nigeria, 281
9/11 (September 11, 2001, terrorist attacks), 65, 98, 309–10
Nineveh, 235, 405
Noah, 34, 35, 87, 88, 91, 93, 141, 144, 145–46, 147, 235, 287, 374, 398
North Korea, 66, 117, 281
Nyquist, Dr. Paul, 111

O

O'Brien, Peter, 133
October 2007 California wildfires, 166–67
Olivet discourse, 265, 274–75
144,000, the. *See chapter 22*, "144,000" (284–97); *also* 231, 267, 274, 322, 356
Open Doors, 213
Oscar (Academy Award), 205–6
O'Shea, Donagh, 75–76
Ottoman Empire, 117

P

Packer, J. I., 196
Palestinians, 10
Parker, Annise, 114
Paul, apostle, 28, 56, 71, 76–78, 81, 82–83, 87, 91, 92–93, 95, 96, 115, 116, 119–36 *passim*, 142, 153, 156–66 *passim*, 169, 171, 174, 175, 176, 179, 183, 184–85, 186, 190, 195, 196, 199–201, 202, 208, 209, 210, 211, 228, 244, 248, 253, 265, 273, 285, 289, 290, 303, 314, 315, 316, 346, 382, 384, 385, 386, 388
peace, scriptures concerning the millennial reign of, 372
Pentecost, J. Dwight, 198, 368
persecution. *See chapter 9*, "Persecution" (110–24); *also* 55, 56, 71, 133, 190, 212–13, 226, 251, 256, 271–72, 277, 281–82, 299, 305–7, 309, 320, 327, 332–33, 337–38
  Christian
    the side effects of, 118–21

  the stages of, 112–14
  the story of, 114–18
  substance of, 112
  three things we can do to prepare for, 122–24
  of Christians
    in the Bible, 115–16
    in history, 116
    today, 116–17
  number of Christians who face high levels of, 213
  number of countries in which Christians face persecution, 213, 281
Persians, 9, 20
pestilence, 40, 157, 238, 241
Peter (apostle), 116, 119, 143, 146–47, 166, 202–3, 213–14, 303, 315, 382, 393, 395, 396, 398
Peterson, Eugene, 115
Petra (city), 322
Philip of Macedon, 20
Phillips, John (Bible expositor), 35, 49, 127, 260–61, 308–9
Pierson, A. T., 166
pilgrimage (*hajj*), 100, 102
Pink, Arthur W., 250
Piper, John, 78–79
plagues, 9, 51, 55, 56, 241, 304–5, 329, 341
Plantinga, Cornelius, Jr., 94–96
Pledge of Allegiance, 63
Pliny, 20
pogroms, 10
Poland, 25, 324
Polycarp, 272
pop culture, 90
population, projected world, 240
Porter, Cole, 85–86
Portugal, 25
prayer (as a spiritual weapon), 135–37
precious stones, 47, 53, 197, 200, 207, 286, 342, 412
Price, Randall, 347–48
prince of Persia, 319, 320
Proposition 8 (CA), 113
prosperity and purity (millennial), 373–74
Putin, Vladimir, 30–32

Q

Qin Shi Huang, 83
Qu'ran (*also* Koran *in text*), 99, 100, 101, 105, 107, 108, 109

R

radical Islam, 64, 66, 71. *See chapter 8*, "Radical Islam" (97–109)

Rahab (harlot), 287

rape of Christian women, 118

Rapture. *See chapter 12*, "Rapture" (155–67); *also* 68, 140, 142, 153, 182, 194, 197, 199, 207, 216, 221, 236, 238, 240, 243, 248, 257, 258, 273, 274, 275, 286, 293, 299, 308, 330, 354, 379, 380, 395, 400

the most concise and logical truth about the, 156–57

origin of the word, 156

sequence of the five aspects of the, 162–65

seven important truths we can know about the, 157–66

six raptures in the Bible, 164

Reagan, Ronald, 31, 57–58, 61, 336

redemption, the (of our bodies), 163–64. *See also chapter 13*, "Resurrection" (168–80)

Reformation, 89, 272

Reid, John, 104

religious discrimination, three countries that have reached a concerning level of, 213

repentance, 146, 245, 275, 302, 303, 308, 308, 356, 389

rest (of the Revelation martyrs), 279–80

restoration of all things, 400, 403–4

resurrection

of the Antichrist, 256, 342

of the body, 399. *See next*

of the dead. *See chapter 13*, "Resurrection" (168–80); *also* 153, 162–63, 165, 216, 380–81, 388

of Jesus, 96, 116, 137, 163, 166, 170, 171, 172–73, 175, 179, 189, 256, 279, 318, 321, 399

of the two witnesses, 308, 309

return of Christ (or, the Second Coming). *See chapter 27*, "Return of the King" (351–63); *also*, x, xi, 14, 47, 76, 87, 139–40, 141, 146, 147, 150, 156–57, 160, 162, 211, 219, 223, 243, 279, 300, 313, 349, 352, 354, 357, 361, 364, 366, 367, 376, 395, 400, 420–21

two characteristics which will dominate society before the, 79–79

reunion with the dead in Christ, 164–65

rewards. *See chapter 16*, "Rewards" (205–17); *also* 120–21, 153, 190, 194–95, 201–3, 367

available to the believer, five, 203

description of heaven's, 208–14

the greatest, 214–17

the kind of religious activity that will result in the loss of, 201–2

for the martyrs of Revelation, 280–81

sample of scriptures that speak of eternal, 206–7

for those who suffer persecution, 120–21

riches, our heavenly, 190

river of life, 415

robes, 20, 223, 279, 293

Roman Catholic Church, 105

Roman Empire, 10–11, 21–28, 64, 133, 213, 255, 338, 339

Romania, 25, 122

Rome, 10, 21, 25, 26, 27, 46, 117, 236, 251, 255, 405, 415

Roosevelt, Theodore, 216

Rosh, 32–33

Rowley, Charlie, 32

Rubinstein, Amnon, 7

Russia. *See chapter 3* (30–43); *also* 1, 10, 64, 71, 88, 99, 213, 272, 337, 343, 361

Russian Revolution, 117

S

Saddam Hussein, 97, 281

Sada, Georges, 97–98, 103, 105

Safa, Reza F., 99–100

saints, scriptures promising Christ's descent with His, 346

Sale-Harrison, Leonard (theologian), 195

salvation, 28, 29, 62, 115, 134, 137, 142, 193, 202, 207–8, 210, 243, 244, 245, 273, 289, 294, 296, 356, 375, 382, 383, 384, 423

Satan (*aka*, the Devil), 49, 55, 56, 126–31, 133, 134, 137–38, 150–51, 156, 177, 187, 212, 213, 231, 242, 246, 247, 250, 251, 254, 256, 257, 261–63, 266, 267, 268, 276, 282, 301, 304, 309, 312, 313–23, 325, 326, 327, 333, 335, 337–38, 357, 359, 360, 370–71, 388, 389, 399–400

deceives, 128

destroys, 129–30

divides, 128–29

meaning of the word, 314

other names for, 129

partners of, 316

personality of, 314–15

power of, 315–16

purpose of, 317–18

Saudi Arabia, 8, 100, 109, 336

Scofield, C. I., 34
sea, the removal of the (new earth), 400–401
sealing
    of Christians, promises of, 289
    Old Testament examples of divine, 287
    of the 144,000, 286–87
seal judgments (*or*, seven seals of Revelation),
    235–36, 259, 395
    first seal, 236
    second seal, 237–38
    third seal, 75, 239–40
    fourth seal, 240–41
    fifth seal, 273, 277, 279
    seventh seal, 236
Second Coming (or, the return of Christ). *See
    chapter 27*, "Return of the King" (351–63); *also*
    x, xi, 14, 47, 76, 87, 139–40, 141, 146, 147, 150,
    156–57, 160, 162, 211, 219, 223, 243, 279, 300,
    313, 349, 352, 354, 357, 361, 364, 366, 367, 376,
    395, 400, 420–21
    angels predicted the, 353
    the application of Christ's, 360–63
    the Bible's description of the glory and
        majesty Christ will display at His, 355
    contrasts between the first and the, 376
    Jesus announced his, 353
    John the apostle foretold the, 354
    number of New Testament references to the,
        156
    the prophets foretold the, 352–53
    two stages to the, 156
Second World War. *See* World War II
second death, 381, 387, 388, 416
secrets, the judging of our, 385–86
secularism, 90, 92
security, the only source of real, 56
Seiss, J. A., 265, 286
self-control, 76, 87, 209–10
self-deception, 96
self-discipline, 209
self-love, 56, 77
September 11, 2001, terrorist attacks (9/11 *in text*),
    65, 98, 309–10
Sermon on the Mount, 75
seven (the number), 328–29
Seven Men Who Rule the World from the Grave
    (Breese), 89–90
Seventh-Day Adventists, 380
Shackleton, Sir Ernest, 361–63
Shadrach, Meshach, and Abed-Nego, 274, 292, 334
sharia law, 105

Shawshank Redemption, The (film), 112
shield of faith, 130, 133, 137
Shi'ites, 101
shoes of the preparation of the gospel of peace,
    130, 132–33, 137
Showers, Renald, 157
signs (from God)
    cultural. *See in general* part 2, "Cultural
        Signs" (chapters 6–11), 71–152
    end. *See in general* part 5, "End Signs"
        (chapters 27–31), 349–418
    heavenly. *See in general* part 3, "Heavenly
        Signs" (chapters 12–17), 153–230
    international. *See in general* part 1
        "International Signs" (chapters 1–5), 1–69
    tribulation. *See in general* part 4, "Tribulation
        Signs" (chapters 18–26), 231–348
    why study? x–xi
Silas, 120, 303
silver, 9, 19, 20, 36, 47, 56, 197, 200, 207, 274, 342
sin, a call to renounce, 422
Sinai Peninsula, 10
Sinatra, Frank, 86
Single European Act, 25
Six-Day War (1967), 10, 37
666 (the number), 327, 328, 329, 330
Skripal, Sergei (Russian spy), 32
Slovakia, 25
Slovenia, 25
Social Darwinism, 90
social media, 182, 307
Sodom and Gomorrah, 41, 263
Solomon (king), 8, 185, 195, 385–86
son of perdition, 128, 265
Soul Winner's Crown. *See* crowns
Soviet Union, 35, 63, 336. *See* Russia
Spaak, Paul-Henri (first president of European
    Parliament), 27
Spain, 25, 101, 272
spiritual warfare, 71. *See chapter 10*, "Spiritual
    Warfare" (125–38)
spiritual weapons, 130–37
Spurgeon, Charles Haddon, 214
steadfastness, a call to, 421–22
Stedman, Ray (late pastor), 42–43, 135
Stephen (NT deacon), 116, 162, 166, 272, 278
stereotyping (of Christians), 112
Stewart, Martha, 77
straw (as a foundation for life building; *aka*
    stubble), 197, 200, 207
streets of gold, 413, 417

Sturgess, Dawn, 32
suffering, benefits in, 118–21
suicide, 67, 88 (teen), 259
suicide bombers, 99, 104
Sunni, 101–2, 105
Sun Tzu, 125–26
Sweeting, George (former president, Moody Bible
   Institute), 196
Sweden, 25
Swindoll, Charles, 88, 241
sword of the Spirit, 130, 134–35
Syria, 8, 10, 35, 99, 270, 336, 344, 347

T

Tada, Joni Eareckson, 178–79
Tajikistan, 34
Talbot, Louis T., 278
tattoos (for Jewish prisoners), 324–25
Taylor, Jack (pastor), 136–37
Temple, William (WWII archbishop of
   Canterbury), 224
terrorism, 7, 61, 97, 98, 99, 104, 348
Tham Luang cave rescue, 298–99
theism, 90
third heaven, 183, 184–85, 187, 407
thorns, 365, 366, 376, 397, 402
threatening (of Christians), 113
"time of Jacob's trouble," 340
Timothy (protégé of Paul), 71, 78, 122, 303
Timperlake, Ed, 66
Titanic, 44–45, 50
tithing, 80
Titus (saint), 158, 303
Tobolsk, 34
Togarmah, 35
Tokyo, 47, 336, 405
total depravity, 87–88
tolerance, 49, 103, 104, 106, 262
Tower of Babel, 45–46
Tozer, A. W., 120, 139, 228
Tracy, Brian, 209
Transfiguration, 171, 174, 301
Treaty of Paris, 24
Treaty of Rome, 24–25
tree of life, 414–15, 416
Tribulation. *See in general part 4,* "Tribulation
   Signs" (chapters 18–26), 231–348; *also* xii, 1, 46,
   49–50, 51, 54, 56, 65, 74–75, 129, 139, 142, 156,
   157, 160, 167, 183, 351, 353, 356, 357, 360, 380,
   381, 395, 400

Truman, Harry S., 3–4, 15–16, 59, 60
Tubal, 33, 34
Turkestan, 35
Turkey, 21, 34, 35, 36, 344, 415
Turkmenistan, 34
Turning Point (TV program), 108
Twelfth Imam, 101, 105–6
two witnesses (of Revelation), the. *See chapter 23,*
   "Two Witnesses" (298–310); *also* 164, 231, 267,
   273, 356
   the death of, 306
   the identities of, 300–302
   the persecution of, 305–7
   the power of, 303–5
   the prophecies of, 302–3
   the rapture of, 308–9
   the resurrection of, 307–8
   the revenge of, 309
tyranny, 61, 306, 326

U

UN Department of Economic and Social Affairs,
   240
unification of Europe, 24–25
United Arab Republic (UAR), 10
United Kingdom, 25
United States of America. *See* America
"United States of Europe." *See* European
   Union
Ur (city), 8, 405
US (United States). *See* America
US Food and Drug Administration, 168
USSR (Union of Soviet Socialist Republics), 31.
   See Russia
US State Department, 281
utopia, 391–92, 394, 404
Uzbekistan, 34

V

vision
   of the apostle John, 48, 74–75, 219, 221–26,
      229, 277, 285–88, 293, 359, 379, 382
   Daniel's first, 22, 23
   Daniel's second, 18, 22–23, 27, 248, 249,
      255
   Nebuchadnezzar's (dream), 18–22
   of Paul, 183
   of Zechariah, 236, 300
Vuchetich, Yevgeny, 372

W

Walvoord, John F. (prophecy expert), 8, 33, 40, 64, 65, 279, 343, 344, 360, 381
Wan, Alex (Atlanta council member), 110–11
war, three ways Satan wages, 125–30
Washington, D.C., 57, 59, 66, 73
Washington, George, 62
Washington Monument, 57
Washington Times, 58, 66, 103
Watts, Isaac, 364–65
weapons of our warfare. See spiritual weapons
Welch, Jack (author of *Winning*), 179
West Bank, 8, 10
West Germany, 24, 25
Whaley, Vernon, 220–21, 229–30
Whitacre, Eric, 295
Whitcomb, John, 302
white horse rider, 236–37
white robes, 223, 279, 293
Whitney, Donald (Southern Baptist Theological Seminary), 136
Wiersbe, Warren W., 194
Wild, Frank, 362–63
Wilkinson, Bruce, 208
Williams, Rowan (archbishop of Canterbury), 105
Wilson, Woodrow, 58, 62
"wings of a great eagle," 312, 322
witnesses (of Revelation)
    the two. See two witnesses
    the 144,000 Jewish. See 144,000, the
woman clothed with the sun, 312–13
wood (as a foundation for life building), 197, 200, 207
word, the judging of every, 386
Word of God (as a spiritual weapon). See sword of the Spirit
world system, precariousness of the, 56
World War I, 238, 405
World War II, 10, 24, 35, 59, 111, 137, 224, 238, 268, 318, 320, 336
worship. See chapter 17, "Worship" (218–30); *also* 94, 203, 215, 253
    in all non-Christian religions encouraged by the false prophet, 261–62
    of the Antichrist, 253–67 *passim*, 341–42
    the center of heavenly, 222–23
    in heaven, 221–26
    is not about here (earth), 227
    is not about the individual, 228–30
    is not about now, 227–28

is not about us, 226–27
services, three integral parts of most modern, 220
for Sunni Muslims, five acts of, 102
the three Hebrew children and image, 334
wrath
    God's, 91, 199, 235, 236, 245, 268, 280, 287, 291, 332
    meaning of the Greek word for (Rev. 12), 321
Wurmbrand, Richard, 122

X

Xerxes, 271

Y

Yancey, Philip, 88
Yeltsin, Boris, 31
Yinxu (city), 405
Yom Kippur War, 347–48

Z

Zacharias, Ravi, 90
Zechariah (prophet), 9, 236, 274, 300, 352–53
Zerubbabel (governor), 300, 303
Zeus, 271
Zimmerman, Carle, 66–67

ACKNOWLEDGMENTS

Beginning in the late seventies and early eighties, I became fascinated with the study of prophecy. I am sure that my friendship with Dr. Tim LaHaye had something to do with my desire to understand and preach these incredible truths which occupy more than one-fourth of the Bible.

I wrote my first book on prophecy with the help of Carol Carlson, the coauthor of Hal Lindsey's *The Late, Great Planet Earth*. From the very first sermon on the book of Revelation and the subsequent writing of six books on prophecy, I have always had one goal: to take these untaught and often confusing subjects and make them live with meaning in the hearts of my hearers and readers.

Earlier this year, my long-time publishing friend Joey Paul came to me with an idea that resulted in the book you have just read. He said, "Why not take all of these many chapters you have written on prophetic subjects and organize them into the order in which the events they describe occur? Why not refresh some of your existing material, write several new chapters as needed, and then combine it all as a new and exciting anthology, accompanied by an exhaustive index? Why not?"

So we did it! And here it is—one of the most exciting and challenging projects of my writing career! I am at the stage of life where I sometimes think of legacy projects, and I am pretty certain that this book belongs under that heading.

Obviously, I could not have done this by myself. I needed the assistance of my literary agent, Sealy Yates, to work out all of the details with HarperCollins Christian Publishing. Our publisher, Daisy Hutton, needed to sign off on this project, and she did way more than that. She led the charge and kept us going when we hit a few bumps along the way. And then there was Sam O'Neal, a new friend and a wonderful editor. We were so blessed to have him assigned to this project.

Finally, I want to express my profound gratitude to Beau Sager, who rides in the front seat of this publishing car with me. When we decided to do this project, we had just finished our last major book and were in recovery mode. We had also agreed to add an additional translation to our Study Bible collection and were in the process of reviewing and renewing our book on Daniel. All of these projects were on Beau's desk when we decided to do *The Book of Signs*. While Beau may have wondered, "What in the world is he thinking?" he grabbed hold of this opportunity with the same enthusiasm he brings to every project we do. Every author should be blessed with someone like Beau!

There were also some others who helped us with the abridgements and editing: Tom Williams, Rob Morgan, William Kruidenier, and Mary Hollingsworth and her team at Creative Enterprises Studio.

Donna is my wife and partner. We have been doing everything together for fifty-five years. I know she wishes I wouldn't run so fast sometimes, but she never complains and always finds some way to be my cheerleader. (By the way, that is what she was when I first met her at Cedarville College.)

There are three other people whose names belong on this page: my oldest son, David Michael, is the driving force behind all we do at Turning Point ministries. He runs the place! And it his understanding of social media and marketing that helps us launch our books. I have said this many times, but I will say it again: Paul Joiner is the most creative person I have ever met. He lives every day in a world of color that I visit only occasionally. Nothing in the world-wide ministry of Turning Point would be the same without Paul Joiner!

Sometimes people ask me this question: "Dr. Jeremiah, you are a pastor, an international broadcaster, and an author. How do you keep it all together?" And I answer them with two words: Diane Sutherland. She is the gate-keeper and the traffic-director who adds sanity to all that we do. Diane, everyone whose name appears in this document takes a moment right now to gratefully bow in your direction. You are amazing!

Finally, I want to tell you how honored and blessed I am to be serving the Lord Jesus Christ for all these many years. Thank you, Lord, for the desire, the energy, the determination, and the enthusiasm You have placed in my spirit. I am fully devoted to You because You first have been fully devoted to me!

David Jeremiah
San Diego—December 2018

ABOUT THE AUTHOR

David Jeremiah is the founder of Turning Point, an international ministry committed to providing Christians with sound Bible teaching through radio and television, the Internet, live events, and resource materials and books. He is the author of more than fifty books, including *Overcomer, A Life Beyond Amazing, Is This the End?, The Spiritual Warfare Answer Book, David Jeremiah Morning and Evening Devotions, Airship Genesis Kids Study Bible,* and *The Jeremiah Study Bible.*

Dr. Jeremiah serves as the senior pastor of Shadow Mountain Community Church in San Diego, California, where he resides with his wife, Donna. They have four grown children and twelve grandchildren.

stay connected to the teaching of

DR. DAVID JEREMIAH

· · · · · · · ·

Publishing | Radio | Television | Online

More Resources from Dr. Jeremiah
· · · · · · · ·

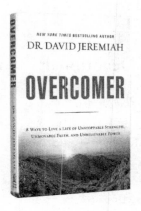

Overcomer
Discover the tools to become an Overcomer in every sense of the word—fully trusting God to prepare you for overcoming the trials and temptations that may cross your path. In this inspiring and practical book, Dr. David Jeremiah uses the armor of God that Paul describes in his letter to the Ephesian church to outline the path to victory.

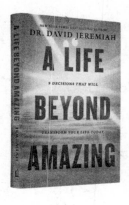

A Life Beyond Amazing
Discouraging headlines, personal adversity, and the toils of daily living often hold us back from living the life God has for us. In *A Life Beyond Amazing*, Dr. David Jeremiah urges us to move past these things, pointing us to a life of blessing beyond our comprehension. He shares nine traits, based on the fruit of the Spirit, that the Church is in need of today, teaching us that God desires for us to live beyond amazing while we await His return.

STAY CONNECTED

· · · · · · · ·

Take advantage of two great ways to let
Dr. David Jeremiah give you spiritual direction every day!
Both are absolutely free!

① *Turning Points* Magazine and Devotional

Each magazine features:

- A monthly study focus
- 48 pages of life-changing reading
- Relevant articles
- Special features
- Devotional readings for
  each day of the month
- Bible study resource offers
- Live event schedule
- Radio & television information

② Your Daily Turning Point E-Devotional

Start your day off right!
Receive a daily e-devotional
from Dr. Jeremiah that will
strengthen your walk with God
and encourage you to live the
authentic Christian life.

Request your devotions today:

CALL: (800) 947-1993

CLICK: DavidJeremiah.org/Magazine